EXPORTING PRESS FREEDOM

EXPORTING PRESS FREEDOM

Economic and Editorial Dilemmas in International Media Assistance

Craig L. LaMay

Transaction Publishers
New Brunswick (U.S.A.) and London (U.K.)

Copyright © 2007 by Transaction Publishers, New Brunswick, New Jersey.

All rights reserved under International and Pan-American Copyright Conventions. No part of this book may be reproduced or transmitted in any form or by any means, electronic or mechanical, including photocopy, recording, or any information storage and retrieval system, without prior permission in writing from the publisher. All inquiries should be addressed to Transaction Publishers, Rutgers—The State University, 35 Berrue Circle, Piscataway, New Jersey 08854-8042. www.transactionpub.com

This book is printed on acid-free paper that meets the American National Standard for Permanence of Paper for Printed Library Materials.

Library of Congress Catalog Number: 2006044468
ISBN: 978-0-7658-0359-7
Printed in the United States of America

Library of Congress Cataloging-in-Publication Data

LaMay, Craig L.
    Exporting press freedom / Craig L. LaMay.
        p. cm.
    Includes bibliographical references and index.
    ISBN 0-7658-0359-3 (cloth : alk paper)
    1. Freedom of the press. 2. Freedom of the press—Developing countries. 3. Press and politics. 4. Press and politics—Developing countries. I. Title.

PN4736.L36 2007
323.44'5091724—dc22   2006044468

To my father, Edward H. LaMay, with love and admiration.

Contents

Acknowledgements

I owe my career, and thus the opportunity even to write this book, to several people whom I count as mentors and as friends: Newton N. Minow, Everette E. Dennis, Michael Janeway, Ken Bode, Burton A. Weisbrod, and the late Margaret Blanchard. Newton Minow, particularly, has been the mentor everyone should have and that I actually do. He is a patient and wise teacher, with a singular talent for getting to the root of problems and proposing bold solutions.

I am grateful also to those who first involved me in the media assistance business. At Duke University I am indebted to the eminent Russian media scholar Ellen Mickiewicz, whose intellectual and administrative talents for linking exacting scholarship with the demands of daily journalism are rare anywhere, and who does it with a diplomatic elegance that always amazes me. At the Vienna-based Institute for the Danube Region and Central Europe I am grateful to former Austrian vice chancellor Erhard Busek, who now serves as the special coordinator for the Security Pact for Southeastern Europe. Together these two have for several years directed the Commission for Radio and Television Policy: Southeast, Central and Eastern Europe, a non-governmental media-assistance organization founded by President Jimmy Carter in 1991 and with which I have been involved as rapporteur since 1995. At the Aspen Institute I thank Charles Firestone and Amy Garmer, and at the Ford Foundation I thank Jon Funabiki. These three engaged me in the International Journalism and Free Expression Roundtable, a three-year program that ran from 2000 to 2003 and which focused specifically on the links between finance and editorial mission in the practice of media assistance. Their persistent, provocative questions on that subject first gave me the idea for this book.

I could not have written any of it without the help of the many publishers, editors and reporters, marketing and sales directors around the world who opened their newsrooms, offices and homes to me. These people shared their business plans, their editorial meetings, their good company. Above all, they shared their hopes for a more democratic future in the countries they call home. Meeting them, in several cases getting to know them, has been one of the great pleasures of my career. I also benefited from long conversations with Harlan Mandel, Sasa Vucinic and Elena Popovic at the Media Development Loan Fund, and Charles Mundale at the Southern Africa Media Development Fund, among many others at both organizations. These four – of whom only one, Vucinic, is a journalist – have done remarkable things to secure press freedom in parts of the world where it otherwise would not exist.

The research for this book was supported by a grant from the Alumna of Northwestern University, which allowed me to travel around the world in 2003 and 2004 to visit almost all of the news organizations profiled or discussed here. I hope the Alumna will be pleased with the result. At Northwestern's Medill School of Journalism, my professional home, I thank professors Loren Ghiglione, Donna Leff, and David Abrahamson for their guidance and encouragement during the writing of this book. At Northwestern's Media Management Center I thank John Lavine and Mike Smith, whose views on the news business I do not always share, but who are skilled and thoughtful teachers. I am also grateful to a former Medill student, Lauren Stone, for her research help and her endless patience with me.

I would not be at this station in life but for the encouragement and support of Karrie Fisher-LaMay, my wife of twenty-three years. My older son Ellis helped me with the technical details of manuscript preparation, and my younger son Owen provided untold happy diversions from writing.

Last, I want to thank my dad, Edward H. LaMay, whose expertise in marketing and finance, coupled with his skepticism for simple answers, were invaluable to me as I gathered and reviewed material for this book. Fortunately, his skepticism failed him when it came to me. No matter what roads I have chosen in life, he has given me love, good humor, and encouragement. I am long past due in honoring him for all he has done for me, and so, though it is inadequate to the task, this book is for him.

Preface

This book focuses on a problem of central significance to both governmental and non-governmental organizations active in international media and democratization projects, namely, how free and independent public affairs media are supposed to sustain themselves – servicing their editorial mission while also paying their bills – particularly in countries where they face a hostile legal or political system on the one hand and the demands of the consumer marketplace on the other. Assistance providers and recipients alike want to know what works: What kinds of projects enhance media independence and professionalism, and which are able to sustain themselves after initial funding sources are exhausted or withdrawn?

The term "media assistance" covers a lot of territory. The U.S. Government Accountability Office, for example, uses the term to include the so-called "public diplomacy" programs that have traditionally been run out of the Department of State since the end of World War II – the Voice of America, Radio Liberty, the many Radio Free services and other, sometimes clandestine broadcast programs. These services have operated with a specific task in mind, to explain the American view of world events to populations that live in authoritarian societies or with whom the United States is trying to establish better relations. Public diplomacy has been characterized both as the worst kind of propaganda and the noblest of public services, but for this book's purposes that debate is not important. Whatever else public diplomacy is, it is a U.S. government owned and operated broadcasting service, not an effort to build indigenous media capacity in developing or democratizing countries.

This second type of assistance is more recent and is the subject of this book. In its official form, U.S. media development aid is primarily the province of the U.S. Agency for International Development (USAID), which justifies media assistance as a tool to prevent social conflict, as an agent of political transparency and accountability, and as an essential component of economic development, the agency's principal mission.

Such assistance also furthers U.S. business and foreign policy interests. USAID notes that its media assistance efforts have "often, though not always, produced the same results that public diplomacy sought to achieve. In many countries, support to independent media created political space that enabled the United States to pursue specific foreign policy goals, such as holding of elections, promotion of human rights, or political reconciliation."[1] In Europe, the European Commission views its media assistance efforts similarly, as do the official development agencies of several (mostly northern) European countries. There are also many private, non-governmental sources of media assistance, including media-based foundations and activist groups, which share some of these goals, in part or in whole, and advance others of their own.

USAID categorizes media assistance by need, which according to the agency is one of three kinds: in "vulnerable countries where conflict may be imminent," USAID focuses on "providing a plurality of voices" as a way of alleviating social tensions; in "areas of active conflict," the agency supports "alternative media" with "short-term grants to provide information and ideas that otherwise would be suppressed"(the form of assistance that most closely resembles public diplomacy); and in "post-conflict and developing countries" the agency seeks "to develop a self-sustaining media sector that is part of the culture of democracy and that supports accountability of other power centers."[2] In real life, of course, the divisions are not so neat. USAID, for example, credits its media assistance to Bosnia for providing "a vibrant media sector...that offers Bosnian citizens a wide range of information and opinions as well as an alternative to the nationalist press."[3] In truth, Bosnia remains a dangerous and divided place, and the media there are overwhelming allied with or dependent on various organized crime interests. Bosnia is a center for trafficking in small arms and women, and reporter access to supposedly public information is typically available only with a bribe. Civil servants, including police, are corrupt and are themselves involved in organized crime. Independent journalists who seek to cover official crime and corruption are routinely harassed, threatened and physically attacked. According to a female reporter from the weekly newspaper *Slobodna Bosna*, some international peacekeepers assigned to the country also participate in the sex trafficking business, and so cannot be counted on to provide journalists with protection.[4] The point is that Bosnia's media "need" is difficult to characterize using USAID's categories. The same could be said of, for instance, Guatemala or Indonesia.

In the early to mid-1980s, media assistance was a relatively small field, but it grew exponentially after the collapse of the Berlin Wall and then of the Soviet Union, with aid going not only to the former communist states but also to post-conflict and democratizing regimes around the world. Media assistance pursues many goals, but the main ones have been journalism training (newsgathering, reporting and editing); media law reform; professionalism (often in the form of journalists' trade unions); and media management training. USAID spent $264 million on media assistance between 1985 and 2001,[5] the great majority of that after 1989, when the agency spent an average of $33 million annually on such assistance, with amounts ranging from a low of $13 million in 1992 to a high of $61 million in 1999[6]; the total of all U.S. media assistance, governmental and non-governmental, is estimated to be at least $600 million over the same period, with the bulk of it going to the former communist countries of Central, Southeast and Eastern Europe.[7] In the most recent year for which data are available, 2004, total U.S. government media assistance was approximately $40 million, with about $25 million of that going through USAID to two independent contractors, Internews ($14.1 million) and the International Research and Exchanges Board (IREX/ProMedia, $11.3 million).[8] The balance of official media assistance for 2004 went through the U.S. State Department.[9] The largest private source of media assistance comes from George Soros' network of thirty-two foundations, led by the Open Society Institutes in New York and London (previously Budapest), which give approximately $20 million annually to media-building projects. The inventory of media assistance donors also includes governmental organizations such as the official development agencies of Sweden, Denmark, the Netherlands, Norway, Finland, and the United Kingdom; international governmental organizations such as the European Union, the United Nations, the Council of Europe, the Organization for Security and Cooperation in Europe (OSCE), and the World Bank; and hundreds of mostly American and European non-governmental organizations.

Over the past decade, the various donor organizations interested in democratization have become increasingly intent on the problem of program sustainability in the non-governmental sectors of transition societies, including media.[10] That problem is economic. A 2003 overview of media assistance by the Netherlands Institute of International Relations defines sustainability as "a process for continuing the benefits of [media] intervention by establishing future indigenous capacity."[11] At one level the sustainability problem is linked directly to general economic development. In 2005, the U.S. General Accounting Office said in a review of USAID media projects that the "sustainability of project recipients" is the key to "the overall success of projects or specific activities at the country level."[12] The World Bank has argued that economic development and democratic transition depend on "the creation of economically viable press enterprises."[13]

At a second level, sustainability in media enterprises is a problem created by the social goods nature of those enterprises, a subject discussed throughout this book. According to Eric Johnson, the Internews administrator for the NIS countries, "The fundamental problems facing independent media in the larger part of the NIS are economic. If you can afford to buy your own building, printing press, TV tower, transmitter, paper, equipment, you're golden. So the keys are to help the media acquire financial viability, try to keep it alive long enough to do so, and provide assistance so that when it does do so it'll be responsible."[14] A recent descriptive overview of media assistance prepared for the John S. and James L. Knight Foundation by journalist Ellen Hume notes that economic sustainability is now at the top of the list of almost any donor conference concerning media assistance and its future challenges.[15] For their part, aid recipients have grown frustrated at what they characterize as ineffective or misguided assistance, and have as a result tried to become more active participants in directing and managing the aid they receive.

Happily, one reason for this changed emphasis is success. The improved political and economic landscape of some regions, particularly in Central Europe, has all but eliminated any sense of need for media aid. Foreign capital investment in Central and even in Southeast Europe has been a transforming factor in the media sectors of those regions, so much so that a few owners, such as the German media company Westdeutsche Allgemeine Zeitung (WAZ), now dominate the newspaper market in Serbia, Macedonia, and Bulgaria. Other American and West European firms, such as the News Corporation, Bertelsmann, Sanoma, and Ringier, have also invested heavily in the East.[16] Elsewhere – in Southeast Asia and in Latin America, for instance – economic growth during the 1990s had a similar damping effect on assistance, even if the political climate for free media in these regions has changed relatively little over the same period.

But another reason for diminished aid is a belief among donors and recipients alike that too many media assistance programs have not produced lasting or worthy results. Perhaps the most famous example of this was Radio UNTAC, a Cambodian radio service created by the United Nations in 1993 to provide voters with reliable news programming prior to the post-conflict, democratic elections in that country. The service was a huge success, credited with helping to ensure an election that was widely perceived as free and fair, and was hailed as a triumph for the use of media in democratization programs. But Radio UNTAC folded with the UN withdrawal from the country, leaving its indigenous journalists to revert to highly partisan and sensational media for employment. The media in Cambodia quickly became instruments of disinformation and social discord, and only fours years after the elections the country suffered a coup.

If Cambodia's experience was extreme, it was not unusual. In many so-called "transition" countries, media and other civil society associations exist in varying states of change, and not always for the better. Often both have weakened. In societies where the experience of totalitarian or authoritarian governments was especially long or brutal, civil society and media freedom remain works in progress. In other cases, key civil society leaders have been lost to new governing coalitions or to simple demobilization. Public-service media that once survived on grants from international donors have found it impossible to service their debt or attract new sources of revenue, principally advertisers, in a newly open and competitive market environment. In other cases, donors have inadvertently created aid dependencies. Konstanty Gebert, a former samizdat journalist in Poland and now a columnist for *Gazeta Wyborcza*, argues that the practice of grant-making that dominated media assistance in the 1990s is counterproductive, if not destructive, a view shared by many others in and out of the donor community. "The grant procedure is dysfunctional and generates undue influence from the grantor, which is pushing its agenda," Gebert says. Worse, grants too often have the effect of focusing the receiving news organization "on how to get the next grant, not how to be independent. This ossifies bad practices, and when the money goes away, the media outlet fails."[17]

After more than a decade of media assistance programs, USAID has reached a similar conclusion:

> Advertising and business investment in media have not developed as needed to support independent media in many post-communist and economically vulnerable societies. Dependence on donors remains a big problem. The emphasis on creating independent media outlets remains vitally important, but it may not be realistic or productive in many places.[18]

USAID goes on to recommend that "the goal of media assistance should be the promotion of the media sector and not the survival of every media outlet."[19]

Against this historical experience and practical background, this book is about the dilemma of sustainability in media assistance programs. The problem is at one level finding adequate and reliable financing, but it is not merely that. If it were, the problem would be easy and the solution uninteresting. Rather the trick is finding adequate economic support for an editorial mission that contributes to democratic processes and to democratic consolidation. Somewhere between these two goals is, presumably, something that might be called "independence." Getting there is the hard part. For many public-service news organizations, whether they work in repressive social and political environments or are finding their way in newly open market economies, independence has become a cruel choice between living forever off grants from international donors or abandoning serious editorial mission to the maelstrom of market competition or, as bad, to political or corporate patronage. Courage, unfortunately, does have a price tag.

Perhaps a dozen or so books and reports exist on the subject of international media assistance, written variously by journalists, scholars and in many cases by aid providers, but few concern themselves with the dilemma of editorial quality and economic sustainability, and none do so at length. The authoritative chronicler of the democracy-promotion industry, Thomas Carothers of the Carnegie Endowment for International Peace, acknowledges media assistance as part of the enterprise, but in his written work rarely does more than link it to "civil society" promotion or to the conduct of electoral campaigns.[20] Other scholarly writers on the democratization industry do not discuss media at all.[21] Some publications produced by or for the media assistance industry or by Western media foundations are essentially narrative overviews of countries or regions,[22] such as the annual reports of the International Press Institute[23] or Freedom House,[24] while others publicize the work of assistance providers (at least in part, presumably, to inform and encourage funders).[25] Official aid sources both national and international also publish on media assistance. The U.S. Agency for International Development, for instance, has a report on the strategic goals of media aid[26] and has published short narrative reports on "best practices"[27] and "programmatic lessons" in the industry.[28] The Vienna-based Representative on Freedom of the Media for the OSCE publishes a biennial report on the status of media freedom across the entire OSCE region, a report that typically includes summaries of media assistance activities and needs.[29] The industry has also produced a number of what might be called guidebooks, essentially how-to volumes on problems associated with media development. Topics include such things as how to report on elections,[30] ethnic and racial minorities,[31] gender issues,[32] broadcast law and regulation,[33] public-service and advocacy campaigns,[34] freedom of information law,[35] and "cyberactivism."[36] There are in addition management primers that cover everything from advertising and audience research[37] to the technical aspects of setting up a radio or television station.[38]

Among the best works on the activities of media assistance are a handful of books and papers by communications law scholar Monroe Price, founder and co-director of the Programme on Comparative Media Law and Policy at Oxford University. He and his colleagues have written about the role of media in both starting and ending violent conflicts,[39] and about the enabling environment for post-conflict media development.[40] Price is also the author of a monograph about the meanings and implications of media sustainability.[41] That monograph was prepared for the International Roundtable on Journalism and Free Expression, an organization in which I participated, and the paper contributed greatly to my interest in and thinking on this subject. The Roundtable, which operated from 1999 to 2003, produced three reports on the subject of media and civil society sustainability.[42]

Of course, a large scholarly and journalistic literature exists on democracy and the media, but most of it focuses on developed Western democracies.[43] A lesser number of scholarly books focus on media in transition states in ways that are theoretically or descriptively interesting but nonetheless fairly remote from the daily problems, reportorial and managerial, that confront journalists in developing democracies and market economies.[44] Other scholars have produced excellent analyses of the role media have played in specific democratic transitions and at the struggle for media control before, during and after transition.[45] At least two good monographs provide descriptive overviews of some of the hundreds of organizations involved in media assistance, what they do and with whom, but so far these have been limited to preliminary mapping efforts.[46] In any case, they are written more from the point of view of donors than recipients (indeed, they were commissioned by donor organizations), and so touch only lightly on the many and varied problems recipients face when trying to convert assistance into sustainable businesses. Finally, there are books and articles on media aid and development that are alike mostly in their lament over the lack of ethical and editorial professionalism among journalists in transition states.[47] While low professional standards are a problem, it is of course not one limited to journalists in developing countries. To the extent these works suggest there are universal normative standards for journalistic practice, the idea finds little support in the historical record, in the variety of legal and regulatory systems for media, or available observation.

This book understands the problems of media assistance primarily but not exclusively as economic ones. It looks at the joined problems of economic viability *and* editorial quality from the point of view of journalists in developing democracies. The economic dilemmas unique to news production are common to all open societies, but arguably they are especially critical in developing countries since the way in which they are resolved there will have a great deal to say about the course and character of democratic progress and consolidation. The book is both descriptive—based on first-hand reporting in Southeast and Central Europe, Latin America, Southeast Asia and Africa--and conceptual. After all, it is not immediately apparent what is meant by "sustainable," never mind "free and independent." Media assistance, like the larger project of democracy assistance, tends to trade in terms whose meanings are at best ambiguous and at worst mere slogans, creating problems that run from distrust to disaster. This conceptual confusion contributes to the operational problem of non-sustainability.

In so far as the problems faced by media assistance are both conceptual and operational, the chapters that follow attempt to distinguish them in that way. Chapter 1 is a more complete discussion of the financial-editorial dilemma discussed in this introduction. To that end, the chapter takes as its central narrative the experience of *El Periodico* and *Nuestro Diario*, two very different newspapers founded in Guatemala after that country's return to civilian rule in 1996. Chapter 2 provides an overview of the democracy promotion industry, its goals and its actors, by placing them within a brief history of U.S. and EU foreign aid programs. Chapter 3 is an overview of the media assistance industry, how it developed in the 1980s and earlier, and how it grew after the 1989 transitions.

Chapters 4 through 5 employ examples from developed and developing countries to examine more closely the editorial and financial challenges faced by the would-be media system architect. The first of these, discussed in chapter 4, is essentially an editorial problem: What is the nature of the relationship between media and civil society in developing democracies, and what does that relationship suggest about media, their likely revenue sources, and their long-term economic viability? The subject is important because both aid providers and recipients commonly link media assistance to civil society promotion, rhetorically and programmatically. But often the term "civil society" is used so casually in media assistance as to be very nearly meaningless. Chapter 5 discusses at greater length the economics of news and the unique problems associated with information goods. It takes as its central case study the piecemeal U.S. approach to public broadcasting and its financing. The United States is virtually alone in the democratic world in having created public broadcasting as an alternative to an overwhelming private, for-profit broadcast system, rather than vice versa. Established by Congress in 1967, the Corporation for Public Broadcasting has had a mixed history, but it has suffered from the start from the two problems central to this book – inadequate sources of revenue and grand confusion about editorial mission.

Finally, chapter 6 looks at several developing-country operational responses to the financial/editorial dilemma. On the one hand it looks at media organizations of different types: an online newspaper in Malaysia, *Malaysiakini*; a national news radio network in Indonesia, Kantor Berita Radio; a radio and multi-media firm in Serbia and Montenegro, B92; and an Internet news magazine in Prague, *Transitions Online*. The experiences of other public-service media are also discussed here, as well as throughout the book. In every case, the goal is to identify and learn from journalists who are striving to make a difference while also trying to make a living, often in political and economic environments that are still difficult for independent media, and sometimes dangerous.

Chapter 6 also looks at two innovative media assistance providers. The first is the New York- and Prague-based Media Development Loan Fund (MDLF); the second is the Gaborone-based Southern Africa Media Development Fund (SAMDEF). Both organizations work essentially as venture capital firms that make below-market loans to quality news and public-affairs media in countries where, for whatever reason, democratic consolidation is stalled or incomplete, or where the market for independent media is severely compromised. The idea in every case is for the participating news organizations to wean themselves from grants and donations entirely and to become full and competitive participants in their markets – that is to say, financially independent. What makes these two organizations unique in the field of media assistance is their commitment to their clients; the award of a loan instead of a grant fundamentally changes the relationship between provider and recipient from one of donor/supplicant to a partnership. The funder takes a long-term interest in the financial and programmatic health of the recipient, which to pay back the loan must develop greater financial discipline and more strategic management.

The usefulness of the assistance models developed by MDLF and by SAMDEF is not universal. Without question, in many parts of the world where democratic transition has yet to take hold or is in retreat (and where, among other things, loans cannot be secured), grants, technical and material media assistance are much needed and in short supply. Elsewhere, however, the MDLF/SAMDEF model provides a good operational benchmark for linking editorial mission to financial performance. As importantly, what these organizations do in transition societies where markets are fragile and political life unstable could also be effective in established democracies where, because of media consolidation, the economic environment for editorially independent media is also hostile. Journalists everywhere who are committed to dispassionate coverage of news and public affairs increasingly find themselves working in media environments that neither encourage nor value their work. In that respect, the discussion about media sustainability, in whatever form, concerns us all.

Notes

1. Krisha Kumar, *USAID's Media Assistance: Policy and Programmatic Lessons* (Washington, DC: USAID Office of Development Evaluation and Information, Bureau of Policy and Program Coordination) January 2004, xii.
2. See Ellen Hume, *Media Assistance: Best Practices and Priorities, Report on a USAID Workshop* (Washington, DC: USAID, Bureau for Policy and Program Coordination, November 2003), 10-12.
3. Kumar, *USAID's Media Assistance*, 2004, ix.
4. Nidzara Ahmetasevic, reporter, *Slobodna Bosna*, author interview, Durham, NC, March 8, 2004.
5. Kumar, *USAID's Media Assistance*, 2004, ix.
6. Government Accountability Office, *Independent Media Development Abroad: Challenges Exist in Implementing U.S. Efforts and Measuring Results*, GAO-05-803 (Washington, DC: GAO, 2005), 9. Hereinafter, *GAO, Independent Media Development Abroad, 2005*.

7. Ellen Hume, *The Media Missionaries: American Support for International Journalism* (Miami, Fl.: John S. and James L. Knight Foundation, May 2002), 1-2. See http://www.ellenhume.com/articles/missionaries1_contents.html.
8. GAO, *Independent Media Development Abroad*, 2005, 9.
9. Ibid.
10. Thomas Carothers, *Aiding Democracy Abroad: The Learning Curve* (Washington, DC: Carnegie Endowment for International Peace, 1999), 207-248.
11. Ross Howard, *International Media Assistance: A Review of Donor Activities and Lessons Learned.* (Amsterdam: Netherlands Institute of International Relations, Conflict Research Unit, June 2003), 21.
12. GAO, *Independent Media Development Abroad,* 2005, 3.
13. Timothy Balding, "Introduction," *A New Approach to Development: The Role of the Press.* (Zurich: World Association of Newspapers/World Bank, June 13, 1999), 3.
14. Quoted in Julia E. Seidler, *Exporting Democracy Without Citizens? Goals and Practices of American Agencies Providing Journalism Assistance Programs in Ukraine* (Iowa City: University of Iowa, unpublished doctoral dissertation, May 2001), 142.
15. Hume, *Media Missionaries,* 2002. Hume lists economic sustainability as the second of her "15 commandments of media development."
16. See Daniela Sussenbacher, "Foreign Ownership in SEE Region," *deScripto: A Journal of Media in South Eastern Europe*, No. 2 (Winter 2005): 11.
17. Konstanty Gebert, columnist, *Gazeta Wyborcza*, author interview, Denpasar, Indonesia, September 10, 2002.
18. Hume, *Media Missionaries*, 2003, 13.
19. Kumar, *USAID's Media Assistance,* 2004, xiii.
20. See, for example, Carothers, *Aiding Democracy Abroad*, 1999; see also Larry Diamond, *Developing Democracy: Toward Consolidation* (Baltimore, MD: Johns Hopkins University Press, 1999).
21. See, for example, Michael Cox, John Ikenberry, and Takashi Inoguchi, eds., *American Democracy Promotion: Impulses, Strategies, and Impacts* (New York: Oxford University Press, 2000).
22. In the 1990s, for example, the now-defunct Freedom Forum Media Studies Center at Columbia University did three overviews of regional media in transition. See Everette E. Dennis and Jon Vanden Heuvel, *Emerging Voices: East European Media in Transition* (New York: Gannett Foundation Media Center, 1990); Vanden Heuvel and Dennis, *Changing Patterns: Latin America's Vital Media* (New York: Freedom Forum Media Studies Center, 1995); and Vanden Heuvel and Dennis, *Unfolding Lotus: East Asia's Changing Media* (New York: Freedom Forum Media Studies Center, 1995).
23. See *IPI Report: 2004 World Press Freedom Review* (Vienna: International Press Institute, 2004). The IPI annual reports are available at www.freemedia.at.
24. See Freedom House, *Freedom of the Press 2004: A global survey of media independence* (New York: Rowman & Littlefield Publishers, 2004).
25. See, for example, the quarterly report of the Knight International Press Fellowships, *Knightline International*, published in conjunction with the International Center for Journalists, knight@icfj.org, or www.knight-international.org.
26. See USAID, *The Role of Media in Democracy: A Strategic Approach* (Washington, DC, US Agency for International Development, Center for Democracy and Governance, June 1999).
27. Hume, *Media Missionaries*, 2003.

28. Kumar, *USAID's Media Assistance,* 2004.

29. See Organization or Security and Cooperation in Europe, *2002/2003 Freedom and Responsibility Yearbook* (Vienna: OSCE, 2003), http://www.osce.org/fom/item_11_13582.html.

30. See, for example, Ellen Mickiewicz and Charles Firestone, *Television and Elections,* first edition (Durham, NC: DeWitt Wallace Center, Duke University, 1992).

31. See Donald R. Browne, Charles Firestone and Ellen Mickiewicz, *Television/Radio News and Minorities* (Durham, NC: DeWitt Wallace Center, Duke University, 1994).

32. See Coleen Lowe-Morna, *Whose News? Whose Views? Southern Africa Gender in Media Handbook* (Windhoek: Media Institute of Southern Africa, 2001).

33. See Ellen Mickiewicz, Charles Firestone, Donald R. Browne, Craig L. LaMay, *Democracy on the Air* (Durham, NC: DeWitt Wallace Center, Duke University, 1999).

34. See *Facilitators's Guide: Media Advocacy Toolkit* (Windhoek: Media Institute of Southern Africa, 2002). MISA is a creation of the 1991 UNESCO Windhoek Declaration. With funds from USAID, it publishes several of these "toolkits," resource books and course guides to be used in public-service campaigns.

35. See Sheila S. Coronel, ed., *The Right to Know: Access to Information in Southeast Asia* (Quezon City, Philippines: Philippine Center for Investigative Journalism, 2001).

36. See Steven Gan, James Gomez and Uwe Johannen, *Asian Cyberactivism: Freedom of Expression and Media Censorship* (Bangkok: Friedrich Naumann Foundation, 2004).

37. See *The Business of News: Running Successful Newspapers in Emerging Free Markets* (Washington, DC: International Center for Journalists, 2000). The report is available through ICFJ at www.idfj.org.

38. The assistance NGO Media Development Loan Fund (MDLF), for example, has published a "Media Manual Series" with several how-to titles. See Sasa Ordanoski, *Are You Sure You Want to Start a Magazine? 100 Things You Need to Know* (New York: MDLF, 2000); Vello Laan, *Radio Tartu: A Case Study in Starting a Radio Station* (New York: MDLF, 2000); and Alexej Fulmek, A *Manual for Survival: A Case Study of the Slovak Opposition Newspaper SME* (New York: MDLF, 2000). Similarly, the Panos Institute publishes *What is Community Radio? A Resource Guide* (Johannesburg: AMARC Africa, 1998).

39. See Monroe E. Price and Mark Thompson, eds., *Forging Peace: Intervention, Human Rights and the Management of Media Space* (Bloomington: Indiana University Press, 2002). See also Price, *Media and Sovereignty: The Global Information Revolution and its Challenge to State Power* (Cambridge, MA: MIT Press, 2002).

40. Monroe E. Price and Peter Krug, *The Enabling Environment for Free and Independent Media* (Washington, DC: US Agency for International Development, 2002).

41. Monroe E. Price, "Sustainability: An Approach Towards a Matrix," discussion paper prepared for the Aspen Institute Roundtable on Journalism and Freedom of Expression, Santiago, Chile, March 13-16, 2001, draft dated February 25, 2001.

42. See Craig L. LaMay, *Journalism and Emerging Democracy: Lessons from Societies in Transition* (Washington, DC: Aspen Institute, 2001); LaMay, *Sustaining Media Pluralism in Democratizing Societies* (Washington, DC: Aspen Institute, 2001); and LaMay, *Democratic Enterprise: Sustaining Media and Civil Society* (Washington, DC: Aspen Institute, 2003).

43. For a recent and thoughtful critique, see Herbert J. Gans, *Democracy and the News* (New York: Oxford University Press, 2003); see also James Fallows, *Breaking the*

News: How the Media Undermine American Democracy (New York: Pantheon, 1996); Robert McChesney, *Rich Media, Poor Democracy: Communications Politics in Dubious Times* (Champaign: University of Illinois Press, 1999); and Jay Rosen, *What Are Journalists For?* (New Haven, CT: Yale University Press, 1999).

44. See, for example, Richard Gunther and Anthony Mughan, eds., *Democracy and the Media: A Comparative Perspective* (New York: Cambridge University Press, 2000); see also Monroe E. Price, Beata Rozumilowicz, and Stefaan G. Verhulst, eds., *Media Reform: Democratizing Media, Democratizing the State* (London: Routledge, 2001); Patrick H. O'Neil, ed., *Communicating Democracy: The Media and Political Transitions* (London: Lynne Rienner Publishers, 1998); and Vicky Randall, ed., *Democratization and the Media* (London: Frank Cass, 1998).

45. Among the best of these case studies is Ellen Mickiewicz, *Changing Channels: Television and the Struggle for Power in Russia* (New York: Oxford University Press, 1997); see also Thomas E. Skidmore, ed., *Television, Politics and the Transition to Democracy in Latin America* (Washington, DC: Woodrow Wilson Center Press, 1993); Elizabeth Fox and Silvio Waisbord, eds., *Latin Politics: Global Media* (Austin: University of Texas Press, 2002); and Richard Gunther and Anthony Mughan, *Democracy and the Media*, 2000.

46. See Hume, *Media Missionaries*, 2002; see also Monroe E. Price, Bethany David Noll, and Daniel De Luce, *Mapping Media Assistance* (Oxford: Programme in Comparative Media Law and Policy, 2002).

47. A book that specifically focuses on low professional standards in developing democracies is Peter Gross, *Entangled Evolutions* (Baltimore, MD: Johns Hopkins University Press, 2002).

1

Democratization and the Dilemmas of Media Independence

"No one can be good for long if goodness is not in demand." – Bertolt Brecht

Since about the mid-1970s, democratic transitions in Latin America, Africa, Asia, and Europe have occurred with important contributions from the civil society sector, including a broad array of media, not just news organizations but also entertainment and public relations media. The questions still confronting many of these countries is whether their transitions are permanent or passing, and if the former what obstacles lie in the way of democratic consolidation. Perhaps the largest obstacle, writes Samuel Huntington, is the recognition that "democracy is a solution to the problem of tyranny, but not necessarily to anything else."[1] Poverty, ethnic and racial conflict, inadequate economic development, chronic inflation with substantial external debt, and political leaders –many of them former dissidents –who are not fully committed to the democratic ideal of lawful and peaceful transitions of power, all militate against successful consolidation. In transition countries as varied in their political, economic and cultural experience as Russia, Indonesia and Guatemala, democracy's hold has been irresolute.

Media assistance is intended in some way to address these problems. For journalists, the idea behind media aid is both obvious and non-controversial – if a people are to be sovereign, they must be able to receive a wide variety of ideas, to criticize the government and, more generally, to circulate information related to public affairs. "Free elections" do not mean much if the government's opponents have been gagged and their platform banned from public discussion. News media make sovereignty meaningful by acting literally as the medium through which actions taken in civil society find their expression in political and economic society and, eventually, their manifestation in public policy. Official assistance providers—such as, in the case of the United States, the U.S. Agency for International Development (USAID) – also endorse the idea that press freedom is a "fundamental" democratic goal,[2] but in practice view media assistance as a more instrumental good. Historically it has been associated with efforts to organize and hold free elections, in which the role of media is to provide voters with information about parties, candidates, polling places and times, and so on. More broadly, the purpose of media assistance, as with other forms of democracy assistance, is to ensure that other, more traditional forms of development aid are used productively and not siphoned off by corrupt or incompetent governments. Official democracy aid, in other words, is supposed to provide at least some measure of transparency and accountability in international economic development. Private providers of media assistance – for example, non-governmental organizations like the Open Society Institute (OSI) or the International Center for Journalists (ICFJ) – will often work to advance these goals as contractors with government aid agencies, but they will also emphasize goals of their own, for example, promoting civil society, advancing women's rights, or securing the rights of free expression and a free press.

The recipients of media assistance –journalists in developing and democratizing countries—typically describe "democratic" media as serving two broad goals. The first is "building a culture of free expression," to which end journalists will talk about a range of issues associated with the "watchdog" role of the press and the need to provide citizens with access to news and information. This conception will often compete with another, quite different one that emphasizes providing citizens access to the instruments of communication, perhaps even against the prerogatives of those who own them, and especially where ownership is concentrated in the state or in private centers of economic power. This conception links media firmly to civil society promotion – "enhancing the bonds of community, building citizenship and promoting individuality," as one Filipino journalist and educator explained it to me.[3] These conceptions are not mutually exclusive, and they are joined in a common inquiry: How does a society create and sustain media that engage the public in democratically centered discourse? From this follows several related questions: What is the role of the state in creating and sustaining an independent and diverse press? What about the seemingly intractable problem of inhospitable environments—from coercive governments, antiquated press laws and marginalized populations on the one hand to public apathy and unfavorable markets on the other? What strategies can journalists in developing societies realistically employ to circumvent, if not overcome, these obstacles free press development?

Unfortunately for the would-be media system architect, there are no good answers to these questions. There exists great disagreement even in established Western democracies about what "free" and "independent" media look like, what purposes they serve, to whom they are held accountable and how.[4] Despite this, it is easy to find in even the academic literature breezy proclamations about the global "triumph" of "Western" journalistic standards.[5] This makes no more sense than it does to talk about "Western-style" democracy. The United States and the United Kingdom, for example, have both very different media systems and quite different ideas of what makes a democracy work. Thomas Carothers has written that "the principles of democracy are quite clear,"[6] but the principles of democracy are also breathtakingly few. "Democracy has no theory to export," Jacques Barzun wrote in 1989, in advance of the democracy aid soon to flow to Central and Eastern Europe, "because it is not an ideology but a wayward historical development."[7] At best, he said, democracy has a theorem: that for people to be free they must also be sovereign, and the necessary conditions for sovereignty are political and social equality. How they exercise that sovereignty, what mechanisms they use to ensure equality and to distribute freedoms, is left to them to decide. As a result, institutional forms of democracy vary significantly. Americans, for instance, would find the social regulatory regimes in Switzerland or Sweden oppressive, the coalition governments of Germany, France, or Italy a hindrance to effective decision-making, and Holland's non-majoritarian, proportional system of party representation incomprehensible. One might seek to copy any of these as a device for the expression of popular will, or invent something completely different.

So while it is fine to talk in broad terms about rule of law, respect for human rights (including free expression), and civil society formation, it is not a theory that makes a democracy so much as it is how the wheels turn. And at the level of machinery, theories about democracy can obscure more than they reveal. Consider, for example, the idea that cultural or religious values are the main impediments to democratization in Asia and the Islamic world.[8] Maybe the problem stems from the way scholarly work gets reduced to television sound-bites by journalists and aid providers, but the effect is the same: to make simplistic what are complex challenges. For example, in Indonesia – an Asian country and the world's largest Muslim nation – the operative values that pose the critical problem for democratization are not Asian "culture" or Islamic "culture" but the many juxtaposed and overlapping "cultures" that coexist within the same political boundaries: tribal communities in Kalimantan and New Guinea; agrarian, semi-feudal communities in the provinces; a growing middle class; and the technology-adept capitalist elite in Jakarta. Add to this that Indonesia stretches across one-eighth of the world's circumference in an archipelago of 17,000 islands containing more than 300 ethnic groups that speak as many or more different languages, and democracy promotion starts to look tricky. If a goal of a public-service media system is, at least in part, to link these many pieces into a coherent whole, how best to do that?

For our would-be architect of free and independent media, there is the additional challenge that media, unlike most other democratic institutions, are rooted not in political or civil society, but in economic society. As an industry, democracy promotion has tended (and still tends) to see media primarily as a component of civil society promotion, which is understandable and fine until aid is exhausted or withdrawn. Then it comes time to pay the bills – for salaries, newsprint, ink, transmitters, videotape, delivery trucks, telephones, computer software, presses and all the rest. Other institutions of governance also have to pay their costs, of course, but many of those have the power of taxation. It is certainly not unheard of for media to rely on tax support – the license fee that sustains many European public broadcasters is exactly that – but as a revenue source it is always troublesome, and in editorial terms its effects can be restrictive rather than liberating. Absent multiple layers of statutory and bureaucratic insulation, media that rely on government support will always be susceptible to government meddling, or worse. Rarely can even the most benign governments be expected to favor any interests but their own. More generally, the idea of government support for media, and thus entanglement with them, can be offensive to the idea of a speech market in which individual actors (and their ideas) are supposed to compete without unfair advantage. In real life, of course, some members of the speech market are hugely advantaged, usually by their economic power. Whether such a system is just or not, it is a principled question to ask whether that power should derive from the government purse. As a practical matter, too, the concept of government media is anathema to people in many democratizing countries, where past experience suggests a bad result, and by no means a "democratic" one.

The business of media assistance, now at least twenty years old, has thus come to recognize a number of dilemmas that are the subject of this book. The central dilemma is economic, between the need to find adequate and diverse sources of revenue while also providing a high-quality editorial product, one that contributes to democratic consolidation and maturity. The argument here is that the problems typically identified in virtually all democratic media systems – the lack of professionalism and even corruption among journalists, the tendency to favor sex, scandal and trivia in print and broadcast – are best understood as economic problems. Public affairs media are, or at least have many of the characteristics of, public goods, and as well media are experience goods. The cost of preparing a television news program, for instance, is the same whether it is broadcast to one person or one million, and no rational person will produce such a program if he cannot recover his average cost of production, that is, the cost of making the program, not the much smaller marginal costs associated with distribution. (The irrational or altruistic person may do this, but not for long.) Recouping those costs becomes more difficult because consumers cannot evaluate a media product without first consuming it. Consequently their decisions about what media to consume are likely to be poorly informed.

A third economic problem for our architect is that the production of this consumption good is an inherently inefficient activity: News is not like automobiles, computers or blue jeans, businesses where in which many fewer workers can now produce more product in less time than they could ten, twenty, or a hundred years ago. Put another way, good journalism is like good music, and is inefficient in the same way. Two hundred years ago, for example, it took four musicians to play Beethoven's String Quartet, Opus 18, No. 4, and it took them about twenty minutes to play it. Today the piece still requires four people and twenty minutes to play. There are some products, and news is one of them, where productivity remains flat or nearly so, notwithstanding the addition of new technologies or other innovations to the production line.[9] Quality journalism – the kind that involves reporters who investigate and report, editors who edit and rewrite – works very much the same way. Good journalism is a hand-made product, and the only way to wring efficiencies out of it is, unfortunately, to eliminate reporters or avoid serious newsgathering, neither of which is apt to improve democracy's chances.

The fourth problem for our architect is that the consumption of public affairs media is also an inherently inefficient activity. As Anthony Downs' posited long ago, the theory of "rational ignorance" suggests that for most people their time and money is more productively spent doing something other than becoming well-informed citizens.[10] For this reason, economist James Hamilton has written, most media engage in "rational omission" with respect to public affairs and investigative journalism, which in addition to being unattractive to audiences is much more costly to produce than sex, scandal, and trivia, and brings lower returns.[11]

It is for these reasons that quality public-affairs media everywhere find it difficult to support themselves financially (a problem discussed in greater detail in chapter 5). In developing democracies, consequently, training programs for reporters and editors, funding to support particular types of coverage, and other well-intended and potentially valuable assistance activities are apt to have little or no enduring value in and of themselves. Someone must pay a news organization's operating costs. Government or private subsidy for those costs, of course, is one solution. So, too, is the market, where media can compete for audiences and revenues. Neither solution is perfect; media under either scenario can be excellent, or they can lose their public good character altogether and even become a drag on the democratic project. As an economic proposition, all that can safely be said is that the availability or unavailability of *any* revenue source will have implications for editorial mission. And editorial mission matters. As a larger popular and academic literature argues, there are in both developing and developed countries many media that are not only financially self-supporting but hugely profitable, but which add little or nothing to democratic decision-making, and in some cases may even undermine it.[12]

The problem for media assistance, then, is to identify worthy editorial missions and then to figure out how to build self-sustaining businesses around them. Unfortunately, this kind of long-term approach is not the norm in democracy assistance, which is often criticized for the attention-deficit disorder of donors. Here also lies second part of the dilemma for our democracy architect. What is a "worthy" editorial mission? Again, economic theory about the impossibility of defining the "public interest" suggests that any answer one provides to this question will be freighted with political assumptions and preferences that will invariably please some members of society while displeasing others. This is particularly so with respect to how media policy understands the rights of the press and of free expression generally, and about the proper involvement, if any, the government may have in the media marketplace. One can choose to dodge these problems entirely, as some media training organizations attempt to do; to describe it in broad normative terms, as some media NGOs do; or to dive headlong into a solution, as some international organizations (like the UN or the OSCE) have been charged to do in post-conflict regions like Bosnia and Kosovo. The solution in any case will always be in some way flawed. As with the problem of financing, this book does not assume that there is a straightforward answer to the problem of editorial mission.

A final challenge facing the would-be democracy promoter, beyond the ambition of this book, is that the very nature of democracy is changing. Even as democracy has become the only normatively acceptable choice at the level of the nation-state, it has arguably been cheapened by its ubiquity. The relationship between decisions that average citizens take at the ballot box and the circumstances of their daily lives grows every more tenuous in a global economy. For journalists and those who wish to assist them, this paradox represents both an editorial challenge and a financial one. On the one hand it prompts the question of how journalists are to understand and explain the challenges facing their countries and communities within the larger framework of global governance. On the other it exposes news organizations everywhere, but particularly in developing societies, to additional competition in the markets for content, production and distribution, and of course for audiences, too.

There is little discussion about the so-called "democratic deficit" in the democratization industry, and to be fair, it is not its concern. Overwhelmingly the industry's practitioners work in and care about places where, against the experience of political repression, ethnic conflict, and war, people are trying to reassert control over the conditions of their own lives, and in many cases to reclaim their dignity as human beings. And at its best the industry is not much interested in the institutions and processes of formal democracy unless they make participatory democracy real—that is to say, they give citizens a voice in government decision-making and provide some measure of social and economic equality. Where the democratization industry focuses on these kinds of places, people, and problems, it is hard not to be impatient both with realists who argue "it cannot be done" and with moralists who underestimate how long and hard the work will be. Though the industry is frequently paternalistic in its thinking and behavior, anti-intellectual and even fad-

dish, it deserves credit for its emphasis on public participation of a kind
that has largely disappeared from advanced representative democracies
(what Robert Dahl, in fact, calls polyarchies[13]), and which is increasingly difficult to resuscitate anywhere, never mind in states struggling to
escape authoritarian or violent pasts. At least some of the uncertainties
that bedevil media assistance are thus derivative of those that bedevil
democracy generally.

A Guatemalan Apologue

In late 2004 I was doing field research for this book when a colleague's
email referred me to a trade magazine article about the Media Management Center, a journalism research and training organization whose home
offices in Evanston, Illinois, are upstairs from my own at Northwestern
University. The Center is the gold standard in media industry executive
training programs, affiliated both with the Medill School of Journalism
and with Northwestern's Kellogg School of Management. Its research
is widely praised and its recommendations carefully noted in the media
industries it serves, not only in the United States, but around the world.
In my visits to news organizations in developing countries, I have frequently referred editors and publishers to the Center's web pages, where
it generously makes its research findings available to anyone who wishes
to examine them.[14] The article in *Editor & Publisher* was another in a
series of accolades. The success story in this case was a Guatemalan
newspaper, *Nuestro Diario*, which since its founding in 1999 has enjoyed
singular commercial success in a market where it competes with five
other dailies. *Nuestro Diario* is especially popular among younger and
less-educated readers, and the article quoted several fourteen year olds
in the tourist haven of Antigua, about forty kilometers out of the capital
city, who claimed to read it "cada dia," every day. "I like the sports, the
stories about soccer, the crime stories, but the main thing is, it's entertaining, a way to pass the time," said one young man.[15]

"*Nuestro Diario*," the article went on to conclude, "is an ironic instance of the student turning teacher, the hottest case study on the international newspaper circuit."[16] The publisher of the paper attributed its
rapid growth in the six years since it opened to marketing and editorial
strategies he had learned at Media Management Center seminars.[17] According to *Editor & Publisher*, *Nuestro Diario* had applied a "rigorous
readership formula with steely discipline,"[18] and it quoted Mike Smith, a
principal in the Center, to the effect that U.S. publishers like the Chicago

Tribune Company were already seeking to replicate *Nuestro Diario's* success with young readers in products like the Tribune's *Red Eye*. And for good reason: *Nuestro Diario* has already nearly doubled the number of Guatemalans who read a daily paper, with a circulation of about 300,000. It is the largest-circulation newspaper in Central America, distributed almost entirely through street and newsstand sales. Compared to its competitors it has relatively few advertisements (with only 8 percent of the national advertising market), but its circulation is more than twice that of its closest competitor, *Prensa Libre*.

What appeals to *Nuestro Diario's* readers, said *Editor & Publisher*, is the paper's "predictability."[19] Part of that predictability is the number of pages, which on most days is thirty-two, making it easy for readers to find features to which they are accustomed while also making limited advertising space more valuable. The paper employs numerous elements of design and presentation – such as leaving the first six pages of the newspaper ad-free – that MMC research has shown are reader-friendly and thus promote sales. The reporting style of the paper, said *Editor & Publisher*,

> is to tell stories with a mix of text, photos and graphics. There are lots of short captions, giving information that is not repeated anywhere else. The main story, always short, almost never quotes anyone. Instead, there are snippets under headshots of the sources, who may be witnesses to a crime or giving an opinion about what happened…. In a package of text and graphics occupying just a third of a page, there might be more than a half-dozen ways to enter the story. On the big story that stretches across pages 2 and 3, there might be 25…. Every page is produced separately and reporting teams compete just to get on it…. Nuestro Diario is also filled with pictures of ordinary people – exactly what readership studies say readers and non-readers want to see.[20]

The article then quoted Smith: "The first challenge you hear to this is that it's 'dumbing down journalism.' I often say to people, well, you try to get that much information in a half-page of text. I don't think that's dumbing down – I think it's smartening up the presentation."[21] Perhaps so. I have worked with and written for the Media Management Center on occasion, enough to know that it mixes scholarly expertise with industry needs in a way that its clients value highly. It has made a science out of the news business.

But of course the news media are not any business. Their products affect how people perceive their choices in a democratic society, and the quality of those products is critical if those choices are to be meaningful. Few would dispute this proposition, even those who honor it in the breach. Beyond that, the implications of the proposition are not clear. Quality is a subjective measure, though presumably it has something to do with the balance of public-affairs information and entertainment available in any one medium. If so, there is the added difficulty that is very nearly impossible to disentangle the "entertainment" aspects of media goods from purely "informational" ones. A soap opera, for example, can be more effective in educating people about a critical public health issue than years of news articles or a barrage of government public-service announcements.

Viewed as an economic proposition, the problem of quality is that the overall character of any good, and particularly media goods, will be dependent on, if not inseparable from, the business constraints put upon it. One such constraint is revenue source, but here, too, there lies conflicting evidence about outcomes. Advertiser support, for instance, is often assumed to be inimical to public service, but with the exception of public broadcasting, the world's exemplary public-service media earn the majority of their revenues from advertisers, not readers or viewers.[22]

The problem of media goods and business constraints has been a matter of debate in developed democracies for a long time, and has been resolved in a variety of imperfect ways, some of them discussed in subsequent chapters. But in developing democracies the problem is new. And where democracies are immature, or where political, social and economic reforms co-vary in potentially destabilizing ways, the problem is especially significant. It is arguably the case, for example, that in a country like Guatemala *Nuestro Diario* makes few or no contributions to public discourse and democratic transition. Put another way, democracy may continue to mature in Guatemala, but the success or failure of *Nuestro Diario* will make small difference to its chances. The paper's business success is remarkable, and that success may even be a sign of social stability in a country where the national psyche is scarred by forty years of military dictatorship, civil war, and genocide. But *Nuestro Diario* is by any reasonable editorial standard a bad newspaper. It is engaging in its way, but to call it a work of reporting is charitable. It is a collection of "captions" and "snippets" and "headshots" that substitute full-color, garish graphics for narrative context and editorial explanation. Its "predictable" editorial features include cartoon-style reenactments of gang killings and political executions (sans the blood and corpses), and lots of sex. Perhaps its most distinctive predictable feature is a daily pin-up girl, printed as a centerfold.

Nuestro Diario is one of five independently published tabloids that comprise the newspaper market in Guatemala. (There is also a government newspaper that publishes official bulletins and announcements, *Diario de Centroamerica*.) *Prense Libre*, at more than fifty years old, is the politically conservative dean of the group and controls 45 percent of the newspaper advertising market. *Nuestro Diaro* is of course the readership leader, with total sales nearly twelve times that of *El Periodico*, an erudite and aggressive investigative paper, and also of *Siglo Veintiuno*, the other elite paper in Guatemala. The fifth paper in the market, *Al Dia*, is aimed at the same poor and mostly young demographic as *Nuestro Diario*, but has not enjoyed nearly the same success, with daily sales of fewer than 45,000 copies.

All the papers distribute nationwide, but distribution is spotty from department to department, and readership is concentrated in and around Guatemala City, where all the papers publish. While doing research for this book, I spent time at *El Periodico*, which I had gone to visit because of its reputation as the country's most vigorous investigative paper, and one that had won, along with its publisher, numerous honors from international press freedom groups for its reporting. It has also survived repeated rhetorical, legal and physical attacks on its reporters and assassination attempts on its publisher, Jose Ruben Zamora. *El Periodico's* newsroom and business offices are in a renovated home in a middle- to upper class residential neighborhood in Zone 13, near the airport. There is no sign identifying the place as a newspaper office, but there are always a few motorcycles and several conspicuously armed men standing at the front entrance. One wears the uniform of a private security service, the others do not. The entrance doors they guard are heavy steel, with a magnetic lock. Like every other house on the block, *El Periodico's* offices are behind an 8-foot concrete wall topped with coils of razor wire. Exterior windows are covered with iron bars to keep out intruders. Here and there, other buildings on the street have signs on their doors announcing themselves as private residences. *El Periodico* draws the attention not only of the authorities but of thugs with the potential to do damage to people and property. Neighbors want to be sure that if someone comes looking for *El Periodico* that they get the right building.

As a business, *El Periodico* struggles. It has tried in various ways to appeal to younger readers, so far without much success. Its staff, ironically, is on the whole young, in their twenties and thirties, about 70 percent of them women. Some of the more senior editors, and Jose

Ruben himself, are in their late thirties or forties, and all began their journalism careers at other papers. Zamora, forty-eight years old when I met him in 2004, is a civil engineer by training. He was a founder of *Siglo Veintiuno* in 1991, but left that paper with his investigative editor, Sylvia Gereda, to launch *El Periodico* in November 1996, shortly after civilian rule returned to the country. The editors and reporters I met at *El Periodico* work there because the paper does what editor-in-chief Anna Carolina Alpirez characterizes as "journalism that matters."[23] Alpirez, like many others on the editorial staff, came to *El Periodico* after having established their reporting careers at other news organizations. For some on the staff, it is a last stop; if *El Periodico* fails, they say, they will leave journalism and do something else. Several of the reporters said they would not work at any other paper, even as they acknowledged that its editorial policies and some of its more pointed editorial features cost the paper both readers and revenues.

On the editorial side, *El Periodico* is two papers in one. The majority of staff work on producing the daily product, and a much smaller group is devoted, full-time, to doing long investigative pieces. In its daily reporting *El Periodico* covers national and local news, including the country's growing importance as a conduit for illegal drugs and immigrants into Mexico and the United States, and the consequent rise of political and drug assassinations that occur in the country. It also covers sport and entertainment, but neither at length, and it does some business reporting. *El Periodico's* cultural reporting includes reviews of pop music, movies and nightlife, but is more likely than other papers to also review high-brow entertainments, including books, a rarity anywhere. And like *Nuestra Diario*, *El Periodico* also has daily "girl photo," though a small and usually modest one (that is to say, fully dressed) that takes up a half page or less. The girl photo is a fixture in Latin American newspapers, even this one. Jose Ruben believes the feature helps to sell the paper. The women on the editorial side see it as incongruous with *El Periodico's* style of journalism. Marketing Director Carolina Marquez thinks it hurts the paper's brand identity. Jose Ruben also elects to publish regularly a columnist whom the entire staff believes is politically and socially regressive, a throwback to the country's militarist past. Jose Ruben publishes him for reasons that no one can fully explain or which, if they did, I did not understand. The idea seems to be that opinion diversity is a social and a journalistic value the paper wishes to promote.

El Periodico competes for readers in a small market – the 20 percent of Guatemalans who do not live in poverty. These readers are educated, middle- to high-income readers who work in government, business and education. The paper's signature work is investigations of corruption in the national civil service and federal government, stories that are accompanied by a strong and reported editorial page. Special sections, done several times a year, examine the history of political violence in the country and its continuing legacy. Jose Ruben writes most of the lead editorials, and his voice stands out as the editorial identity of the paper. In 2003, when former Army General Efrain Rios Montt ran for president as candidate of the Frente Republicano Guatemalteco (FRG) party, despite a constitutional provision barring former military officers from holding that office, *El Periodico* was the paper that most vigorously reported about and editorialized against his candidacy and the court that authorized it. The law notwithstanding, Rios Montt was hardly the ideal chief executive for a country on the mend. A former Army chief of staff, he had seized the presidency in a 1982 coup and ruled Guatemala for a little more than a year until he was himself deposed in August 1983. In his short tenure in office, Rios Montt had implemented a counter-insurgency plan modeled on the French experiences in Algeria and Vietnam, destroying hundreds of rural villages and often slaughtering their civilian inhabitants. By the end of 1982, the policy had driven approximately a half million refugees either into Mexico or into Guatemala's slums.[24] More than 200,000 had died or disappeared.[25]

In 2003, Rios Montt was serving as president of Congress, a position that provided him immunity from prosecution. In 1990 and 1995 he had sought to run for president, but both times his candidacy had been barred by the Constitutional Court. In July 2003, however, a Constitutional Court packed with FRG judges approved his candidacy, a decision a *lower* court stayed days later as an affront to rule of law. When it did, Rios Montt gave a radio address urging his followers into the streets. By then the campaign had already turned violent, with twenty-two people connected to political parties having been assassinated. It would soon get worse. Several hundred FRG supporters, many recruited from rural departments, came to Guatemala City wielding guns, machetes and clubs. On July 24 and 25, approximately five months before the election, the capital city was the scene of violent riots in which masked and armed men sacked office buildings, fired machine guns from roaming trucks, burned piles of tires in the streets, took hostages, and attacked journalists covering the riots, killing one. Both the U.S. Embassy and the UN mission in the city were forced to close. The Guatemalan government, led by President and FRG party leader Alfonso Portillo, took no action to quell the riots, and indeed members of the Army and the police participated in them.[26] Mayan peasants in the highlands, fearing the return of a military regime, began streaming toward the Mexico border, where they were either turned away or herded into refugee camps.

A month before the riots, on the morning of June 24, a dozen armed men had gone to Zamora's house posing as investigators from the public prosecutor's office. They forced their way in, then stripped, tied up and blindfolded Jose Ruben, had him kneel with a pistol to his head, and beat his children in his presence. Throughout the attack, the men took orders from someone on the telephone. According to Zamora, one of his attackers told him, "If you value your children stop bothering the people above. I don't know who you've annoyed high up the ladder, but we have orders that someone up high despises you. Whatever you do, do not report this."[27]

The attackers left after three hours. They demanded money and promised to return if it was not paid. Zamora sent his wife and children out of the country for the duration of the campaign, and continued with his work. "We are all vulnerable to delinquency in this country," he said, "and I have a duty to carry on."[28] International human rights and press groups rallied to *El Periodico's* cause, and the World Association of Newspapers and the U.S.-based Media Development Loan Fund urged the State Department to express its dismay about the attack on Zamora to the Guatemalan government. It did, with the result that police security around the newspaper's offices increased. Three months later, in December 2003, General Rios Montt was eliminated from the ballot in the first round of voting after polling only 19 percent. As well he lost his congressional leadership position, exposing him to prosecution both in Guatemala and in Spain. Throughout it all, *Nuestro Diario* remained silent on the critical constitutional questions surrounding the general's attempt to recapture the presidency, though it ran photographs of the riots and their aftermath, along with plenty of "snippets."

It has to be noted that *El Periodico* was not the only news organization that suffered violence during the run-up to the 2003 elections. Other journalists covering the riots, particularly television reporters, were also attacked, and one was killed when he suffered a heart attack while being chased. Journalism is a dangerous enterprise in Guatemala, and the more dangerous for those that take it seriously. If *El Periodico* is on the hard road to independence, it has chosen to be there. The paper was at one time in a business partnership with *Prense Libre,* and together the two created *Nuestro Diario.* As part of the deal, *Prense Libre* held 60 percent ownership of *El Periodico.* Eventually the joint venture fell apart because *El Periodico* could not meet its financial responsibilities to *Nuestro Diario*, leading *Prense Libre* to take *El Periodico's* shares in the paper as payment. In the deal, *El Periodico* also lost access to its printing press. Zamora and his partners could have solved their financial problems by selling the paper outright to *Prense Libre*, thus becoming the "high end" product in a group that would have served virtually the entire Guatemalan newspaper market. (*Al Dia*, for example, was created for this purpose, a joint venture of *Siglo Veintiuno* and Costa Rica's *La Nacion*.) But had it done so, the thinking went, *El Periodico* would have had to abandon its commitment to investigative reporting; at any rate, a sale would have turned Jose Ruben and the rest of the staff into someone else's employees. So instead they negotiated a loan from the Media Development Loan Fund, and bought back their shares from *Prense Libre.* Though the three papers are no longer legally or financially linked, *El Periodico* and *Nuestro Diario* still occupy adjoining buildings. From the outdoor patio that separates *El Periodico*'s newsroom from its business offices, one can look through several windows into *Nuestro Diario's* spacious and well-appointed newsroom.

Somewhere in the wide editorial space that separates the two newspapers lies the dilemma that faces journalism enterprise everywhere, but that is especially acute in developing democracies: The more closely a media product takes on the social and economic characteristics of a public good, as *El Periodico*'s investigative reporting does, the less support it will find in the market; as a media product loses its public good character – as with *Nuestro Diario's* murder-as-entertainment features and pin-ups – the more likely it is to be financially sustainable, but the less its sustainability matters to the outcome of democratic transition.

Admittedly, this formulation of the dilemma is overdrawn. *Nuestro Diario's* ability to engage young people, especially the many who are poorly educated and employed, can hardly be a bad thing – even if the content falls short of some desirable minimum of public affairs reporting – and especially so in a country where because of its genocidal wars the population is overwhelmingly young. Moreover, and as discussed elsewhere in this book, one sign that a country has begun the process of democratic consolidation is that its media cease to be predominantly oppositional, but instead begin to feature a broader array of choices, including lighter and more entertaining fare for more diverse audiences. Viewed in that light, *Nuestro Diario* may be more important for what it represents than for what it produces.

El Periodico, on the other hand, is important for what it produces. Investigative reporting is what press freedom is *for*. It gives that freedom its *raison d'être*, and it requires skill and tenacity. Done well it also requires money and time, sometimes a lot of both. That is why many news organizations, no matter where they are located, rarely do investigative work. It is cheaper and less risky to cover official statements, news conferences and other events specifically designed for news coverage – Daniel Boorstin's "pseudoevents."[29] Anywhere it is done, investigative reporting is based on the premise that real news does not happen on TV talk shows or in press conferences, but in places that are often mean, grubby and sometimes dangerous. The reporting of real news also invites recrimination and even revenge. In a country like Guatemala, where rule of law and civil society support are still weak, the decision to do investigative journalism requires extraordinary courage and ingenuity.

Of course, none of that matters a wit if one cannot keep the lights on. To survive, better to become profitable, *El Periodico* needs to be a well-managed business, and where possible it must learn from its competitors. Juan Luis Font, the young managing editor of the paper, spends a great deal of his time thinking about new editorial features or promotions that might attract readers or advertisers, all while protecting the core investigative and editorial functions of the paper. So, too, does the paper's sales manager, Juan Carlos Velazquez, an old university friend of Jose Ruben and with him a founder of *Siglo Veintiuno*. Like their colleagues at *Nuestro Diario*, Font and Velazquez have studied the findings from the Media Management Center's "Readership Institute" study, and both believe that *El Periodico* could and should make productive use of the study's recommendations.[30] But not all of them. One Readership Institute paper specifically questions whether investigative reporting is "relevant" to young adult readers, an empirical challenge that strikes at the heart of the paper's editorial mission.[31] Other Readership Institute reports do not discuss investigative reporting at all, but do say repeatedly that stories which are "too long" or "cover too much" are "inhibitors" to readership.[32] Obviously individual news organizations will decide for themselves what these findings imply for their business, but it is certainly possible to conclude that the kind of reporting that is central to *El Periodico's* social mission is, simply, a poor business choice. Former *Chicago Tribune* foreign correspondent and Chicago Council on Foreign Relations Executive Richard Longworth reports anecdotally that newspapers across the American Midwest have read the Readership Institute findings to conclude that they should no longer publish *any* international news or even national news, but instead focus on the same sort of quick-hit local features than have made *Nuestro Diario* so successful.[33]

In 2004, according to Juan Carlos, *El Periodico* was in the red, though both he and the paper's general manager, Carlos Gonzales Campo, expected the paper to become profitable in 2005. Another problem was cash flow. About 10 percent of the paper's revenues in 2004 came from advertisements paid a year in advance, and though the paper grew its circulation in 2004, the growth was not that significant. In any case, Juan Carlos was tied to advertising rates he had negotiated months earlier. He believes *El Periodico* must grow its subscription to 50,000, almost double the current figure. When I ask him how he would do that, he smiles and says, "I suppose we have to change the product."[34] Juan Carlos believes the paper needs more entertainment features, and he specifically suggests advice columnists and comics. He tells me he has argued with the editors for a regular supplement geared to young readers, and in 2005, led by Juan Luis and investigative editor Sylvia Gereda, the paper launched a once-weekly supplement for kids. The paper's young marketing manager, Carolina Marquez, is even more frustrated. She believes she can offer valuable guidance on features readers want – and as importantly what they do not – but is rarely consulted on the matter. *El Periodico's* mostly male and mostly middle- and high-income readers, she says, are insufficient to sustain the paper over the long term. Carlos Gonzales, a retired banker and an old friend of Jose Ruben, agrees. "Our 'elite' is not economical," he says, "but it is an elite that likes to read. The biggest challenge is to increase readership, but we're not getting anywhere. We're stuck."[35]

There is a third way to sustainability, but *El Periodico*, like virtually all of the media examined in this book, has chosen not to take it: The paper could choose to survive by relying on grants from regional and international media and human rights NGOs, from official aid organizations and from whomever else might choose to donate money or material to keep it going. In effect, *El Periodico* would thus operate as a not-for-profit firm on the implicit if not explicitly legal presumption that its core activity is neither profitable nor self-sustaining. Given its reputation for quality, this would not be that hard to do, at least in the short term. From the beginning, *El Periodico* has benefited from outside donations of money and technical expertise, and at crucial times it would have gone out of business without them. Such revenue sources, however, are both unreliable and often linked to donor expectations that the paper's management believes could compromise – or could appear to compromise – its independence. And as a matter of principle, Zamora and his colleagues believe that if they can make the paper a market success they will also make a statement about Guatemala's progress toward democracy.

It is easy to find media in the developing and democratizing world that are supported by grants from non-governmental or international governmental organizations (NGOs and IGOs), as well as media that are staffed and operated by NGO or IGO personnel for the express purpose of supporting some other democracy-enhancing goal, for instance developing civil society, promoting public health or supporting national and local elections. Often, however, donor-supported media wither and die when aid is withdrawn, redirected or exhausted – as eventually it always is. Some of these media firms are supposed to die: at least in the judgment of their funders they have served their purpose. Other media firms that have survived have done so by becoming so aid-dependent as to have forfeited any meaningful claim to editorial independence. Rather they constantly re-tool their editorial mission as they till for donors. In the process, these media frequently lose public credibility, thus undermining the case for their continued existence, and they fail to develop the managerial capacity to survive on their own. In the meantime, their presence can have the unintended and undesirable effect of competing in the market for audiences and advertisers against other media that are trying to reinvent and reestablish themselves as independent voices in a changed political, social and economic landscape.

Of course, donor-supported media do not have to collapse into editorial irrelevance, and some can be excellent, far superior in quality to anything else available. This is especially so in societies where legal protections for the press are weak or nonexistent. In Cambodia, for example, where hopes for democracy collapsed after the 1997 coup, the not-for-profit *Cambodian Daily* has emerged as one of two papers of record (the *Phnom Penh Post* is the other) and is dependent on financial donations. This kind of sustainability works at least until the donors' money or interest runs out, and then the calculus changes.

The dilemma of sustainability was first summed up for me in 1999, in a conversation with Sheila Coronel, a distinguished investigative reporter in the Philippines who is now the executive director of the Philippine Center for Investigative Journalism in Manila. Today, Coronel said, good journalism that survived in the worst of political and social conditions now has to succeed financially against competition from a variety of other outlets, including many that trade in entertainment and sensationalism, and others that are subsidized by governments. Reflecting on her time working as a journalist during the Ferdinand Marcos era, she said, "Tyranny of the state may be better than tyranny of the market. As journalists we knew what to do with the state – you topple it. But what do you do with the market?"[36]

The same problem exists in other democratizing regions. A 2005 article in *deScripto*, the professional journal of the Southeast Europe Media Organization, or SEEMO, notes that

> since the media requires (sic) two markets to survive economically (audience and advertising), it has to be interested in financially successful management, but at the same time it must irritate the economic status quo because of its duty to research such themes as part of investigative journalism. So it may and often does happen that journalists are challenged to research subjects that may not be in the best interests of people or organizations which are stake or shareholders in the media. Economically speaking, media ownership is not an easy position. On one hand, media entrepreneurship is encouraged in a very difficult and complex market, and on the other hand, it is the source of independence problems, often negatively impacting freedom, the open media market, and above all, media culture. Ownership is the position at which economy, quality, money, and public communication values meet and where all those factors come into a difficult crux in a democratic culture.[37]

This "crux" is of course not unique to developing and democratizing states. Western journalists confront it daily, if in a different context. In a 1997 speech to a roomful of Russian journalists (then still enjoying freedoms that have largely eroded under President Putin), *Washington Post* columnist Jim Hoagland talked about the erosion of Western journalism standards under the onslaught of financial pressures that he said were "redefining the market – downward."[38] In the United States, he said, "our lowering of standards and refocusing of reporting is being subliminally, subtly dictated by market concerns in a rapidly and at times violently changing global economy."[39] Exempting only the Public Broadcasting Service – a not-for-profit – Hoagland charged that the financial markets' demand for steadily increasing quarterly profits had gutted news organizations of their core purpose and most editorially important features, and in the process posed a "threat to democracy."[40] And then he corrected himself: "I realize to my Russian colleagues I must sound something like a cry-baby. Here I am, complaining of the problem of too much money while they strive to find enough resources and moral support within their own society to establish and pursue independent reporting and editing. If they are successful, perhaps years from now they will get to the point of having the problems I have complained about today."[41]

In fact, they already do. Though a host of factors affect the sustainability of a news organization, and some critically so, the economic dilemma in news production is much the same in both developed and developing states: The character of some information goods is such that few if any for-profit firms will choose to produce them, with the result that they may not be produced at all. Put another way, in an open and free society, media independence is largely a function of revenue sources, and irrespective of how one characterizes that relationship, it colors any definition of "independence" one chooses to use. And in societies where markets have greatly liberalized but significant political and social barriers to press freedom continue to exist, as in Guatemala, the twin goals of financial and editorial independence can be especially elusive. *Nuestro Diario* is a market success largely because it avoids the high expenses and low returns associated with serious news production. *El Periodico* has won international editorial acclaim, but struggles for audiences and revenues in its own market.

What is Press Independence For?

Framed as a question, the dilemma faced by *El Periodico* – and for that matter by *Nuestro Diario* – is this: *How are professional news media supposed to sustain themselves financially without giving up or deeply compromising their editorial independence?* Again, the dilemma is not unique to developing states; the economics of quality journalism is a subject that currently receives much professional and academic commentary in the United States and Western Europe, and the broad contours of that discussion are discussed in chapters 4 through 6. What that experience suggests for developing democracies will depend in the first instance on how one characterizes media "freedom" or "independence." But the social consequences of the dilemma may be particularly worrisome in states where civil society is weak or impaired, where economic stability and security are fragile, and where rule of law is a work in progress – in short, where democratic consolidation is incomplete and large segments of the population have yet to see their lives significantly improved by political transition.

It is for these reasons that official and private sources of financial aid to media development will so often link their support, rhetorically if not also programmatically, to civil society development. The assumptions behind that linkage are again interesting for what they imply about editorial mission and the meaning of editorial "independence," and those assumptions are discussed in subsequent chapters. For now, it is sufficient to note that the after-effects of political transition on the media sector mirror those in civil society generally. Those effects include, above all, a shift in purpose. Media that once existed as sources of political opposition, for example, must now contend with the practical challenges of democratic governance, and more immediately of running a business. Speaking in Chicago in early 2005, for example, South African journalist Mathatha Tsedu said that since 1994 the news media in his country

> have gone for well-off blacks and forgotten the poor. They no longer serve as watchdogs for the weak and the poor. The poor are not a market, but a liability. Nobody covers them. It is the same in the United States, but here the poor are a minority and the middle class is the majority. In South Africa, the poor are the majority. If no one is interested in them, how do we represent them? How are they part of our democracy? It is the dilemma of existence versus the need of the media to survive…. At the same time we have had an exodus of skilled journalists who have left to join government and business. The result is less coverage of our country's democratic story even as it gets more difficult to tell.[42]

Tsedu was one of South Africa's leading opposition journalists during the apartheid era, a role that is evident today in the physical scars he carries from detentions and beatings. For a brief 14 months in 2002 and 2003, Tsedu served as editor of the *Sunday Times*, South Africa's largest paper (with a Sunday circulation of 3.5 million) but not one known for being the voice of the powerless. He was eventually fired by the paper's owner, Johnnic Communications, which claimed his performance was unsatisfactory, and specifically that he failed to produce an "independent quality newspaper that sustains our democracy, is trusted by its readers and advertisers, is targeted at those people in Living Standards Measures categories 6-10 in South Africa and Southern Africa, and is profitable."[43] But as one South African commentator noted after the firing, the question is not why Tsedu was fired, but why Johnnic ever hired him in the first place:

They knew he came from a deeply embedded tradition of Black Consciousness activism. They knew that Africanisation was important to him. They knew that he had a strong change agenda, including getting rid of the popular and lucrative – but controversial – "extra" editions…. They knew that the slogan he often annunciated was: 'Journalism must serve the poor and the powerless.' But having selected him, Johncom management must have known that this would mean a disruption in staff, readership, sales, advertising and revenue. Why did they appoint him if they did not want to go down this road?[44]

What makes Tsedu's firing particularly notable is that Johnnic Communications is itself one of South Africa's most visible democratization projects. Formerly known as Times Media Limited, Johnnic is today a publicly traded firm, owned by a coalition of black business groups and trade unions known as the National Empowerment Consortium. Johnnic's executive staff and board of directors are overwhelming composed of blacks and representatives of other "previously disadvantaged communities." Johnnic owns several publishing and entertainment properties, but the *Sunday Times* is the money-making machine at the heart of the enterprise. And because the controlling Consortium is itself deeply in debt, it is also highly sensitive to changes in share prices and profit levels. According to the commentator above:

Tsedu's dismissal is not about media freedom, for no one is suggesting it was an attempt to stifle his views. It is not about race, much as this provides the cover for those who want simple and crude explanations. It is about the complexities, contradictions, limitations and difficulties of transformation in an empowerment media company. It raises questions about what transformation is intended to achieve. Is the goal to maximize the profitability of empowerment shareholders? Does it mean closing a New York bureau and opening one in Lagos? Does it mean getting rid of the 'ethnic' editions, which were conceived in the sin of apartheid but are popular and lucrative? Does it mean hiring political editors who have no experience? How does one weigh the demands for change against shareholders' demands for growth? Which takes priority?

One thing is clear: there is no point to transformation if the end-product is not a healthy and profitable newspaper. There is little value to empowerment if you have been empowered to control a shell. All of this takes place in an increasingly competitive market. The *Sunday Times* used to be the undisputed king of the English-language weekend, but now it has to fight off the *City Press, Sunday World, Sunday Sun* and *Sunday Independent*, some of whom are eating away at the top of the market, others at the bottom.[45]

The sustainability dilemma is thus important not only for what it suggests about financial viability, but because it is also a way of thinking about a more fundamental question: *What is media independence and what is it for?* Media assistance programs, whatever their purpose, rarely address this question head on. When they do, the answer tends to be understandably short and abstract. The sum of it is usually that journalism is a means to an end: to promote fair elections and universal suffrage; to develop political parties; to guide legal, judicial and administrative reform; to strengthen civil society; to support public education and social services; and perhaps most often, to promote free-market economies. The relationship between journalism and civil society is of special concern to media assistance programs mostly because donors believe the two are symbiotically joined. It is not uncommon to hear that free and independent media are a necessary, even sufficient, condition for sustaining civil society, and it is very nearly impossible to find literature on media development that does not include (mostly vague) assertions about its importance to civil society development.

Even assistance organizations that are founded, funded and run by journalists and journalism organizations tend to shy away from any but the most general statements about the goals of press freedom and independence. American journalists are particularly wary of this discussion. Media assistance, after all, is an undeniably political activity, but because their professional norms frown on anything that might be characterized as advocacy, journalists tend to characterize what they do as training, largely neutral as to matters of content or editorial mission. A common refrain one hears from Western media trainers, for instance, is that they show aid beneficiaries "how" to cover the news, but do not presume to tell them "what" to cover. One commentator calls this an "occupational ideology of professionalism"[46] that in itself is assumed to enhance democracy.

Other media assistance providers are bolder in stating their objectives. USAID's published materials on media assistance are notable and praiseworthy in this regard; they are far more explicit about basic questions of journalistic purpose and media system architecture than anything in American press law. Some private sources of media assistance are also advocates for particular ideas about press freedom and its purposes. That they are should not be surprising. In most places that receive media assistance the point of the assistance is to publicize, perhaps to remedy, gross social inequities and injustices, up to and including the legacies of political torture and mass murder. Professional norms notwithstanding, "neutrality" concerning fundamental human rights violations is immoral. In any case, media assistance providers can hardly ignore the reasons for their own existence. To do so makes any discussion about the field incoherent. And in the absence of explicit consideration of editorial

Figure 1.1
Enabling Conditions for Press Freedom

Peace, stability, and tolerance
Pluralistic society
Basic conditions for survival
Favorable economic conditions for the media
Sufficient resources/equipment & infrastructure
Physical safety of journalists
Constitutional reform
Independent judiciary
Access to information
Access to media
Diversity of media outlets
Independent journalism associations
Self-regulation / ombudsmen/ critical culture in journalism
Courage

Figure 1.2
Limiting Factors for Press Freedom

Government repression/archaic laws/emergency regulations
Religious suppression
Non-state repression/gangs and paramilitary
Partisan political corruption of journalists
Self-censorship
Lack of journalism training/unprofessionalism
Imbalance of media in urban and rural areas
Unsupportive culture/lack of public support
Unsupportive market/market fragmentation
Inadequate investment in public and journalism education
Dangerous work environment/conflict and war
Media concentration/opacity of corporate ownership
Privatization of public service media
Commercialism in media

purpose (and assuming political violence is not a factor), the market will determine how the media system operates, which media it sustains, and what they produce. For some that will be enough. Depending on what one takes "independence" (or for that matter, "democracy") to mean, perhaps it should be.

Definitions: What Does a "Free" Press Look Like?

Among the critical component of democratic norms are rights of free expression. Robert Dahl long ago postulated that freedom of expression and freedom of information were two of seven criteria most useful for evaluating any state wanting to call itself a democracy.[47] In its most tangible form, Dahl said, the exercise of those norms comes down to the existence of a "free and responsible" press system – an economical measure but not an easy one to make operational. What does a free and responsible press system look like? Especially since the end of the Cold War, and pushed along by changes in communications technology, both developing and developed nations have had the opportunity to ask this question in both normative and legal terms. And for countries emerging from various forms of authoritarian rule there is there is the additional question of what news media practices promote democratization. As with the post-World War II period, some media restructuring over the last decade has been the result of international military intervention (as in Bosnia and more recently Kosovo and Iraq), but since the mid-1980s most has been the result of a significant effort by the democratic West to export ideas about press freedom to Central and Eastern Europe, Latin America, Southeast Asia and to a lesser extent Africa. That effort has involved the provision of either bilateral or multilateral financial and material assistance from donor countries (such as the United States, Britain, Germany or Sweden); IGOs such as the Organization for Security and Cooperation in Europe (OSCE), the European Union (EU) or the African Union (AU); and international and regional NGOs, of which dozens concern themselves almost exclusively with media and free expression issues.[48]

Both donors and recipients of media aid have historically used terms like "independence," "freedom," "responsibility," "professionalism," "diversity," and "sustainability" to mean a great variety of things, depending on their historical experience, social norms and practices. Media scholarship also uses these terms casually, and sometimes non-sensically. One widely used academic text in international journalism studies, for example, defines "independent" journalism as anything that is not government funded.[49] This will surely come as a disappointment to the British Broadcasting Corporation (BBC) even as it confirms the deeply held convictions of FOX News viewers in the United States. In the business of media assistance, donors and recipients alike tend to define independence by what it is not – it is *not* monopolistic control over the instruments of mass communication. Beyond that, it is not clear what independence means, never mind "free," though presumably both terms have something to do with the source and predictability of a media organization's revenues, and its autonomy from government control over editorial decisions.

Often these terms are defined by ideological or strategic objectives. In the 1970s, for example, a body set up under the United Nations Educational, Scientific, and Cultural Organization (UNESCO), the MacBride Commission, defined media freedom as communication in the service of economic development. The Commission recommended citizen rights of access to the media, the development of locally managed, alternative channels of communication, and the participation of non-professionals in media production. Western countries, and the United States in particular, rejected the report as an attack on editorial judgment (and thus free expression). By 1991 UNESCO appeared to have changed its own views on the subject in the Declaration of Windhoek:

> We mean by an independent press, a press independent from governmental, political or economic control…. By pluralism, we mean the end of monopolies of any kind and the existence of the greatest possible number of newspapers, magazines and periodicals reflecting the widest possible range of opinion within the community.[50]

This is language that most journalists would agree with, but it is not very useful to a discussion of sustainability: A press independent of governmental, political or economic control does not exist. The press must be dependent on *something* for its viability; the press *cannot* be free, but is locked into a cycle of interdependence. In authoritarian societies the interdependence is easy to understand: governments employ strict censorship to control the flow of information to the general public, and journalists exist as mouthpieces for the government. In democratic societies the interrelationship is much more variable, in part because theory is less important to democracy than how freedom is lived and perpetuated.[51] Ideally, the role of the media in a democracy is to ensure the existence of a broadly and equitably informed citizenry that can hold elites accountable and ensure popular control of government through free and competitive elections. To enable the press in that role, at least two conditions have to obtain: Citizens must have some sort of constitutional or statutory right to political information, and media have to be protected from the arbitrary exercise of government power. Most democracy scholars also argue for a third condition, that media pluralism – by which they mean a broad array of media forms and outlets offering a variety of political viewpoints – has to be ensured through legal means, for example restrictions on ownership.

These descriptions are to some degree caricatures. Totalitarian regimes never succeed in suppressing all speech, nor is their control over information complete and omniscient. Democratic societies almost all have some measure of government control over, or at least government involvement in, their media systems. At one level this theoretical dichotomy is a relic of a Cold War framework in which democratic media systems, whatever they were, were clearly different from and freer than authoritarian ones. That framework is long overdue for reassessment, and to some extent the current emphasis on "sustainability" in media aid – to the extent it concerns itself with other goals conterminous with or dependent on sustainability – can be read as the beginning of such a process. Though that inquiry usually focuses on developing societies, it has been helped along by growing criticism in developed democracies that the media in general and broadcasting in particular are undermining representative democracy rather than enhancing it.

This book understands sustainability to mean *financial sustainability joined with a public-service editorial mission*. Financial sustainability means the ability of a media firm to be economically viable in a country where the enabling conditions for sustainability – above all the rule of law – are in more or less in place. Unfortunately, in many transition states one of more enabling conditions is frequently absent. At a 2000 meeting of journalists from more than two dozen transition states (and convened by the Ford Foundation and the Aspen Institute) participants identified the principal enabling conditions for a healthy media sector as those shown in figure 1.1; the same group identified the obstacles to a healthy media sector shown in figure 1.2, obstacles that most knew from personal experience.

It can be inferred from these figures that what journalists themselves identify as the critical enabling conditions for media development and sustainability are much the same as those that scholars and donors identify as important for democratic transition generally: the rule of law, a healthy civil society, and favorable economic conditions.[52] With respect to media development, at least, these things are not mutually exclusive. Criminal libel laws, licensing schemes and value-added taxes, for example, function both as legal and economic restraints on the press. Religious repression, ethnic conflict, paramilitary threats and rural poverty function both as civil society and economic barriers to media sustainability. Official corruption and organized crime inhibit civil society, economic and rule of law development.

Where any one of these important enabling conditions for press freedom is absent in a debilitating way, it makes less sense (and sometimes none) to talk about sustainability in terms of market viability. In Zimbabwe under Robert Mugabe, currently, media sustainability is not a problem money can solve. There and elsewhere sustainability has to be understood in terms appropriate to the functions of media in those societies. Monroe Price and Bethany Davis Noll have argued that in many states those functions are not so different from what they were a decade or more ago, [53] and therefore that sustainability can take on multiple meanings depending on the goals of assistance, for example:

- *Crisis sustainability*, in which the goal is to keep media financially afloat during periods of violent conflict and post-conflict, or in the aftermath of natural disasters. Here sustainability will almost certainly be dependent on outside donors.

- *Incubator sustainability*, in which the goal is to nourish a variety of new media with the expectation that some will survive and some will not. Most common in post-conflict or transition societies where the enabling environment is still a work in progress, incubator sustainability will also have supplemental goals, such as promoting professionalism among journalists and developing a legal framework that promotes free and responsible expression.

- *Strategic sustainability*, in which the goal is to further some political and economic goal, much in the way public diplomacy does. In November 2001, for example, the United States created Radio Free Afghanistan to promote democratic values in that country. Such media may not – and are not intended to – outlive their strategic purpose.

- *Election sustainability*, in which the goal is to enable citizens to make an informed choice about candidates, as in the post-conflict elections in Cambodia, Bosnia-Herzegovina or East Timor.

For at least three of these forms of sustainability – crisis, strategic and election – the critical disabling condition is failure of rule of law. Without it, any discussion of financial sustainability is going to be highly conditional, and extreme cases very nearly pointless. Profits provide little protection against police raids and mobs. Rule of law essentially means that the government abides by its legal obligations under the constitution; that the police and military are accountable to civilian authorities; that the work of both legislative and administrative procedures are transparent and public; and that an independent judiciary provides the public an effective way to protect its civil rights against encroachment by the government or concentrations of private power. The value of rule of law, in short, is predictability and fairness. Without it, journalism lives under constant threat of arbitrary state action. At a minimum, the law has to ensure journalists the freedom to gather and disseminate news without fear of criminal prosecution or violent attack.

Ideally, a host of ancillary rights flows from that basic freedom, above all, perhaps, a right of access to public places and proceedings, and also to government information. The rule of law also requires a regulatory framework that imposes as few burdens on speech as possible so that media firms can serve their audiences, develop their markets, and ensure their financial independence. Where regulations are necessary – in determining how political candidates may acquire and use broadcast time during elections, for example – they must be clearly written, process-based and narrowly drawn. Non-media regulations that have the effect of skewing the speech market – tax laws and licensing schemes are notorious in this regard – are undesirable.

Of course no bright line separates "stable" or "mature" legal systems and transition states from back-sliders. Thomas Carothers, among others, has argued that a great many so-called transition states are not transitioning to anything, but instead are stuck in a vast "gray area" between authoritarianism and democracy.[54] At any given time, it can be difficult to tell where on the continuum one of these gray-area states lies, and the judgment will vary depending on the measures one chooses to employ. Several independent variables comprise democratic progress, though none may be susceptible to easy measurement. For official purposes, and sometimes as well for journalistic ones, the most popular indicator of democratic momentum is a successful election (and ideally more than one) that is free and fair, and in which a majority of eligible voters participate. Elections have tangible qualities: they are usually bound by rules and fixed by time, they can be observed, votes counted and observations about process compared to electoral outcomes. Elections, in other words, can be evaluated more or less objectively. But of course an election by itself is no guarantee of democracy. Iraq, Ukraine and Indonesia all held national elections in 2004 and 2005, elections whose eventual outcomes were generally judged to be fair (if in some other way seriously flawed). Each country still suffers from a battery of other critical problems, however, ranging from official corruption to criminal violence – in short, inadequate rule of law development. By what other objective measures would one determine these countries' progress toward democracy?

In sum, then, it is one thing to identify clear threats to the press, quite another to identify the essential contours of press independence. In 1985, researcher David Weaver and his colleagues argued that trying to apply the same model of press freedom to many countries was simply not credible, especially when a model seeks to compare industrialized countries with developing ones.[55] All of the major press freedom and sustainability indices (discussed in detail in chapter 3) rely on values that are, if not subjective, at least not universal. And the measure most amenable to quantification, financial sustainability, is often subject to restraints that have less to do with economics than with near-ideological faith in the market. It may well be that the market is a better devil to deal with than the government, and markets when they work properly are at least predictable in their ruthlessness. Moreover, journalists in developing democracies typically have little or no experience of benign government involvement in the media sector, and so for them market independence is the *only* conceivable choice. But the judgments of the market may be no more kind to high-quality "independent" journalism than was the old authoritarian state.

Notes

1. Samuel P. Huntington, *The Third Wave: Democratization in the Late Twentieth Century* (Norman: University of Oklahoma Press, 1992), 263.
2. See Lorne W. Cramer, "Promoting Free and Responsible Media: An Integral Part of America's Foreign Policy," U.S. Department of State, 2003, at http://uninfo. state.gov/journals/itgic/0203/ijge/gj01.htm (accessed June 15, 2004). Cramer was Assistant Secretary of State for Democracy, Human Rights and Labor in the first George Bush administration. He is currently president of the International Republican Institute.
3. Melinda Quintos de Jesus, Executive director, Center for Media Freedom and Responsibility, Manila, Phillipines, author interview, Denpasar, Indonesia, September 10, 2002.

4. See Denis McQuail, *Media Performance: Mass Communication and the Public Interest* (Newbury Park, CA: Sage Publications, 1992); see also Daniel Halin and Paolo Mancini, *Comparing Media Systems: Three Models of Media and Politics* (New York: Cambridge University Press, 2004).

5. See, for example, William A. Hatchen and James F. Scotton, *The World News Prism: Global Media in an Era of Terrorism,* 6th ed. (Ames, IA: Blackwell Publishing, 2002), 168.

6. Thomas Carothers, *Critical Mission: Essays in Democracy Promotion* (Washington, DC: Carnegie Endowment for International Peace, 2004), 262.

7. Jacques Barzun, "Is Democratic Theory for Export?" *Society* (March/April 1989): 16-23, 23.

8. Any number of journalism commentators have discussed the idea that Asia and the Muslim world are for cultural reasons poorly suited for democracy. For an academic discussion of the subject, see Huntington, *The Third Wave*, 1992.

9. The problem of productivity lag in inherently inefficient enterprises is known as "Baumol's cost disease" after William J. Baumol, the economist who first identified it using the analogy of a string quartet and the performance of a musical work. See William J. Baumol and William G. Bowen, *Performing Arts: The Economic Dilemma: A Study of Problems Common to Theater, Opera, Music and Dance* (New York: Twentieth Century Fund, 1966).

10. See Anthony Downs, *An Economic Theory of Democracy* (New York: Harper Books, 1957).

11. See James T. Hamilton, *All the News That's Fit to Sell: How the Market Transforms Information Into News* (Princeton, NJ: Princeton University Press, 2004).

12. See, for example, Herbert J. Gans, "Journalism, Journalism Education, and Democracy," *Journalism and Mass Communication Educator* (Spring 2004), 10-16; Gilbert Cranberg, Randall Bezanson and John Soloski, *Taking Stock: Journalism and the Publicly Traded Newspaper Company* (Ames: Iowa State University Press, 2001); James Fallows, *Breaking the News: How the Media Undermine Democracy* (New York: Vintage, 1997); John S. Carroll, "The Wolf in Reporter's Clothing: The Rise of Pseudo-Journalism in America," *Los Angeles Times*, May 6, 2004, www.latimes.com/news/opinion/commentary/la-050604ruhllecture_lat.story.

13. Robert Dahl, *Democracy and its Critics* (New Haven, CT: Yale University Press, 1989).

14. Readership Institute research and publications are available at http://www.readership.org/.

15. Mark Fitzgerald, "Born in the USA," *Editor & Publisher* (December 2004): 48-51.

16. Ibid.,48,49.

17. Ibid., 49.

18. Ibid.

19. Ibid., 50.

20. Ibid., 51.

21. Ibid.

22. See Leo Bogart, *Commercial Culture: The Media System and the Public Interest* (New York: Oxford, 1995). See also John C. Merrill "International Media Systems: An Overview," in *Global Journalism: Topical Issues and Media Systems*, eds. Merrill and Arnold S. de Beer (Boston: Pearson, 2004), 32-33. Merrill identifies the "great" "quality" newspapers of the world as *Asahi* (Japan), *El Pais* (Spain), *Frankfurter Allgemeine* (Germany), the *Independent* (U.K.), *Le Monde* (France), *Los Angeles Times, Neue Zuercher Zeitung* (Switzerland), the *New York Times,*

Sueddeutsche Zeitung (Germany) and the *Washington Post*. Whatever the merits of the list, one thing can be said of it: All of the papers earn most of their revenues from advertising.

23. Anna Carolina Alpirez, executive editor, *El Periodico*, author interview, Guatemala City, October 14, 2004.
24. For a brief history of Guatemala's experience between the U.S.-backed 1954 coup and restoration of civilian rule in December 1995, see Andrew Reding, "Democracy and Human Rights in Guatemala," World Policy Institute, April 1997, http://www.ciaonet.org/wps/rea01/index.html.
25. Official, unofficial and academic sources report the number of dead and disappeared under Rios Montt's rule between 19,000 to 200,000. The 200,000 figure comes from the U.S. State Department. See http://www.state.gov/r/pa/ei/bgn/2045.htm.
26. An August 30, 2003, report by Guatemala's Human Rights Ombudsman (Procuraduria de Derechos Humanos, or PHD), determined that public officials had planned and executed the riots.
27. David Brewer, "Guatemala press freedom alarm," *BBC News World Edition*, June 28, 2003, http://news.bbc.co.uk/2/hi/americas/3028928.stm (accessed June 2, 2004).
28. Ibid.
29. Boorstin coined the term "pseudo-event" to refer to events that were prepared and staged for news coverage. He first developed the idea in a 1960 article, the same year as the first televised presidential debates between John Kennedy and Richard Nixon. See Daniel Boorstin, *The Image: A Guide to Pseudo-Events in America* (New York: Vintage, 1961).
30. Readership Institute, http://www.readership.org/.
31. "Auditing Your Newspaper's 'Experiences,'" Readership Institute, July 2004, 3, http://www.readership.org/new_readers/data/auditing_experiences.pdf.
32. See, for example, "Key Newspaper Experiences," Readership Institute, July 2004, 3, http://www.readership.org/new_readers/data/key_experiences.pdf.
33. Richard Longworth, executive director, Global Chicago Center, Chicago Council on Foreign Relations, author interview, Evanston, IL, April 16, 2005.
34. Juan Carlos Velazquez, sales manager, *El Periodico*, author interview, Guatemala City, September 16, 2004.
35. Carlos Gonzales Campo, general manager, *El Periodico*, author interview, Guatemala City, September 15, 2004.
36. Sheila Coronel, executive director, Philippine Center for Investigative Journalism, author interview, Queenstown, MD, May 31, 2000.
37. Thomas A. Bauer, "Two Schools of Thought," *deScripto: A Journal of Media in South Eastern Europe*, No. 2 (Winter 2005): 4.
38. Jim Hoagland, "Media: Democracy in Jeopardy?" in *Freedom and Responsibility Yearbook, 1998/99* (Vienna, Austria: Organization for Security and Cooperation in Europe, Representative of the Media, 1999), 109-112.
39. Ibid.
40. Ibid.
41. Ibid., at 110.
42. Mathatha Tsedu, remarks at the Medill School of Journalism, Northwestern University, Evanston, IL, March 7, 2005.
43. "Media statement by Johnnic Communications Chief Executive Officer, Mr. Connie Molusi," November 10, 2003, http://www.prnewswire.co.uk/cgi/news/release?id=111560.

44. Anton Harber, "The hiring and firing of Mathatha Tsedu," *Business Day* (November 14, 2003)., http://www.journalism.co.za/modules.php?op=modload&name=News &file=article&sid=884 (accessed January 26, 2006).
45. Ibid.
46. James Miller, "Democratization and 'Fact-Based' Journalism: Donor Politics in East Central Europe," paper presented at an International Conference of the Association for Education in Journalism and Mass Communication, London, January 5, 2002.
47. Robert A. Dahl, *Democracy and its Critics* (New Haven, CT: Yale University Press, 1989).
48. For excellent overviews of the universe of media assistance, see Monroe E. Price, Bethany Davis Noll, Daniel De Luce, *Mapping Media Assistance* (Oxford: The Programme in Comparative Media Law & Policy, 2002); Ellen Hume, *The Media Missionaries: American Support for International Journalism* (Miami, FL: John S. and James L. Knight Foundation, May 2002), http://www.ellenhume.com/articles/ missionaries1_contents.html; and James Miller, *Democratization and Fact-Based Journalism: Donor Politics in East Central Europe* (New York: Council for European Studies, 2001), http://www.europanet.org/conference2002/abstracts/j1_miller. htm.
49. Hatchen and Scotton, *The World News Prism,* 2002, 32.
50. UNESCO, *Declaration of Windhoek*, Windhoek, Nambibia, May 3, 1991, http:// www.unesco.org/webworld/com_media/communication_democracy/windhoek. htm.
51. For a wonderful explanation of democracy and its conflicting theories, see Barzun, "Is Democratic Theory for Export?"1989.
52. See Monroe Price and Peter Krug, *The Enabling Environment for a Free and Independent Media.* (Washington, DC: United States Agency for International Development, 2002), http://pcmlp.socleg.ox.ac.uk/enablingenvironment.pdf.
53. Monroe E. Price and Bethany Davis Noll*, Media Sustainability: Democracy and Development* (Washington, DC: Aspen Institute, 2002), http://www.aspeninst. org/c&s/nonpub/20020909/price_noll.pdf.
54. Thomas Carothers, "The End of the Transition Paradigm," *Journal of Democracy* (January 2002): 5-21.
55. David H. Weaver, J.M. Buddenbaum and J.E. Fair, "Press Freedom, Media, and Development, 1950-1979: A Study of 134 Nations" *Journal of Communication*, Vol. 35, No. 2 (1985): 104-117.

2

Democracy Promotion in Foreign Assistance

"This whole tendency to see ourselves as the center
of political enlightenment and as teachers strikes
me as unthought-through, vainglorious, and unde-
sirable." – George Kennan

In the heady year of 1989, as the United States government and various private organizations began to send people and money into Central Europe to help with the democratic transition, historian Jacques Barzun published a brief essay in *Society* in which he asked just what these missionaries proposed to teach. Democracy has no commanding orthodoxy, he wrote. The great writers on the subject do not agree, and taken together their writings do not form a system: "The Federalist writers are afraid of democracy; John Adams disputes Tom Paine and goes only part way with Jefferson. Burke and Rousseau sound like direct contraries. Tocqueville calls for so many of the special conditions he found here that his conclusions are not transferable. Bagehot does the same thing for Great Britain: you have to be English to make the English Constitution work."[1] And it gets worse. The democratic theorists wrote on a few similar subjects but employed an enormous variety of terms peculiar to their own experience and institutions. When they *did* use the same terms, they frequently meant very different things. The "array of ideas and devices cannot but be daunting," Barzun wrote, "Which are essential? How should they combine?"[2]

Until recently, the answers to these questions did not matter much. Two decades ago, no one needed a theory to know that democracy, however defined, was preferable to the military dictatorships of Central and Eastern Europe, Asia, and Latin America, or to South Africa's apartheid police state. Democratic theory mattered less than democratic survival, and for that it was enough to be steadfastly anti-communist, even if that required occasional and emphatically anti-democratic means. For democrats in a dangerous world, foreign aid operated within a fairly narrow set of national security objectives.

Then the Soviet Union collapsed in 1991, in the midst of Huntington's "Third Wave" of global democratization. The wave began in the mid-1970s, and since then some sixty countries have changed from various forms of non-democratic regimes to nominally democratic ones. As well, several new countries have joined the world community, so many that the number of independent countries in the world is open to dispute. By most accounts there are 193 now, though somehow 201 "National" Olympic Committees sent teams to Athens in 2004. Freedom House counts 192 sovereign states in the world; it categorizes 121 as "electoral democracies," eighty-eight as "free," and another fifty-five as "partly free."[3] By Freedom House's calculations, then, as many as 60 percent of the world's countries are now democracies—almost twice as many as in 1985, though for a dozen or more, that label almost certainly claims too much. Forty-six percent of them are "free," the highest percentage since Freedom House began its surveys in 1972.[4] More telling, half of those "free" states have enjoyed that status for fewer than fifteen years[5]; several of those are in Asia, a region that still has its share of authoritarian states but was once thought to be wholly unreceptive to democratic change. In 2004 alone there were national elections in Taiwan, Indonesia, South Korea, the Philippines, Malaysia, Sri Lanka, India, and Japan. The first four of those were dictatorships two decades ago. In South Korea, Taiwan, Malaysia, and India, voters in 2004 punished extremist opposition parties with authoritarian tendencies.

As with the post-World War II period, democratization's most visible successes have occurred in Europe. Arguably, the Cold War's concluding chapter was written in November 2002, when at their summit meeting in Prague the nineteen members of NATO invited seven former communist countries to enter the alliance in 2004, those to follow three others—Poland, the Czech Republic, and Hungary—that had become NATO members in 2000. One month later the fifteen European Union members invited eight former communist countries, plus Malta and Cyprus, to become members, which they did in spring 2004. Another entity, the Organization for Security and Cooperation in Europe (OSCE), has constrained conflict from Central Asia to Southeast Europe and has created a forum for security and human rights that includes both the United States and the Russian Federation. Americans have paid little attention, but these developments are important because for most of its history Europe has existed in an almost natural state of war. What began in 1951 as the European Coal and Steel Community was of course never about coal and steel, but about peace between France and Germany; whatever its shortcomings, the EU is today also about creating a new community of democratic nations. As such, the EU constitutes an important balance of influence (if not power) to the United States, and one object of that influence will be the future of democratization efforts in Southeastern and Eastern Europe, the Middle East, Asia, and Africa.

For better or worse, that future has been transformed by the foreign policy of President George W. Bush, who came to office scorning his predecessor's "soft" use of U.S. military power in the service of nation-building and peacekeeping, but by November 2003 seemed to have reversed himself, declaring, "The advance of freedom is the calling of our time. It is the calling of our country."[6] This moralistic approach to international politics long predates Bush, with antecedents in Woodrow Wilson's arguments for the right of national self-determination. More recently, the United States and its NATO allies employed similar logic in Kosovo for the stated purpose of enforcing UN Security Council resolutions, but without Security Council authorization. President Bill Clinton said at the time that the bombing was necessary "to prevent the slaughter of innocents on [NATO's] doorstep,"[7] in effect asserting moral justification for what was often called a "humanitarian war." In Iraq, Bush has claimed the same justification (among many others), but against enormous international opposition. In Iraq, the United States has also engaged in the historically unique project of democracy-building at the point of a gun. The most closely comparable modern efforts are the rebuilding of Japan and Germany after World War II, but both of those were defeated enemies who had engaged in a war of open aggression against others; less favorable are comparisons to the U.S. efforts under presidents William McKinley and Wilson to "liberate" and then democratize the Philippines and Mexico, respectively. Whatever one's view of the Iraq war, it has made a hash of the moral and strategic judgments that have always combined in U.S. foreign policy. As the *New Yorker* put it during the heated campaign summer of 2004, "The war has everyone from George Will to Michael Moore sounding like an unsentimental realist with no patience for any American involvement overseas."[8]

At the same time, Huntington's wave has largely receded, and only a few, relatively affluent countries once thought of as transitional have successfully consolidated. In addition to those in the Baltics and Central Europe, there are about a dozen others scattered across Latin America, Africa and Asia. In a disproportionately large number of other countries, however, transitions have effectively stalled; their governments are neither dictatorial nor democratic, but instead exist in what Thomas Carothers calls a "political gray zone."[9] Marina Ottaway has characterized these states as "semi-authoritarian";[10] Larry Diamond calls them "competitive authoritarian" regimes.[11] Some of these countries have elections in which two or more parties compete for and share power, but in every other respect democracy is a dead letter. The state itself is weak and generally unable to address the country's problems; public participation extends little beyond elections, and the public perceives politicians and government officials as corrupt and self-interested. Many Latin American countries fit this profile, but so do countries in Europe (Ukraine), Asia (Nepal) and Africa (Sierra Leone). In every case, the defining feature of this stagnation is that the political elites are, in Carothers' words, "profoundly cut off from the citizenry."[12] They compete for power and they may even collude to acquire it, but they use it only to promote their own interests, often through a vast patronage system.

In other gray zone countries, one group of elites – whether a party, a family or an individual – has come to dominate, such that the distinction between the state and the ruling elite is almost indistinguishable. These dominant-power countries have open elections, but they are often marred by fraud, and the institutions of governance – in particular the judiciary – are hard-pressed to maintain independence. Citizens are free to vote but see little point in doing so, and the economy is often hobbled by corruption and cronyism. Such dominant-power countries are common throughout sub-Saharan Africa, where once-pluralistic regimes have essentially ossified into one-party states (for example, Cameroon, Burkina Faso, and Tanzania), and in some of the former Soviet states of Central Asia – for example, Armenia, Kazakhstan, and Turkmenistan. Some Middle Eastern countries that have liberalized – Egypt, Algeria, Jordan – also fit the bill, having transformed themselves from authoritarian countries to dominant-power states, but the Middle East as a whole remains the region least open to democracy. Whatever energies exist to counter the ruling regime in these gray area states, Carothers says, usually reside in civil society groups and independent media that depend for their survival on Western funding.[13]

For advocates of democracy promotion, then, Barzun's questions from seventeen years ago still linger: Is democracy for export, and if it is, what specifically should aspiring democracies copy? Barzun was skeptical. Those of us who live in open societies value our freedoms and can name their advantages, he wrote, but that does not make us models for others: "A democracy cannot be fashioned out of whatever people happen to be around in a given region; it cannot be promoted from outside by strangers; and it may still be impossible when attempted from inside by determined natives. Just as life on earth depended on a particular coming together of unrelated factors, so a cluster of disparate elements and conditions is needed for a democracy to be born viable.... The parts of the machine are not detachable; the organism is in fact indescribable, and what keeps it going, the 'habits of the heart,' as Tocqueville called them, are unique and indefinable. In short, we cannot by any conceivable means 'show them how to do it.'"[14]

Despite such cautions, a large industry based primarily in the United States and northern Europe now promotes democracy around the world. In the 1990s, Western sources pumped billions of dollars into democracy-promotion programs in Central and Eastern Europe, Latin America, and to a lesser extent Asia and Africa. The United States government alone is estimated to have spent more than $1 billion during the 1990s on democracy assistance in Europe, with private sources contributing millions more.[15] As a percentage of U.S. foreign aid, democracy assistance is small, accounting for only about 16.5 percent of total official aid to Central and Eastern Europe during the 1990s, and about 3.5 percent of the total to Russia and the Newly Independent States over the same period. According to Carothers, democratization assistance from all sources, public and private, now totals approximately $2 billion per year (not counting post-war assistance to Iraq).[16] This chapter is a largely descriptive one about the democratization industry – the "parts of the machine," including media assistance.

Development Aid During and After the Cold War

Histories of democracy promotion in foreign aid reasonably begin in the middle twentieth century, with the creation of the United Nations and the Bretton Woods institutions. These are the institutions, created by the United States and its allies after World War II, whose combined emphasis on human rights and economic development shaped the modern world. The principal concern of this book – media assistance – is a category of aid unto itself, but it is an offshoot of democracy assistance, which is part of the larger category of development assistance. Development assistance includes both bilateral and multilateral government aid – or Official Development Assistance (ODA)—and private giving from a wide range of organizations – churches, universities, foundations, corporations, advocacy groups, and even some wealthy individuals. ODA is defined as the "transfer of resources on concessional terms,…[which is] undertaken by official agencies; has the promotion of economic development and welfare as its main objectives [at least outwardly]; and has a 'grant element' of 25 percent or more."[17]

Today, global non-military foreign aid is an industry that channels tens of billions of dollars to developing countries, and employs hundreds of thousands of people.[18] Aid can be bilateral – provided from one country directly to another – or multilateral – provided by several countries to another country or region, usually through an intergovernmental organization like the United Nations or the International Monetary Fund (IMF). About 25 percent of the world's foreign aid is multilateral; the rest is bilateral.[19] To oversimplify somewhat, aid can be given as a grant of money or material, with no requirement for repayment, or as a loan. Both bilateral and multilateral aid can be "tied" or "conditional," though these features are much more common in bilateral aid. About 30 percent of the world's foreign aid is tied,[20] that is, it requires the recipient to spend at least a portion of its assistance on goods and services produced by the donor nation. As such, tied aid is as much or more a product of domestic policy than of foreign policy, since it is intended to create (or protect) jobs and export industries in the donor nation, and in particular to avoid the possibility that tax dollars might be used to subsidize foreign competition.[21] One history of foreign aid says flatly that the only constant in international assistance is that "the development objectives of aid programmes have been distorted by the use of aid for donor commercial and political advantage."[22] Bilateral aid is also more likely than multilateral aid to be conditional, or based on some kind of quid pro quo. Requirements might be based on the strategic needs of the donor country, such as access to military bases or natural resources; or based on the need to satisfy a domestic political constituency, such as U.S. prohibitions on the use of development aid to counsel women about birth control.[23] During the Cold War, when both the United States and the Soviet Union used aid in their various proxy battles around the globe, conditional aid sometimes had the perverse effect of promoting official corruption in recipient countries, retarding economic, administrative and political development, and derailing democratic accountability.

Bilateral aid is sometimes characterized as a form of exploitation, and in particular a process that redirects aid to benefit the donor countries themselves, whose companies charge noncompetitive and excessively high prices – thus reducing aid effectiveness and limiting the potential for sustainable development in the recipient country. Multilateral aid, by contrast, has been thought to be less susceptible to these problems, and more focused on humanitarian concerns. Certainly from a recipient country's point of view, multilateral aid is more flexible because it allows governments to shop internationally for the best prices on products and services. Put in practical terms, multilateral aid is like getting a VISA card instead of a Sears card – the card holder can use it in more places, and thus negotiate a better deal.

As a part of U.S. and international policy, development aid began with post-war planning for the reconstruction and stabilization of Europe. The immediate task, of course, was to thwart the advance of Soviet communism, and so initial aid to the region came in the form of emergency grants. The first such grants, more than $4 billion, went to Southern and Eastern Europe through the United Nations Relief and Rehabilitation Administration (UNRRA), established in 1943. A handful of non-governmental organizations were also created to deliver this assistance. Oxfam originally worked specifically with Greek refugees in the Balkans and Europe, and CARE – originally known as the Center for American Relief in Europe, was created in 1945. (Today CARE stands for Center for American Relief Everywhere.) In 1947, to avert crisis in Western Europe, U.S. Secretary of State George Marshall announced a reconstruction plan that in the next four years distributed more than $12 billion to the region through the Organization for European Economic Cooperation (now known as the Organization for Economic Cooperation and Development, or OECD). To support long-term reconstruction projects, the Bretton Woods system, led by the United States, created the World Bank – known officially as the International Bank for Reconstruction and Development[24] – and the IMF. By 1949, total U.S. foreign aid, military and non-military, totaled 2.75 percent of U.S. Gross Domestic Product.[25]

That same year the Chinese revolution, followed shortly thereafter by the Korean War, led the United States to provide aid to several countries in Central and Southeast Asia. The success of the Marshall Plan in Europe had led the U.S. government to understand foreign assistance as a way to create market economies that would generate jobs and capital, and an educated middle class that would create political pressure for popular participation in matters of governance, especially in those regions of the world in which Soviet influence was a concern. The geography of concern increased dramatically in the 1950s and 1960s with the independence of European colonies in Africa, Asia and Latin America, and the emergence of the non-aligned movement. The World Bank's first loan to a developing country went to Colombia in 1950, and throughout the decade the United States led the world in the provision of foreign aid, accounting for 60 percent of the total. In 1956 the Soviet Union began its own bilateral aid program, and by 1966 was providing $6 billion annually in technical and economic aid to developing nations.[26] Thereafter development aid, already closely linked to strategic security objectives, was bound to them. That linkage continues to this day, with the largest portion of all U.S. foreign assistance going to the Middle East.

As bilateral aid grew, so did multilateral aid. The first multilateral aid organizations were the UN and the Bretton Woods institutions, though none focused on development until several years after their creation. The IMF is not technically a development organization at all, though its activities have in many ways come to mirror those of the World Bank. In the 1960s and 1970s, regional development banks came into existence and grew to prominence, among them the Inter-American Development Bank, the African Development Bank, the Asian Development Bank and the Arab Fund for Social and Economic Development.

In 1960, W.W. Rostow's influential book *The Stages of Economic Growth: A Non-Communist Manifesto*, argued that by doubling investment rates, underdeveloped countries could "take off" into self-sustained growth.[27] Acting on this conviction, the Kennedy administration increased foreign aid by a third and in 1961 created the United States Agency for International Development (USAID), the Peace Corps, and, to promote economic development in Latin America, the Alliance for Progress. Aid to the newly independent, developing states of Africa followed on the same basis. The goals of these initiatives, as President Kennedy described them in his inaugural address, was to reach out to the people in "huts and villages across the globe, struggling to break the bonds of mass misery" and to "pledge our best efforts to help them help themselves for whatever period is required."[28] Not coincidentally, Rostow served under both Kennedy and Lyndon Johnson, a time when

U.S. non-military foreign aid reached an all-time high of 0.6 percent of U.S. GDP.

For at least thirty years then—until the collapse of the Berlin Wall in 1989 and then of the Soviet Union two years later—U.S. foreign aid, though controversial, had at least three identifiable objectives. The pre-eminent goal was strategic, to contain communism and other left-ist-populist movements and, where they had found footing, to combat them through U.S. influence. The two secondary goals were to promote economic growth in poor countries and to provide humanitarian relief to the victims of natural disasters and man-made crises. The three goals were discrete, but in obvious ways also inter-related and even, at times, contradictory. Individual countries, regions and international organiza-tions received different amounts of U.S. aid, to be spent in different ways, depending on a calculus that took all three factors into account.[29] In some regions, most infamously Latin America, American "assistance" did more to strangle democratic development than to advance it.

With the sudden and unexpected demise of the Soviet Union, the central pillar of U.S. foreign aid disappeared almost overnight (and, with it, a major source of the world's development aid), and before long even the developmental rationale for assistance seemed less convinc-ing than it once had been. In Asia and Latin America, particularly, the 1980s and 1990s were a period of rapid if uneven economic growth, with corresponding increases in literacy rates and life expectancy, and decreases in poverty and infant mortality. This growth was fueled in part by the surge of global private capital flows that for the first time included developing countries.[30] Partly in response to these changes, both conservative and liberal members of Congress heightened their criticism of USAID, particularly, as ineffective and unnecessary. The administrations of presidents George H.W. Bush and Bill Clinton sought to cut the foreign aid budget as part of general deficit reduction, though Clinton was far more aggressive in this regard. Total U.S. bilateral and multilateral aid peaked in 1991, mostly the result of aid to Central and Eastern Europe, and then began a steady decline. In November 1993, Clinton announced that foreign aid would no longer focus on client states and allies, as it had during the Cold War, but on approximately seven global objectives: promoting peace, sustainable development, trade and investment, and democratization; providing humanitarian assistance; improving health and environmental standards; and assisting with the transitions in Europe.[31]

Despite this shift in emphasis, U.S. non-military foreign aid expenditures in the 1990s actually decreased. In 1994, the total of all U.S. foreign aid – primarily bilateral economic and military assistance and funding to the World Bank and the International Monetary Fund – was approximately $13.7 billion.[32] That year President Clinton proposed cutting total foreign aid by 10 percent, though the proposed cuts fell unevenly; Clinton did not propose cutting the $5 billion then provided annually to Israel and Egypt, nor did he propose increasing aid to Russia and the NIS region (then $2.5 billion, with Russia itself getting only about 15 percent the amount given to Egypt). Other regions and countries – Central America, Pakistan and Turkey – saw very large aid reductions.[33] The Republican Congress that came to office in 1994 sought to cut aid even further, and that year the State Department proposed a merger with the USAID, then with an annual budget of about $6 billion. Vice President Al Gore killed the idea, leading North Carolina Senator Jesse Helms to attempt, unsuccessfully, to legislate a merger. Foreign aid would not begin to increase again until 1998, and when it did the primary causes for the increase were peacekeeping missions in the Balkans and humanitarian relief programs in Central America after the devastation caused by Hurricane Mitch. Still, by 2000 U.S. official development assistance (ODA) had fallen to just under $10 billion annually,[34] not to increase again until after the September 11, 2001 attacks.[35] Late that year, the United States gave a $600 million disbursement to Pakistan, and by 2003 non-military foreign aid had reached $15.3 billion, or about .14 percent of U.S. GNP.[36] U.S. aid in terms of GNP percentage is the lowest of any industrialized country among the thirty member states of the OECD, though since 2001 the United States has provided the most aid in absolute terms.[37] USAID assistance in 2001-2002 was $9.2 billion,[38] and since then USAID has also provided approximately $3.6 billion in assistance to Iraq.[39] In 2002, President George W. Bush pledged to increase foreign aid 50 percent by 2006, though even that increase, were it to happen, would leave the United States far short of the target of .7 percent of GNP adopted by the OECD.[40] Such a target is probably unrealistic; only five countries – Denmark, Luxembourg, Norway, the Netherlands and Sweden – have ever managed to meet it.

Throughout the 1990s, a number of critics from across the ideological spectrum urged that the entire apparatus of U.S. foreign aid be re-examined. As one might expect, the criticisms of foreign aid varied enormously, but a common theme in all of them had to do with the political motivations for aid, and whether they were the right ones. Partly for this reason, USAID itself has historically been uncomfortable with democratization programs, which it sees as political rather than economic activity. At the same time, critics of USAID have argued that responsibility for its development programs should be given to the international development banks, the World Bank and the International Monetary Fund. The banks are but one of several multilateral assistance organizations with which the United States is involved, and the two where its influence is particularly strong. The World Bank's president is by tradition an American nominated by the president; the International Monetary Fund's president is traditionally a European, but its second-in-charge is always an American. The United States is also a major contributor to the United Nations Development Program (UNDP), the Inter-American Development Bank, and the Asian Development Bank; and it is a member of inter-governmental organizations (IGOs) for which democratization and media development are core concerns, among them the Organization of American States (OAS) and the OSCE.

Finally but importantly, the greatest part of U.S. foreign aid today is non-governmental, approximately $35 billion annually.[41] The Europeans and the Japanese give primarily through their governments, though Americans give far more through private means and non-profit organizations. In 2000, according to USAID, the largest single source of private U.S. assistance were the $18 billion in remittances sent by foreign nationals in the United States to their home countries.[42] Global remittances of $50 billion are roughly equal to global ODA, and that figure is expected to increase as electronic banking services replace inefficient and costly money transfer companies. Remittances to Latin America, most of them from the United States, are about $14.5 billion annually, more than what the region receives from multilateral development agencies.[43] In 2000, U.S.-based NGOs provided another $6.6 billion in grants, donations and volunteer labor. Religious organizations provided $3.4 billion in health care and educational assistance, relief and literacy programs; U.S. businesses sent $2.8 billion overseas; and private foundations provided another $1.5 billion in international assistance.[44] Much of the growth in private international giving in the 1990s came from foundations, which grew in number from 32,000 to 56,000 during the decade; in 2003 those foundations accounted for about 11 percent of total grants – approximately $3 billion, about four times as much as foundations gave in 1990.[45]

Those totals are probably skewed somewhat by the emergence of mega-foundations such as the Bill and Melinda Gates Foundation, but the growth is significant all the same. Though it is obviously an important point that private-sector foreign aid from the United States is greater than government aid, comprising about 60 percent of all assistance, it is hard to know how accurate these figure are. USAID's data are based on its own records, reports of the U.S. Office of Management and Budget and the OECD. But it is certainly possible that the figures with respect to private giving are overstated. As discussed below, government aid monies are often distributed through NGOs, which are retained as contractors to provide programs and services. Some NGOs, particularly in the democracy-promotion business, receive almost all their funding from government grants and contracts. In this sense, to call them private is technically correct but fundamentally misleading.

The Democratization Industry

Democracy assistance is the model of a globalized industry, built on a network of national development agencies, inter-governmental organizations and non-governmental organizations. These participants can be donors or recipients of aid monies, or both. The United States and several European countries, for instance, act as bilateral donors, providing assistance to other states or regions where they have historic or strategic interests. IGOs like the European Union or the World Bank act as multilateral donors, but are also dependent on their member nations for their operating and program costs. The United States, for example, is the single largest contributor to the World Bank's lending funds. Transnational corporations also participate in democracy assistance, both directly and through their corporate foundations. In the United States, corporate charitable giving overseas was once illegal, but now includes cash and non-cash grants, employee volunteer programs, and cause-related marketing. According to former USAID administrator Carol Adelman, the U.S. industries that provide the most foreign aid are pharmaceuticals, telecommunications and computers.[46] But there are many others. In Africa, for example, where USAID reports the trend of private and corporate assistance is *least* developed, the roster of private foundations and corporate grantmakers includes several Fortune 500 firms, among them General Electric, General Motors, Chevron, Minnesota Mining & Manufacturing (3M), Monsanto, Dell Computer Corporation and Eli Lilly.[47] Corporate giving focuses almost exclusively on economic and agricultural, environmental, health and nutrition programs; democracy and governance programs are the province of private foundations and other NGOs.

NGOs in the democratization industry also act both bilaterally and multilaterally, and they range from professional, technically sophisticated, international firms to the thousands of regional and local organizations scattered around the globe. Some NGOs are little more than service providers – subcontractors that carry out development programs of their own and for other organizations – and some are primarily advocacy, research or monitoring organizations. In that respect many NGOs are not interested in democratization per se, but on some enabling element of democracy. Human Rights Watch, for example, was founded specifically to be an international clearinghouse for information and activity related to the abuse of human rights. In the field of media assistance, the Brussels-based European Institute for the Media monitors the performance of media in elections for the European Commission, and also acts as a research organization that helps donors, governmental and non-governmental, identify funding needs.

All of these actors – national governments, IGOs and NGOs – are linked in a web of one-to-many relationships; from any point on the network there is one or more linkages to other actors in the system. The institutional relationships are often hierarchical; the actual flow of aid resources from donors to aid recipients or program implementers typically flows from governments and IGOs through regional and local NGOs and businesses. Monroe Price and his colleagues, for example, graphically represent the media component of the democratization industry as a triangle, with governments and IGOs and a few large NGOs at the top distributing resources downward through international, regional and local intermediaries and "local partners" who in effect bid for contracts by responding to funders' requests for proposals.[48] The distribution of influence in this pyramid is less hierarchical. For example, the publicity activities of NGOs, acting cooperatively or independently, can have powerful effects on the agendas and activities of the major donor states and IGOs, and not always for the better. Regional and local NGOs can also take the initiative in identifying specific assistance needs, then independently prepare proposals for funding to meet those needs.

Mapping Democracy Promotion

In the United States, the official locus of democracy-promotion aid is USAID, the grant-making agency created when the Foreign Assistance

Act of 1961 merged two existing agencies, the Development Loan Fund and the International Cooperative Administration. As an independent federal agency, USAID must ask Congress for its funding each year as part of the executive department's budget requests. The agency works both on its own initiative and in some cases cooperatively with other federal offices, in particular the U.S. departments of State, Defense and Justice. As a government agency engaged in bilateral aid, USAID has counterparts throughout the developed democratic world – the European Commission, the Canadian International Development Agency, the British Overseas Development Agency, the Swedish International Development Agency, and similar state agencies in Norway, Finland, Denmark, Germany and Japan, among others in the membership of the OECD.

Another major source of U.S. democracy-promotion assistance are the major government-funded NGOs in the field – the Asia Foundation, the National Endowment for Democracy (NED), and the Eurasia Foundation, all three of which are private, not-for-profit organizations funded almost entirely by the federal government to promote democracy overseas, and all three of which will carry out contracts for USAID.[49] Government support to private NGOs is not new; it dates to federal assistance to the Red Cross during the Civil War in the mid-19th century. More recently, NGOs have been the product of U.S. government efforts to promote its domestic and foreign policy objectives during World War II and the Cold War. During World War II, for example, the federal government licensed relief agencies and provided them with money and goods for distribution; in return, the State Department required its licensed charities to supply regular reports on their finances and operations, including of course all aid disbursements. When the war ended, many of these same organizations received agricultural surpluses from the government, a policy that had two benefits. It kept domestic prices for agricultural products suitably high, and it sought to ensure that, by providing aid through intermediary organizations rather than directly, assistance would not be used to subsidize or otherwise benefit Soviet relief efforts, especially in Africa and Asia. Eventually, some officials concluded that NGOs could serve as surrogates for the U.S. government in countries where existing U.S. aid was either limited or non-existent, or where an official U.S. presence was diplomatically sensitive or impossible.

It was partly on that theory that the federal government created the Asia Foundation, the NED and the Eurasia Foundation. The Eurasia

Foundation, begun in 1992, was intended to work in the countries of the former Soviet Union where an official U.S. presence would have been unwelcome. One of Eurasia's founders, former USAID officer and University of Michigan Professor Charles Greenleaf, told researcher Julia Seidler in 2000 that in many of the NIS countries in the early 1990s "it wasn't a good idea to have the U.S. government involved.... [The democratic institutions in another country] were in many ways too delicate and too sensitive."[50] In response to a memo by then Secretary of State James Baker, Greenleaf submitted a proposal for what became the Citizen Democracy Corps, the forerunner to the Eurasia Foundation. The foundation continues to get the largest part of its funding from the federal government (90 percent in 2002, according to publicly available tax records), though it also receives funding form a huge variety of other government and private sources, among them George Soros' foundations, the Pew Charitable Trusts, and the Norwegian government.

According to another of its founders, Eugene Staples, the Eurasia Foundation was modeled after an earlier government creation, the Asia Foundation, created in 1954 to provide aid to China and Southeast Asia and which for many years was secretly funded by the Central Intelligence Agency. The purpose of these organizations, Staples said, was to "pursue either social development or political development or economic development objectives, making quite small grants and with a much closer set of communications and contacts with grassroots organizations because you're not involved in high-level government policy."[51] The goal of the Eurasia Foundation, Staples wrote, was the "slow but widespread creation and growth of new economic and political institutions responding to the reform efforts of many thousands of NIS citizens."[52] Today the Eurasia Foundation's mission for the region is to fund "programs that build democratic and free market institutions in the twelve New Independent States (NIS) of the former Soviet Union."[53]

Each of these three nominally private organizations has its own mission, regional focus and strategy, and each fulfills its remit in significant part by subcontracting work to other organizations. NED, for example, has provided grants to independent NGOs such as Transparency International and to IGOs like the International Development Law Institute. These grantees, in turn, provide financial, technical or other kinds of assistance through contracts with any of hundreds of smaller NGOs around the world whose work may focus on a single goal or project, such as registering women to vote or training journalists in investigative reporting techniques. Some of these contracts are true partnerships in which two or more organizations, through cooperation or joint ventures, are able to meet their missions more effectively; others are more accurately characterized as simple subcontracts, in which an NGO wins a bid to perform a particular task.

At times, the federal government's funding of overseas democratization organizations and programs has been controversial, and at times even embarrassing. In addition to funding the Asia Foundation, for example, the CIA also secretly funded both Radio Free Europe and Radio Liberty, a fact known to key members of Congress and also to many journalists, but not to the American public until 1967, when the *New York Times* first chronicled the connection. The immediate result of the story was a public relations fiasco, because the radios had for several years solicited donations from the public through an advertising campaign known as the Crusade for Freedom. In 1971, Congress terminated CIA funding for the stations and arranged for their continued existence by open appropriations. CIA support for the Asia Foundation was made public around the same time, with much the same result. Such secrecy, critics argued, effectively undermined the very message of democratic openness these programs were intended to convey – especially in their media broadcasts to closed, totalitarian regimes.

By the 1970s federal government subsidies to NGOs were three times what they had been in the 1940s. As Brian Smith writes, NGOs of whatever character became "a logical conduit for increased U.S. public assistance for three reasons. Congress wanted to ensure that a greater amount of foreign aid reached the poorest abroad. It also wanted to regain the confidence of the American people in foreign aid after the Vietnam War. Finally, it was easier to convince Third World governments that U.S. foreign policy henceforth was to emphasize alleviation of poverty and equitable development, not popular revolutions or U.S. intervention in the internal political affairs of foreign countries."[54]

Suspicion abroad and criticism at home are still a problem, however. A ready example of the problem is the National Endowment for Democracy. Created by Congress in 1983 at the urging of President Ronald Reagan, the NED was intended to support democracy programs overseas that were specifically forbidden to USAID and to other government aid agencies by their charters. The idea was that the NED would be less hindered by legal and political restrictions, and that as an ostensibly private organization it would escape any stigma that might otherwise attach to programs clearly identified with the U.S. government. Critics of the NED argue that it has functioned as a slush fund for its four primary grantees: the National Democratic Institute for International Affairs (the Democratic Party), the International Republican Institute (the Republican Party), the Free Trade Union Institute (FTUI) of the AFL-CIO, and the Center for International Private Enterprise operated by the U.S. Chamber of Commerce.[55]

Criticisms of NED are many. Most seriously, the NED has in numerous instances been accused of allowing its core grantees to act as their own "mini State Departments,"[56] sometimes in ways that effectively under-mine official U.S. policy.[57] Practically from the moment it was funded, the NED has meddled in other countries' elections – in Nicaragua, Costa Rica, Chile, Czechoslovakia and even France – in ways that would be illegal for foreign groups operating in the United States.[58] Only a year after its founding, for example, the NED funded a military candidate, Nicholas Ardito Barletta, for president of Panama, despite official U.S. policy to oppose military rule in the country. When U.S. Ambas-sador to Panama James E. Biggs learned of the NED's involvement, he wired the White House demanding that "this hair-brained project be abandoned before it hits the fan."[59] Shortly thereafter, NED gave financial support to opponents of Costa Rican President Oscar Arias because of his criticism of President Reagan's policies in the region, particularly his support of the Contras in Nicaragua. Arias was both a Nobel Peace Prize winner (for his efforts to end the civil wars in the region) and the leader of Central America's most stable and enduring democracy. In addition to receiving financial support from NED, Arias' political opposition was supported by Panamanian dictator Manuel Noriega. In the French case, the AFL-CIO's FTUI approved a $1.5 million grant to "defend democracy" in France on the grounds that Francois Mitterrand's socialist government was "threatened by the Com-munist apparatus."[60] One of the organizations funded by FTUI was the French National-Inter-University Union, a right-wing extremist group. When the French newspaper *Liberation* exposed these activities, the U.S. government was quick to disavow them.

The important point about NED's activities is that the place of de-mocracy promotion in foreign assistance has always been defined by numerous tensions, and specifically the fact that democracy assistance, unlike other forms of aid, is an explicitly political activity. Congress has had to dance around this fact from the beginning. Title IX of the1961

Foreign Assistance Act required USAID to assure "maximum participation in the task of economic development on the part of the people of the developing countries, through the encouragement of democratic private and local government institutions."[61] Congress did not, however, set aside any funds for this purpose, and so what specific forms participation was to take, and whether they were political or economic, was a matter left to USAID, which saw itself as an economic development agency and was both administratively unprepared for and institutionally wary of any activities that involved electoral politics.

It eventually became apparent, however, that Rostow's modernization theory had a fatal flaw: Aid unaccompanied by pressures for political accountability did not work very well, and sometimes had the perverse result of entrenching and enriching powerful and autocratic rulers and their parties. Worse still, if unattended by pressures for economic accountability, U.S. assistance created incentives for corrupt governments to make inefficient use of aid in order to qualify for *additional* aid. To be fair, these problems were often the result of political calculations beyond the control of USAID, a product of the mission conflict present in U.S. aid from the beginning. Political economist Jeffrey Winters, for example, has described the process by which Indonesian dictator General Suharto received enormous loans from the World Bank because, with its oil and other natural resources, Indonesia was one of the dominoes the United States sought to defend against communist insurgency in Vietnam. Suharto's credentials as an anti-communist were sufficient to sustain huge inflows of aid despite his regime's violence and well-known corruption. In 1966 and 1967, the Indonesian army killed more than 1 million communists (mostly ethnic Chinese), the largest such mass killing outside of Russia, but the killings had no effect on U.S. aid, which actually increased. Suharto, in turn, diverted untold billions of dollars to himself and his family, leaving Indonesia with a debt it cannot repay (and Suharto's family extremely wealthy).[62]

A similar pattern repeated itself throughout the Cold War: U.S. assistance intended to promote democracy was frequently combined with or even subverted by manipulatively political forms of "aid" from the Central Intelligence Agency, often for purposes that were anti-communist and anti-democratic. In Guatemala, for instance, the Defense Department and CIA in the 1970s and 1980s provided support to the Guatemalan military's vicious campaign against political opposition or criticism of virtually any kind in its war against "communism." In 1982 and 1983, under dictator General Rios Montt, the Guatemalan military wiped out entire Mayan villages, murdering as many as 200,000 people and burying them in mass graves. At the same time, amazingly, USAID was funding programs to train rural community leaders how to more effectively participate in politics. A later study commissioned by USAID to evaluate its work in the region revealed that more than 750 of those trained under the USAID program were murdered, many of them by the Guatemalan military.[63]

It was these kinds of abuses that had led President Jimmy Carter put human rights at the center of his administration's foreign policy when he came to office in 1976. Today the scope of human rights norms and human rights law reaches to include a variety of things that may or may not be universally understood as "rights" (for example job security and health care), but in 1976 the focus was much more narrow, in particular on torture, murder and other forms of political violence and coercion. Carter's understanding of human rights, therefore, did not include democracy promotion and it did not rely on increased aid. The administration was also decidedly non-interventionist, in part because previous American political intervention, particularly in Latin America, was even by 1976 a cause for shame rather than celebration. Carter was therefore left with moral suasion and diplomatic pressure as his only real policy options, and he used them to great effect, emphasizing the record of violence and abuse in the world's repressive regimes. In particular, Carter was able to create breathing space for political opposition in the military regimes of Latin America, and he used the 1975 Helsinki Accords to expose the human rights abuses of the Soviet Union.

What Carter began Ronald Reagan continued, though Reagan's idealism was of a completely different kind, in concept and in practice. Reagan announced his administration's determination to bring down the "evil empire" of the Soviet Union, and early in his first term Reagan launched "Project Democracy" to counteract what he viewed as dominant Soviet ideological influence in the Third World. Project Democracy was run out of the White House and relied on conferences, international exchanges and increased international broadcasting by the Free Radio services and Voice of America (then both under the auspices of the U.S. Information Agency) to promote American ideas about democracy. At the same time, and independent of the administration, a bipartisan congressional effort to promote democracy around the world took shape in the form of the NED. In 1982, Reagan spoke publicly and proudly of these efforts in a speech to the British Parliament, saying that he wanted to "foster the infrastructure of democracy, the system of a free press, unions, political parties, universities, which allows a people to choose their own way to develop their own culture, to reconcile their own differences through peaceful means."[64] Eventually the Project Democracy folded for want of congressional funding, but NED received initial funding of $18 million in 1983 and was formally launched in December of the same year. In its initial grant-making, NED focused less on democracy than it did on anti-communism, some of it little more than gratuitous pay-outs suited to the political preferences of its member organizations.

Concurrent with these efforts, the Reagan administration developed a vigorous military component to its democratization goals, supporting "freedom fighters" in places like Angola, Afghanistan and Nicaragua. In his 1985 State of the Union address, Reagan emphasized that "We must not break faith with those who are risking their lives to defy Soviet aggression,"[65] and his administration exercised that faith nowhere more vigorously than Latin America, where it worked to topple left-leaning governments both openly, as in the invasion of Grenada, and covertly, as in his administration's secret funding of the Nicaraguan paramilitary contras. Reagan's eagerness to engage right-wing but anti-communist dictators in Central America effectively reversed Carter's policy toward the region. Though Reagan talked about democratization in the region in electoral and even human rights terms, he chose to fund (in addition to the contras) violently repressive military regimes in El Salvador, Guatemala and Honduras. In some cases that funding included aid for elections and for justice reform, but such aid was typically politicized and in some cases even undermined by covert U.S. efforts to assure the outcome of elections. In 1984, for example, USAID provided aid for voter registration to El Salvador, ostensibly to ensure the credibility of that year's elections, even as the CIA provided funds to ensure that the administration's favored candidate, Christian Democrat Jose Napoleon Duarte, won the election.[66]

Despite these conflicts between hard-line anti-communism and progressive democratization in Latin America policy, electoral and justice reform emerged as permanent and important features of U.S. democracy assistance in the late 1980s, not only in Latin America, but also in the Philippines and South Korea. Carothers suggests the evolution was more practical than political.[67] When, for example, the State Department was forced by public pressure to investigate the 1981 murders in El Salvador of four American women missionaries and the 1980 murder of Archbishop Oscar Romero, it found the country's judicial and police systems so inept and corrupt as to be an impediment to the investigation. As a result, the State Department in 1983 undertook a $9.2 million program to reform El Salvador's judiciary. USAID later established two large judicial reform projects, one for Central America and another for the Caribbean, and at the urging of the State Department in 1986 created an assistance program to teach investigative skills to regional police. In the latter half of the 1980s, as elections swept dictators from office throughout Latin America, U.S. electoral assistance in the region also grew significantly. To this day, however, suspicions linger in Latin America about U.S. motives in providing such aid. Some U.S. credibility was regained when it abandoned its support for the Philippines' Ferdinand Marcos in 1986 and, a year later, when it compelled South Korean President Chun Doo Hwan to fulfill his promise for open elections that removed him from power. But as recently as August 2004, the heavy involvement of the NED in funding groups opposed to Venezuelan President Hugo Chavez renewed old fears in the region about the United States' commitment to democratic norms.

U.S. Democracy Promotion after the Cold War

By the end of the 1980s, U.S. democracy assistance in support of fair elections and judicial reform had reached an annual level of between $100 million and $150 million.[68] By 1999, total U.S. government democratization assistance had more than quadrupled, to approximately $700 million annually[69]; USAID democracy assistance had reached more than $530 million annually[70] and had expanded to include two new program areas, governance and civil society, both of which are now far larger, in the dollars given to them, than electoral aid, now the smallest of USAID's four core assistance categories.[71] After coming into office in 1993, President Clinton identified "building sustainable democracies"[72] as one of USAID's central goals, and in 1994 created a research and consulting office within USAID, the Center for Democracy and Governance, "to help USAID officers design and implement democracy and governance programs that are strategic and objective."[73] By the end of the decade, smaller democratization programs were being run through the

Department of Defense (in the form of human rights training mandated by Congress as part of the International Military Education and Training Program, or IMET); the Department of Justice (which provides training to police investigators and judges), and the State Department (which as of 2000 assumed the public diplomacy duties of the U.S. Information Agency). In addition to the already existing NED and the Asia Foundation, Congress in 1993 created the Eurasia Foundation to work in Russia and the NIS regions.

The growth in democracy assistance in the 1990s was driven in significant part by the collapse of the old anti-communist rationale for foreign aid. Suddenly there was more breathing room for idealistic pro-democracy ideas, though the more dramatic and accompanying shift was to a policy of encouraging free markets. Beginning in his first term, President George H. W. Bush and Congress established several aid programs to the transition states of Europe, including Support for Eastern European Democracy (SEED, created in 1989) and a number of smaller programs for the states of the former Soviet Union (mostly Russia and Ukraine) under the 1991 Freedom Support Act. Only a small portion of the funds in these programs was for democracy promotion – most was for more traditional forms of economic and social aid – but the total amount of direct U.S. democratization aid to Central Europe and the former Soviet Union was nonetheless significant, approximately $1.2 billion between 1990 and 1998.[74] Indirect U.S. aid, through the NED and the Eurasia Foundation, brought the aid total for the region to approximately $1.5 billion for the decade.[75]

Much of that aid, of course, flowed under the administration of President Clinton, who established an Interagency Working Group on Democracy to try to coordinate different elements of the policy as they were carried out by the State Department, the Commerce Department and USAID.[76] During the Clinton administration, the hazy policy of "democratic enlargement" became, nominally at least, a centerpiece of U.S. foreign policy.[77] Clinton had focused on the global democratization movement in his 1992 campaign, in which he criticized President Bush for his starkly realist approach to the world and what Clinton characterized as a willingness to coddle dictators. To Clinton, the key to democratization was market reform, and his foreign policy focused most clearly on American economic objectives and developing open markets abroad. In March 1993, Clinton told his State Department that the principle foreign policy goal of his administration would be to advance

U.S. economic power and to "make trade a priority element of American security."[78] A few months later, Clinton gave a keynote address to the United Nations in which he declared that America's "overriding purpose" was "to expand and strengthen the world's community of market-based democracies."[79] In almost every other respect his foreign policies were sharply criticized by those who believed that his administration's emphasis on "soft power" – the persuasiveness of ideas and the value of good examples – was both directionless and indecisive on matters related to the real world of political and military power.

Clinton, however, was willing to tolerate authoritarian regimes "when other security needs or economic interests"[80] made it expedient to do so. Most notably, his administration angered many members of Congress when it chose to embrace increased trade with China over the strong objections of those in both parties critical of China's human rights record. In other countries – for example, Peru with Alberto Fujimori, Indonesia with Muhamed Suharto, and throughout the Middle East – the Clinton administration maintained economic and diplomatic ties with governments that were strongly autocratic and in some cases violently repressive. Clinton was thus no more willing or able than his predecessors to ignore U.S. strategic concerns. President George W. Bush has established military bases across north central Asia – in Turkmenistan, Uzbekistan, Tajikstan and Kyrgyzstan – all authoritarian regimes in the strategically important, oil-rich Caucasus.

U.S. democracy assistance in the 1990s also grew in sub-Saharan Africa, where South Africa was the shining democratic success but more than forty other countries received assistance totaling more than $700 million,[81] and in Asia, where the overwhelming focus of aid in the decade was on economic development. Annual democracy assistance expenditures to Latin America actually declined in the latter part of the 1990s, after the largest single expenditure for democratization aid in the region went to Haiti in the aftermath of U.S. military intervention to restore President Jean Bertrand Aristide to power in 1994.[82] Otherwise U.S. democratization efforts in the region have been largely diplomatic. With two important exceptions (Venezuela, in 2002 and Haiti in 2004), U.S. administrations have been publicly critical of any attempts in the region to seize power through violent means. The record of these democratization efforts around the world are decidedly mixed: for the success stories like South Africa and Chile, there are also some marked failures. Cambodia has been the largest recipient of democratization aid in Asia,[83] but suffered a military coup in 1997. Haiti, despite $100 million of U.S. aid, experienced a coup in 2004.

Today democracy promotion at USAID remains a subsidiary part of "an integrated development agenda,"[84] and is viewed as important primarily because of the recognition that bad and corrupt governments are an impediment to the broad range of economic development goals – economic growth, population growth, health and nutrition; environmental protection; crisis and disaster prevention, and so on. USAID's official view is that "the strategic long-term domestic and foreign policy objectives of the United States are best served by enlarging the community of democratic nations worldwide. Establishing democratic institutions, free and open markets, an informed and educated populace, a vibrant civil society, and a relationship between state and society that encourages pluralism, participation, and peaceful conflict resolution – all these contribute to the goal of establishing sustainable democracies."[85] A related idea, according to a 1998 USAID report, embraces the democratic-peace hypothesis: "Democratic governments are more likely to advocate and observe international laws and to experience the kind of long-term stability which leads to sustained development, economic growth, and international trade. Countries that are experiencing economic growth and are actively engaged in trading relationship are less likely to engage in acts of war."[86]

USAID is not alone in this thinking; most aid providers share the view that democracy promotion and economic development are interdependent. In 1989, for instance, the World Bank blamed Africa's developmental failures on poor governance.[87] Since then the Bank, like many other international aid sources, has tried to make closer conceptual and programmatic connections between economic development and competent governance. Over the same period, a growing number of international NGOs have brought technical and research expertise to the subject of democratization, focusing on such things as government transparency and accountability, legal and regulatory reform, and a broad array of human rights concerns. Many of these NGOs are also extremely effective advocates for their political goals, and many are also essential to the worldwide distribution of humanitarian assistance in all its forms. Approximately 1,600 of them are registered contractors for the United Nations, and organizations like the World Bank and the IMF now include NGOs as participants, and sometimes as partners or operational intermediaries, in a variety of development projects.

The European Approach to Democracy Promotion

Europe also emerged as a major source of democracy assistance in the 1990s. Among individual states, Germany was the largest funder, by 1998 giving €200 million annually, about half of that through its party foundations (*politische stiftungen*), to "state and civil society work." The same year the United Kingdom's assistance to "human rights and governance" was more than €100 million; the Dutch government was splitting €140 million annually between "human rights" and "good governance and peacebuilding"; and France and Denmark each was giving €70 million to "human rights and democracy." Sweden typically devotes the largest percentage of its foreign aid budget to democracy work, a little more than 10 percent.[88]

The European Union was slower than the United States to respond to the global democratic opening that occurred in the 1980s, even though its most celebrated moment came on European soil in 1989. Between 1990 and 1998, the EU increased its funding for democracy assistance three-fold, such that by the end of the decade total EU democracy assistance roughly rivaled that of the U.S. at approximately €800 million annually, or about 2 percent of the overall EU aid budget (an overall budget that is significantly larger than the United States foreign aid budget, in which democracy assistance accounted for about 10 percent of all aid at the end of the 1990s). Like the U.S. the EU devoted by far the greater part of its assistance to economic development, and until mid-decade the EU, like the United States, gave most of its dedicated democratization assistance to elections activity; later it trimmed its elections programs to less than 20 percent of its aid budget and took a strongly "bottom-up" approach to democratization, favoring civil society programs and the participation of local, indigenous NGOs. The notable exception to this policy was in the Balkans, where the 1995 Dayton Accords and later the Kosovo settlement gave the EU specific remit, under the international authority of the OSCE, the UN and NATO, to engage in political work.

The regional distribution of U.S. and EU democracy assistance over the 1990s was very similar, though there were some important differences. In the early part of the decade, the European Commission's Democracy Initiative directed more than 50 percent of its assistance to two regions, Latin America and the countries of Sub-Saharan Africa, the Caribbean and the Pacific (known to the Commission as the "ACP countries"). By the second half of the decade, assistance was more widely distributed. Between 1996 and 1999, the greater part of EU democracy assistance went to Central Europe, the Balkan states and the NIS region (35 percent) and to the ACP countries (21 percent) and Latin America (17 percent). Over the same period, 14 percent of EU democracy assistance went to North Africa (where U.S. assistance outside of Egypt was negligible), and only 1 percent of EU aid went to Asia.[89]

Strategically, the notable difference between EU and US assistance in the 1990s was the European preference for funding for civil society development through the funding of local NGOs and other grass-roots and service-delivery organizations. In its media assistance programs, for instance, the overwhelming share of EU aid went to freedom of expression NGOs whose primary task was improving local press coverage of various human rights issues. The EU focus on NGOs, according to one source, was chosen because it was "seen likely to play the crucial role in igniting democratizing momentum in pre-transition states, and the best means of counter-balancing the power of elites in semi-democratic contexts and still-fragile post-transition states…. This approach was seen by policy-makers as addressing the often-advanced criticism that Western donors were unduly concerned with the formal institutional features of democracy rather than its more substantive social elements."[90] Distinctly different than the American approach, the European strategy "was 'non-prescriptive' in terms of 'institutional end-goals.' Rather it was concerned with expanding the scope of individual sites of democratic process, and aimed, in the words of one policy maker, at 'constructing a political will for democratic policy-making' rather than implanting 'institutional forms.'"[91]

With respect to substance, EU assistance in the decade differed from American assistance in that it was less conspicuously geo-strategic in its policies and, pushed by the European Parliament, was far less interested in governance funding and much more aggressive in promoting human rights. In every region except Sub-Saharan Africa, where the principal funding focus remained on elections, the lion's share of the EU assistance budget – typically 80 percent or more – went to fund human rights NGOs.[92] A common criticism of such funding, even within the EU itself, was that such funding was too ad hoc and lacked any kind of overarching vision.[93] Another criticism was that funding went to a fairly narrow range of favored causes and organizations – excluding, for example, religious groups, which were important to transitions in both Central Europe and Latin America – and sometimes focused too heavily on a single social issue.[94] In Morocco, for instance, one-third of the assistance provided through the Euro-Mediterranean Partnership (MEDA Democracy) went to women's rights NGOs.[95] In 2000, 75 percent of the EU budget for Latin America went to a single project to create a network of development and human rights NGOs.[96] By 2001, EU assistance in Central and Eastern Europe was also focused heavily on the rights of ethnic minorities; an internal Commission report said critically that the effect of such aid was limited to "raising the visibility of recipient NGOs."[97] Another Commission report made the criticism that in Eastern Europe the EU favored a few well-connected and high-profile NGOs whose activities muted or competed with work by local organizations.[98] By 2000, EU Development Commissioner Poul Neilsen worried openly that too great a focus on NGOs might even have the undesired effect of undermining the formation of democratic institutions in transition societies.[99]

By the end of the 1990s, the focus of EU and US assistance had largely converged on matters of substance. Most significantly, both continued to see economic and market reform, coupled with administrative capacity building, as the essential and most productive driver for broader political reform. Within Europe (and with the notable exception of Turkey), the EU has been far more likely to recognize and reward economic reforms than political ones as a condition for EU membership (or membership consideration). Unfortunately, it is also the case that both the EU and the United States, in aggressively protecting their comparative trade advantages over poor developing countries, have probably done a lot to limit the capacity for economic growth and political liberalization in many of the countries where they otherwise purport to support these goals.[100] At the end of the 1990s, the US had also joined the EU in giving civil society development a higher profile; as noted earlier, it is now the largest of USAID's four program areas in dollar terms.[101]

With respect to how programs actually operate, the EU has remained less goal-oriented than the United States and more likely than the United States to engage local people in project design and implementation. Americans, by contrast, are known to send a visiting consultant who arrives on the scene with plans in hand and a staff at the ready. The American approach is also defined, in every category of aid, in terms of objectives.[102] Though most objectives are highly qualitative in nature, the American approach aspires to produce results that can in some other way made susceptible to quantitative evaluation. With respect to elections, for example, the goal of USAID media assistance is that "media fulfills role as watchdog in the electoral process,"[103] an objective that is to be evaluated through content analyses that measure the "number of media outlets providing critical assessments" and the "accuracy of media critiques."[104] With respect to civil society assistance, the overarching goal of media assistance is to enhance the "free flow of information," an objective that is itself the sum of four subsidiary goals each with its own definition, evaluation criteria and data collection methods.[105]

Finally, the EU approach to democracy assistance has relied on deeper and more formal relationships in its assistance framework, favoring partnerships with local and regional organizations. With important exceptions, the United States is more likely than the EU to act independently of any partners. In Latin America, for example, the United States is a member of the OAS, but in the context of election monitoring has often stepped outside its role in that organization to adopt unilateral measures against specific states, something the EU has chosen not to do in a similar role in the Euro-Mediterranean Partnership. From one point of view, the EU democratization project is thus more concerned with building normative support for democratic reforms (including in the process of EU enlargement) than is the United States; from an American point of view, the EU's approach can seem piecemeal and irresolute.

What Works? The Problem of Program Evaluation

A final problem for democracy assistance, and thus also for media assistance, is program evaluation. Perhaps the most obvious feature of democratization projects, public or private, is their tendency to speak of their programs' successes in almost breathless terms, and more generally to assume that relatively small and isolated achievements are representative of broader positive trends. At least part of that tendency can be attributed to the need for good publicity, and more specifically the fact that most organizations in the democratization industry, governmental and non-governmental, must constantly be making the case for their own continued funding.

But the fundamental problem is devising objective measures of success: finding evaluation criteria that are clear, finite, and which can be applied consistently in different settings; and identifying causality between programs and outcomes. As a USAID report noted in 1997,

Democracy objectives are often multidimensional and not easily captured by a single measure. Indicators of performance may differ depending on the state of a country's democratic development. Sometimes, performance data can be too expensive to collect at frequent intervals. Finally, performance in other sectors can affect democracy programming. Centrally, the Agency continues to look to the development of quality indicators for assessing the performance of democracy objectives.[106]

The evaluation process in democracy-promotion is subjective for the same reason it is in any activity devoted to fulfilling a social mission or providing a public good: In economic terms, the positive externalities of public goods are diffuse and difficult to measure. Or, as Carothers says, "the value of democracy programs is often not their specific effects on institutions but the way they reshape the attitudes or ideas of individuals."[107] Add to this the varying conceptions of democracy – what it requires, what its essential institutions are, how it works, and cultural and historical circumstances that will everywhere be unique—and useful evaluation in democracy assistance begins to appear impossible. To take an obvious example, the steps of transition and the measures of success in a country that is democratizing in the aftermath of violent conflict will likely be different than those where transition is the result of a peaceful negotiated settlement. Civil society assistance, which focuses precisely on the kinds of broad social attitudes Carothers emphasizes, is thus particularly hard to evaluate. Media assistance, which is almost always either linked to civil society programs or part of them, presents even more difficulty, relying as it does on complex and abstract notions of press freedom and press responsibility. These are subjects of endless debate and disagreement in established Western media systems. It is hard to imagine how they might be made both understandable and quantifiable in countries where democracy is both new and unstable, the swirl of social, political and economic change unpredictable. As a practical matter, too, many democratizing countries will be profoundly influenced by their neighbors, whose problems and people cross borders. Recognizing these kinds of factors and controlling for them in evaluation is difficult.

For all this, however, evaluation is critical. In its absence, there is ample room for inefficiency and worse. Carothers writes that:

> Many democracy groups evaluate their efforts informally and haphazardly, with many projects not evaluated at all. To some extent this is due to the belief common among democracy promoters that their work is of unquestionable value and needs no assessing. Then, too, starting with the slew of democratic openings in the late 1980s and early 1990s, democracy groups got in the mode of hurrying from one country to the next, launching programs on a crash basis. Painstaking retrospective analysis appeared an unaffordable luxury.[108]

For government assistance programs supported by taxpayers, however, evaluation is a statutory obligation. The Government Performance and Results Act of 1993 requires U.S. agencies to produce annual statements that describe their goals and their progress in meeting them. The law also requires federal agencies with common or overlapping interests to explain how they will coordinate their activities, including those of the large democracy-promotion NGOs that receive U.S. funds.[109] The General Accounting Office (which in 2004 changed its name to the Government Accountability Office) has been critical of U.S. agencies – particularly USAID, the State Department and the Justice Department – for what it consistently characterizes as poor evaluation, noting, among other things, that:

> the relationship among implementing agencies has often been characterized more by competition than by cooperation, which has led to fragmented programs that are not always mutually supportive in achieving common goals…. Furthermore, by not addressing and building on potentially complementary programs of other donors – some of which receive considerable funding from the United States – agencies risk overlooking critical resources that can be used to meet the strategic goal of democracy promotion. U.S. agencies implementing democracy assistance projects have also not consistently evaluated project results, thus missing opportunities to highlight lessons learned and to share best practices and information…. Consequently, GAO found few project reviews that were useful for transferring knowledge about the impact and sustainability of projects in different countries.[110]

At the broadest level, USAID, the EU and other democracy funders evaluate programs against the development indicators established by the Development Assistance Committee of the OECD at the G-8 Birmingham summit in January 1997. Several governmental, intergovernmental and nongovernmental organizations collect and publish data on those indicators, including those that purport to measure democratic progress. Freedom House, for example, does an annual survey of human rights and civil liberties around the world, then compiles its data in such a way as to rate countries as either "free," "partly free" or "not free." USAID uses the Freedom House rankings to judge the impact of its programs, a method it has acknowledged is imperfect and for which it has been criticized by the U.S. Government Accountability Office.[111]

Until 1993, USAID's formal evaluations of its programs relied on internal teams who would visit project or country sites, interview project participants and write a summary report. Critics of the agency charged that this approach to evaluation essentially measured progress by the amount of money USAID spent and, according to the General Accounting Office, relied too heavily on the none-too-disinterested reports of USAID subcontractors.[112] The method was narrow in scope, often limited to people with a material stake in the program (and thus, often, hopeful of receiving additional aid disbursements), and tended to focus on short-term results in what is by nature a long-term enterprise.

Beginning in 1993, in response to critics both within the government and outside it who wanted to sunset USAID as part of a general reduction of the U.S. foreign aid budget (and to a federal statute, the Government Performance and Results Act), the agency began a strategic planning approach to its programs that it called "managing for results" and which was fully implemented throughout the agency by 1997.[113] The managing for results approach established a system of multi-year goals for each program and a series of quantitative and qualitative goals to be tested annually against several democracy "indicators."[114] In 2001, the agency folded managing for results into a purportedly more comprehensive programming policy that includes "customer focus," "teamwork and participation," "empowerment and accountability," and "valuing diversity."[115] Managing for results, according to the agency, "means making intended results explicit; ensuring agreement among partners, customers, and stakeholders that proposed results are worthwhile; and organizing our daily work and interactions to achieve results effectively." Whatever this means, in practice managing for results strongly favors quantitative measures; where they are not available – and they are rarely available – qualitative ones "must be defined so as to permit regular, systematic and relatively objective judgment regarding change in the value of status of the indicator."[116] USAID normally forgoes formal project evaluation unless a program appears to be either unusually successful or unsuccessful (in which case the point of formal evaluation is to explain the anomaly); rather each USAID mission submits an annual report summarizing the progress toward whatever goal or goals it has defined for its individual missions, and requesting whatever additional resources it believes necessary. Carothers calls the managing for results protocol "pseudoscientific efforts that are worse than [no evaluations] at all."[117] He also believes that despite the complex system of indicators, the system works pretty much like the old one did, that "although the monitoring component of the system is designed to keep track of the progress of projects, it has ended up operating as an evaluation mechanism – the results of the year-by-year monitoring exercises are used to make decisions about whether to continue projects and as general measures of success."[118]

The Government Accountability Office has criticized the strategic plan, arguing that USAID's "missions still have difficulty linking their activities to the broad indicators of development"[119] and urging the agency to develop more sophisticated and appropriate indicators, and if at all possible more precisely quantitative ones. More generally, the GAO has urged all federal agencies engaged in democratization projects to "address how U.S. agencies will cooperate with each other and other major donors to achieve greater impact and sustainability in these programs; establish a strategy for periodically evaluating democracy assistance projects that is consistent across agencies, countries, and types of programs; and establish a systematic mechanism to share information on development approaches, methods, materials, and results from democracy assistance projects among U.S. agencies and implementers."[120]

On their face, these recommendations appear difficult to implement: USAID's strategic objectives are frequently cast in terms of "more this" or "less that" – for example, "greater public debate and discussion on critical issues"[121] – and qualified with a host of modifying adjectives and adverbs. In its cooperative media programs with the NGO IREX/ProMedia, for example, USAID's strategic objective is "increased, better-informed citizen participation in community, political and economic decision making," the indicators for which are "more unbiased public information available to citizens"; "readily available public information repositories established"; and "better independent news coverage."[122] Even where quantitative indicators are used as sub-indices – for example, increases in newspaper subscriptions – there is, of course, no necessary relationship between the indicator and the goal.[123] Rather causal relationships have to be inferred or assumed. Media programs pose special difficulties; not only are their results difficult to measure, but the relationship between media and democracy is complex enough that some USAID missions are reluctant to engage in media work at all.[124]

USAID's efforts to better measure the effects of its work are in obvious respects laudable. The agency attempts to verify program and mission results, rather than merely make claims for them, and in doing so holds both itself and the NGOs it funds more financially and operationally accountable. At the same time the managing for results system is constitutionally inadequate to its task, and one suspects that with its layers of indices it has the potential to distort results or to create perceptions that are misleading or even wrong. In one well-known example, the USAID mission in Phnom Penh in 1997 reported significant democratic progress in Cambodia, only to have the government overthrown by a military coup the same year.[125] More generally, aid that is tied to quantitative performance indicators can create corruption, as aid recipients up and down the chain learn to master bureaucratic reporting requirements that may reveal nothing, and conceal much, about actual performance. Meanwhile, potential aid recipients who lack the staff or the expertise to meet USAID reporting requirements are apt to find themselves unable to compete for funds that only large, professionally staffed organizations are prepared to compete for.

Carothers notes that many USAID officials and aid recipients dislike the managing for results system, which they view both as dismissive of their own professional judgments and ineffective. He urges an evaluation system that is on the one hand much more documentary – that produces information about programs, their implementation, effects, strengths and weakness, and what he freely admits are public relations materials that "can be used convince others that the aid programs are a worthwhile investment" – and on the other, more scholarly and more entrepreneurial. Carothers urges aid providers to "engage in deep learning" about democracy assistance even as they "look for new approaches, and understand how the assistance is perceived and valued."[126] An evaluation system with these broad requirements, or something like it, is familiar to anyone, including academic institutions, that relies on grants for a significant part of program expenses. Typically reports to funders list program outputs, publicity for those outputs, and the ability to attract additional funders as evidence of successful grant outcomes. Whether such an approach is enlightening (for donor or recipient), or serves simply to satisfy donors depends entirely on the rigor applied in the actual process of evaluation. The missing ingredient in these evaluations is usually any kind of careful audit of program participants or examination of program operations that goes beyond either a participant evaluation form or a quick site visit. Carothers recommends both as the kind of "long-view" approach to evaluation necessary to democratization work, and notes that both involve significant time and expense. In the end, he argues persuasively if unhappily that in the democracy business there are simply no easy measures of success that can "substitute for in-depth, qualitative analysis."[127]

The problems of evaluation are not unique to USAID, of course; the agency's various NGO partners and other grant-making organizations share them. They share as well the natural preference for quantitative indicators of success, and the tendency to infer causality where it may not exist. For example, the Eurasia Foundation believes its media grants should "further the principles of objectivity and pluralism; and improve business and management skills of media organizations."[128] Eurasia's approach to evaluating its progress toward these goals is fairly typical: it relies on outside consultants; visits to program sites by its own field staff; and the reports of grantees themselves. Outside consultants review about 15 percent of Eurasia's programs, usually by spending several days at a program site talking with grantees, reviewing their work, and assessing its impact on the target community. Foundation staff members with oversight responsibilities for specific programs will visit program grantees about once every six weeks. For their part, grantees qualify for assistance in the first place only when they draw up a list of defined program objectives, and once they receive a grant must file regular (usually quarterly) reports with the foundation as a condition of receiving their funds, which are paid in tranches. In these reports, grantees are expected to describe any tangible products they have produced, such as an ethics guide or a market survey, as well as any other "project accomplishments to date."[129] Grantees' summary reports, due at the close of a program, include their responses to a mix of qualitative questions – for example, who benefited from the program and how? – and quantitative ones – for example, what was the mix of gender or ethnic groups involved in the program?[130]

Third parties also engage in evaluation, though they, too, will find themselves falling back on what are essentially broad qualitative assessments. A 2000 report by the Democracy and Rule of Law Project at the Carnegie Endowment for International Peace, for example, came to the harsh conclusion that NGOs in the democratization industry have essentially tried to replicate Western models in places where they are simply inappropriate, and that their claims of success are hugely overstated: "Like the broken clock that tells the right time twice a day, at some point, a strategy applied to many places is bound to 'fit' somewhere."[131] NGOs have played a "large and important role" in building new, democratic-looking institutions, the report said, but these efforts had done little to affect how these institutions, and the societies of which they are a part, actually function and, perhaps most importantly, are in most cases not sustainable. "Political parties, regular elections, independent media, and local NGOs are all now part of the political landscape in many states across Central Europe and Eurasia and their links with foreign groups are robust," the Carnegie report said, but these same institutions "function poorly with weak links to their own societies."[132]

The Carnegie report concluded by urging major funders and their partner NGOs to "increase funding for democracy assistance or stay home. Business as usual will support the development of institutions that are not sustainable."[133] Similar assessments are easy to find, and some are even harsher. One commentator writing in a 1999 issue of the *Journal of Democracy* wrote that in Central and Eastern Europe "a lot of money was spent on introducing agendas from the outside and creating non-governmental organizations that pleased external donors."[134] The good news about this misguided policy, the author wrote, was that the "effort did not work."[135]

Notes

1. Jacques Barzun, "Is Democratic Theory for Export?" *Society* (March/April 1989): 16-23, 16.
2. Ibid.
3. Freedom House rates as "free" those countries with an average score of between 1 and 2.5 on a combined 7-point scale of political rights and liberties. See Adrian Karatnycky, "2003 Freedom House Survey," *Journal of Democracy*, Vol. 15, No. 1 (January 2004): 82-84.
4. Karatnycky, "2003 Survey," 2004, 83.
5. Ibid., 92.
6. George Packer, "A Democratic World," *New Yorker*, (February 16 and 23, 2004), http://www.newyorker.com/printable/?fact/040216fa_fact1.
7. David Rieff, "A New Age of Liberal Imperialism?" *World Policy Journal*, Vol. 16, No. 2 (Summer 1999): 1-8; see also Adam Roberts, "NATO's 'Humanitarian War' Over Kosovo," in Larry Minear, Ted van Baarda, and Marc Sommers, eds., *NATO and Humanitarian Action in the Kosovo Crisis* (Providence, RI: Thomas J. Watson Jr. Institute for International Studies, Brown University, 2000): 121-160.
8. George Packer, "Wars and Ideas," *New Yorker* (July 5, 2004): 30-31.
9. Thomas Carothers, *Critical Mission: Essays in Democracy Promotion* (Washington, DC: Carnegie Endowment for International Peace, 2004), 262.
10. See Marina Ottaway, *Democracy Challenged: The Rise of Semi-Authoritarianism* (Washington, DC: Carnegie Endowment for International Peace, 2003).
11. Larry Diamond, "Assessing Global Democratization a Decade After the Communist Collapse," address to the Workshop on Democratization organized by the New Europe College and the Romanian Academic Society, May 6, 2002, Bucharest, Romania, 5.
12. Thomas Carothers, "The End of the Transition Paradigm," *Journal of Democracy* (January 2002): 5-21, 11.
13. Ibid., 13.
14. Barzun, *Is Democracy for Export?* 1989, 19, 23.
15. Thomas Carothers, *Aiding Democracy Abroad: The Learning Curve* (Washington, DC: Carnegie Endowment for International Peace, 1999), 41.
16. Carothers, *Critical Mission*, 2004, 2.

17. Robert Cassen, *Does Aid Work? Report to an Intergovernmental Task Force, 2nd edition* (New York: Oxford University Press, 1994), 2.

18. The actual number of people engaged in foreign aid is unknown, but a single institution – the World Bank – employs several thousand people by itself and finances the work of more than 40,000 people just in Africa.

19. Peter Boone, "Politics and the Effectiveness of Foreign Aid," *European Economic Review*, Vol. 40, (1996): 289-239.

20. Ibid., 290-91.

21. David William Gillies, *Commerce Over Conscience? CDAS Discussion Paper No. 48* (Montreal: Centre for Developing-Area Studies, 1987).

22. Peter Hjertholm and Howard White, "Survey of Foreign Aid: History, Trends and Allocation," discussion paper, Institute of Economics, University of Copenhagen, 3. Presented at "Foreign Aid and Development: Lessons of Experience and Directions for the Future," a conference held in Copenhagen, October 9-10, 1998.

23. Under current U.S. law, foreign aid may not go to family planning groups overseas that "promote" abortion, even when using non-U.S. funds.

24. The World Bank Group comprises five separate entities: the International Bank for Reconstruction and Development, founded in 1945; the International Finance Corporation, 1956; the International Development Association, 1960; the International Centre for Settlement of Investment Disputes, 1966; and the Multilateral Investment Guarantee Agency, 1988.

25. See R.E. Wood, *From Marshall Plan to Debt Crisis: Foreign Aid and Development Choices in the World Economy* (Berkeley: University of California Press, 1986).

26. Hjertholm and White, 1998, 8.

27. See W.W. Rostow, *The Stages of Economic Growth: A Non-Communist Manifesto* (New York: University Press, 1960).

28. John F. Kennedy, Inaugural Address, January 20, 1961.

29. Carol Lancaster, "Foreign Economic Aid," *Foreign Policy in Focus*, Vol. 5, No. 42 (December 2000a); see also Lancaster, *Transforming Foreign Aid: U.S. Assistance in the 21ˢᵗ Century* (Washington, DC: Institute for International Economics, 2000b).

30. Ibid, 2000a.

31. "Tell Me the Old, Old Story: Foreign Aid," *Economist*, (July 23, 1994): 26.

32. Ibid.

33. In 2002, before the Iraq war, the top ten recipients of U.S. foreign aid were, in order, Egypt, Russia, Israel, Pakistan, Serbia & Montenegro, Colombia, Ukraine, Jordan, Peru and Afghanistan. See the Organization for Economic Co-Operation and Development (OECD) data for the United States at http://www.oecd.org/dataoecd/42/30/1860571.gif.

34. See the Organization for Economic Co-Operation and Development's Aid Statistics Web page at http://www.oecd.org/statisticsdata/0,2643,en_2649_34447_1_119656_1_1_1,00.html. See also USAID data on sources of U.S. foreign assistance at http://www.usaid.gov/fani/ch06/objectives02.htm. The $10 billion ODA figure includes the budgets of USAID and the Peace Corps, U.S. contributions to the World Bank, and some State and Defense department humanitarian assistance.

35. In 2000, another $12.7 billion of aid fell outside of ODA guidelines: aid to Israel, Russia, the NIS states, and support for the National Endowment for Democracy and the International Monetary Fund.

36. Non-military aid includes all USAID assistance, food aid and "other economic" assistance. See U.S. Overseas Loans and Grants, colloquially known as the government's "Greenbook," at http://qesdb.cdie.org/gbk/index.html. The world's

largest bilateral foreign aid program, based on the size of the country's economy, is Finland's.

37. Foreign assistance data for the United States and other developed countries are available from the web site of the Organization for Economic Co-Operation and Development (OECD), at http://www.oecd.org/home/.
38. Ibid.
39. See USAID's Iraq post-war accounting at http://www.usaid.gov/iraq/updates/oct04/iraq_sum02_101304.pdf.
40. In 1949, when U.S. foreign aid peaked, there was no such measure as Gross National Product (GNP), but only Gross Domestic Product (GDP). The difference between them is that GDP refers to the value of all goods and services produced within the United States. GNP, a measure introduced in 1991, reflects changes in the global economy and refers to the value of all goods and services produced by labor and property supplied by U.S. residents, whether in the United States or elsewhere in the world. A U.S. factory in Vietnam, for example, contributes to U.S. GNP. Official Development Assistance, or ODA, is measured in percentages of GNP.
41. Carol C. Adelman, "The Privatization of Foreign Aid: Reassessing National Largesse," *Foreign Affairs* (November/December 2003): 9-16.
42. Ibid.
43. Ibid.
44. See USAID data on sources of U.S. foreign assistance at http://www.usaid.gov/fani/ch06/objectives02.htm.
45. Adelman, "Privatization of Foreign Aid," 2003.
46. Ibid.
47. See USAID, Africa Bureau Office of Sustainable Development: "Private Foundations and Corporate Grantmakers in Africa" (Washington, DC: USAID, September 2001).
48. See Monroe Price, Bethany Davis Noll and Daniel De Luce, *Mapping Media Assistance* (Oxford: The Programme in Comparative Media Law & Policy, February 1, 2002), 5.
49. Both the Asia Foundation and the Eurasia Foundation get the largest part of their funding from tax-based sources, a fact they do not hide but do much to play down in their literature; approximately 88 percent of the Asia Foundation's 2003 income and 90 percent of Eurasia's 2003 income come from public sources. Both the Eurasia and Asia Foundations undertake democratization projects that range from civil society development to promoting free media.
50. Julia E. Seidler, *Exporting Democracy Without Citizens? Goals and Practices of American Agencies Providing Journalism Assistance Programs in Ukraine* (Iowa City: University of Iowa, unpublished doctoral dissertation, May 2001), 96.
51. Ibid.
52. Eugene Staples, "A Note from the Founder," *Eurasia News*, Spring 1997, 2.
53. See the Eurasia Foundation at http://www.eurasia.org/.
54. Brian Smith, *More Than Altruism: The Politics of Private Foreign Aid* (Princeton, NJ: Princeton University Press, 1990), 70.
55. Martin Morse Wooster, "This is No Way to Promote Democracy," *Wall Street Journal* (July 17, 1991): 23.
56. David Corn, "Beltway Bandits: Better Dead Than NED," *Nation* (July 12, 1993): 56.
57. David Pallister and Andy Weir, "Britons Get Reagan 'Slush Money,'" *Financial Times* (December 9, 1985): 17.

58. See generally Paul E. Kanjorski, "Group Cloaked in Secrecy Meddling in Foreign Affairs," *Atlanta Constitution* (May 24, 1991): A17; and Mary McGrory, "Dollars for Democracy," *Washington Post* (August 5, 1993): A2. See specifically Shirley Christian, "Group is Channeling Funds to Parties Opposing Pinochet," *New York Times* (January 15, 1988): A1; John S. Nichols, "Get the NED Out of Nicaragua," *Nation* (February 26, 1990): 268; Stephen Engelberg, "U.S. Grant to 2 Czech Parties is Called Unfair Interference," *New York Times* (June 10, 1990): A8; Robert S. Greensberger, "U.S. Group Aided Arias' Costa Rica Foes," *Wall Street Journal* (October 14, 1989): A11; and Stanley Meisler, "Allocation of Funds in France Embarrassing," *Los Angeles Times* (February 6, 1986): A25.
59. Pallister and Weir, "Britons Get Reagan 'Slush Money,'" 17.
60. Meisler, "Allocation of Funds in France Embarrassing," 1986.
61. *Foreign Assistance Act of 1961*, 75 Stat. 424, § 281.
62. See Jonathan R. Pincus and Jeffrey A. Winters, eds., *Reinventing the World Bank* (Ithaca, NY: Cornell University Press, 2002).
63. See Creative Associates International, *A Retrospective of AID's Experience in Strengthening Democratic Institutions in Latin America, 1961-1981* (Washington, DC: Creative Associates International), v-10. See also Carothers, *Aiding Democracy Abroad*, 1999, 26.
64. Ronald Reagan, "Promoting Democracy and Peace," address to the British Parliament, London, June 8, 1982.
65. Ronald Reagan, "State of the Union Address," Washington, DC, January 31, 1985.
66. See William M. LeoGrande, *Our Own Backyard: The United States in Central America, 1977-1992* (Chapel Hill: University of North Carolina Press, 1998), 249.
67. Carothers, *Aiding Democracy Abroad*, 1999, 40.
68. Ibid., 48-49.
69. Ibid., 54.
70. Ibid.
71. USAID's four program areas are listed as "Strengthening the Rule of Law and Respect for Human Rights"; "Promoting More Genuine and Competitive Elections & Political Processes"; "Increased Development of a Politically Active Civil Society"; and "More Transparent and Accountable Governance." For budget details, see USAID's "Democracy and Governance" web site, www.usaid.gov/our_work/democracy_and_governance/.
72. Bill Clinton, "State of the Union Address," Washington, DC, January 25, 1994.
73. USAID, Center for Democracy and Governance, "Democracy and Governance: A Conceptual Framework," Document PN-ACD-395 (Washington, DC: USAID, November 1998a).
74. Carothers, *Aiding Democracy Abroad*, 1999, 49 -54.
75. Ibid.
76. Stephen Hook, "Building Democracy Through Foreign Aid: The Limitations of United States Political Conditionalities, 1992-1996, *Democratization*, Vol. 5, No. 3: 156-180, 169.
77. See the White House, *A National Security Strategy of Engagement and Enlargement* (Washington, DC: U.S. Government Printing Office, 1996). See also Douglas Brinkley, "Democratic Enlargement: The Clinton Doctrine," *Foreign Policy* (Spring 1997): 111-127.
78. Bill Clinton, "American Leadership and American Diplomacy," U.S. Department of State Dispatch, March 1, 1993.

79. Bill Clinton, "Address to the UN General Assembly," New York, September 27, 1993.
80. Bill Clinton, "Democracy in America," speech at the University of Milwaukee, Wisconsin, October 1, 1992.
81. Carothers, *Aiding Democracy Abroad*, 1999, 51.
82. Ibid., 42-44.
83. Ibid., 43.
84. USAID, *Democracy and Governance*, 1998a, 5. With respect to democratization as a "discrete subculture" within USAID, see also Carothers, *Aiding Democracy Abroad*, 1999, 47.
85. See USAID's "Democracy and Governance" web site, www.usaid.gov/our_work/democracy_and_governance/
86. See USAID, *Democracy and Governance*, 1998a, 1.
87. Stephen Knack and Gary Anderson, "Is 'Good Governance' Progressive?" (Washington, DC: World Bank, 1999).
88. See Commission of the European Communities, *European Initiative for Democracy and Human Rights, 1999*; *EU Annual Report on Human Rights 1998-1999*; Commission of the European Communities, *Report on the Implementation of Measures Intended to Promote the Observance of Human Rights and Democratic Principles in External Relations 1996-1999,* 2000. The Commission reports give aid figures in euros, even though the European Monatary Union did not begin until January 1, 1999.
89. Richard Youngs, "Democracy Promotion: The Case of European Union Strategy" (Brussels: Center for European Policy Studies, Working Doc. No. 167, October 2001) 5.
90. Ibid., 10
91. Ibid.
92. Commission of the European Communities, *Report on the Implementation of Measures Intended to Promote the Observance of Human Rights and Democratic Principles in External Relations 1996-1999* (Brussels: European Commission, 2000).
93. See Danish Foreign Ministry, *Evaluation: Danish Support to Promotion of Human Rights and Democratisation, Vol. 1, Synthesis Report* (Copenhagen: Danish Foreign Ministry, 1999), 11.
94. Gordon Crawford, "European Union Development Co-operation and the Promotion of Democracy," in Peter Burnell, ed., *Democracy Assistance*: International Cooperation for Democratization (London: Frank Cass, 2000), 110.
95. Richard Youngs, *The European Union and the Promotion of Democracy* (New York: Oxford University Press, 2002).
96. Youngs, "Democracy Promotion," 2001, 10.
97. Ibid.
98. Commission of the European Communities, *Evaluation of the Phare and Tacis Democracy Programme, 1992-1997: Final Report* (Brussels: European Commission, 1997), 42
99. Youngs, "Democracy Promotion, 2001, 16.
100. See M. Smith and S. Woolcock, "European Commercial Policy: A Leadership Role in the New Millennium?" *European Foreign Affairs Review, No. 4* (1999): 419-62.
101. See USAID's "Democracy and Governance" web site, www.usaid.gov/our_work/democracy_and_governance/
102. See USAID, Center for Democracy and Governance, "Handbook of Democracy and Governance Program Indicators," Document PN-ACC-390 (Washington, DC: USAID, August 1998b).

103. Ibid., 57.
104. Ibid., 88.
105. Ibid., 115, 139-143.
106. USAID, *1997 Agency Performance Report* (Washington, DC: USAID, 1998), v.
107. Carothers, *Aiding Democracy Abroad*, 1999, 283.
108. Ibid., 285.
109. U.S. General Accounting Office, *The Results Act: An Evaluator's Guide to Assessing Annual Agency Performance Plans*, GGD-10.1.20 (Washington, DC: GAO, April 1, 1998).
110. U.S. General Accounting Office, *Foreign Assistance: U.S. Democracy Programs in Six Latin American Countries Have Yielded Modest Results*, GAO-03-358 (Washington, DC: GAO, March 2003), 13.
111. See U.S. Government Accountability Office, *Independent Media Development Abroad: Challenges Exist in Implementing U.S. Efforts and Measuring Results*, GAO-05-803. Washington, DC: Government Accountability Office, July 2005, 9-10.
112. See General Accounting Office, *The Results Act: Observations on USAID's November 1996 Draft Strategic Plan*, July 11, 1997, GAO/NSIAD-97-197R. See also General Accounting Office, *Foreign Assistance: USAID's Reengineering at Overseas Missions*, GAO/NSIAD-97-194 (Washington, DC: GAO, September 12, 1997).
113. USAID, "Statement of the Administrator," *Congressional Presentation FY1998* (Washington, DC: USAID, 1998).
114. USAID, *1998 Agency Performance Report* (Washington, DC: USAID, March 31, 1999), v.
115. USAID, Programming Policy, E200.3.2.1. "Managing for Results," ADS 200 *Introduction to Programming Policy*, 2004.
116. USAID, Quality of Performance Data, E203.5.5 "Performance Monitoring," *ADS 203 Managing for Results: Monitoring and Evaluating Performance.*, 1997.
117. Carothers, *Aiding Democracy Abroad*, 1999, 301.
118. Ibid., 288.
119. GAO, *Foreign Assistance: USAID's Reengineering at Overseas Missions*, 1997.
120. GAO, *Foreign Assistance: U.S. Democracy Programs in Six Latin American Countries Have Yielded Modest Results*, 2003, 14.
121. A list of USAID program objectives for media in transition societies is available at USAID, Office of Transition Initiatives: Media Programming, http://www.usaid.gov/our_work/cross-cutting_programs/transition_initiatives/focus/media.html.
122. IREX/PROMEDIA, *USAID Professional Media Program Semiannual Report, January 1-June 30, 1998*, 65.
123. Ibid, 5. Intermediate indices for USAID objectives for the period included: "publishers and managers effectively and efficiently manage media enterprises"; "supportive legal and regulatory environment established to promote independent media"; "journalism education formal and informal stresses importance of unbiased reporting"; "increase in the number of independent and sustainable media institutions." Sub-indices used to measure these intermediate indices included: "media networks exist"; "media outlets have strategic business plans"; and "media outlets use market research to increase advertising."
124. USAID, Center for Democracy and Governance, *The Role of Media in Democracy: A Strategic Approach*, PN-ACE-630 (Washington, DC: USAID, June 1999), 1.
125. See USAID Cambodia, *Results Review and Resource Request* (Phnom Penh, Cambodia: USAID Cambodia, Feb, 1998).
126. Carothers, *Aiding Democracy Abroad*, 1999, 300.

127. Ibid., 302.
128. Nick Deychakiwsky, Eurasia Foundation official, quoted in Seidler, *Exporting Democracy Without Citizens?* 2001, 200.
129. Seidler, *Exporting Democracy Without Citizens?* 2001, 201.
130. Ibid., 201-202.
131. Sarah E. Mendelson and John K. Glenn, "Democracy Assistance and NGO Strategies in Post-Communist Societies, Working Paper No. 8." (Washington, DC: Carnegie Endowment for International Peace, Democracy and Rule of Law Project, February 2000), 17.
132. Ibid., 6.
133. Ibid.
134. Irena Lasota, "Sometimes Less is More," *Journal of Democracy*, Vol. 13, No. 1 (January 2002),:125-128, 126.
135. Ibid.

3

The Origins and Goals of Media Assistance

The last great American export is our journalistic
freedom and freedom of speech. —David Halberstam

Efforts by U.S. sources to promote ideas about press freedom overseas date to efforts by the Associated Press to include in the Treaty of Versailles language about providing journalists unfettered access to news. The AP's motivation was not altruistic, but economic. In the early twentieth century the company was a member of a global press consortium in which all foreign news was gathered and disseminated by national press monopolies like the AP in the United States, and, in Europe, Reuters, Wolff and Havas. Each covered its section of the world, and each in its reporting often shaped the news to comport with national interests. This club system worked until the arrival of United Press International in the United States, which, because it was not part of the consortium, did not play by its rules. As a result, UPI reporters regularly scooped the AP on important European news, and it was this competitive disadvantage that the AP sought to remedy with its proposal to open foreign territories to all journalists. The effort failed. The Versailles Treaty included no provisions for free access to news, in effect leaving informational walls around the world's major powers until the end of World War II.[1]

Two decades later the American Society of Newspaper Editors promoted the idea of "international freedom of the press" in the 1943 United Nations charter.[2] In response, the UN established a special Subcommittee on Freedom of the Press, led by the eminent American First Amendment scholar and Harvard Law School Professor Zechariah Chafee, Jr. The subcommission was almost immediately mired in disagreement over its purpose. The central disagreement, between the Americans and other members of the subcommission, was whether their charge was to draft a statement on press freedom or press responsibility.[3] A second dispute concerned who would qualify as a "journalist" for any consequent newsgathering privileges the group might recommend.[4]

Chafee organized an international convention to resolve these problems, to meet in Geneva in 1948. Tensions between the Europeans and Americans were high, each suspecting the other's motives. Europe journalists desperately needed newsprint at the war's end, and journalists from non-aligned nations with representatives on the subcommission were also short of paper. Both parties looked to their American counterparts, the world's biggest consumers of newsprint, for donations. But the Americans refused, fearing the lost advertising space and revenues that would result from running smaller editions. The Americans even refused the British, the United States' staunch ally, leading British journalists to question their American colleagues' sincerity in their advocacy for global press freedom.[5] The international delegates on the subcommission also complained about the shortcomings of American reporters, whom they thought had no respect for other nations, were too sensational and unprofessional, and above all simply ignorant. They did not know enough about the countries they covered, did not care to learn, and did not worry about the misperceptions they created through bad reporting. A State Department memo to the U.S. delegation warned that "a world whose communications facilities were shattered by the war looks with apprehension at US preponderance in terms of both facilities and know-how. These war-torn countries fear a flood of American material which they believe may engulf their own cultures. They are apprehensive lest their own people be turned into gum-chewing Americans."[6]

If American members of the delegation were insensitive to perceptions created by their behavior, the federal government did its part to reinforce them. It refused, for example, to allow reporters for the *New York Daily Worker*, a socialist newspaper, to travel to Geneva, requiring the American press delegation to point out that the ban violated the very stand on freedom they were going to Geneva to defend. At the same time, international journalists with communist affiliations, including many from Western Europe, were not allowed into the United States to cover UN business. Those who were given entry faced several travel restrictions, most commonly confinement to New York City.[7] In the end, the Geneva Convention was a failure. It drafted three international agreements – one concerning rights of newsgathering, a second on freedom of information, and a third proposing a mandatory right of reply for those attacked or criticized in news reports. All of the proposals failed, ridiculed by communist, non-aligned and democratic nations alike.[8] Later, Carroll Binder, the editorial page editor for the *Minneapolis Tribune*, would replace Chafee as subcommission chair, in which capacity he tried unsuccessfully to write an international code of journalistic ethics. Carroll himself eventually ended that effort when he concluded that virtually every proposal would have the effect of restricting American press freedom not only abroad, but at home.[9] American journalists would later launch the American Press Institute (API) , which today brings foreign reporters to the United States for training. The API, in turn, would have a hand in the creation of the Vienna-based International Press Institute, which monitors freedom of the press worldwide. But the experience of the immediate post-war efforts seemed to suggest that American ideas about press freedom were not readily exportable, or even welcome.

Before the 1990s, then, U.S. media assistance had not much to do with democracy promotion or even press freedom. Official assistance, if it could be called that, was limited mostly to the public diplomacy programs run out of the State Department and the U.S. Information Agency, as well as other smaller programs run quietly or even covertly out of NED or the Asia Institute. USAID media programs of the day were understood primarily as a means to realize other economic development goals. A 1985 essay by USAID's Clifford Block (at the time the agency's associate director for development communications) noted that what the agency then called "communications aid" had grown significantly over the past decade not as the result of any external pressures, but instead "almost entirely by successful research and development, which has demonstrated, compellingly, the power of communications in achieving fundamental development tasks.... USAID does not support the growth of communications as an end in itself, but rather as a facilitator of programs in other sectors – food production, population, health, nutrition, education – for which Congress allocates funds as specific major budgetary items each year."[10]

In the late 1960s, USAID had invested in instructional television as a tool for education reform in El Salvador on the theory that "a completely modernized system of instruction, with new curricula and teacher behaviors, could be built around classroom TV delivery."[11] Within a few years, USAID expanded this concept to South Korea, Kenya, Nicaragua,

Thailand and the Dominican Republic, but using radio instead because of its low cost and the relative ease with which it made possible two-way communication, thus enabling student interaction with instructors. USAID also adapted radio for the provision of public health, family planning and nutrition programs and services in Tanzania, Gambia and Honduras; and for its agriculture programs in Latin America and Africa. Beginning in 1974, USAID started experiments in supplementing its foreign assistance efforts through satellite communications, and in 1978 began its Rural Satellite Program, a pilot project that provided higher education courses and audio-conferencing to rural areas of Indonesia and the Caribbean.[12] More widely, as USAID shifted its focus in the mid-1970s to rural areas in developing nations, it began to invest in media of "low cost, simplicity and broad coverage."[13] Overwhelmingly that meant aid for radio and "simple print materials,"[14] much less for television, and virtually none for newspapers or book publishing, both of which were then and remain today largely confined to the urban areas of developing countries.

Even as this work went on, sharp disagreement had developed between Western nations, particularly the United States, and developing ones on basic questions of press freedom. The UN Subcommission on Freedom of the Press had lost its charter in 1952, but the controversies it had engendered returned in the 1970s in a new body, set up under the United Nations Educational, Scientific, and Cultural Organization (UNESCO), the MacBride Commission.[15] Chaired by Sean MacBride, a founder of Amnesty International and a Nobel Peace Prize recipient, the new Commission evaluated the communications needs of the non-aligned Third World and defined media freedom as communication in the service of economic development, a characterization that came with implications for free expression norms. In its final report, the Commission recommended citizen rights of access to the media, the development of locally managed, alternative channels of communication, and the participation of non-professionals in media production. The report rejected proposals for licensing journalists and providing them with special privileges, but it conspicuously did not give private ownership of news media and other communications facilities the same status as public control, a decision that Western journalists, news organizations and governments construed and rejected as a direct attack on independent editorial judgment (and thus free expression). Coming in the middle of the Cold War, that rejection was at least partly due to the belief that the

Commission's recommendations were socialist economic theory dressed up as media policy. Despite these differences, both the U.S. government and several western press groups, led by the American-sponsored World Press Freedom Committee, continued to give significant donations of money and equipment to media in Africa, Asia and Latin America and sponsored internship programs for foreign journalists. The U.S. government also provided the developing world with free transponder time on Intelsat. In the end, however, basic differences on how news should be managed and for whose benefit – combined with East/West political confrontations and North/South economic ones – led the United States to withdraw from UNSECO in 1985.

In the same year, and obviously recognizing the controversy caused by the MacBride Commission and the UNESCO meetings that followed it, Block argued that USAID "has defined its role in the continuing New World Information and Communications Order as helping to generate constructive approaches for the development of communications in the Third World – that is, dealing with an underlying cause of the rhetorical fireworks."[16] A year earlier, USAID had formally embraced that role by issuing a Policy Determination on Developmental Communications that urged increased attention among field officers to the potential uses of communications technologies in assistance projects, and especially with respect to the "public education" aspects of those projects.[17] While the Policy Determination did not encourage the use of funds for communications infrastructure development, it did not rule it out when such development was both "critical" and "affordable."[18] Block, in his assessment of USAID's communications work, echoed the MacBride Commission:

> As communications systems expand throughout the developing world, there is the opportunity to shift the way information is viewed, from an assumption of extreme scarcity to one of broad accessibility. A concomitant shift can occur in the ability of people throughout the world to empower themselves and to improve the quality of their lives. Fundamentally new institutional models are possible, with communications as a catalyst.[19]

It was the events of 1989 that finally unhinged media assistance from its near-exclusive association with economic development and associated it explicitly with democracy promotion. For USAID, the changed emphasis was a direct result of the 1989 Freedom Support Act and the Support for East European Democracy Act,[20] both of which significantly increased funding for democracy assistance in Central Europe and

Eurasia. Following the 1989 transitions, USAID at first carried out its media assistance programs through its regional Bureau for Europe and Eurasia. Later the agency would shift media assistance to the Office of Transition Initiatives (OTI), in the Bureau for Humanitarian Response, and the Democracy and Governance Center in the Global Bureau, both created in 1994 with different objectives. OTI's job is to provide the initial response to media needs in political emergencies and post-conflict situations – for example, support for newspapers, magazines, television and radio stations and programming in places as varied as East Timor, Angola, Rwanda, Liberia and Kosovo – then when stability returns to hand over the work to other USAID program officers or to an NGO. The Democracy and Governance Center (now the Office of Democracy and Governance, or ODG) is much more focused on long-term media assistance needs and planning; it therefore concerns itself with research and evaluation and has become an important source of information and coordination on media assistance programs of all kinds. Additionally, USAID's Bureau for Democracy, Conflict and Humanitarian Assistance (DCHA) manages democratization programs in fragile or post-conflict states, but the media programs for DCHA are administered by either OTI or ODG.

According to USAID, its media programs have legal and moral authority in Article 19 of the Universal Declaration of Human Rights, which states that "Everyone has the right to freedom of opinion and expression; this right includes the freedom to hold opinions without interference and to seek, receive and impart information and ideas through any media and regardless of frontiers." The agency stated in 1999 that the two goals of media aid are to "ensure that citizens make responsible, informed choices rather than acting out of ignorance and misinformation," and to provide a "'checking function' by ensuring that elected representatives…carry out the wishes of those who elected them."[21] By 2002, a USAID statement on this mission had infused it with rhetorical force, identifying the media's role in democracy as "being a 'watchdog' over government and educating people about the issues that affect their lives," and going on to quote Thomas Jefferson on the force of public opinion.[22] Assistant Secretary of State for Democracy, Human Rights and Labor Lorne Craner asserted in 2003 that U.S. foreign policy is to assist media development because "the right to a free press, and the freedoms of thought and speech that free press entails, are fundamental and universal human rights that ought to be enjoyed by all people based on their humanity. This belief is displayed in the U.S. Constitution, in the Universal Declaration of Human Rights, and in the United States' history of combating censorship and media control domestically and abroad."[23]

The problem with these rhetorical flourishes is that the essential contours of a free media system are no more evident today than they were in 1948. This is a policy problem that no development agency can or should resolve. And there is the additional economic problem, central to this book, that media cannot perform their democratic role if they cannot first find adequate and dependable sources of revenue. For these reasons as well as historical ones, USAID as well as other national and international aid organizations continue to link media sector support to general economic development. USAID stated in a 2003 report on its foreign assistance mission, "there are many reasons some countries have not made more development progress, but common to almost all of them is bad governance."[24] The report concluded, therefore, that a healthy media system is necessary not only to ensure good governance, but to advance the primary development goals of poverty reduction and the creation of human and social capital.[25] In 2002, the United Nations Development Program, as part of its Poverty Reduction Strategy Paper (PRSP) process, released a report, *Deepening Democracy in a Fragmented World*,[26] in which it emphasized the importance of public knowledge and participation as factors in sustaining economic reform and growth. According to the report, that process involves soliciting public views about national economic policy and increasing the transparency and accountability of policy-making institutions. The same year, the World Bank's World Development Report discussed the contributions that a healthy media sector can make to the development of functioning market, saying that the "media need to be independent, accountable, and able to provide relevant information and reflect diverse social views."[27] Implicit in all these reports is that well-informed citizens make successful development possible, and thus that the presence of quality media is both predictive of and synonymous with public participation in politics and the economy. The opposite is also true, as Derick Brinkerhoff and Arthur Goldsmith note in an analysis of media programs for the World Bank:

> Unstructured and unmanaged participation may lead to disharmony and confusion, not necessarily to good policy.... Costless and risk-free participation is impossible. Managing it is complex and may fail or lead to unexpected outcomes. Bringing external groups into policy decisions puts many demands on public managers. It also takes time, which can impede rapid decision-making. If handled improperly,

participation may produce policy stalemate, or worse, social conflict and societal division if actors cannot agree or compromise.[28]

To the extent that social cohesion and peace depend on the performance of the media, this is a burden few media in developing countries are prepared to bear. Neither are most governments, even the most well intentioned of which are not likely to see the development of an informed citizenry as a priority. As a result, writes Ann Hudock, "what one finds [in developing democracies] is that 'independent' and 'sustainable' media do not necessarily or by definition contribute to democracy. Media that are independent of government control often suffer from corporate influence. Economically sustainable media may rely heavily on entertainment programming that draws large audience shares and advertising revenues while doing little to serve the public interest."[29]

This economic dilemma applies with equal force to media in the world's developed democracies, but in developing democracies the problem is particularly acute, and a number of other aid practitioners working in IGOs and NGOs have emphasized the point. Tim Carrington and Mark Nelson of the World Bank write that, "As more analysts recognize a functioning media to be a 'development good,' capable of contributing to improved accountability, efficient markets, and information-rich societies, it is important to recognize that all these benefits are derived from the media's financial independence. And that independence, in turn, is a function both of the surrounding economy and a particular media company's ability to turn a given economic environment to its advantage."[30] Relatively few media are able to do this, however, because "behind the often passionate debates over media rights and responsibilities is a simple fact too often overlooked by the international organizations shaping media support projects: The media is [sic] a business."[31]

That oversight has consequences for news coverage. A 2002 Panos Institute report on the PRSP process notes that in weak media markets there is often little or no coverage of national or local development issues and choices, which take a back seat to political and entertainment reporting or, worse, to patronage reporting in which news organizations demand payment as a condition of (favorable) news coverage. Even if journalists wanted to cover development issues, the report says, they often lack the technical skills and knowledge to do so. Moreover where news media are primarily urban-based, as they often are in developing countries, they are apt to see poverty as a rural issue irrelevant to their audiences.[32]

Media Assistance After the European Transitions

In 1990, Everette Dennis and Jon Vanden Heuvel published one of the first important overviews of Central and Eastern Europe's news media in a report for the Gannett Foundation (now the Freedom Forum), a report that included assessments to guide the imminent flow of assistance to the region.[33] The report's central conclusions concerned the twin problems of sustainable financing and capable management in newly competitive and unstable markets. In a brief foreword to the report, Foundation chairman Allen Neuharth praised the "new-found freedom" in the region's media and singled out "economic realities" as the major obstacle to their further development.[34] For their part, Dennis and Vanden Huevel identified the "market economy and privatization" as the most significant macro-level areas requiring aid, needs that were coupled with immediate assistance for "management training and expertise."[35] They also criticized early media assistance efforts in the four countries as "well-intentioned, but fragmented and inadequate."[36]

Throughout the 1980s, the greater portion of USAID media assistance had gone to Latin America, but by the mid-1990s the agency had shifted its attention to Europe and Eurasia, where is still spends 60 percent of its media assistance dollars.[37] Before the transitions, Western media aid had flowed to Central Europe in the forms of small grants and equipment to underground publications and the few broadcasters, such as B92 Radio, then a student-run university station in Belgrade, that provided an alternative to state-controlled news outlets. After 1989, aid came first in the form of training, much of it from USAID and through the now-defunct United States Information Agency (USIA, whose activities were absorbed into the State Department in 1999),[38] and also funds for or donations of basic materials needs like newsprint and computer terminals. In the democratic euphoria of the day, USIA sponsored several needs-assessment studies and short-term internships that brought foreign journalists to the United States for editorial and management training programs. Around the same time, another U.S.-government funded organization, the International Media Fund, was created by former Secretary of State James Baker and funded by Congress, the NED and USIA; its goal was to provide advice to private donors wanting to get involved in Central and Eastern Europe, as well as to make some grants of its own. The NED funded a series of projects in the early 1990s in partnership with the NGO Freedom House in Czechoslovakia, Bulgaria and Romania. In Poland, NED provided support to Solidarity through its Fund for Free Press and Publishing. The Voice of America (VOA), which was in 1990 an operation of USIA, also operated a number of training programs for Central and Eastern European journalists, both in the region and in Washington, D.C. Many of these training programs still operate – Reuters, the BBC and International Center for Journalists best known among them – and their work is generally admired in the developing world.

Several of these training programs were done in partnership with private U.S. press groups such as the American Society of Newspaper Editors (ASNE), and what was then the Center for Foreign Journalists (now the International Center for Journalists, or ICFJ) and the Soros Foundation Network. American journalism schools at Northwestern University, the University of Missouri, Northeastern University and the University of Georgia also participated in the needs-assessment and training programs, as did several news organizations and journalism foundations: Reuters and the BBC World Service operated training programs that continue to this day; the John S. and James L. Knight Foundation, in cooperation with ICFJ, began a fellows program that sends reporters with significant experience working for U.S. news organizations on training assignments overseas.

In 1990, the World Press Freedom Committee convened a "Voices of Freedom" conference to review the landscape of Central Europe's media needs and propose what it the conference report called "doable projects."[39] The European representative for the Committee, Ronald Koven, cautioned his colleagues at the conference that "parts of what Westerners have to offer are not yet useful or transferable,"[40] but went on to argue that the Western journalism training "provides the biggest bang for the buck."[41] In its overview of ongoing work, the conferees counted funding for dozens of smaller conferences and seminars in the region; subscriptions to American newspapers donated to newspapers, libraries, and training centers; efforts to "twin" Central European newspapers with American and Canadian newspapers; and several small donations of equipment, textbooks, software and newsprint, and journalism "handbooks."[42] Of the many training programs cataloged at the conference, most were described in the vaguest of terms – for example, "professional training for the coming generation"[43] or "advising local broadcasters on the needed legal framework"[44] – and most also proposed sending American journalism professors and journalists to the region to, as one conferee put it, "look at the context of American journalism and how it fits into their societies."[45] Some of these assessment and teaching trips, it turned out, involved multiple-city tours with only two-day stops in each city.[46] The only long-term training project described in any concrete terms at the conference were the six-month internships then offered by the Center for Foreign Journalists in Reston, Virginia. The Center had been established in 1984 with the specific objective of bringing international journalists to the United States for training opportunities at U.S. newspapers and television stations, and by 1990 had already passed twenty-three Central European journalists through its program.[47] The amounts of money discussed at the conference were small, usually well under $100,000, and again most of it to be disbursed not to Central European journalists, but to Western news organizations and NGOs that would provide training. In dollar terms, the largest aid proposal at the conference was $1.2 million to provide a used printing press to a newspaper in Romania.[48] Of all the proposals at the "Voices of Freedom" conference, perhaps the most curious was for a "Freedom Bus" that would drive rotating teams of American journalists around Central Europe, carrying with them a "single movable library of sample newspapers and magazines."[49]

Viewed in retrospect, the proposals from the "Voices of Freedom" conference captures in a nutshell both the early enthusiasm for what could be done, and a central reason for the disappointment that followed. Western aid providers – Americans particularly – have focused on training and demonstration programs because they believe them to be an "apolitical" activity. As James Miller has written, "Professionalized 'world' journalism is a kind of clinical instrument, depoliticized, depersonalized, whose rational rules of practice have emerged and diffused along with liberal democracy.... Journalism's craft skills can be adapted – 'reinvented' by adopters, in the jargon – to make them fit recipients' preferences. Such reductability and adaptability are said to place the transferred knowledge outside the realm of politics and relationships of domination."[50] It is common to hear Western journalists who have worked in assistance programs say they taught others how to gather and report news, not what to gather and report. Such a claim seems suspect on its face. It is hard to imagine, for instance, how one would teach another to cover a national political campaign without at some point broaching the subject of what makes a candidate newsworthy, particularly in a developing democracy where there are likely to be several (if not dozens) of parties and candidates vying for news attention, some of them openly nationalist, religious, militaristic or racist in their views, but commanding significant public support.

Another reason for the continuing emphasis on training programs is the persistent belief, common to both media assistance providers and, as well, to many aid recipients, that a lack of professionalism among journalists is the most persistent obstacle to press freedom in democratizing countries. Peter Gross has written, for example, that even in the relatively successful states of Central Europe the media do not need to be further democratized but to professionalize: "They need to become morally and professionally accountable to their audiences. They need to supply accurate, balanced, complete, and verifiable information that allows citizens to debate issues, come to conclusions, and make decisions. And they need to educate their audiences both in the uses of objective, verifiable information and in the standards that make news gathering and reporting useful to them as citizens. Only by doing so can the media directly facilitate the process of democratization."[51]

Where training programs are developed with the specific needs of local and regional journalists in mind, where providers know a country and its media environment, and where the purported beneficiaries of the training believe that the provider is committed to the work, such programs are almost always welcome. Where the opposite is true, such programs stir resentment. Aid recipients are tired of what they scornfully call "parachute professors," big NGOs and others who are often, as they see it, the true beneficiaries of media assistance programs. Throughout much of the 1990s, their experience was that financial and material assistance was often too little and too piecemeal, that it came from multiple providers that had joined together for the purpose of winning a grant, but that brought to their programs no strategy and no real concern for ensuring long-term success. To be fair, it was awareness of this experience that led many providers to rethink their programs and to emphasize sustainability. (Another, more practical reason, is that many donors have grown tired of or disillusioned with media assistance; others have simply changed their grant-making focus to other areas.)

All this has also led some aid recipients to emphasize sustainability, but on their own terms. Sasa Vucinic, a founder of B92 Radio in Belgrade and now the director of an assistance NGO, the Media Development Loan Fund (MDLF, discussed at length in Chapter 6), says he got the idea for MDLF after attending one too many aid-coordination conferences in New

York. For significantly less than the cost of flying two dozen European journalists to the United States and housing them for a week, he says, he could have purchased several pieces of desperately needed equipment for B92. It was time, he said, for a new approach.

The Organization of Media Assistance

Today the map of global media assistance providers looks very much like the map of democracy assistance providers, at least at the top, where the same national aid agencies and international organizations dominate the field. The principal IGOs providing media assistance are the European Commission, the Organization for Security and Cooperation in Europe (OSCE), UNESCO, the United Nations Development Programme (UNDP), and, most recently, the World Bank. There are other IGOs in the business, as discussed below, though some of newer ones have been created by these larger bodies to meet special needs. Among the leading national providers of media assistance (in addition to USAID), the most well known (and among aid recipients, the most respected) are the official aid agencies of several northern European countries – Sweden, Norway, Denmark, the Netherlands, Germany and Britain – along with Canada. At the level of NGO involvement in media assistance there are also repeat players—the Eurasia and Asia foundations, for example – but as indicated above the field also includes many other organizations, of widely varying sizes and missions, many of them founded by journalists, news organizations or media foundations.

Categorizing Media Assistance

USAID now develops its media assistance programs to fit the political character of the countries where it works, which it categorizes as one of five types: closed; semi-democratic or developing; war-torn; post-conflict; or transition. In two of these categories – closed and war-torn – there is little USAID can reasonably do. Media assistance to these societies, if any, is likely to be in the form of public diplomacy programs or direct material assistance to underground or opposition media. The most promising political environment for media assistance, in USAID's view, is the transition state, which is assumed to be moving steadily away from authoritarianism and toward democracy, and where both social and economic development are advanced enough to support additional political progress. Semi-democratic/developing societies are those that are stalled or back-sliding into old habits – Carothers' "gray area" states – and where as a result press freedom is tenuous and media independent of the state are still fragile. Post-conflict states are those like Bosnia-Herzegovina or perhaps Serbia, where a legitimate government has come to power and there is the opportunity, as well as the need, to re-tool the entire media system, and in some cases (for example Kosovo) to build one from the ground up.

In each of these settings, both official and private media assistance will go to an enormous variety of organizations and objectives. A 2005 study by the U.S. Government Accountability Office[52] and a 2002 study for USAID and the World Bank by Price, Noll and DeLuce identify several discrete categories of media assistance,[53] including:

- Journalism training and education that runs from teaching the basic elements of reporting and writing to covering more complex topics like economics or the environment. Training can also include the development of journalism schools, "press centers" and "media institutes and associations." Price and his colleagues note that "there is increased demand for longer-term training conducted 'on-site.'"
- Management training "aimed at helping media outlets become commercially viable and sustainable." Such training typically includes programs in and varies in its depth and effectiveness.
- Training in journalism ethics and professionalism intended to ensure media "accountability" and which can include quantitative instruments like market and public opinion surveys, and qualitative ones like ethics codes and press councils.
- Material assistance "aimed at helping build the infrastructure needed to ensure continued media independence." Often this kind of assistance is technical, the provision of everything from email to printing presses necessary to collect and publish news, but it can also include financial operating assistance, for example subsidizing subscriptions to photo or news agency services.
- Assistance in developing networks of independent broadcast media. The idea is to link developing broadcast media in joint ventures of various kinds that allow them to make the most efficient use of limited production, distribution and management resources.
- Assistance in developing "democratic legal and regulatory frameworks" for media. This remains an ongoing need in many transition countries and occurs at several levels, from IGO and NGO provision of advice, background documents and draft laws to the training of local lawyers and judges in media law issues, and in

funding for free expression advocacy groups. Related activities noted by Price and his colleagues include providing assistance to non-media organizations that monitor and report on government abuses of press and expressive freedoms; and direct assistance for legal counsel to media and journalists subject to state harassment.

- Assistance to help created professional journalists associations and other media trade groups that can create common cause for press freedoms.
- Assistance to help "educate journalists about reporting on alienated communities and overcoming religious, ethnic or national prejudice," as well as to help them report objective about violent conflict with "balance" and "fairness."
- Assistance to help develop community radio and journalism that will encourage "social and cultural development."
- Assistance for digital "new communications" and the development of various distribution mechanisms that are difficult for governments to control.
- Assistance to provide "security training" for journalists working in conflict zones, and to provide counseling for journalists suffering from the psychological trauma of covering violent conflict.

In USAID's formulation, "a media sector supportive of democracy would be one that has a degree of editorial independence, is financially viable, has diverse and plural voices, and serves the public interest. The public interest is defined as representing a plurality of voices both through a greater number of outlets and through the diversity of views and voices reflected within outlet."[54] In practice, the agency says, this means moving "the media from one that is directed or even overtly controlled by government or private interests tone that is more open and has a degree of editorial independence that serves the public interest."[55] It also means figuring out who holds economic and political power in the media sector, where that power is located and how it is used. In related fashion, it means developing media strategies appropriate for mobilizing important publics, whether illiterate rural farmers or educated urban professionals, businesses, universities or NGOs, to challenge that power. The strategies available for assistance will vary with geography: the mission's financial and staff resources; the local economic environment; the capacity of local actors to implement a program; and perhaps most important the presence or absence of political will in the country to create change. The goals that USAID has for media assistance, the strategies it uses to reach them and even the measures it uses to evaluate them vary from country to country.

This variation is obviously both a virtue – USAID is often unfairly accused of employing an identical template everywhere it works – and a shortcoming, making overall evaluation of USAID media programs difficult.[56]

Organizationally, USAID support for media programs is conceptualized in the same way other agency democratization programs are, with stated goals and a series of indices and sub-indices by which the agency proposes to measure progress (or the lack of it) toward those goals. Importantly, the agency's media assistance programs are in not a category of their own, but rather are a component of agency goal number 2, "Democracy and Good Governance," and more specifically a means to achieve "Strategic Objective 2.3," which calls for "increased development of a politically active civil society."[57] It is in the area of civil society promotion that one finds "intermediate result 2.3.4," – "enhanced free flow of information" – and thus the justification for media programs. Branching downward from there is a listing of instrumental "media sector" activities, such as training journalists, and environmental ones, such as media law reform. The sub-indices (or success measures) for result 2.3.4 are four: "plural array of independent sources of information encouraged"; "improved investigatory reporting"; "increased use of new information technologies"; and "improved financial and management systems in media entities."[58]

For evaluation purposes, each of these sub-indices has its *own* series of indicators, and each of those is described in terms of its relevance to the goal, how it should be measured, and potential problems of interpretation. These media activities, as USAID understands them, are about journalism, and thus distinguishable from other "media" activities, such as public health or civic education campaigns, that might contribute indirectly and even substantially to media development, but are not based in journalism. USAID's journalism-based programs, of course, are thought to benefit the agency's other democratization initiatives, for example, by reporting on the various branches of government (promoting transparency, accountability and rule of law), and informing the public about candidates for public office (ensuring open and competitive elections). Moreover, other USAID objectives have media components; most noticeably, agency objective 2.2 – "More genuine and competitive political processes" – includes among its many sub-indices the expectation that "media fulfills (sic) role as watchdog in the electoral process."[59]

If all this sounds confusing, the European approach is even more dizzying, reflecting not only the European Commission's preference for working with local NGOs and its emphasis on human rights, but the complex and often confusing nature of EU governance, with multiple layers of institutional authority. The EC, like the United States, partners with major IGOs like the OSCE and the Council of Europe (each of which has its own media programs), and also has its own media delegations. On policy matters with regard to democratizing countries outside of Europe, the EC works through the Foreign Relations Directorate-General, under whose auspices are both the Development Directorate-General and the European Community Humanitarian Office. The implementation of assistance programs is the responsibility of EuropeAid, whose job is to identify needs, solicit proposals, award grants, monitor and evaluate programs. EuropeAid works with the programs of the Foreign Relations Directorate General, but also with its own eight directorates, five of which focus on different regions of the globe. Directorate A, for example, is concerned with Europe, Caucasus and Central Asia.

The EC has also supported programs targeted to specific challenges within or adjacent to Europe. TACIS is a democratization and development program for twelve countries in Eastern Europe and Central Asia that includes media development as one of several "social development and democratization" objectives. On Europe's fringes – in North Africa and the Middle East – the EC's MEDA programs have included civil society and free expression programs as part of a larger development package for the twelve Mediterranean states targeted by the programs. In the former Yugoslavia, for example, most EC media assistance came through the European Reconstruction Agency, and the EC has provided reporting and ethics training to journalists in the region through its support for the Association for Democracy in the Balkans.

The European-based IGOs are important not only for the aid they provide but for the influence they wield. In particular the Council of Europe (with forty-three members and focused on its member states and future member states); the OSCE (with fifty-five members, including the United States and states in Central Asia, well beyond the remit of the Council); and the Stability Pact for South Eastern Europe provide important forms of media assistance. The oldest of these organizations is the Council of Europe, whose Media Division emphasizes media and general expressive freedoms as part of a broader Council emphasis on human rights; the Division's charge is to implement the European Standard in the Area of Freedom of Expression and the European Convention on Transfrontier Television, both derivative of Article 10 of the

European Convention on Human Rights. In practice, the Media Division is a supporting instrument for the Council's focus on legislative reforms in ascension countries, where presumably such reforms depend on corollary reforms in other democratic institutions, including the media. The Council's human rights emphasis also includes special attention to the rights of ethnic and racial minorities, and its 2001 Framework Convention for the Protection of National Minorities includes an article on media practices and obligations in this regard. "Because integration into Europe is seen, from the transition societies, as such an important goal," Price writes, "and because gaining CoE approval is perceived as a first step toward such an integration, the Council commands a certain amount of authority and influence."[60]

Like other IGOs, the Council works directly with the governments of its member and ascension states and with NGOs. Governments are encouraged by the Media Division to make requests for assistance, which are then drafted into proposal for review by the Council's Committee of Ministers. For ascension countries, this proposal includes both carrot and stick. In 2001, for example, Ukraine was threatened with expulsion from the Council for a variety of media-related offenses, but particularly because the repressive policies of President Leonid Kuchma, who was implicated by a tape recording in the murder of a prominent investigative reporter. To redeem itself, Ukraine made several proposals for media assistance to the Council, in effect submitting to its oversight, and the Media Division responded with a two-year program of reforms for Ukraine's media policies. Because of the political sensibilities involved in this kind of near-obligatory assistance, the Council (like USAID) will sometimes choose to channel its aid through an intermediary NGO. NGOs advise the Council's Media Division on its work, and also submit proposals for funding to the Division. Importantly, Council assistance does not depend on the approval of the target country, which may or may not be consulted about the project.

The other major European-based IGO, the OSCE, is a more recent creation than the Council. The OSCE is the successor to the Commission for Security and Cooperation in Europe, itself an outgrowth of the 1975 Helsinki Accords on human rights. The OSCE has been most publicly visible in the last decade through its activities in Bosnia-Herzegovina and Kosovo, where its responsibilities have included, in effect, rebuilding media systems that were deeply compromised by hate speech and, in Kosovo's case, physically destroyed by war. In both cases, the OSCE's media work was supportive of international agencies, including NATO and the UN, working to secure open and free local and national elections, of which fair and expansive media coverage was viewed as an essential part. In that role, and particularly with respect to broadcasting, the OSCE found itself in public disagreement with other international organizations and with Western media, particularly the *New York Times*, which sharply criticized some of the OSCE's policies in the region. Elsewhere the OSCE has been an effective watchdog on abuses of media and expressive freedoms across a region – Eastern Europe and Central Asia – where such abuses are common, publishing annual reports on its member states and the development of their media law and policy, and the legislative and administrative bodies responsible for them.

The Stability Pact for South East Europe, chaired by former Austrian Vice Chancellor Erhard Busek, is the most recent of the European IGOs to provide media assistance. Funded by more than forty countries and several IGOs, the Stability Pact was created at the instigation of the EU in 1999 to help reconstruct and stabilize the Balkans after the wars of the previous decade,[61] the Pact is comprised of three "working tables": democratization and human rights; economic reconstruction, development and cooperation; and security matters. The Pact's media work is located in the human rights table, where the charge includes "civil society building" and the development of "free and independent media," and a task force identifies needs and likely governmental and non-governmental donors that might meet them. The Pact's activities, which range from technical assistance to communications policy advice, extend not only the countries that comprised the former Yugoslavia, but Albania, Bulgaria, Hungary and Romania.[62]

NGOs in Media Assistance

In part because of the various and confusing uses of the term "NGO," the total number of NGOs active in media assistance is probably incalculable. That said, in the regions of the world where assistance is needed it is not hard to count heads. In Southeast, Central and Eastern Europe, where international media assistance during the 1990s was perhaps most vigorous, the media office of the OSCE identified forty-nine different international, regional and local NGOs operating in 1998. The count included the Paris-based World Association of Newspapers and Reporters Sans Frontieres; two of the German political party foundations; the

London-based International Federation of Journalists; the Toronto-based International Freedom of Expression Exchange Clearing House; the Dusseldorf-based European Institute for the Media; the Vienna-based International Press Institute; Press Now, from Amsterdam; and the U.S.-based International Center for Journalists, the Committee to Protect Journalists, Freedom House, the American Society of Newspapers, Accuracy in Media, Fairness and Accuracy in Reporting, the World Press Freedom Committee, and the Freedom Forum, among others. Among the regional or local NGOs at work on press freedom issues, the OSCE identified the Belgrade-based Association of Independent Electronic Media, and Media Center Belgrade; the Moscow-based Glasnost Defense Foundation; and the Human Rights Center of Azerbaijan. A number of international NGOs focused broadly on human rights issues – Human Rights Watch, Amnesty International, Article 19, the Czech Helsinki Committee, the Andrei Sakharov Foundation, and others – also had media assistance programs in the region.[63]

Of the major media-assistance NGOs, three – the International Research and Exchanges Board (IREX/ProMedia); Internews; and the Open Society Institute (OSI) – are truly global. All are U.S.-based, and all use a strategy that can be characterized as a going local: They open branch offices in countries where they operate – for example, "Internews Georgia" or "Internews Middle East"—hiring expatriates and local advisors to provide advice on program development and implementation. The idea is to both to support indigenous media wherever possible and to avoid the inefficiencies and local resentments often associated with remotely conceived and managed forms of assistance, and particularly U.S. government assistance. (There are financial benefits, too: The act of becoming a legal "Ukrainian" or "Russian" or "Indonesian" entity sometimes makes an organization eligible for funding from other international donors.) In Russia, for example, Internews has administered the USAID-funded Media Development Program (MDP) in partnership with the Russian American Press and Information Center (RAPIC), the goal of which is "to speed the development of a commercially viable media sector" in the country. MDP, in turn, has funded the Glasnost Defense Foundation, which monitors and reports on the abuse of journalists' rights; the Moscow Media Law and Policy Center, which encourage media freedoms through media law courses, conferences and publications; and the Standing Commission on Freedom of Information, which advocates for the right of public access to government and corporate information.

Like Internews, OSI is known for localizing its programs. It has national foundations in twenty-nine countries, in Kosovo and Montenegro, and regional foundations in southern and western Africa that provide assistance in a total of twenty-seven African countries. Unlike Internews, OSI gets the lion's share of its funding from its founder, Hungarian-born financier George Soros, who has been described in press accounts variously as a visionary for a global democratic order and a megalomaniac. A 1995 *New Yorker* profile of Soros characterized him as "an unregulated billionaire with a messiah complex."[64] A 1994 *New York Times Magazine* article described him as having "cast himself as an international policy guru and a savior of nations."[65]

Because Soros' personal interests vary so widely, media assistance is actually a relatively small part of OSI activities. Nonetheless, Soros has media assistance programs in Africa, Central, Eastern and Southeastern Europe, Eurasia, Southeast Asia. Most but not all of these programs are under the OSI moniker – OSI's media assistance agency in Ukraine, for example, is known as International Renaissance Foundation. In Southeast Asia, assistance from Soros' philanthropies will often get channeled through other, intermediary organizations because of the official perception, advanced by former Malaysian Prime Minister Mahathir, that Soros' currency trading caused the 1998 debt crisis in the region. All OSI programs are autonomous and are led by local boards of directors and staffed primarily with indigenous people, though there is no doubt that Soros himself is an active participant in evaluating the programs and their work.[66] As Gordana Jankovic, OSI's media programs administrator, explained to me in 2003, "We are unlike other media assistance organizations, other foundations, in that we have a living donor."[67]

Each of these large NGOs relies heavily on partners – with one another, and with overlapping circles of governmental, intergovernmental and non-governmental agencies. Many key personnel in these organizations have worked in more than one media-assistance NGO, and some have experience working for government assistance agencies. So intertwined are the activities of many media assistance organizations, large and small, that they will occasionally squabble over who should get credit for a particular project. Sometimes they will also duplicate efforts. In a 2005 review of USAID media programs, for example, the Government Accountability Office found instances where multiple NGOs were funded for the same work, with no clear chain of command in place.[68] In one case, the State Department and USAID each funded different NGOs to rebuild radio stations that had been wiped out by the tsunami, with the result that ground crews found themselves fighting over who was authorized to complete the work.[69]

Still, the benefit that comes from this network of donor and NGO relationships is a shortened learning curve. In recent years, the media assistance community has sought to record its successes and map out best practices. USAID's strategy paper on media assistance specifically identifies several NGOs with best practices in several areas of media assistance: analyzing and drafting media legislation; monitoring and reporting on media restrictions; lobbing for journalists' rights; removing barriers to media entry, and to the means of media production and distribution; supporting independent media in a transition environment; community broadcasting; coverage of ethnic minorities and women; reporting on executive and legislative activities; providing low-interest loans; improving journalism education; and others.[70] Both USAID and its Office of Transition Initiatives also publicize the various "lessons learned" from assistance projects.[71] IREX/ProMedia, Internews and the Soros foundations share information with other divisions within their own organizations; each has developed a kind of benchmarking system that identifies best practices for possible adoption or adaptation in media development projects in other countries and regions. Finally, the International Center for Journalists publishes a regular electronic bulletin, the International Journalists Network, which very helpfully catalogs media assistance projects around the world.

An important feature of media assistance, as with democracy assistance generally, is that there is such extensive interaction between governmental and non-governmental sectors that it can be difficult to say whether some NGOs are truly independent of governments.[72] As noted already, several of the biggest NGOs in the democratization industry get significant funding – and sometimes almost all of their funds – from the U.S. government, often through contracts with USAID or the State Department.[73] Among the major U.S. NGOs in media assistance, this is true not only of the Eurasia and Asia foundations, but Internews, IREX and ICFJ. IREX/ProMedia, for example, receives financial support from several sources, though its journalism programs are funded entirely by USAID. Internews established Internews Europe in 1995 and Internews International in 1998, both based in Paris. Originally the organization received most of its funding from USAID and USIA, though today it receives funds from several public and private sources in the United States and Europe; indeed, Internews' U.S. tax returns show that it has the greatest variety of donors of any of the big NGOs working in the NIS region.

Aside from concerns about program coordination and duplication, it seems fair to say that any NGO which receives government funding is an instrument for pursuing governmental goals. Economists describe all governmental contracting out, or privatization of government services, as exactly that. It is a separate question, not for discussion here, whether such contracting is also a mechanism for withholding information from the public about governmental activities, though presumably it has that benefit with respect to both domestic and international publics. The important point is that Internal Revenue Service samples of the tax returns of 501(c)(3) non-profit organizations show that instances in which government revenues comprise upwards of 90 percent or more of a non-profit organization's funding are well outside the norm, and yet such percentages are common among these big democracy- and media-assistance NGOs.

A number of European NGOs also receive the bulk of their funding – well more than half – from governments. The World Service Trust of the British Broadcasting Corporation (BBC) has since 1989 been a major provider of overseas journalism training programs, which the Trust establishes as local institutions in the countries where it operates. These journalism "schools," as they are sometimes called, focus both on substantive training – for example, how to cover armed conflict, elections or ethnic minorities – and on technical skills – courses on ethics, reporting and production skills, and news management. Like most large NGOs, the Trust works in partnership with other donors and government institutions like the Danish Foundation for International Development, the OSCE, the EU and the European Journalism Center.

Another significant source of nominally private European media assistance are the German political foundations, or *politische Stiftungen*, which have sponsored media assistance programs in Europe, Latin America, Africa and Asia. The foundations, of which there six major ones, are each linked to a particular party and each funded primarily by the German government, though the foundations act independently in identifying and funding media projects. Consistent with other European approaches to democracy aid, the political foundations often carry out projects in full partnerships with regional and local NGOs. Other European governments also fund their own democracy-assistance NGOs, most with some kind of media activity. Until early 2005, for example, Denmark supported the Baltic Media Center, which promoted "democracy, social development and a peaceful international cooperation through the active participation of the media."[74] Press Now, established in 1993, is another Danish NGO that works on a range of media assistance projects in Southeastern and Eastern Europe; its funding comes variously from the Danish government, from political foundations and from independent NGOs like OSI. Other European governments – Switzerland, Norway, Sweden, Austria – in addition to having official aid agencies, also fund independent NGOs for whom media assistance of some kind is a major mission.

The process by which governments make media assistance grants to NGOs varies, but will depend to a great degree on the specific purpose for which democratization funds are authorized and who is approved to receive them. Congress gives money to USAID, for example, under broad rubrics such as "civil society building," which USAID then subdivides into more detailed activities. The agency will then prepare a request for applications (RFA) for programs to meet its designated goals; the RFA is typically twenty or more pages long, excluding the material about USAID standards, application forms and instructions, and with details about the nature of the proposed work, whom it is supposed to serve, and any special restrictions with respect to eligibility and personnel.

The USAID RFA process is typically limited to a select group of large organizations, both other government agencies and NGOs, that meet USAID's criteria for eligibility and which will act as program implementers. The most important operational criteria for eligibility are the financial and organizational capacity to staff and manage a program satisfactorily; ability to work with other NGOs or government agencies; and the ability to meet USAID's reporting, monitoring and evaluation requirements. Additionally USAID looks for knowledge of the media environment and contacts in the region, requirements that sometimes translate into personnel requirements. In the NIS states, for example, USAID in 1995 made the none-too-demanding requirement that program directors have at least five years of "relevant work experience," knowledge of both the U.S. media environment and that of Central and Eastern Europe, and be able to recruit advisors to help implement the program.[75] Language skills, the RFA said, were "desirable but not essential."[76] Completed proposal applications go to a technical panel at USAID, which reviews them and makes a recommendation to the office that put out the RFA. Once USAID awards a grant, the decision about who else participates in the program, whether as beneficiaries or as partners, is largely left to the grantee; outside of its general budgetary restrictions, USAID does not specify how money is to be spent.

A common USAID requirement for media programs is that eventual program participants be independent, by which USAID means that no "media entities that are under the control of any level of government, or that receive a government subsidy"[77] are eligible. Many NGOs choose to impose a similar requirement on program participants, whether or not they receive USAID funds (and many NGOs would prefer to avoid USAID funds when they can, precisely because of the restrictions imposed on them). The Eurasia Foundation, for example, also includes media "independence" as a criterion for grant eligibility, but is more generous than USAID in defining the term, emphasizing the importance of not being dependent on any single governmental or private source of revenues. Internews, does much the same.

In large part these policies reflect the difficulty, particularly in the NIS countries but in other regions as well, of figuring out who actually "owns" the media, particularly broadcast media. Still, such requirements are an interesting feature of organizations that are themselves often heavily dependent on governmental funding, and for whom that funding presumably has some impact on organizational mission, if not also on program selection, design and implementation. A central assumption of all media assistance is that revenue sources are a key measure of and influence on editorial independence, an assumption that presumably has a corollary for incentives and outcomes among those organizations that actually provide the assistance. Price notes that "NGOs prefer grants or flexible arrangements that allow a maximum of autonomy and flexibility in the field. On the other hand, government agencies often prefer close supervision of a project through explicit contractual arrangements."[78] The result, he suggests, is a constant tension between government funders and recipient NGOs, each of which approaches a project with different knowledge and expectations.

USAID also acknowledges this tension in its strategy document on media assistance, where it confronts the possibility that truly independent media may well be critical of the United States, sometimes harshly so. This is a problem that must be "creatively managed," according to the agency:

> On the one hand, support for programs comes from U.S. taxpayers' money so it is naïve to think that there would be political support for activities which appear, at

face value, to develop voices critical of the United States and its policies. On the other hand, the ultimate goal of journalism training or outlet support is to develop the capacity for professional, objective reporting. If this reporting is critical of the United States or its policies, then in some respects this should be seen as a sign of success. When relying on intermediaries to channel U.S. funds for media activities, the instrument for doing so is very important to protect the beneficiaries from excessive U.S. interference. Where grants are used instead of contracts, more flexibility is allowed, and less oversight expected. Many field missions, however, use contracts to hire intermediaries so that they can have direct influence in programs and even participant selection, and, as a result, manage the activities in such a way as to avoid raising concerns.[79]

"Local Partners"

The most diverse arena of media assistance is at the delivery level, where there is a mix of both aid beneficiaries and what Price and his colleagues call the "local partners"[80] to the major donors and intermediary organizations. Those local organizations include media organizations – print, broadcast, magazine, on-line – but also professional journalism associations, freedom of expression NGOs, financial-assistance NGOs, journalism schools, and other indigenous training and monitoring programs. Some of these organizations are genuinely local and indigenous, while others are local only in the sense that wherever they are from they are the ones on-site to recommend, implement or manage a project, and usually but not always there because of their technical or regional expertise. Still others are regional organizations with local chapters, and some "chapters" are in fact a few people, or even a single individual, who function as the eyes and ears of a larger grant-making body.

"Local partner" is a term of art, and not a very precise one. Local does not necessarily mean small, for example. Both the Eurasia and Asia foundations, for example, with their extensive knowledge of and experience in their respective regions, identify likely recipients for grants and loans and thus act as *de facto* local partners to many smaller NGOs based in the New York, Washington or Western Europe. Conversely, there are an untold number of small NGOs across the globe engaged in some aspect of media work. A good way to get a feel for the number and variety of them is to look through the tax returns of major funders like the Eurasia Foundation or OSI, which show grants and loans ranging from a few a few thousand to many millions of dollars and awarded to hundreds of organizations, many of them truly local in composition and focus, and even to individuals. Other "local partners" are probably better described as intermediaries whose role is to manage aid projects, from delivery to evaluation. IREX/ProMedia, for example, lists among its "strategic" partners in Europe and Eurasia the BBC World Service Trust, the American law firm of Covington & Burling, the Cox Center at the University of Georgia, the European Journalism Centre, InterMedia, International Newspaper Financial Executives, the University of Missouri School of Journalism and the World Association of Newspapers. IREX/PROMEDIA also lists as media assistance partners in the region the American Bar Association, Baltic Media Center, the Council of Europe, the Danish School of Journalism, the Independent Journalism Foundation, the Institute for War and Peace Reporting at New York University, Internews, Norwegian Peoples Aid, Management Systems International, the Media Development Loan Fund, the Media Diversity Institute, Medienhilfe, OSI, the Network Media Program, the OSCE, Press Now, Soros Local Foundations, the Swedish Helsinki Commmittee, the Thomson Foundation, Transparency International, the Media Task Force for Stability Pact for Southeast Europe, the UK Department for International Development, and the World Bank Institute.[81]

It is not the point of this book to review or comment on the hundreds (perhaps thousands) of media assistance organizations in the world or to describe all the ways in which they interact. Still, a description of a few notable ones provides a sense of the range of activities these NGOs undertake:

- The *Philippine Center for Investigative Journalism* (PCIJ), based in Quezon City, was founded in 1989 to provide training fellowships, seminars and financial assistance to reporters and news organizations that want to do investigative stories on the environment, public health, governance and other complex subjects. The PCIJ publishes its own investigative magazine, *i*, and its investigative reports have won numerous awards and international acclaim. The Center also produces excellent guidebooks on public policy issues affecting journalism, such as the 2001 book *The Right to Know: Access to Information in Southeast Asia*, a guide to access law in all nine countries of the region.
- The *Southeast Asian Press Alliance* (SEAPA) was founded in Bangkok in 1998 for the purpose of uniting various journalists' associations in the region under a larger organizational umbrella that could advocate for press freedom and protect journalists against violence and intimidation. SEAPA operates throughout the region, but has been particularly active in Malaysia and Indonesia. SEAPA is itself the creation of several other NGOs: PCIJ; the Thai Journal-

ists Association; the Alliance of Independent Journalists; the Indonesian-based Institute for Studies in the Free Flow of Information; and the Center for Media Freedom and Responsibility.

- The *Media Institute for Southern Africa* (MISA) is a Namibia-based NGO with chapters in eleven of the twelve countries that comprise the Southern Africa Development Community (SADC). MISA was created in 1992 to fulfill the goals for independent and pluralistic media outlined in the 1991 Windhoek Declaration; to that end, MISA focuses on legal reform and the defense of journalists and news organizations, civil society development and journalist training. Institutionally related to MISA is the Southern Africa Media Development Loan Fund, or SAMDEF, discussed in more detail in chapter 6.

- The *Roma Press Center* (RSK) in Budapest, founded in 1995, is a good example of an NGO concerned with a specific civil society problem, in this case the treatment of a scorned minority. RSK is a subdivision of another NGO, the Roma Rights Foundation. The Center is essentially a press agency; it works to increase objective news coverage of the largest ethic minority in Central and Eastern Europe, and it provides training to Roma journalists. The Center's news stories and features are distributed to national dailies and local newspapers throughout the region. The Center has partner organizations in Slovakia, the Czech Republic and Romania. One of them, the Roma Press Agency in Bratislava, publishes all its materials online with support from OSI, the American Embassy's Small Grants for Democracy Development program, the Dutch Embassy and the European Commission.

- The New York-based *Independent Journalism Foundation*, founded in 1991 by James L. Greenfield, a member of the *New York Times* editorial board, focuses on human capital development, primarily by offering training that allows journalists to upgrade their reporting and technical skills. The IJF created the Centers for Independent Journalism first in Prague (1991), then in Bratislava, Bucharest, Budapest and, in 2001, in Phnom Penh. The Prague Center closed in 2001, though the remaining IJF Centers, all staffed by local and regional journalists, have become important assistance partners for other media assistance funders and NGOs. According to its materials, the IJF's training programs are intended to "encourage effective, fact-based responsible journalism" based on "international professional standards and ethics."

- The Brussels-based *European Journalism Centre* (EJC) was created in 1993 and trains journalists primarily in issues related to the project of European Union, from migration to security. The EJC works with European journalism schools organized under the banner of the European Journalism Training Association, and its programs are supported largely by grants from national development agencies and European bodies like he EC and the Council of Europe. The EJC has also been active in Central and Eastern Europe, where it has run numerous training programs in partnership with national and regional press associations, and with the BBC World Trust, OSI and the Eurasia Foundation.

- The Washington, DC-based *International Center for Journalists* (ICFJ), founded by former *Boston Globe* Editor Thomas Winship in 1984 as the Center for Foreign Journalists, is arguably the international standard for comprehensive journalism training programs. The Center emphasizes its "real world" programs for journalists in print and broadcast media on "best practices" in areas ranging from business management to environmental reporting to journalism ethics. With financial support from the Knight Foundation, the Center sends about twenty U.S. journalists overseas for this purpose each year; the Center also brings foreign journalists to the United States to work in U.S. newsrooms. The Center produces training manuals in several languages to supplement all of its training programs, and as noted above it operates the International Journalists' Network, a regular online newsletter with stories about media assistance programs, threats to media independence, additional training opportunities, and so on.

- *Developing Radio Partners* is one of the newer NGOs in the field of media assistance, created by William Siemering, one of the founders of National Public Radio in the United States, and a long-time contributor to the radio projects of the Open Society Institute. DRP began operations in 2002, with a mission of "supporting independent radio stations in countries transitioning to democracy through professional development in journalism, programming, station management and finance." Most of DRP's current programs are in Africa and Asia, and all emphasize the cost-effectiveness and accessibility or radio programming over virtually all types of media, as well as their ability to serve rural and illiterate populations. DRP also emphasizes long-term financial sustainability in its projects, and so publishes case-studies and best practices guides.

- Several free expression and journalist advocacy NGOs, though they are not important as grantmakers, are nonetheless important to media assistance for their role in publicizing limitations on expressive freedoms around the world. Some of these organizations also award prizes for distinguished reporting, a process that can have the effect of insulating journalists from government or private-party harassment, while also legitimizing their work. Among the notable NGOs of this type are Article 19, the Committee to Protect Journalists (CPJ), the International Press Institute (IPI) and Reporters sans Frontiers (RSF). All are advocacy organizations that monitor and report on the conditions for free and vigorous reporting around the globe. In the United States, a number of private foundations and trade groups also perform in this role, among them the McCormick Tribune Foundation, the John S. and James L. Knight Foundation, the MacArthur Foundation, the Ford Foundation, the Freedom Forum, and the American Society of Newspaper Editors.

Many if not most of these NGOs partner with other aid providers, including one another. Developing Radio Partners, for example, works with both the International Center for Journalists and Independent Journalism Foundation. Ultimately, of course, the local partners that matter most in the field of media assistance are the small, independent news organizations struggling to do good journalism in political and economic climates that are, if not hostile to their existence, indifferent to their survival. These news media are the critical piece in the assistance pyramid, since of course it is their success that is the point of assistance.

It is also at this level that problems are most apparent. Recipients of media assistance are frequently skeptical about the goals and the kinds of assistance they receive, particularly from the larger international NGOs. They will sometimes fault programs for being culturally inappropriate or even chauvinistic, but more common is the view that too many aid programs serve primarily to benefit the donor and as a result have few lasting benefits. Indonesian journalist and former Neiman Fellow Andreas Harsono, for instance, says that some prominent assistance organizations, governmental and non-governmental, may mean well but "are not always helpful and sometimes are presumptuous. The people they send do not know a country's culture or history. Many international NGOs do not have a long-standing interest or purpose in a country and so do nothing to build local capacity. They often bypass local democratic processes, and so do not solve problems but make them worse."[82]

Anecdotes about waste in media assistance are easy to find – everybody has one. Kabral Blay-Amhere, president of the West African Journalists Association in Ghana, described to me a £15,000 British training program in Ghana in which, he charged, only £2,000 went to actual training—the rest, he said, went to overhead, including the cost of supporting two tutors sent from the United Kingdom.[83] Lin Neumann of the Southeast Asian Press Association (SEAPA) tells of an NGO operating in the region that received a $500,000 grant (from a donor he declined to identify) for no other reason than that the grantor was under deadline pressure to find a grantee.[84] Some NGOs and IGOs come in for sharper criticism than others, most commonly because of a perceived attention-deficit disorder in donors who seem more interested in their own needs than those whom they are putatively there to help.

When asked to explain why Western aid can be so clumsy, a common response from aid recipients is that media assistance, like development aid generally, is driven by two things: the domestic politics and strategic interests of donor states, and international news coverage. For government donors, recipients believe, a major concern is translating domestic political concerns into the international arena, a view that is consistent with any number of assessments of foreign aid. With respect to media, for example, the post-911 increase in funding for Voice of America and other public diplomacy efforts in the Middle East is a result of both domestic concerns about terror and a foreign policy that is deeply engaged in the region militarily. Donors themselves will often cite the need, indeed the duty, to export "the values enshrined in the First Amendment of the Constitution,"[85] though when pushed for particulars aid providers are not always clear on what those values are or where they apply. The Arab broadcaster Al Jazeera, for instance, is the embodiment of First Amendment values as they are commonly understood in American law and among American journalists – independent, entrepreneurial and frequently courageous in its reporting, Al Jazeera is partisan, inflammatory and frequently irresponsible in its talk shows and commentary. Nonetheless, Al Jazeera's influence in the Middle East – its exercise of First Amendment "values" – is routinely cited as the reason why the United States government should fund counter-programming in the region.[86] Meanwhile the U.S. government has urged the government of Qatar, which subsidizes Al Jazeera, either to sell the station or reign in its programming.[87]

Aid recipients also believe (whether it is true or not) that governmental and non-governmental donors respond to the so-called "CNN effect"— the process by which international attention and money are directed to a region by virtue of television news coverage. When this happens "the response to crisis is then often blown out of proportion," says Sharmini Peres, executive director of the Canadian Journalists Association, which operates the International Freedom of Expression Exchange. "There is a flood of support and afterward there is total abandonment."[88] The consequences of the intervention may nonetheless linger, says Basma El Husseiny, a former Ford Foundation media program officer in Cairo: "International agencies come in and reorder priorities, sometimes harmfully."[89]

Finally, Monroe Price and his colleagues have characterized the various types of media aid in the same way that development aid generally
is described, either as "top-down" or "bottom-up."[90] The top-down approach is usually associated with multi-lateral governmental assistance;
it creates under IGO control alternative sources of information that are,
both structurally and in their content, "neutral and peace-oriented."[91] The
bottom-up approach, more commonly but not exclusively the domain
of NGOs, focuses on "strengthening local, indigenous media outlets,
particularly those that strike a new voice, in the hopes of building a
public sphere, a civil society, and the long-term machinery for peace
and reconstruction."[92]

Both approaches have problems that affect the long-term prospects
for successful outcomes. The top-down approach to media development
is apt to alienate locals, including journalists, who see it as foreign, offensive or even hostile to their interests. Moreover where the approach
succeeds it may do so at the cost of weakening indigenous media that
cannot compete with a heavily subsidized, well-equipped news organization. Should that organization later collapse when international support
is withdrawn, the net effect of the assistance may be a media system as
weak or weaker than existed at the point of intervention. The bottom-up
approach to media assistance, on the other hand, must by design find its
way through a media environment where, particularly in post-conflict
societies, media organizations are likely to be partisan rather than independent, and reporting standards are often low or in decline. Often, what
passes for independent reporting in these environments is really just a
proxy for the interests of the donor. Finally, of course, these categories
are not mutually exclusive. Bilateral government assistance, for example,
will sometimes have top-down goals but employ a bottom-up strategy.
USAID, as discussed already, will seek to promote civil society goals by
funding indigenous media organizations, though as one would expect in
a way consistent with the political and strategic priorities that the U.S.
government has identified for the region.

Whatever the merits of these many criticisms, a few points seem
obvious. NGOs and IGOs can indeed become large, agenda-driven institutions, and most need to maintain a funding base; as result they can
become highly competitive, and may at times work at cross-purposes.
They can also be parochial in their views, and remarkably unsophisticated
in their understanding of the media systems and values they wish to export. That does not mean the people working for them are inexperienced

or unknowledgeable. Quite the contrary. Many current and former journalists working in or with media assistance programs are accomplished and skilled professionals of extraordinary personal integrity and are personally and deeply committed to their overseas work. Moreover those working in the field can spend an inordinate amount of time negotiating with political, cultural and military authorities at the local, national and, in some cases, international level, making even straightforward programs difficult to operate and even incremental successes hard to achieve. In this regard, not the least of problems for the media assistance donor community are errors of fact and outright misrepresentations by aid recipients, particularly in regions where media are themselves divided into competing camps. Finally, of course, the value of any particular program – never mind the division between "real training" and "overhead" – will always be subject to second-guessing.

Measuring Results: Evaluating Media "Independence"

As the foregoing suggests, the problem of objective measurement that applies to democracy promotion programs applies with equal force to media assistance and to its goal of creating a sustainable, "free" and "independent" media sector. Adding to the problem is that national and international donors will employ complex, multi-layered funding patterns of the kinds described above, and at the same time use differing definitions of "independent media development," making it very nearly impossible to identify aggregate funding levels with any precision, never mind evaluate program success.

Nonetheless, there is a long history of researchers attempting to measure press freedom using quantifiable measures. In the mid-1960s, for example, scholar Ralph Lowenstein developed the Press Independence and Critical Ability (or PICA) Index, linking data on government restrictions on the media with data on economic impediments to press viability, specifically national data on industry concentration and competitive markets.[93] Today at least three internationally known indices exist that purport to rate media freedom and, explicitly or implicitly, media sustainability. The oldest is the annual "Survey of Press Freedom" done by the NGO Freedom House and which includes rankings for almost all of the world's countries; the second is a "Media Sustainability Index" (MSI) created jointly by USAID and IREX in 2000; and a third, more recent entry to the field, is the "Press Freedom Index" from the European NGO Reporters sans Frontières (RSF). Both USAID and the U.S. State

Department use the Freedom House rankings together with the MSI as an evaluation tool in all their media programs, and in some instances have used the MSI as the *only* evaluation tool.[94] The Government Accountability Office has in the past praised these indices, and particularly the MSI, but in 2005 noted that while they "are useful for measuring the state of the media in countries... they are of limited utility in measuring the specific contributions of U.S-sponsored projects toward developing independent media in countries when used alone."[95]

The MSI is arguably the most useful of the three indices, though because it is so new it has no baseline data from before 2001 and cannot be used to evaluate long-term trends. The MSI is an ordinal scale measurement developed to evaluate the progress of media development projects in Europe and Eurasia, but its markers could presumably be used to evaluate any media system. The MSI focuses on five attributes that IREX says characterize a "successful" media system, one of which is the degree to which "media are well-managed businesses, allowing editorial independence."[96] The other key environmental measures favoring media sustainability are "legal and social norms" protective of free speech and access to public information; journalism that meets "professional standards of quality"; the availability of "multiple news sources" that provide "reliable and objective news"; and "supporting institutions" that serve the "professional interests of independent media." Two discrete groups evaluate a country's media according to these sub-indices. The first is composed of country experts: "representatives of local media, nongovernmental organizations, professional associations, international donors and media development implementers."[97] These experts meet together with one or more members serving as a panel moderator; together they hash out a score for each rating attribute, and the moderator writes an analysis of the discussion. Separately, IREX staff based both in-country and in IREX's Washington, D.C., offices conduct a similar review. The scores of the two panels are then combined to obtain final scores for each country.

The MSI develops a score for each of these sub-indices by employing seven to nine "indicators." The indicators for judging whether media are "well-managed businesses, allowing editorial independence" are these:

- Media outlets and supporting firms operate as efficient, professional, and profit-generating businesses.
- Media receive revenue from a multitude of sources.
- Advertising agencies and related industries support an advertising market.

- Advertising revenue as a percentage of total revenue is in line with accepted standards at commercial outlets.
- Independent media do not receive government subsidies.
- Market research is used to formulate strategic plans, enhance advertising revenue, and tailor products to the needs and interests of audiences.
- Broadcast ratings and circulation figures are reliably and independently produced.[98]

A virtue of the MSI, apparent in the indicators above, is that it evaluates a country's media sector as a whole, without focusing on any single medium. As such, it allows for the possibility that editorial independence can take different forms, not only within a media system, but between different systems. The problem with the index is that it implicitly ignores the economics of news and public affairs provision. Assuming Guatemala's *Nuestro Diario* is a sign of democratic progress in that country, for example, it is easy to see how it fits in the environment described by the MSI indicators. It is much harder to see how *El Periodico* fits, if it fits at all. At best, the MSI describes a media system whose essential feature is the absence of government. This is understandable but inadequate. "Efficient, professional and profit-generating" is not an editorial mission. To confuse it with one does no favor to journalism, or to democracy.

The survey conducted by Freedom House has the advantage of being the most comprehensive, ranking 192 countries. And because the survey has been done since 1979, it provides some longitudinal observations not possible with the other two indices. But the media ranking system used by Freedom House is remarkably vague about its methodology and its definitions, and it is not clear just how it scores its indices. Its survey scores rely on evaluations of three broad categories that are remarkable mostly because they mirror the critical enabling conditions for press development discussed in chapter one, which Freedom House categorizes as the legal, political and economic environments. Under its economic environment category, Freedom House claims to measure "the structure of media ownership; transparency and concentration of ownership; the costs of establishing media as well as of production and distribution; the selective withholding of advertising or subsidies by the state or other actors; the impact of corruption and bribery on content; and the extent to which the economic situation in a country impacts the development of media."[99] Freedom House rates each country in these categories on a score of zero to 30 (though political environment has a larger range, zero to 49), with zero being a perfect score. The organization then adds the scores from each category to get an overall score. "Free" media systems are those with scores of between zero and 30, "partly free" are those scoring between 31 and 60, and "not free" those with scores of 61 to 100.[100] Of relevance to this book's inquiry, the category that provides for the most consistent downward pressure on press freedom scores is the economic one.

In 2002 a third press freedom index appeared on the scene, this one from the Paris-based Reporters sans Frontières.[101] RSF is probably best known for its defense of journalists who have been attacked, either rhetorically or physically, and its index reflects that preoccupation. Unlike the other two indices, it gives special emphasis to the efforts that governments make to protect journalists from obvious outrages like imprisonment and murder, and lesser ones like confiscation and various forms of official and unofficial censorship. Economic variables are less critical to the RSF evaluation (though the methodology is not clear how any variable is evaluated). Finally, RSF does not sort countries into categories in the way Freedom House does, but simply ranks states (166 of them in the current survey) from first to last according to score.[102] Readers must come to their own conclusions about where in the ranking free media decline and then disappear into the ranks of "not free" media.

Each of these three indices is valuable in its way, and in the case of the MSI, particularly, is used as a guide to further funding for USAID media projects, both as to kind and place.[103] Each index also has either qualitative or quantitative limitations, too. The Freedom House and RSF rankings, because they involve so many countries, necessarily neglect the factual detail and cultural nuances that are the specialty of the MSI (which evaluates only about twenty countries in Europe and Eurasia). Moreover to be taken seriously, any effort to compare truly large numbers of countries at some point requires quantitative research methods and the availability of adequate and comparable data. Perhaps an inherently subjective matter like press freedom is not susceptible to such an inquiry (the availability of reliable data would be impossible in many states) but that is just the problem. The subjective nature of all these indices leads to conclusions about press freedom that, viewed either by themselves or in comparison to one another, are very nearly incomprehensible. The RFP, for instance, finds that the freest press systems in the world are the Nordic countries of Finland, Iceland, the Netherlands and Norway.

Freedom House in its 2004 survey find Denmark, Sweden and Iceland tied for first. And yet media in each of these states, print and broadcast, receive extensive government support – tax reductions, reduced postal rates, newsprint subsidies and so on.

The MSI, by comparison, with its explicit assumption that government subsidies are inimical to press freedom, adopts a uniquely American point of view – and not a very accurate one at that. The American media are of course subsidized in all kinds of ways, most obviously in terrestrial broadcasting, where television and radio licensees use the publicly owned electromagnetic spectrum without paying a fee to do so. Magazines and newspapers benefit from and in many cases would not survive without second-class postage rates. In Europe the tradition of state broadcasting is both long and rich, if now under economic assault from cable and satellite competitors. Whatever their problems, the world's more notable public broadcasters – in the United Kingdom, Germany, Japan, Austria, and elsewhere – are famous above all for the independent character of their news programming. The MSI emphasis on the market as the best guarantor of editorial independence, combined with its suspicion of forms of ownership other than private and for-profit, ignores both the public good character of news and public affairs information and the possibility that such products might be most sustainable in the not-for-profit sector of the economy. And of course the not-for-profit sector, under whatever name it goes, because it is tax-exempt, is state subsidized.

Finally, each of these indices makes assumptions about free speech norms that are not universal even in established democracies. Freedom House, for instance, assumes that Germany's ban on Nazi speech, not much different except in detail from hate speech regulations found in other countries, is a threat to press freedom. So, too, are regulations on obscenity and violent content on the Internet. The French media are penalized because of the extensive state support they receive, and because of the French practice of registering journalists through the *Carte de press*. Anywhere political parties have even partial ownership of media – not uncommon in Western Europe—that, too, is assumed to be inimical to press freedom. Another feature of media law in Europe, written into state constitutions in several cases, are regulations promoting public access to and content diversity on the media. Such regulations admittedly put the government in the precarious role of having to actively promote press freedom without smothering it with good intentions. Nonetheless, many societies accept the view that governments have a responsibility to ensure through structural and even content regulation the core of a "free" and "independent" media system. Not so in the United States, where the constitutional and arguably the normative assumption is that the speech market should be the exclusive domain of private and self-interested actors. Sometimes even attempts at self-regulation are viewed with suspicion. Lowenstein's PICA-Index, for example, penalized countries that had press councils, viewing them as restraints on free expression. Today the MSI includes no measures for self-regulation among its eight sub-indices for evaluating "professional journalism."[104]

To be fair, neither IREX nor Freedom House makes any claim that its index is an appropriate tool for evaluating media assistance programs, and neither was designed for that purpose. In the absence of these indices, however, the alternative is anecdotal evidence of even less usefulness, or quantifiable measures that infer causality where none may exist. Researcher Julia Seidler describes the shortcomings of evaluation methods in an analysis of USAID's programs in Ukraine in 1995 and 1996, when, during the agency's transition to strategic planning, the media program's objective, as part of the civil society portfolio, was changed "to increase and better informed citizens' participation in political and economic decision making."[105] The primary indicator for this goal was the extent to which citizens were exposed to non-government and politically unaffiliated news sources, and the availability of such news coverage. The indicator was measured by the "number of hours of independent TV programming (excluding daily news programs) broadcast in the 30 largest cities in which USAID-sponsored Internews training had taken place."[106] A second indicator was increased program "quality," measured by total number of cities with daily, non-governmental newscasts.[107] "These indicators indeed show that [Ukrainian] citizens may be more informed," Seidler writes, "however, it is hard to see the link between the hours of television programming and citizen participation in elections."[108]

USAID nonetheless saw signs of success in these measures, with help from its grantees. In defense of its claim that Ukrainians are "clearly...being presented with more than one point of view" and have "greater exposure to non-government news sources,"[109] USAID's 1997 report on Ukraine essentially catalogued the variety of Internews and IREX/ProMedia training and support activities at independent television stations in the country. The hourly data on independent television programming, the measure for the first indicator, were supplied by Internews. Seidler concludes that "grantees, mainly Internews, IREX/ProMedia and the Eurasia Foundation, are still relied on to provide USAID with information on the success of its media programs,"[110] and that success appears to be a simple function of how many journalists, technicians and other media employees received training from these organizations. In its 1997 report on the country, for example, USAID cited as evidence of its success the network of non-governmental television stations and the International Media Center established by Internews.[111] In effect, the evidence of progress was the mere existence of active grantees with ongoing programs.

Obviously USAID must be accountable for its democratization programs and the business of measuring media effects on those programs will always be difficult. Moreover Ukraine's political and economic environment is still overwhelmingly hostile to non-state media, which face political harassment and economic pressures from both central and regional government officials. On balance, then, the presence of USAID and its program partners in the country has to be judged a good thing. Seidler reports that USAID-funded programs at Internews and IREX/ ProMedia have also been effective challenging government restrictions or harassment; in one case she discusses, IREX/ProMedia publicity was instrumental in restoring a television station to the air after the government shut it down during a parliamentary election.[112] Internews-trained broadcasters have successfully reorganized and professionalized their newsrooms, uncovered stories of government waste and corruption, and USAID has been willing to stay the course when local government officials have responded with licensing fees, threats and outright censorship.[113] It may nonetheless claim too much to conclude, as USAID did in its 1997 summary of its Ukraine grants, that "such programs are building for the future and helping to create the kind of human and institutional capacity that will be needed to build a civil society from below." [114]

The consistent shortcoming of program evaluation in media assistance is the same as in democracy assistance generally, confusing output with outcomes. The only real solution to this problem is dedicated research that requires elaborate data collection and a variety of assessment methodologies, and that is time-consuming and expensive. Few if any aid providers (including USAID) have the budget to do this kind of work. As a consequence, the fall-back solution has been an effort among many aid providers, acting on their own or collectively, to confer on best practices and publish results – in short, to learn from a decade and a half of intensive experience. Many NGOs, for example, now hold regular annual or biennial conferences to which they invite their local program partners for several days of case studies and collegiality. USAID and the World Bank in 2002 brought together media assistance providers from national development agencies, international organizations and several leading NGOs to discuss the problems of program coordination and program sustainability in the sector. A background paper prepared for that meeting, by Monroe Price and his colleagues, marked a first step in mapping the field conceptually and programmatically.[115] The next year, the Netherlands Institute of International Relations published a similar overview of the field that drew eight case studies Asia, Latin America and Africa.[116] Some NGOs now also make case studies, open-source software tools and other products of their experience available on their web sites.

Notes

1.   See Margaret Blanchard, "The Business of a Free Press," *Gannett Center Journal* (Fall 1990): 17-29.
2.   For a complete discussion of American media assistance efforts in the early part of the Cold War, see Margaret A. Blanchard, *Exporting the First Amendment: The Press-Government Crusade of 1945-1952* (New York: Longman, 1986).
3.   Blanchard, "Business of a Free Press," 1990, 22.
4.   Ibid.
5.   Ibid., 24-25.
6.   Ibid., 23.
7.   Ibid., 23-24.
8.   Ibid., 25.
9.   Ibid., 25-26.
10. Clifford H. Block, "Bilateral Aid in Communications: The U.S. Agency for International Development," *Journal of Communication* (Spring 1985): 27-33, 27, 28.
11. Ibid, 30.
12. Ibid, 30-34.
13. Ibid., 29.
14. Ibid.
15. The commission was named for its chairman, Sean MacBride of Ireland, winner of both the Lenin and Nobel Peace prizes.
16. Block, "Bilateral Aid in Communications," 1985, 36.
17. USAID, *Policy Determination: Development Communication* (Washington, DC: U.S. Agency for International Development, February 1984).
18. Block, "Bilateral Aid in Communications," 1985, 37.
19. Ibid., 38.
20. See Public Law 102-511 and Public Law 101-179, respectively.
21. USAID, Center for Democracy and Governance, *The Role of Media in Democracy: A Strategic Approach* (Washington, DC, June 1999).
22. Frederick W. Schieck, "Independent Media's Role in Building Democracy," *Global Issues*, Vol. 8, No. 1, February 2003). http://usinfo.state.gov/journals/itgic/0203/ijge/ijge0203.htm.
23. Lorne W. Craner, "Promoting Free and Responsible Media: An Integral Part of America's Foreign Policy," *Global Issues*, Vol. 8, No. 1 (Washington, DC: U.S.

Department of State, February 2003) http://usinfo.state.gov/journals/itgic/0203/ijge/ijge0203.htm.

24. USAID, *Foreign Aid in the National Interest: Promoting Freedom, Security and Opportunity* (Washington, DC: USAID, January 2003), 6.
25. Ibid.
26. United Nations Development Program, *Human Development Report 2002* (New York: Oxford University Press, 2002). The report is available at http://hdr.undp.org/reports/global/2002/en/.
27. World Bank, *World Development Report 2002, Building Institutions for Markets* (New York: Oxford University Press, 2002), 182.
28. Quoted in Ann Hudock, "Hearing the Voices of the Poor: Encouraging Good Governance and Poverty Reduction Through Media Sector Support" (Washington, DC: World Learning, 2003), 2.
29. Ann Hudock, "Democratizing the Media," unpublished paper prepared for the Aspen Institute/Ford Foundation International Roundtable on Journalism and Freedom of Expression, Queenstown, MD, November 12-14, 2003, 3.
30. Tim Carrington and Mark Nelson, "Steps to a Free, Financially Viable Media," *Global Issues*, Vol. 8, No. 1, 2003), http://usinfo.state.gov/journals/itgic/0203/ijge/ijge0203.htm.
31. Ibid.
32. Panos Institute, *Reducing Poverty: Is the World Bank's Strategy Working?* (London: Panos Institute, 2002), 28.
33. Everette Dennis and Jon Vanden Heuvel, *Emerging Voices: East European Media in Transition* (New York: Gannett Center for Media Studies, 1990). Several other reports on Central and Eastern European media were also published about the same time. See, for example, Ronald Koven *Survey of Needs of Emerging News Media in Central and Eastern Europe* (New York: World Press Freedom Committee, 1990).
34. Dennis and Vanden Heuvel, *Emerging Voices*, 1990, i.
35. Ibid.
36. Ibid.
37. Government Accountability Office, *Independent Media Development Abroad: Challenges Exist in Implementing U.S. Efforts and Measuring Results*, GAO-05-803 (Washington, DC: GAO, 2005), 1.
38. By the end of the 1990s, USAID had become the locus of U.S. government media assistance, replacing USIA, whose principal job – public diplomacy – had withered after the communist collapse of 1989, not to be revived until after the attacks of September 11, 2001. For that reason, the agency was merged into the State Department's Bureau of Education and Cultural Affairs (BECA) in October 1999, and today BECA is once again primarily in the public diplomacy business, reporting to the State Department's Under Secretary for Public Diplomacy and Public Affairs.
39. World Press Freedom Committee (WPFC), *Voices of Freedom '90: A Coordination Conference on News Media Aid Projects in Central and Eastern Europe* (Washington, DC: World Press Freedom Committee) 1990, 28-31.
40. Ronald Koven, "The New Media in the New Democracies," in WFPC, *Voices of Freedom, 1990*, 5.
41. Ibid., 6.
42. Malcolm F. Mallette, "Assistance Programs," in WFPC, *Voices of Freedom*, 1990, 11-12.
43. "Report of Marvin Stone, Chairman and President, International Media Fund," in WFPC, *Voices of Freedom*, 1990, 20.

44.   "Report of Julia Fuller, Program Officer, National Endowment for Democracy,"
in WFPC, *Voices of Freedom*, 1990, 18.

45.   "Report of Hewson Ryan, ASNE Journalists Exchange Program," in WFPC, *Voices
of Freedom*, 1990, 20.

46.   "Report of Jerry Aumente, Director, Journalism Research Institute, Rutgers University," in WFPC, *Voices of Freedom*, 1990, 12.

47.   "Report of George Krimsky, Executive Director, Center for Foreign Journalists,"
in WFPC, *Voices of Freedom*, 1990, 15.

48.   "Report of Anca Hassing, National Strategies Inc.," in WPFC, *Voices of Freedom*,
1990, 19.

49.   WPFC, *Voices of Freedom*, 1990, 29.

50.   James Miller, "Democratizing East Central Europe: Is Western Journalism Uni-
versal? Ahistorical? A Human Right?" Paper presented at the Association for
Education in Journalism and Mass Communication (AEJMC) Research Session
"Europe and the World: Comparative Mass Communication Research," London,
January 5, 2002, 7-8.

51.   Peter Gross, *Entangled Evolutions: Media and Democratization in Central Europe*
(Washington, DC: Woodrow Wilson Center Press, 2002), 174.

52.   GAO, *Independent Media Development Abroad*, 2005, 4.

53.   Monroe E. Price, Bethany Davis Noll, Daniel De Luce, *Mapping Media Assistance*
(Oxford: The Programme in Comparative Media Law & Policy, February 1, 2002),
2-5.

54.   USAID, *The Role of Media in Democracy*, 1999, 3.

55.   Ibid.

56.   The absence of uniform measures for USAID media assistance programs was a
central finding in GAO, *Independent Media Development Abroad*, 2005.

57.   For details on USAID's results frameworks, see USAID, *Handbook of Democracy
and Governance Program Indicators*, PN-ACC-390 (Washington, DC: USAID,
August 1998). See in particular the section on civil society, 115-121. The handbook
is available online at http://www.usaid.gov/our_work/democracy_and_governance/
publications/dgtpindx.html#pnacc390.

58.   Ibid., 115.

59.   Ibid., 57, 61.

60.   Price, et al., *Mapping Media Assistance*, 2002, 12.

61.   The Stability Pact was a result of UN Security Council Resolution No. 1244,
adopted on June 10, 1999.

62.   The Security Pact's web page is available at http://www.stabilitypact.org/.

63.   "Where to find those who help the media – NGOs in the OSCE world," *Freedom
and Responsibility Yearbook, 1998/1999* (Vienna: OSCE, Representative on
Freedom of the Media, 1999), 251.

64.   Connie Bruck, "The World According to Soros," *New Yorker* (January 3, 1995): 77.

65.   Lyle Crowley, "George Soros," *New York Times Magazine* (April 3, 1994): 27.

66.   Aryeh Neier, "President's Message," *1997 Soros Foundations Report*.

67.   Gordana Jankovic, Open Society Institute, author interview, Queenstown, MD,
November 14, 2003.

68.   GAO, *Independent Media Development Abroad*, 2005, 25.

69.   Ibid.

70.   USAID, *Role of Media in Democracy*, 1999, 18-35.

71.   Ibid. See also USAID Transition Initiatives: Media Programming at http://www.
usaid.gov/our_work/cross-cutting_programs/transition_initiatives/focus/media.
html.

72. See David Hulme and Michael Edwards, "NGOs, States and Donors: An Over-view," in *NGOs, States and Donors: Too Close for Comfort?*, eds. David Hulme and Michael Edwards (New York: St. Martin's Press, 1997), 8.

73. See GAO, *Independent Media Development Abroad,* 2005, 5-8.

74. The Danish Baltic Media Center closed for financial reasons in February 2005.

75. USAID, Bureau for Europe and the New Independent States, *Request for Applications: Professional Media Program, Central and Eastern Europe*, DHR-95-A-001 (Washington, DC: USAID, June 15, 1995), 29.

76. Ibid.

77. Ibid.

78. Price, et al., *Mapping Media Assistance*, 2002, 22.

79. USAID, *Role of Media in Democracy*, 1999, 9-10,

80. Price, et al., *Mapping Media Assistance*, 2002, 29.

81. See http://www.irex.org/media/index.asp.

82. Andreas Harsono, managing editor, *Pantau*, author interview, Queenstown, MD, June 1, 2000.

83. Kabral Blay-Amihere, Ghana program officer, Ford Foundation, author interview, Queenstown, MD, June 1, 2000.

84. Lin Neumann, SEAPA, author interview, Queenstown, MD, June 1, 2000, 17.

85. David Hoffman, "Beyond Public Diplomacy: Weapons of Mass Communication," *Foreign Affairs*, (March/April 2002): 83; see also David Anable, "US-style free press – best bang for buck in foreign aid," *Christian Science Monitor* (February 9, 2005) www.csmonitor.com/2005/0209/p09s01-coop.html (accessed August 11, 2005).

86. Hoffman, "Beyond Public Diplomacy," 2002.

87. Steven R. Weisman, "Under Pressure, Qatar May Sell Jazeera Station," *New York Times* (January 30, 2005): A1.

88. Sharmini Peres, IFEX, author interview, Queenstown, MD, June 2, 2000.

89. Basma El Husseiny, Egypt program officer, Ford Foundation, author interview, Queenstown, MD, May 30, 2000.

90. Monroe E. Price, ed., *Restructuring the Media in Post-Conflict Societies: Four Perspectives, the Experience of Intergovernmental and Non-Governmental Organizations.* (University of Oxford: Programme in Comparative Media Law & Policy, Centre for Socio-Legal Studies, May 2000), 1-4.

91. Ibid, 2.

92. Ibid.

93. Ralph L. Lowenstein. *PICA: Measuring World Press Freedom* (Columbia, Mo.: Freedom of Information Center, School of Journalism, University of Missouri, 1966).

94. GAO, *Independent Media Development Abroad,* 2005, 11.

95. Ibid.

96. See the "Media Sustainability Index" at www.irex.org/msi.

97. Ibid.

98. Ibid.

99. Freedom House, *Freedom of the Press, 2004* (New York: Rowman & Littlefield, 2004), xi.

100. Ibid., xii.

101. See the most recent RSF Worldwide Press Freedom Index at http://www.rsf.org/article.php3?id_article=11715.

102. Ibid.

103. GAO, *Independent Media Development Abroad*, 2005, 3.

104. See the "Media Sustainability Index" at www.irex.org/msi, xxiii.

105. Julia E. Seidler, *Exporting Democracy Without Citizens? Goals and Practices of American Agencies Providing Journalism Assistance Programs in Ukraine* (Iowa City, Iowa: University of Iowa, unpublished doctoral dissertation, May 2001), 193.
106. USAID/Western NIS Mission, *1997 Results Review and Resource Request (R4),* March 9, 1998, 93.
107. Ibid., 94.
108. Seidler, *Exporting Democracy Without Citizens?* 2001, 194.
109. USAID, *Results Review*, 1998, 94.
110. Seidler, *Exporting Democracy Without Citizens?* 2001, 195.
111. USAID, *Results Review*, 1998, 25.
112. Seidler, *Exporting Democracy Without Citizens?*, 2001, 199.
113. Ibid., 220-224.
114. Ibid.
115. Price, et al., *Mapping Media Assistance*, 2002.
116. Ross Howard, *International Media Assistance: A Review of Donor Activities and Lessons Learned.* (Amsterdam: Netherlands Institute of International Relations, Conflict Research Unit, June 2003).

4

The Civil Society Problem: Media Freedom and the "Public Interest"

"The problem of the press is confused because the critics and the apologists expect the press to...make up for all that was not foreseen in the theory of democracy." – Walter Lippmann

If media assistance is attached to democracy promotion by its importance to civil society development, just what is the nature of this relationship? The idea is this: Civil society is that realm of voluntary social relationships that exists apart from the administrative or economic spheres of life. It is where citizens are made, bound together by norms of belief and behavior. Free media and civil society are each a necessary condition for the other: media are, literally, the medium through which people express and contest their ideas; and a diverse, active civil society is presumed to be supportive of a diverse, vibrant media market. Media also connect civil society to the more formal, administrative "public sphere," where ideas and values are transformed into policies and programs. Without healthy media and civil society sectors, the theory goes, the system gets inadequate or corrupted inputs and democracy does not work properly. The system may continue to function, but it is likely produce outputs that are distinctly undemocratic.

If this sounds like a heavy burden to place on a media system – never mind the lowly journalist – it is. If it sounds unclear and unhelpful, it is that, too. Anyone who has observed conferences devoted to democratization generally and media assistance particularly has heard the term "civil society" tossed about so casually as to wonder if anyone thinks the term means anything certain. Often as not it is a proxy for other interests, including the self-interest of the speaker. That said, no one disputes the idea that civil society, whatever it is, is important to democracy, which after all is not merely a collection of institutions and formal processes. If Jacques Barzun is right that democracy is "about how the wheels turn," citizens presumably have a role in the turning that goes beyond just showing up on election day. If citizens do not turn all the wheels, or even the most important ones, they can do a lot to gum them up, and without them, democratic governance loses its democratic character, even its legitimacy. It is the crisis of citizenship in the global order of international organizations, governmental and non-governmental, that has given rise to the term "democratic deficit." The term was first coined to describe the bureaucratic superstate that is the European Union, in which decisions taken in Brussels or Strasbourg are far removed from the daily concerns of voters in Stuttgart or Toledo. Indeed, as David Held has written, the business of democracy assistance exists within a "democratic paradox":

> From Africa to Eastern Europe, Asia to Latin America, more and more nations and groups are championing the idea of democracy, but they are doing so at just that moment when the very efficacy of democracy as a national form of political organization appears open to question. As substantial areas of human activity are progressively organized on a regional or global level, the fate of democracy, and of the independent nation-state in particular, is fraught with difficulty.[1]

The United Nations puts the matter similarly:

> Democracy is widely argued to be essential for the fulfillment of individual and collective aspirations, the articulation of interests, and the nurturing of civil society. Globalizing forces have underpinned the dissemination of this message. The spread of democratic governance seems inevitable. Yet the march of democratization is highly contested, and there is little consensus on what democracy is or should be. While the leading international actors are pursuing a rigorous liberal agenda based upon the belief that democracy and market-oriented economics are conducive to a peaceful "international society," many voices are resisting the model of democracy that this presumes. The proliferation of democracy defies a universal model. Moreover, this proliferation cannot obscure the problems that have appeared in many democratic countries. Established democracies are increasingly mired in disillusionment, stagnation, and bureaucratic overload. The procedural tenets for democracy may well exist, but the spirit of democracy - a public sphere of debate in the context of political transparency, accountability and representation - is questionable.
>
> The parallel transition to free-market economics and democracy has likewise posed difficulties for many countries. A number of democratic experiments are in jeopardy, and democracy has not been able to meet all the demands that confront these transitional societies. In some circumstances, democratization has proved to be a politically destabilizing and socially uncomfortable process.[2]

The sum of it is that as democracy has become more ubiquitous, it has also become weaker, both conceptually and objectively. At the level of global governance, Keohane and Nye use the term "networked mini-malism" to describe the matrix of nation-states, IGOs, NGOs and trans-national corporations that run the world, however imperfectly.[3] In this matrix, only nation-states are sovereign within the ordinary, democratic meaning of that term—that is to say, accountable to voters. But states are less powerful than they used to be; Robert Dahl has compared their role in the international system to that of local governments within nation-states.[4] In normative terms, the problem for global democracy is figuring out who "we the people" are, how they might meaningfully participate as citizens, and how representation should operate, if it operates at all. Sociologist Herbert Gans has questioned "whether today's representa-tive democracy even has much need for citizens other than on election day."[5] A common way to measure democratic legitimacy, for example, is to look at political inputs and outputs, but in the international arena the link between popular activity and policy is tenuous at best. Consider the fact that the protests of some 11 million people in 800 cities around the world on February 15, 2003 – what the *New Yorker* characterized as the largest one-day protest in history – had absolutely no effect on the decision of the U.S. and British governments to attack Iraq a few weeks later. An alternative view might emphasize the work of NGOs and other activist groups, but as Ann Florini and P.J. Simmons write it is hardly democratic to argue that "global problem solving [should] be left to a loose agglomeration of unelected activists."[6]

With respect to political outputs, which give elected governments legitimacy, citizens care about such things as economic and personal security. But, as Fritz Scharpf argued in his 1999 book *Governing in Europe*, such forms of security are steadily disappearing.[7] For more than two decades, government spending on public goods (schools, basic research, health services, transportation) and on the social safety net (jobs programs, unemployment insurance, pensions) has been in de-cline in Western democracies, pressured by the global financial markets and by political and economic policies that have strongly favored the privatization of what were once largely state functions. In many cases, these policies have led to innovation, better services, and lower prices for consumers, most obviously in telecommunications and air travel, but they also deny citizens many of the services they most expect from government. The Germans term this process *amerikanische Verhaltnisse* – "American conditions." In developing nations, these socioeconomic policies, enforced by the World Bank and the International Monetary

Fund, have forced governments to cut social spending as a condition of assistance. Everywhere, state regulation has been challenged by the market as the best determinant of the public interest--and as most consistent with "freedom"—in areas such as environmental quality, food safety, workplace safety, and financial services. With some important exceptions (Russia, for example), the only area of public spending that has remained conspicuously untouched around the world, and in some cases has been significantly increased, is spending for military and police forces.

Taken together, these trends raise questions about what purposes the withered state is supposed to serve, and more particularly about what popular sovereignty is supposed to mean. Presumably even weakened states will always be able to command some loyalty from their citizens, but it may be loyalty of the most destructive and undemocratic kind. As former European Parliament President Klaus Hansch once said with respect to Europe, at the very moment when governments are losing their ability to deliver the goods and services their citizens need, citizens are growing ever more nostalgic for the sense of "belonging" that is at the root of nation-state identity.[8] Against all this, the global security challenge to democratic governments in the aftermath of September 11, 2001, is to identify, assist, and reclaim the world's so-called failed states – Afghanistan, Sudan, Liberia, Sierra Leone, the Democratic Republic of Congo, Somalia, and others – from the desperation that produces global terrorism, and to prevent other states – such as Zimbabwe, Colombia, and Sri Lanka – from failing. It is not clear how established democracies are supposed to do this even as they are busy rewriting the terms of their obligations to their own citizens.

At least two things are notable about these developments. One is that they draw attention to the many and often unsatisfactory uses of the term "democracy." Journalists and politicians will often use it in the most casual way to describe a country that has managed to hold an election (or, better, two) more or less free of fraud. Others use the term formally, to describe a system that combines universal suffrage, regular fair and free elections, governmental agencies accountable to elected officials, and a legal system that protects against arbitrary state action and provides for free expression. Neither of these usages speaks to whether and how citizens engage with their government, or to how power is distributed among citizens, and so both ignore the modern emphasis on civil society and participatory democracy. With that in mind, what follows is first a discussion of civil society, what it is and how it varies in different kinds of post-transition societies. After that we consider the separate but related problem of the "public interest" and its implications for how media systems are structured, whom they should serve, and how. Western assistance providers and certainly many U.S. journalists assume that in a democracy a healthy, functioning media system is a more or less natural thing. It's not. Media systems are the products of political choices, and few if any can be merely defended by appeals to the public interest.

Media Freedom and Civil Society

It is common to read in the literature on media and democratization generalized descriptions of the public interest, some of them quite thoughtful. Hudock, for example, defines democratic media systems as those "that provide space for expression of diverse views, supply relevant and timely information to citizens, and hold the government to account by serving as a check on elite power."[9] James Curran has defined the ideal democratic media system similarly, but with greater emphasis on public participation, saying it "should be organized in a way that enables diverse social groups and organizations to express alternative viewpoints.... It should assist collective organizations to mobilize support; help them to operate as representative vehicles for the views of their supporters; and aid them to register effective protests and develop and promulgate alternatives."[10]

In the business of media assistance, this focus on public participation explains both the emphasis on civil society and the attention to reforming media institutions. Each contributes to the larger, substantive goal of democratization: to "contribute to a more competitive or participatory political system as well as to the institutionalized diffusion and fragmentation of political power conferred by the electorate upon a chosen group of representatives."[11] A recent Dutch overview of the media assistance industry describes media and civil society programs as virtually one in the same:

> In the process of democratization, a reliable media and supportive infrastructure operate in symbiotic relationship with a healthy civil society.... Donors have increasingly funded indigenous and international media rights-watching organizations monitoring and lobbying against censorship and infringements upon media freedoms as well as journalists' professional and personal freedoms. In addition, media programmes have supported organizations monitoring media content and performance as a reflection of a society's political freedoms and level of democracy. The international community has also directed support to the creation of self-governing councils among journalists and media owners in order to encourage professionalism and to recognize good journalism. Although often not considered part of media assistance, other initiatives

aim at fostering a more mature information culture. In such a culture, NGOs and citizens are more confident in having recourse to the media to communicate their views and in using the media as a forum for debate.[12]

While by no means all aid providers think of media assistance this way (certainly many journalists and journalism NGOs do not), many do link civil society to media development, both conceptually and programmatically. The majority of USAID's media assistance programs fall under its civil society portfolio, and many large NGOs that do media work will also justify media programs, implicitly if not explicitly, as agents of civil society formation. If objectionable in some ways, the link is understandable: No matter how one understands the role of the media in a democracy, a primary purpose is to inform the public on issues of importance and thus to make public participation in elections meaningful. Secondarily, of the many challenges journalists face in consolidated democracies, democratizing states and of course also in semi-authoritarian countries, one they all share is a policy, regulatory and social environment they perceive to be, in one way or another, hostile to independent, professional journalism. By the power of their voices, journalists presumably have the ability to change that environment through their engagement with and support of civil society associations.

The idea of civil society has its origins in the Scottish Enlightenment of the eighteenth century, though it received new visibility and celebrity when the political opposition to authoritarian governments in Central and Eastern Europe embraced the concept in the years preceding the collapse of the Soviet Union. Over the past two decades untold aid monies and conferences have been devoted to civil society, and a large literature has bloomed on the subject. Some of that literature is analytically helpful; much is conceptually muddy at best. Scholars debate the definition of the term; journalists use it to mean a variety of things (including simple civility) and have invoked it as a remedy for any number of political and professional ills in both developing and developed media systems. One commentator notes that "rarely has so heavy an analytic cargo been strapped on the back of so slender a conceptual beast."[13]

If the term "civil society" covers a vast conceptual ground,[14] it can be summarized as that realm of voluntary association outside the state and the market which acts as an organized counterweight to the power of the state, and whose existence is thus presumed to be a critical component of democratic transition and consolidation, perhaps – in so far as civil society functions as a stand-in for public participation in political life

– the critical component. [15] Lester Salamon and his colleagues equate civil society with the non-profit sector, defining civil society organizations very broadly as those that are private (institutionally separate from the state), non-profit and self-governing. [16] Understood this way, civil society is one of the major actors in global governance, along with nation states and international government organizations, and a multi-trillion dollar industry that comprises one-eighth of the world economy. [17] In the literature on democratization, political scientist Juan Linz defines civil society as "that arena of polity where self-organizing groups, movements and individuals, relatively autonomous from the state, attempt to articulate values, create associations and solidarities, and advance their interests." Civil society can include large social movements (most notably, today, feminism, environmentalism and human rights), and in its modern form places renewed emphasis on ethnic, racial and religious identities and includes a wide array of single-issue groups with varying commitments to pluralism and democracy. [18] So far as democracy and democratization are concerned, Linz says, civil society is important because it is where political pluralism comes from – again, where citizens are made. [19] At the level of global governance, international NGOs are often identified the locus of international civil society, though their claim to representation is not altogether convincing. [20]

At the level of state governance, the institutions that comprise the non-governmental sector of society – churches, neighborhoods, families, clubs and civic groups, and so on – are especially important to civil society because they perform a number of important social functions: they provide a buffer between the individual and the power of the state and the market; they create social capital; and they develop democratic values and habits. Civil society, in short, provides to democracy what the law, with its rules and sanctions, cannot – social trust, social authority, civic virtue and vision – the stuff of citizenship. At its best, civil society is about social responsibility. Indeed, the idea as it has developed in modern times stands in opposition to the Western tradition of liberal individualism and its tendency to see people either as bundles of legal rights and entitlements, cut off from any higher moral claims, or as consumers motivated only by economic self-interest. [21]

Even accepting all this, it is not clear precisely why civil society is critical to democratization or how it actually connects citizens to the machinery of governance. Perhaps most troublesome is the view of civil society as a tolerant and cooperative space, when in fact its oppositional and fragmented character might just as easily be an obstacle to democratic consolidation, particularly where governments are weak. Ample evidence suggest that civil society can be anti-democratic, even disastrously so.[22] And even where it is benevolent, it is something of a mystery how civil society's benefits are supposed to find their way into the more formal realm of "political society."

In the democratization business, the concept of civil society can be even more confusing. Anyone who has spent much time in or around meetings of aid providers might be forgiven for thinking that civil society is a kind of catch basket, a category of last resort for any of a multitude of unique and complex social, economic and political problems that do not fit under any of the industry's other rubrics. Its presumptive neutral character, too, can be a useful place to advance as democratic principles what are in fact the political preferences of aid providers, program implementers and recipients.

Leaving aside problems of definition and application, journalism and civil society would seem to have some obvious common interests. Both produce information and churn meaning from it. News organizations act as informal hubs in civil society networks, taking in information and sending critical bits of it back out in every direction, in the process composing a coherent (if not necessarily an accurate) profile of public attitudes and values. Civil society associations and independent media organizations are thus interdependent, and may even overlap. In developing and transition states this is especially common. A social group or NGO might have its own publicity arm, for instance, and distribute its own newspaper or radio program; a media organization might actively seek to identify and serve specific communities of interest, for example an ethnic or racial minority, women or immigrants, farm laborers or factory workers. The Lebanon-based Human Rights Media Network (HRMN), for example, is a network of local and regional human rights groups and individual activists that report and distributes information about human rights abuses and achievements across the Middle East and North Africa. HRMN was founded and is directed by Kamal el Batal, a civil engineer by training. The Network's website publishes in both English and Arabic the work of stringers throughout the region, as well as reports from national and international newswires. The goal of HRMN and other organizations like it is to weave expressive freedoms, including press freedom, into a growing democratic fabric. Media and civil society each is presumed to be each a necessary condition for the other.

In practice, however, they are not always viewed this way. USAID, as noted in the previous chapter, places media development in a supporting role to civil society promotion in the hierarchy of its democratization objectives. That is to say, independent media are primarily a means to an end, not an end in themselves. It is not at all uncommon to hear aid workers, particularly those whose work does not include media development, describe media this way, often with a distinct tone of impatience for journalists whose view of their independence does not include acting as the publicity arm of civil society groups and their causes. Journalists, in turn, will sometimes find themselves facing the most severe pressure on their editorial decision-making not from governments, but from civil society groups angered by what they view as unfair news coverage, and whose dedication to the cause of freedom does not extend so far as to tolerate inquiries into their own activities. This can be especially true in countries such as Bosnia-Herzegovina, where the enormous number of international NGOs, IGOs and local NGOs located there together form a kind of *de facto* government. Very often these organizations do not see themselves as the legitimate subject of critical news coverage, and many of them – despite their professed dedication to transparency in governance – are not themselves very transparent. Local journalists, of course, will see the situation quite differently, and often will complain that these civil society organizations are unprofessional, uncooperative and even disingenuous in discussing their programs. Civil society and independent media may therefore be necessary conditions for each other, but neither is a sufficient condition for the other. Their interests may overlap, but they are not the same.

Journalism fits awkwardly into the mix of institutions that comprise civil society, though the fit will depend on how one understands journalism's core purpose in a democracy. As Premesh Chandran, the CEO of *Malaysiakini*, the only independent news source in Malaysia, explained it to me, civil society's job is to "blow the whistle" when the government acts in ways that are repressive or irresponsible, and it is then the journalist's job to pursue and report the story. This view, or something like it, is not uncommon in democratizing states, and it is one reason both journalists and aid organizations consider civil society formation so important. In their view, the journalist's job is both to build civic consciousness and social solidarity (as in the "civic" or "public" journalism movement in the United States, for example) and to expose government corruption and incompetence.

In important ways, however, Chandran's formulation runs directly contrary to the Western "fourth estate" or "liberal" view of journalism, which follows closely on Western free expression theory and sees journalism as institutionalizing the expressive freedoms that provide a moderating influence on sources of power. Because those sources of power include civil society, this model is the least deferential to it. Put another way, in the fourth estate formulation, the journalist "blows the whistle" and civil society acts on the information. (In real life, of course, these roles are not exclusive, and journalists and NGOs will act both as "whistle-blower" and "investigator.") Finally, civil society can fit comfortably with a conception of journalism that is essentially developmental, which understands its role as promoting socio-economic change through education, economic expansion, and growth. The problem with this view is in the way governments typically use it. In Asia particularly, but also Africa and Latin America, nominally democratic governments continue to justify strict controls of the news media in the name of socioeconomic development and political stability. Those controls include restrictions on ownership, national security and sedition laws, and annual licensing requirements.

Of course, these conceptions of journalistic purpose are not exclusive of one another. In either a consolidated Western democracy or in an Asian transition state, for instance, a news organization might understand its mission as promoting public engagement in civic life *and* promoting free expression *and* supporting economic development. *Malaysiakini*, for example, is an online newspaper in a country where print publications are restricted to the handful of companies with licenses to print them, and licenses go overwhelmingly to party-affiliated newspapers, few of them worth reading.[23] *Malaysiakini* exists only because it has exploited the government's decision not to regulate the Internet as part of its policy to make the country an attractive site for information-technology industries. In that respect, *Malaysiakini*'s future is closely linked with the success of the government's economic development policies – policies that to succeed will presumably compel the ruling Barisan Nasional coalition to allow an increasingly freer and larger space for information exchange.

In the democratization industry, civil society and media are linked in yet another way: their fortunes will often seem to co-vary. That is to say, an active and idea diverse media is apt to co-exist with an active and idea diverse civil society. Discussions on both topics, therefore, typically turn on a few core concerns. With respect to civil society, the primary problem is (and presumably for some time will remain) building civil society; in many countries and regions, civil society is for one reason or another weak or non-existent, and sometimes where it does exist it is not very pluralist, or worse, it is anti-democratic. Elsewhere the problem is how to reinvigorate a civil society sector that in the years after democratic transition has withered.

Civil Society, the State and Democracy

Scholarship on democratization argues that the character and strength of civil society institutions depend above all on the type of regime that preceded the transition period. Political scientist Juan Linz, for example, has argued that the paths to democratic transition and consolidation vary according to whether the deposed regime was authoritarian, totalitarian, post-totalitarian or sultanistic.[24] So far as civil society is concerned, the defining characteristic of totalitarianism is the complete lack of political, economic or social pluralism, all of which the state has tried systematically to obliterate. Post-totalitarian regimes allow the emergence of some forms of social pluralism, but usually that pluralism is located within the regime itself, such as an opposition faction within the ruling party. Authoritarian regimes typically have civil society institutions that evolve outside the regime – in the private space of culture, art, religiosity, and also in the economy – and which can be very strong but are not necessarily democratic in impulse. China, for example, has seen its civil society sector grow dramatically in recent years, but that growth has not been accompanied by any significant democratization movement. In sultanistic societies, Linz writes, the defining characteristic of the regime is unrestrained personal leadership of the kind that typified Marcos' Philippines, Haiti under the Duvaliers, Mobutu Sese Seko's Zaire (Congo), Suharto's Indonesia or Iran under the Shah. In such societies all forms of pluralism are precarious, and civil society, where it exists, is subject to the whims of the ruler, for whom the state and the military are personal instruments to be used at the ruler's discretion. With each type of non-democratic regime, Linz argues, the most important element in the development of civil society after the transition is the concurrent development of the rule of law and the guarantee of civil liberties.

The implication of this argument is important, and sometimes lost on media assistance providers: The most effective guarantee of a healthy civil society is a strong state, and the struggle between civil society and the state is not a zero-sum game. Indeed in the absence of a strong state civil society can easily erupt in civil war – most of the armed conflicts since the end of the Cold War have been intrastate affairs in ethnically and religiously pluralist countries where the proliferation of civil society associations devoted to narrow causes threatened or destroyed democratic transition. In a 1998 editorial sharply critical of "civil society romantics," the Indian newspaper *The Hindu* observed that "civil society finds as much space for casteist, class, communal and patriarchal projects as for movements challenging all these, and dominant structures in civil society can neutralize democratic agendas."[25] Indonesian journalist Bimo Nugroho speaking of his own country's experience, has observed that weak or corrupt states can politicize civil society (as Suharto, for example, did in the years before the 1998 collapse by creating Islamic youth groups as a token form of political pluralism) and thus exacerbate rather than ameliorate social differences.[26]

This is as true in global governance as it is in national governance. Several commentators have noted that the global activities of many NGOs and IGOs have played a role in triggering ethnic nationalism and religious fundamentalism, both of which tear at the state, encourage human rights violations and provoke humanitarian crises. In short, civil society gains that come at the expense of a weakened state, while predictable and perhaps even healthy in the short term, may not be supportive of democratization in the long term. Political theorist Michael Walzer writes,

> The state itself is unlike all the other associations. It both frames civil society and occupies space within it. It fixes the boundary conditions and the basic rules of all associational activity. It compels association members to think about a common good, beyond their own conceptions of the good life.... And across the entire range of association, individual men and women need to be protected against the power of officials, employers, experts, party bosses, factory foremen, directors, priests, parents, patrons; and small and weak groups need to be protected against large and powerful ones. For civil society, left to itself, generates radically unequal power relationships which only state power can challenge.[27]

That is not to say that civil society joined with a strong state automatically results in political pluralism. Even where governments are strong and ostensibly liberal they are not necessarily supportive of civil society. Running roughly concurrent with the most recent global wave of democratization has been the rise in Western developed societies of what some scholars call "authoritarian liberalism," the process by which the role of the market in social organization has been maximized and that of civil society diminished, sometimes with strong impetus from governments.[28] The British government under Prime Minister Margaret Thatcher, for example, attacked the conditions of civil society by trying to restrict the activities of trade unions, to limit press freedom (including in particular that of the British Broadcasting Corporation), to curtail the rights of criminal defendants, to make local authorities more responsive to the central government, to politicize the police, and so on.

Among authoritarian states, many – China, Vietnam and Iran, to name a few – have allowed political, social and economic liberalization to enlarge the space for civil society operations, but only because the government views those operations as central to its own goals of control. In China, for example, privately published newspapers now far outnumber state papers and engage in investigative reporting and muckraking. Journalists have to carefully self-censor themselves, but not always; when the ruling party began its own highly publicized anticorruption campaign in the late 1990s, it encouraged the private print press to join in. Chinese television features live news, call-in programs and celebrity interviews, and the government allows a great deal of general news and entertainment programming to enter the country, but the growth of electronic media is largely the result of market reforms and the government's desire to invest in growth industries, and the government does not hesitate to jam international broadcasts critical of the regime or to shut down popular Internet sites. Groups that represent broad portions of the population (such as women's groups) and whose aims are not clearly focused on officially stated goals typically have a harder time establishing themselves. Often when they do it is because they undertake some "acceptable" activity; the government looks favorably upon groups that give support to women living in poverty, for example, but not to those that object to the official economic policies that keep them there.[29]

Many democratization studies note that in some regions of the world – Pacific Asia and the Middle East, particularly – the dividing line between the government and society is neither clear nor immutable. The Chinese language, it is said, has multiple terms for "state," but none for "civil society." Nomenclature aside, a number of scholars argue that civil society does not really exist in Pacific Asia, at least not in the liberalizing sense in which Western political theorists use the term. The thrust of the argument focuses on an "illiberal middle class" that emphasizes "community rather than autonomy and moral certainty rather than tolerance" and which has a substantial economic stake in the stability of the public sector.[30] One piece of evidence in this theory is the extent to which press freedom is curtailed throughout the region; self-censorship is common and where it fails, as one commentator put it in a description of the South Korean media, the state is regularly "on hand to offer Confucian guidance."[31]

Journalists throughout the world describe similarly illiberal civil society tendencies in their own countries or regions. In Egypt, says Basma el Husseiny, a former Ford Foundation media program director, society itself is "nonplural" and thus there is fairly low tolerance among the public for diverse ideas or even free expression generally. At present, she says, the most potent elements of Egyptian civil society are the Islamic groups that "provide educational institutions, provide services to the community, and work on conservative legislation."[32] One measure of their effectiveness can be found in the 2001 decision by Cairo's al-Azhar University, for a millennium the unrivaled center of higher education in the Islamic world, to embark on a campaign to weed out "vice" from Arabic literature, film, theater, music and scholarship.[33] In Malaysia and Indonesia, Islamic civil society groups bring pressure of various kinds – legal and extralegal – on news organizations whose views on issues from immigration to women's rights they find offensive. Konstanty Gebert, a former *samizdat* journalist and now a columnist for *Gazeta Wyborcza* in Warsaw, has made a similar observation about the political influence of Catholic and Jewish fundamentalists in Poland and Israel, respectively. The same could be said of Catholic, Protestant and Jewish groups in the United States, many of which monitor news organizations, universities and NGOs for the expression of ideas and opinions they view as hostile to their own religious or political beliefs.

Media and Civil Society: The Chilean Experience

To the extent that media freedom and civil society development are in fact interdependent, what goals do they have in common? Journalists and democracy promoters in transition states will typically name two. The first is the creation of social capital—"enhancing the bonds of community, building citizenship and promoting individuality," as one Filipino journalist described it to me. The second is "building a culture of free expression," a process that usually emphasizes encouraging the "watchdog" role of the press and providing citizens with access to news and information. A quite different conception of the media's contribution to civil society focuses on providing citizens access to the instruments of communication, perhaps even against the prerogatives of those who own them, and especially where ownership is concentrated in the state or in private centers of economic power. These general concerns are joined in a larger one: How does a society actually do these things, that is, create *and* sustain media that engage the public in democratically centered discourse?

A useful case study for considering this question is Chile, a country typically regarded as one of the true successes of the third wave, and economically the most vibrant state in Latin America. Chile emerged from bureaucratic authoritarian rule with the election of a Christian Democratic President, Patricio Aylwin, in 1989, around the same time much of South America returned to civilian rule after more than a decade dominated by right-wing military governments. The modern Latin American political experience is unique in many ways, not least in the fact that the generals who ruled there did so with the aid of the United States government, which in the name of democracy helped to launch numerous dictatorships. Officially, U.S. policy in Latin America in the years following World War II was to fight communism. In 1961 President John F. Kennedy had announced an "Alliance for Progress," a sort of Marshall Plan for the region. For several decades the United States provided direct military, financial and political support as part of its Pan-American alliance against communism, and particularly, in Latin America's case, against internal "enemies of freedom": labor, the poor, the intelligentsia.[34]

Chile's experience was particularly tragic. "No other Latin American country could equal Chile's record of constitutional government," writes historian John Charles Chasteen. "For years, Chilean democracy had negotiated major ideological differences,"[35] but following the presidential victory of socialist-communist Salvadore Allende and his Popular Unity coalition in 1970—and despite the fact that Allende disavowed violent revolution in favor of constitutional process—the U.S. Central Intelligence Agency adopted a "firm and continuing policy," in the words of the agency itself, "that Allende be overthrown by a coup."[36] The United States embarked on an economic war against Chile, and in 1973, under General Augusto Pinochet Ugarte, the Chilean military overthrew Allende's constitutional government in what turned out to be "the bloodiest takeover in the history of Latin America."[37] The country would not emerge from military rule until Aylwin took office in 1990, though the military—and Pinochet—have remained powerful figures in the Chilean transition, and Chileans continue to reconcile themselves with their legacy.

The experience of Chile in the final years of the Pinochet regime illustrates the surge of civil society and media activity that often precedes political transition as well as the difficulty of sustaining that level of mobilization after the non-democratic government has been toppled. Faride Zeran, director of the journalism school at the University of Chile, says that a vibrant "independent press helped Chilean society to overcome dictatorship at the ballot box and made it possible for people to overcome their fears,"[38] but since 1989 the independent press has withered. During the decade of transition that followed the 1988 elections, Zeran said, "We did away with what Pinochet could not undo in 17 years."[39]

Much of the independent press of which Zeran speaks had had an organic relationship with political parties that were illegal under the Pinochet government. As such it was also an elite press, its audience limited to the upper strata of Chilean society. Without question those media were important incubators of dissent and principled opposition to the military regime, but most students of the Chilean transition point to television, the country's only true mass medium, as the more critical element in Pinochet's electoral defeat. Ironically, television's rise to prominence was at least in part the result of Pinochet's efforts to modernize the country's communications system, to place it in private hands, and to orient it toward the market and away from a politically focused print press that depended heavily on the state. One consequence of that modernization was a six-fold increase in television set ownership between 1970 and 1983, such that television penetration had reached 95 percent at the time of the 1988 plebiscite.[40]

It was that geographic and demographic reach more than its editorial content that made television singularly important to democratic transition. Until 1988 Chilean television had offered no political debate; broadcast news under the Pinochet regime was whatever the regime said it was and typically showed political opponents only in a judicial context, where they were portrayed as criminals. Editorially independent broadcasting had ceased following the 1973 coup, when radio stations, magazines and newspapers belonging to Unidad Popular, the left-wing coalition that had supported Allende, had been confiscated and either held by the military government or sold to private firms. Media belonging to other parties, such as the Christian Democrats, were not officially closed but rather hounded out of existence. The state television network, TVN, and all other television broadcasters came under the control of Pinochet-appointed university presidents. Within a few years the military government ended the practice of providing public financing to television, and in 1977 ended all restrictions on television advertising, thus creating a unique situation where state-controlled channels were financed by the private sector.[41]

In 1987 this state of affairs began to change with the visit of Pope John Paul II, the first ever papal visit to the overwhelmingly Catholic country. Though the government tried to orchestrate television coverage of the visit in its favor, it was hard put to deny or suppress the pope's public call for a return to Chile's democratic traditions. "The result," writes one commentator, "was to legitimate an ethos antagonistic to the authoritarian regime, an ethos that would eventually serve as the basis for the victory of the 'No' side in the 1988 plebiscite."[42] In advance of the plebiscite and under the rules of the government's National Television Council, the opposition received fifteen minutes of airtime each day, though it was otherwise banned from news and public affairs programs. The opposition's brief message was juxtaposed with the government's own fifteen-minute message in thirty-minute programs that aired between 10:45 P.M. and 11:15 P.M. on weekdays, noon and 12:30 P.M. on weekends, time slots the government had chosen to ensure the smallest possible audience. To the government's great chagrin, the program drew enormous audiences and became the topic of public discussion throughout the country, thus allowing the opposition to surmount the enormous obstacles to defeating Pinochet at the ballot box: It had to overcome the negative images that the regime had used to portray it as inefficient and violent, even as it offered no candidate or program of its own; it had to convince people cowed by fifteen years of state terror that a "NO" vote against the government would not result in reprisals; and it had to explain that even if Pinochet lost the plebiscite he would remain in power for a full year before there would be a presidential election.[43]

To meet these challenges the opposition turned its media campaign over almost entirely to a team of producers, advertising executives, reporters and political scientists who chose to attack Pinochet with the modern techniques of democratic campaigning: focus groups and polls designed to ascertain voters' concerns, and public relations strategies for targeting undecided voters, especially women and the young. Instead of trying to counter the government's relentless negativity and scare tactics, the opposition chose the motto "We are more" and was positive and issue-focused. Rather than devote its entire fifteen-minute broadcasts to single topics, it did short vignettes on issues ranging from poverty and health to exile and torture, all hosted by a well-known personality and featuring musical jingles, comic sketches and the personal testimony of common citizens. Pinochet became a target of humor intended to dispel his image of political invincibility, and painful subjects such as the "disappeared" were treated respectfully, as the basis for national reconciliation rather than division.

So successful was the television campaign that it became a news story in its own right, covered by the nation's print media. Importantly, where the opposition's television campaign had made the conscious decision not to respond to the government's attacks, the print media covering the campaign *did* respond, disputing the government's arguments and thus providing a valuable complement to the television campaign. This activity underscored the fact that while the television campaign was critical to political mobilization, the print media performed the essential task of providing information. In that role the print media were among those associations that laid the groundwork for mobilization in the realm of civil society, contributing to and interacting with the social organizations and the political opposition that Pinochet had tried to eradicate, then ignored and finally misjudged. The television campaign, in turn, reinforced activity that went on in communities and in face-to-face contact with voters.

With few exceptions, says Zeran, the dynamism that existed among media in the years immediately before and after the plebiscite is now gone. Among the principal alternative weeklies that promoted democratization were *Cauce*, *Analisis* and *APSI*, all now defunct. Much of the opposition press had depended for a significant portion of its financing on grants from foundations and political parties, and when those sources dried up circulation and advertising revenue did not suffice to pay the bills. Some print media that campaigned for democracy did for a time successfully appeal to broader and more diverse audiences, but they, too, have closed. The last of the important opposition weeklies, *Hoy*, closed for financial reasons in 1998, as did the independent daily *La Epoca*, which had been founded in 1987 and was generally credited for high-quality reporting leading up to the election. *La Epoca* was unable to service its debt from sales and unable to attract advertisers after the transition because of advertiser discomfort with the paper's editorial view. Today Chile's newspaper market is dominated by two large and conservative conglomerates, El Mercurio, S.A., publisher of the Santiago daily *El Mercurio*, and Consorcio Periodistico, S.A. (COPESA), whose flagship paper is *La Tercera*. Both organizations gave political support to and received financial support from the former military government.[44] Allende had tried unsuccessfully to nationalize the newspaper industry, and had had a particularly hostile relationship with *El Mercurio*, which received financial support from the CIA.[45] A March 2005 report commissioned by the Chilean government on the human rights abuses of the Pinochet years stated unequivocally that *El Mercurio* and *La Tercera* knew about the torture of political prisoners by the military regime, and knowingly lied about it in news reports.[46]

There are a few "alternative" voices in Chile's print press today, mostly famously the *Clinic*, a magazine created in 1998 by the political alliance Concertacion (on behalf of presidential candidate Ricardo Lagos) when a Spanish judged ordered Pinochet's arrest and extradition upon the ex-dictator's visit to the London Clinic (hence the paper's name). The *Clinic* was to serve an openly political purpose – to derive political capital from Pinochet's detention – and Concertacion abandoned the paper four months and eight editions after launching it. Today the *Clinic* survives as a garish and outlandish bi-weekly that earns almost all its revenue from kiosk sales; mainstream advertisers shun the publication because it is bizarre. The *Clinic* is primarily tabloid spectacle—photographs of nude women and outlandish, made-up stories – with sporadic bits of political satire and real news thrown in. According to publisher Pablo Dittborn, it is because of its obvious outrageousness that the paper escapes libel suits from Chile's famously hypersensitive public officials.[47] But the *Clinic* also covers topics like abortion and divorce that the mainstream media will not, and, unusual in Chile, it shows little respect for Catholicism. When Pope Benedict XVI was elected in May 2005, for example, the *Clinic*'s cover photograph depicted the new pontiff with the head of a German Shepard.[48] More notably, the *Clinic* was the only periodical in the country to cover the 2005 government report that linked *La Tercera* and *El Mercurio* (and particularly *El Mercurio's* owners, the Edwards family) with the abuses of the old regime. According to Chile's Circulation and Readership Verification Association, the *Clinic* is now the sixth-highest circulation among magazines in the country (with more than 230,000 readers) and the second-most read publication of any kind in Santiago behind the Sunday *El Mercurio*.[49]

Another more traditional (six-day-a-week) newspaper, *Diario Siete*, appeared in early 2005 as the successor to the now defunct independent investigative magazine *Sieto+7* and quickly made its mark with a series of stories on the foreign bank accounts and corporations around the world where Pinochet and his family hid more than $27 million earned from off-budget spending and kick-backs from arms sales when the general was president. *Diario Siete's* ownership is divided evenly between the original investors from *Sieto+7* and COPESA, which handles printing and distribution. In the spring of 2005, some Chilean observers speculated that COPESA's investment was a strategic one in advance a presidential election. Juan Pablo Cardenas, director of Radio Universidad de Chile and a former editor at *Analisis*, said:

> COPESA is simply doing business. They are doing business for the Concertacion. [COPESA owner] Saich sees that [conservative candidate] Lavin's campaign is weak enough that it could mean the fourth consecutive Concertacion government, so he releases a new newspaper for a while, to do a good business and to be in favor of what could be another Concertacion government. But if he finds out Lavin could win, he might let the newspaper fold.[50]

In January 2006, Socialist Michelle Bachelet, the Concertacion candidate, became Chile's first woman president. Bachelet is the daughter of a an Air Force officer who was arrested, tortured and killed by the military regime in 1984, and as a child she had been held with her mother at the detention center at Villa Grimaldi.

Television, which in Chile as throughout Latin America came of age in a period dominated by military governments, has since 1989 increased its standing as the nation's principal mass medium. TVN is now self-financing and subject to the same ratings pressures as other private broadcasters and cable channels. At the same time, TVN is subject to government oversight and interference, just as all media are subject to prosecution under the country's media laws, most notably its "contempt of authority" provisions in the criminal code, the state security law and the code of military justice. All these provisions (known in the region as desacato laws) allow public officials, including judges and military officers, to bring criminal charges against news organizations for virtually any kind of criticism.[51] Under pressure from the United States, the Chilean legislature has since 2001 debated either repealing or reforming seven different provisions, but as yet has made little progress.[52]

Most worrisome, says Sebastian Brett of Human Rights Watch, is that Chileans do not seem to care much that their news media are so singularly conservative and uncritical, nor do they perceive their relative lack of choice in this regard or the government's punitive hostility to criticism as a threat to or limitation on their own expressive rights. "If freedom of speech is the oxygen of democracy," Brett asks, "why are there not people in the streets asking for air to breathe? I remember in the early 1990s there were people wearing gags on their faces standing outside of court buildings protesting. The Chilean Journalists Union led this protest. Now, ten years into democracy, no one is in the streets anymore. What's the reason?"[53] According to Zeran, the problem is that of the country's forty journalism schools, thirty-three are "controlled by the economic right" and "the question of freedom of expression is not on their curriculum."[54]

Zeran's observation raises recurring and fundamental questions about "democratic" media: What constitutes "media pluralism" in a society, and what role should governments and markets play in creating and sustaining it? One could argue, for example, that Chile's media *are* both modern *and* pluralistic. Indeed, unlike most democratizing countries Chile did not witness any fundamental changes in its communications system after the fall of the old regime. Rather, the process of privatization that began under Pinochet has continued under subsequent, democratic governments, most notably with the privatization of Radio Nacional in 1994. Chilean television, at least, has also been globalized: Megavision is owned partly by the Mexican broadcasting giant Televisa, and the television operation of the Universidad de Chile is now 49 percent owned by the Venezuelan consortium Venevision. All of this activity has had the effect of reducing the government's involvement in the operational aspects of communications – from the point of view of many free expression advocates an essential task of any meaningful transition to a democratic media sector. It is not the only goal, of course. With respect to editorial matters, the country's evolving but still often hostile press laws combined with the pressures of the market have had the undesirable effect of driving viewpoint diversity from the Chile's media, though clearly that perception depends on how one defines viewpoint diversity.

Several of the journalists I met in Santiago, for example, pointed to *El Mostrador*, in 2001 a fairly new on-line business publication. Their criticism of *El Mostrador,* while not explicit, centered on its "elite" character as an online-only service and, more obliquely, on its non-oppositional approach to public affairs. But *El Mostrador*'s general manager, Federico Joannon, made it clear to me that he and his partners were in business to turn a profit, not to serve as an opposition center to the government. "We care about recovering democracy," Joannon said, but that is not our key issue. We created the company and risked our capital in the belief that the Internet will become the fundamental medium. We are not committed to the government, the church or the business community. We are not a refuge for alternative groups—that is legitimate, but not the crux of what we do. We want to provide information to the majority of people – they have the right to be well informed, too – and are trying to be a watchdog on power, a viable business activity in the center of the business world.[55]

Not long after I returned from Santiago, a *New York Times* editorial on Latin American media praised *El Mostrador* for being "daring and innovative," but closed with the charge that in Chile "as elsewhere in Latin America, the market has more often produced media that unquestioningly support the powerful in society, failing the public they are supposed to serve."[56] Charges like these – especially when they come from large, private and profitable Western media firms – are difficult to evaluate. The leading public affairs media in developed democracies throughout the world, almost without exception, are private firms that earn the bulk of their revenues from advertising, not circulation.[57] More generally, while it may be true that Chile's media do a poor job of covering public affairs, it is also true that the low levels of political involvement and political polarization in the Chilean public are at levels characteristic of consolidated democracies.[58] In short, what some may view as public apathy and a diminished media market – that is, democratic failure – others may fairly regard as measures of successful democratic transition. That transition has been aided by the country's economic success. By the time Pinochet stepped down in 1989, Chile had the strongest economy in the region, one that enjoyed broad popular support. The Christian Democratic presidents that followed the dictator, Patricio Aylwin and Eduardo Frei, and most recently Socialist Ricardo Lagos, all emphasized social justice but none introduced significant economic changes. Arguably, the economic stability that Pinochet brought to Chile has provided some of the social stability necessary for the continuing investigation of and national reckoning with the dictator's crimes.[59]

Clearly there are multiple valid and important measures of media pluralism, and where, as in Chile's case, the state wields significant powers of censorship and control, pluralism will suffer. It may be circumscribed further where major sources of news and information are controlled by non-media sectors of the economy with links to the government or large stakes in public policy. COPESA, for example, is controlled by a group tied to Chile's banking industry—just as in the United States the television network NBC is owned by General Electric, a large defense contractor, and in Italy (until 2006) the country's prime minister ownedthree television networks. But as to the practical problems of *which* voices to sustain in a transition society and *how* to sustain them, journalists and many aid providers hold conflicting views on the role that governments and NGOs should play on the one hand, and the market on the other. With respect to the "how" question, Sebastian Brett notes that in the early 1990s left-wing members of the Chilean legislature proposed to enforce pluralism by statute, essentially guaranteeing financial support for media unable to find sufficient footing in the market. The Chilean Supreme Court declared the law unconstitutional, a decision that Brett calls correct. "Judges should not have that responsibility,"[60] he says, though he clearly supported the spirit of the legislation.

The Chilean experience is unique in many respects unique, but not in all. A common problem with civil society is how to sustain it in something other than a purely oppositional form after the early period of democratic transition. Several scholarly and political commentators looking at transition societies from Central Europe to Latin American have commented on the processes of civil society take-off, stagnation and institutionalization – in short, the gradual inclusion of civil society into the state after transition, and the consequent weakening of the civil society sector.[61]

One commentator describes these processes as "demobilization" and "decapitation."[62] Demobilization occurs when democratic transition follows on a negotiated settlement between the old regime and civil society. This is precisely what happened in most of Eastern and Central Europe in 1989-1990, where national round-table negotiations were critical to transitions in Poland, Hungary, Czechoslovakia and East Germany. In the course of negotiations, some of the enmity that exists between the state and civil society softens, and in any event the immediate reason for civil society's intensity – exclusion from political life—disappears. Very often the decision to demobilize is a conscious one, taken to make way for the development of democratic politics. In Chile, for example, much of the civil society movement that unseated General Pinochet was in fact the creation of the outlawed Christian Democrat and Socialist parties. In the period after the 1988 plebiscite these parties were again able to participate legally in politics and consciously chose to demobilize so they could get on with the business of governing. Decapitation occurs when, as in Poland and the Czech Republic, many of civil society's most articulate and active spokespeople are drawn into the new government, thus depriving civil society organizations of their leadership. The irony is that decapitation is most likely where civil society has been most successful in promoting democratization.

In some transition societies, demobilization and decapitation are particularly troublesome because civil society is weak to begin with. In post-Communist European states, even those that liberalized in the years following Stalin's death in 1950, many civil society organizations had little opportunity to escape state scrutiny and harassment or to engage in autonomous social action. So long was the experience of repression that civil society organizations were simply crushed out of existence and, as important, out of memory. In Latin America, by contrast, the bureaucratic authoritarian regimes that ruled virtually the entire region in 1970 were also relatively short-lived; following democratic transition about a little more than decade ago, political parties, trade unions and other repressed organizations were resurrected, often with the same leadership that existed before dictatorship. More generally, most Latin American countries had had experience with the political and institutional elements that are essential to civil society survival: an accountable executive, a capable bureaucracy, laudatory experience with civil and political rights, the rule of law, and transparency in political decision-making.

In Central and Eastern Europe, civil society has been further strained by economic reforms that while necessary have effectively created dual societies, one economically and socially far better off than the other. Dual societies commonly exist in other developed and developing countries, but in Central and Eastern Europe the duality is particularly divisive because so many of the old structures of socialist production now co-exist with large sectors of the economy that have adapted to the competitive market. Not all of these factors argue against the creation and sustainability of civil society, and some are short-term problems. New leaders will eventually replace old ones, for instance. Other problems are more serious. By its nature, civil society is about the creation of social unity through fragmentation and conflict, but in dual societies such conflict is apt to have less to do with governance than with the allocation of state resources. Where governments are weak, this kind of civil society discord can be anti-democratic and destabilizing.

The Problem of the Public Interest

The expansion of democracy has provided an opportunity to ask just what "public interests" media systems are supposed to serve, and, consistent with "freedom," how they should be structured to accomplish those ends. There is a large and rich literature on this subject regarding Western media systems, particularly with respect to the broadcast media, and there is no attempt here to summarize it except to state what few commentators on the subject ever do: There is no natural equilibrium of interests that defines the public interest. We know from the work of economist Kenneth Arrow that *a* public interest does not exist, that in any situation offering more than two choices there is no rule that will take people's individual preferences and aggregate them into the social welfare. Market advocates will argue that the invisible hand performs such a function, including if not especially in speech markets, but that assertion is incorrect. The invisible hand does not measure preferences so much as it does willingness to pay. I may prefer a Harley Davidson, for example, but am only willing to pay for a Honda.

Arrow explained the problem of the public interest with his "impossibility theorem," which starts with understanding what economists and political scientists call transitive and intransitive preferences.[63] Preferences are transitive if they can be put in a sensible and predictable order; that is to say, if I prefer peanuts to walnuts and walnuts to almonds, it should follow that I prefer peanuts to almonds. But if the reverse turns out to be true – that given a choice I prefer to almonds to peanuts – then my choices are intransitive. What Arrow was trying to do was to create a voting system that was consistent, fair, and would lead to transitive (orderly and rational) group preferences when there were more than two options to choose from. In the process, he proved that such a system was impossible. If, for example, there are three candidates, A, B and C, and we have three citizens choosing among them, their individual voting preferences might be ABC, CBA and BCA. Under these conditions, whichever candidate is selected, the winner may not have a plurality of the vote, and a majority will prefer someone else. Put another way, there is no single election procedure that can always fairly decide the outcome of an election (or other public choice) that involves more than two candidates or alternatives. Since we cannot rule out conflicting orderings, we cannot say a voting system will go from individual to group preferences unless we impose some kind of restraint on the choice – for example, the restraint of majority rule – or we violate basic norms of fairness. These conditions have especially worrisome implications for democracy, since they can lead to group decisions that are simply nonsensical or to decisions about governance that are manifestly undemocratic. As political scientists Ken Shepsle and Mark Bonchek have written, "The group is either dominated by a single distinguished member or has intransitive preferences."[64] "Single distinguished member" is just a nice way of saying "dictator," and so Arrow's theorem is also known as the dictator theorem.

The conclusions we can reach from Arrow's theorem are two and straightforward, even if the theorem is mathematically complex. First, every method of determining the public interest is imperfect, and though each method will have its advantages, each is *guaranteed* to have some of the disadvantages – that is to say the sometimes-incomprehensible results – required by Arrow's theorem. The challenge for policy makers and citizens is to choose the system that produces those results the least often. The second conclusion is that any absolute claim about the public interest is, by definition, a defense of the indefensible. Such claims are not indefensible in any moral sense, but rather in an empirical one. We simply cannot say how economic and policy abstractions will play out in real life. If, for example, the president's chief economic advisor says that job outsourcing is good for the economy, such a statement is consistent with what every student learns about trade in Economics 101, but in fact the real world is more complicated than that. The same can be said for assertions about the public interest in media markets.

To take an easy example, both Britain and the United States are democracies, but their understanding of what constitutes the public interest in broadcasting could not be more different. Britain's system is built around a state-funded, not-for-profit national service, the British Broadcasting Corporation; private, commercial and for-profit television was added only recently. The American system has from the beginning been based on private, for-profit, and for the most part local broadcasters; a small and weak public broadcasting system was created in 1967 to remedy supposed market failures in the commercial sector. Today these two systems are nominally alike in that they are a mix of private and public firms, for-profit and nonprofit firms, but philosophically, on the big questions of editorial mission, they are profoundly different. Each system has its clear advantages and defects, and both are presumably consistent with the public interest as each country understands it. And yet the differences between these systems are striking, not of degree but of kind. How can this be? It comes down to Arrow's theorem, and a public policy decision, consistent with basic rules about fairness, that seeks to produce the greatest public benefit with the fewest undesirable

outcomes. One can argue, of course, about whether either policy succeeds. Arrow himself recommended John Rawls' test for a just society:
Would one be willing to be thrown into it at random?

From a journalistic point of view, the proper balance of "public" and
"private" media in a media system is only one of the structural dilemmas
that have important consequences for editorial mission. Several others
follow and are equally difficult. For example, how much competition,
between which competitors and in which marketplace (for example,
local or national), is required to adequately represent the various public
interests in a democracy? In many transition states the problem of too
much competition – or conversely, too little of it – may not immediately
exist, but as media systems and economies mature, policies that were
once sufficient to promote press freedom and independence may quickly
become irrelevant or even counterproductive.

There are still more dilemmas for the media system architect trying to
enable a democracy: What legal rights of access, if any, exist for content
producers, political candidates or for the general public to media infra-
structures, state or private? Are general anti-trust and fair competition
laws sufficient to guarantee "democratic values" in a media system, or
does the protection of those values require additional regulations? If so,
what regulations? Can foreign companies own part or all of domestic media companies? If so, do different rules apply to different media? On the
one hand, there is an arguable public interest in limiting foreign ownership
on the assumption that domestic owners may be more sensitive to public
concerns, particularly in a crisis. In broadcasting especially, restrictions
on ownership might be and often are defended as a means of protecting
and promoting national cultural identity. Restrictions on ownership can
also be used to protect significant minority identities, whether religious,
racial, ethnic or something else. Viewed in this way, ownership restrictions
or preferences can be defended as a kind of benign government intervention in the speech marketplace, a structural adjustment intended to protect
viewpoint diversity. Seen another way, of course, these restrictions are
just a form of government subsidy for favored speech, and as such its
claims, no matter how well intentioned, are offensive to media freedom.
And where governments are not benign, foreign ownership may be less
susceptible to government bullying and can provide points of view otherwise unavailable in countries dominated by state-owned media.

Finally, of course, there are the micro questions concerning media
and the public interest. Consider a practical example that confronts all

would-be democracy builders in developing states: Who should get access to broadcast time in national referendums and elections for public office?[65] This straightforward question, presumably critical to the quality and quantity of public participation in governance, begs countless other questions with no single, satisfactory "democratic" answer:

- Do candidates or parties or both get access? Do all candidates get access, or only some? If there are multiple candidates, what threshold requirements, if any, must they meet to qualify for broadcast time?
- Is airtime free to the candidates? If it is, who bears the cost of production? Are broadcasters compensated in any fashion for candidate time, especially if there are several or even dozens of candidates?
- Do candidates get equal time, or are specific times and length of time allotted by formulae? If so, what formulae, devised by whom? How should the formulae deal with minority parties?
- May broadcasters sell time? If so, on what terms? Must they sell time to any and all candidates for office – in effect compelling them to associate with ideas and with people with whom they may strongly disagree—or may they exercise their independent editorial judgment (presumably a cornerstone of any system of free expression) and choose not to sell time to some candidates?
- What about content requirements? For example, whether the airtime provided to candidates is unpaid or paid, must candidates themselves appear on their on behalf, or can others represent them? Must candidates identify themselves in any way with promotions aired on their behalf? Can political advertising be bound by time restrictions that specify either a minimum or maximum number of seconds, minutes or hours? If candidates are allowed to purchase airtime, must they disclose the source of their funding?

All of these questions apply as well to the possibility that the public – whether in the form of individuals, civic groups, trade associations, unions, for-profit and not-for-profit firms, representatives of racial and ethnic minorities, political action committees, the expatriate community, and so on – is also entitled to airtime during elections. A final regulatory difficulty is how to make principled and understandable distinctions between candidate time, of whatever type, and legitimate news coverage of candidates, their activities and policies. Broadcasters and politicians everywhere understand that "objective" news stories about "newsworthy" events – many of them manufactured to portray candidates and their policies as favorably as possible – are more essential than political advertising to their electoral success. Incumbents especially enjoy an enormous advantage in this respect, since presumably their regular participation in public events of all kinds is newsworthy. Conversely, both broadcasters and politicians understand that the decision by a broadcaster to portray a candidate negatively, or worse simply to ignore him, can effectively kill a politician's campaign – and his career.

The point of these examples is to underscore that media systems are not acts of nature but the result of conscious choices by governments and policy makers. The choices governments make (or that aid providers promote) can a result in media systems that are more or less equally "democratic," but which emphasize very different expressive values. Moreover it will almost always be the case that in making those choices the decision to maximize one expressive or "democratic" value will result in a less than optimal emphasis on another.

Consider just one example from the United States' experience with these issues: the law regarding public information access and newsgathering. Though there exist both federal and state statutes on access to government information and public facilities, those laws fall under constitutional guidelines that the U.S. Supreme Court devised in the span of two days in June 1974, in three separate cases. Two of those cases involved journalists claiming a right of access to prisons, one against the California Department of Corrections[66] and the other against the Federal Bureau of Prisons.[67] In both cases, journalists claimed rights of access on behalf of the public, to go into detention facilities and interview specific inmates. On June 24, 1974, the court denied the journalists' claims in both cases on the theory that there was no generalized public right of access to prisons, and thus no such right for journalists either; when joined with the government's interest in security and the efficient operation of its prison system, the Court said, the access claim was unsustainable.

On June 25, the Court ruled in a distinctly different kind of access case, this one involving a Florida statute that compelled newspapers to publish rebuttals by political candidates whom the papers had criticized in their editorial pages.[68] The statute had been modeled as a print media corollary to a now-defunct federal rule that applied to broadcasters (the Fairness Doctrine), but was challenged by the *Miami Herald* as an unconstitutional infringement on its editorial discretion. The Justices unanimously agreed with the *Herald*, noting that it was the distinctive technological and natural-monopoly characteristics of broadcasting that justified such an access rule in that medium. Despite the plaintiff's claims that print publishers also exercised a *de facto* monopoly on public debate, such a rule could not apply to newspapers, the Court said: "The choice of material to go into a newspaper, and the decisions made as to limitations on the size and content of the paper, and treatment of public issues and public officials – whether fair or unfair – constitute the exercise of editorial control and judgment."[69]

Taken together, writes First Amendment scholar Rodney Smolla, the three cases constitute a stark doctrinal bargain on the question of access in the American media system.[70] On the one hand, the First Amendment is not a freedom of information act; journalists cannot use it to compel access to documents or places. On the other, the First Amendment will not permit the public to use the media as bulletin boards. Put simply, news organizations have no constitutional right of access to the workings of government, and the public has no right of access to news organizations. The glue that holds this bargain together, Smolla says, is the Court's historical unwillingness to read the First Amendment's speech clause independent of its press clause. If it did, this historic bargain might well have been struck the other way: The press, acting on behalf of the public, could have been given special rights of access to public facilities; the public, in turn, could have been given a limited rights of access to the instruments of mass media. The result of such a bargain would be to reallocate freedoms in the speech marketplace, increasing freedom for some while decreasing freedom for others. There would still be inequities in the speech market, just as there are now, but with the balance of freedom struck in a dramatically different way.

Would such a reallocation be any less "free" or "democratic"? This is not just a theoretical question. It comes up constantly in democratizing societies, where local NGOs, ethnic and racial minorities, and citizens generally are apt to believe, as a matter of fairness, that rights of expression cannot be limited to media owners, particularly when those owners are identified with the old non-democratic regime. This is especially so with broadcasting, where governments are unavoidably involved and interested in decisions about licensing. The way in which this is done is invariably political. In 1996, for example, the U.S. Telecommunications Act, though it made significant changes in most industries, allowed only incumbent television broadcasters to receive digital spectrum allotments, which were awarded at no cost and for extended terms. Potential challengers for digital spectrum were shut out, as was the public generally. The Netherlands, by contrast, takes public participation to the other extreme, guaranteeing a number of political, cultural, trade and religious groups access to television time.

So given these limitations, what does a free media system look like? How does it engage citizens in discourse and link their concerns to political society?

Theorizing a Free (and Accountable?) Press

A common criticism of both U.S. media assistance and the public diplomacy services is that they seek to export the normative values and practices of the American media system to countries where they are inappropriate or of little use. James Miller, for example, has argued that U.S. media assistance seeks to export an "occupational ideology of 'professionalism.'"[71] This ideology holds that journalists must be:

> as free as possible from what they perceive to be the self-interested influence of their sources, their audience, their employers and their media's advertisers. Especially, journalists keep their distance from politics, by which they generally mean overt allegiance to party partisanship. They also vigorously resist the capacity of non-journalists to sanction their work through such means as press councils, licensing, formal codes of ethics, and even, to the extent possible, the law. They are committed to what they see as truth-telling about public affairs, which is to say chiefly that they seek informational balance and factual accuracy in news accounts whose most desirable subject is the revelation of hidden wrong-doing.... Freedom of the press, in these terms, is nearly synonymous with freedom itself.[72]

"Professionalized, 'world' journalism is thus a kind of clinical instrument," Miller writes, "depoliticized, depersonalized, whose rational rules of practice have emerged and diffused along with liberal democracy."[73] This criticism is fair in some respects, off the mark in others. Certainly not all media assistance providers regard themselves as the global standard-bearers for journalism practice and for free expression values. And most journalists, whether they work in Indonesia, Guatemala, Serbia or anyplace else, find the Miller's conceptualization of their task as generally agreeable. Few would think his characterization uniquely American or Western, and many would be offended at the suggestion that they were. Journalists disagree about the particulars of professional practice and above all about their social responsibilities, but good journalists everywhere want a few basic things: They want to be free from outside editorial interference, they want to tell their stories as truthfully and completely as possible, and they don't want to be punished for doing it. What they *would* debate, vigorously, is the best way to make these norms operational, and not merely a collection of platitudes. So the important thing about these norms is how they are enabled by the legal and institutional architecture of a media system.

Even in developed democracies, reports Denis McQuail, there has long been "a state of considerable confusion and conflict over the norms which should apply to communication arrangements and to performance from the point of view of 'society.'"[74] In democratic media systems, McQuail argues, the central conflict since about the mid-twentieth century has been between established authorities (governmental, religious, educational) and demands for unrestricted free expression. This conflict has at least two important subtexts. The first concerns the debate between those "elites" who argue that the media should advance cultural and educational goals and those who see the media primarily as a business. The second concerns the tug of war between those who control the media (owners, editors and journalists) and those among the public who want control over the media, or access to them, for their own purposes.

Other scholars, among them James Carey and J.B. Lemert, have identified a number of critical approaches to these conflicts: Marxist; cultural/critical studies; social responsibility and empiricist.[75] These approaches can and do overlap in the work of individual theorists (McQuail, for example, is a social scientist interested in measures of social responsibility). The social responsibility school of thought, however, is the one most commonly understood and accepted both by those who work from *within* the media industries – journalists – and those who interact with them – academics, government officials, and the public. Allowing for any number of important exceptions, the other approaches are the domain of scholarly study, and while they have produced many insightful and intellectually rigorous contributions to the literature on media and democracy, they have had arguably (and unfortunately, as Carey has noted) the least impact on media practice or on public debate about media practice.

The social responsibility approach to media studies also fits neatly with the democratization industry, where, as discussed in chapters 2 and 3, media are one in a chain of institutional elements necessary to promote and ensure good governance, and good governance is valued primarily, though not exclusively, because it ensures that aid provided for economic development is spent effectively and accountably. Only more recently has media assistance has been linked to civil society development and mobilization, and to broader concerns about free expression rights and responsibilities. Where media assistance follows on civil conflict or war, these concerns are magnified. In the literature on media development, theorists say that the role of the media in a democracy is to ensure the existence of a broadly and equitably informed citizenry that can hold elites accountable and ensure popular control of government through free and competitive elections. To enable the press in that role, at least two structural conditions have to obtain: Citizens must have some sort of constitutional or statutory right to political information, and media have to be protected from the arbitrary exercise of government power.[76] Most democracy scholars also argue for a third condition, that media pluralism – by which they mean a broad array of media forms and outlets offering a variety of political viewpoints – has to be ensured through legal means, for example restrictions on ownership.[77] In her overview of the subject, Beta Rozumilowicz concludes that a fourth condition is necessary, a system in which "access is both equally and effectively guaranteed."[78]

One detailed attempt by a former journalist to revise the old Cold War media classification system (devised in 1961 by Frederick Seibert, Theodore Peterson and Wilbur Schramm)[79] has been undertaken by South African media scholar Guy Berger, who describes democratic media as conforming to one of four types distinguished by their editorial and social missions:[80]

- *Liberal*, or the classic Fourth Estate model, in which journalism is an independent source of social power that provides a check on both state and private power. The liberal model sees journalism primarily as a private enterprise rather than a state one, and as such the common criticism is that its independence is too easily compromised by private interests – owners, advertisers, public relations firms and others.
- *Neoliberal*, in which journalism is the primary advocate for cultural pluralism, giving voice to minority and dissident voices against the dominant political views in the media system and society. The neoliberal model is premised on public debate, and in much of the world has been a response to authoritarian political regimes.
- *Social democratic*, in which journalism performs a public role more akin to guide than guardian. In this view, journalists do not stand in an adversarial role to power so much as frame the terms of citizenship, define and shape democratic culture. The social democratic model is epitomized by large public-service state broadcasters like the BBC or NHK.

- *Participatory*, in which journalism is neither guide nor guardian, but actively promotes the voluntary associations and political habits of civil society. Where social democratic journalism concerns itself with the formation of the nation, participatory journalism concerns itself with the formation of communities. And unlike neoliberal journalism, which sees citizens primarily as consumers of politics, the participatory model sees them as political actors. Participatory journalism is relatively new; it is exemplified in the United States by the public (or civic) journalism movement, and around the world by attempts to use the Internet has a tool of political organization and action.

These models overlap in obvious ways. Many state broadcasters, for example, see themselves not merely as nurturing their nation's culture, but also as serving as a watchdog on government (liberal) and, as many state broadcasters are required to do, giving voice to minority viewpoints (neoliberal). Similarly, those who see journalism as a Fourth Estate are likely to believe that their work increases public knowledge and thus makes citizen participation in government meaningful. What makes these models useful as tools of analysis is that they function differently in developing democracies than they do in developed ones. In developed nations, for instance, it is increasingly difficult to see how some of these models function at all except as idealized norms. Throughout the developed world journalism has become a small part of a larger media environment that includes entertainment, sports, music, advertising and direct marketing; in that environment, the mixing of content and purpose puts journalism in an increasingly competitive market for audiences and has the effect of privileging news content that is most easily leveraged across multiple media platforms. These trends are only amplified by globalization and media deregulation, both of which have unleashed additional competitive forces that militate against liberal journalism's watchdog tradition. That tradition is not dead—it lives in some elite media and also in some decidedly un-elite media, primarily on the Internet, that report on both public affairs and on the alleged failings of the established press.

In much of the developing world the liberal journalistic tradition is not only alive and well, but owes its existence to the very factors that repress it – above all inept or corrupt governments. One of the ironies of democratic transition, and an observation one hears often from journalists in transition countries, is that journalism was in some key respects better when it was officially suppressed. A major reason for the success of media under authoritarian regimes, of course, is foreign assistance, which often diminishes or disappears altogether after the political transition. For better or worse, the liberal journalistic tradition, with its aversion to state control of the media sector, assumes that sector belongs to the competitive market. It assumes as well, Rozumilowicz observes, that "economic criteria of success should prevent tyranny of opinion,"[81] an assumption that does not square either with economic theory or, in many places, easy observation.

For journalists in developing societies, the larger problem with the liberal and neoliberal journalistic traditions is that they are not necessarily conducive to democratization. The liberal tradition, for example, supports vigorous and effective monitoring of the government, and its emphasis on private ownership provides a needed counterweight to what are often government-held monopolies in media. The neoliberal push for pluralism is also essential to democratization, if not also to civil society. At the same time, however, there is nothing about the liberal model that makes it inherently democratic, and the ethical excesses of the liberal model may undermine public support for free expression. This is a subject of growing concern in Western journalism, and particularly in the United States, but it has corollaries everywhere. Maciej Wierzynski, director of Voice of America's Polish Service, has described a situation in which Poland's two small private television networks curried political favor in order to insulate themselves from competition. "One of the private networks," Wierzynski said, "bribed the whole parliamentary caucus to preserve the 30 percent limit on foreign investment and block the flow of foreign capital to the media market."[82]

Private media can subvert democratic impulses in other ways. If, for instance, the media see their role primarily as promoting economic development or social stability, they can devolve into nothing more than a mouthpiece for an undemocratic government. The effect is to further entrench established interests, both in government and in the private sector. Rosa María Alfaro of the Asociación de Comunicadores Sociales (CALANDRIA) of Peru has said that in Latin America "political parties and government buy journalists with advertising,"[83] effectively securing favorable treatment through patronage. "Envelope journalism" – in which journalists routinely accept bribes in return for favorable coverage – is still common even in democratic and developed Asia. At the other extreme, liberal journalism can threaten democratization when it becomes a source of political opposition in its own right or, as often happens, when a nominally independent press becomes the tool of politicians opposed to the government, as happened with the late Massoud Abiola in Nigeria. When this happens, journalistic values are subverted to political agendas, even more so when the opposition press scores a victory at the ballot box and becomes the government press – and thus loses its liberal character entirely, to the point where it may retard or subvert democratization.

In developed media systems, one response to the excesses of the liberal journalism model has been to give renewed emphasis to the social democratic model typified by public broadcasting. More recently, some journalists, academics and policy makers have called for developing a public-service infrastructure of digital media using revenues from public resources, in particular from the sale or lease of electromagnetic spectrum.[84] The policy idea is that through direct or indirect intervention, government may—among other things—promote public access to the means of communication, encourage and regulate competition, and subsidize high-quality news, public affairs and cultural fare that the market may not support.

To the extent those in transition states understand this social democratic ideal, they often reject it. Typically journalists in those countries have at best mixed feelings about the government's ability to play a positive role in news and public affairs because of their experience of media as a tool of state domination. Even where governments are ostensibly acting in the "public interest," says Wierzynski, the legacy of state control makes for an uneasy partnership. "Anytime we try to discuss the role of government in media it leads to political questions," he says. "Who controls? Who sets the priorities? In the case of Poland, state-owned media have played the decisive role in electronic media on the rationale that they are protecting 'national culture' against foreign television. As a result we have a situation where national culture is not so much protected, but the government makes political appointments to state radio and television."[85] For other societies, their experience with privatization has been little better and sometimes worse, effectively removing any possibility of public scrutiny of the news media.

If social democratic journalism has few champions, Professor Berger's final model, participatory journalism—much scorned as "civic journalism" by journalists in the United States—has obvious appeal in developing societies. It emphasizes the kinds of citizen associations that are thought to promote civil society, and, much more than the other models, acknowledges implicitly that in societies emerging from authoritarian pasts no single institution, and certainly not the press, can advance the cause of democratization by itself. Participatory journalism also reaches out to the large numbers of people, particularly in rural areas, who have traditionally been both socially marginalized and beyond the reach of virtually every public affairs medium except state radio. Critics of participatory journalism charge that it is susceptible to abuse, and that may be especially true in societies whose media experience is one of monopoly state control. Further, the impediments to independent journalism in developing societies—poverty, high illiteracy rates, scattered populations and poor infrastructure development—are particularly injurious to the goals of participatory journalism.[86] The Internet, for example, has been widely praised as the first mass medium that allows for interactivity and community-building—and thus ideally suited to participatory journalism—but poverty and limited information infrastructure make the Internet unavailable to a majority of people in many developing societies.

Nonetheless, Berger's analysis is helpful for thinking about the different media sector-government relationships possible in a democracy, and also about the media's roles with respect to promoting, creating and guiding public participation in governance. And as noted above, these conceptual models can overlap and co-exist within the same media system. Even in the United States, for example, where the liberal model is most dominant, the regulatory scheme that governs broadcasting contemplates that terrestrial radio and television should have statutory public duties – for example, to make themselves available on favorable terms to qualified candidates for public office – that print media do not.

Similar to Berger, James Curran has theorized an integrated, "five-sector" approach to media development that in effect combines most of the features of Berger's media types into one system.[87] At the core of that system is a state-financed public broadcasting system. A "civil sector," as Curran calls it, would address the concerns of pluralists by providing assistance to support media that serve ethnic and racial minorities, and other underserved social groups such as women or children. A "professional" sector would provide support to journalists so that they could engage in their craft without regard for either government or market support, and a fourth sector, the "social market," would operate as a point of entry where new voices and points of view can hone their craft and rise to prominence. Only the "private enterprise" sector depends exclusively on the judgments – and the financial support – of the market. The virtue of the model, Rozumilowicz writes, is that it balances competitive and participatory interests, and "seems to recommend the existence and promotion of at least two media sectors, each with different funding sources, organizational principles and end goals."[88]

Obviously whether any of these normative models is workable depends the first instance on the extent to which political conditions exist to support them. Assuming they do, it is an economic error to assume, as virtually all of these theories do, that functionally discrete media sectors do not compete with one another for audiences, content, editorial and other talent, and above all for revenues. They do. Where will the money come from to support them all, and particularly those that purport to serve some social goal?

Markets, Regulation and Free Expression Values

Price and his colleagues have defined media sustainability in terms of "reasonable objectives," and whether sufficient and varied revenues exist to meet them.[89] Some objectives may be perfectly reasonable (maximizing audiences, for example) but make little or no contributions (balanced and complete reporting, presentation and discussion of opposing political views) to the information needs of a healthy democracy and civil society association. The choice of objectives is critical: Because news and public affairs reporting may cost more to produce than other kinds of content and, at the least, competes for time or space that could otherwise go to more lucrative fare (e.g., entertainment), a newspaper or television station that provides news and information may find that the *level* of revenues necessary for sustainability is higher, and as well that the *sources* for those revenues are either fewer or significantly different (for instance, in the distinction between not-for-profit and for-profit firms).

So while sustaining a variety of media may be important as a general democratic goal, it matters a lot what *particular* goals a country's media policy is supposed to serve. In the United States, for example, stated policy goals for broadcast media include "diversity." USAID also refers to media diversity as a development goal, and often as well uses the term "media pluralism." It is rarely clear in either context what these terms mean. Robert Entman and Steven Wildman have pointed out that diversity might be measured in economic terms by the number of media choices available to consumers (*product* diversity); in normative terms by point-of-view variation (*idea* diversity), or with the goal of ensuring that all ideas get adequate time and emphasis (*access* diversity).[90] Again, the easiest of these terms to understand and use is product diversity, both because it is quantitative and, from a free expression point of view, facially neutral with respect to content. It is the least subject to second-guessing. It may also be the least important if the goal is promoting "civil society" or encouraging the habits of democratic society.

In practice, "diversity" and "pluralism" are likely to mean any or all of these things, sometimes in combination. Talking about media coverage of the second Intifada, for example, Daoud Kuttab of the Institute of Modern Media at Al-Quds University in Ramallah emphasizes the development of Arab satellite stations, local television and radio stations, and their importance in how the world, and especially Arabs themselves, view the Palestinian-Israeli conflict. Where the major wire services are often biased and Arab state television tightly controlled, Kuttab says, satellite stations have allowed people to see "professional Arab journalists working for the BBC or other western agencies reporting on how the conflict was affecting the Palestinians, and also giving time to Israeli officials who speak Arabic."[91] At the community level, he says, local stations during the second Intifada have had the "unique opportunity to literally stick their cameras out the window, sit under the table, and give the audience an amazing show."[92] Arab television audiences thus have both product and idea diversity – more channels to choose from, and several of them offering a perspective other than the government's.

A number of thoughtful critics have argued that product diversity, while it may not be a sufficient measure of pluralism, is not a bad thing – certainly so far as democratic values are concerned.[93] In the United States, in Western Europe and Latin America, and in parts of Asia and Africa, the twin policies of deregulation and privatization have without question fueled growth, innovation and competition in the communications industries. No one can seriously argue that these developments – the result of diminished state control over the media sector—are not a net plus for media freedom. Radio, for example, has been re-born as a democratic medium throughout the developing world. With governments giving up monopoly control of the airwaves, hundreds of new commercial FM and community-owned stations are now on the air. Usually owned or controlled by locals and run on a non-profit basis, community radio has flourished in Latin America and parts of Africa, owing in significant part to its very low start-up costs. Talk shows are a staple of community stations, and while many are shrill or entertainment-oriented, many others feature political interviews, listener call-ins and other formats that have enlarged the space for political debate. Radio is probably the most "civil-society" oriented of all media in the developing world, in significant part because of its value to rural areas where newspapers are nonexistent. In Indonesia, for example, community radio is the mainstay of ethnic music, programming that in such an ethnically and geographically scattered country is otherwise unable to sustain itself. Commercial stations in the country prefer to play Western pop music.

In the last decade, deregulation and privatization have also spurred technological innovations that have significantly changed the role of media in democratization. Satellite television, the Internet and mobile telephony, in particular, provide geographically disparate people access to information and permit them to share ideas, organize and affect policy, including at the level of global governance. So-called "countrynets," for example – electronic mailing lists, Usenet groups, web pages – unite activists and expatriates opposing authoritarian regimes in countries that ordinarily do not rate coverage by mainstream international media like CNN or the BBC. BurmaNet, for instance, is funded by the Open Society Institute and provides exhaustive coverage of Burma's military government and its human rights abuses. Sierra Leone's Expotimes.net has more than 70,000 users around the world; there as across Africa, Internet use and development has been driven by Africans in the Diaspora. Similar countrynets operate in China, Kenya, East Timor, the Balkans, the West Bank and countless other places.

Not all of these Internet uses can be characterized as democratic, nor does their existence signal political liberalization – often quite the opposite.[94] Most countrynets trade in advocacy, not dispassionate analysis. But many also provide useful information for those who want it and a way for disenfranchised citizens of those countries and regions to make themselves heard.[95] Equally important, it is difficult (though not impossible) for governments to control their citizens' ability to get and share information using these new technologies.[96]

A third important consequence of liberalization is that people everywhere now receive much more foreign media content than they once did. The Internet is part of that phenomenon, but international media like CNN, the BBC and Bloomberg are now very nearly ubiquitous, and some national media have become regional or even global. For Americans, Al Jazeera is probably the best-known example of this, but there are others. Millions of Arabs read the daily *Al Sharq Al Awsat*, which contains reports and opinions from the *New York Times, Washington Post, Los Angeles Times* and *Christian Science Monitor*. The paper is edited in London and delivered by satellite. The South African satellite service Multichoice serves subscribers across the continent, and in South Asia Star TV, Zee TV, Sony TV, Gemini and the Sun – all based in India – have established footprints that cover the subcontinent.

These global information flows have at least one positive consequence, denying all but the most determined governments the ability to control completely what their citizens see, hear and read. But they can also make it harder for local media to compete for audiences (except the most parochial variety) and thus decrease the coverage given to local and even national issues, especially issues that affect rural areas, ethnic and racial minorities, and the poor. To the extent that state broadcasters have lost their monopolies, they are also affected by this competition; many have tried to replace lost public revenues with advertising revenue, and in doing so have weakened or abandoned whatever public mission they may once have served – forgoing multi-language programming, programs in education, health care, agriculture and so on. Many of these media markets are quite strong – the question is whether the media that are economically sustainable are really worth sustaining.

A growing body of academic and popular literature argues that liberalization has failed to nurture the kinds of news and public affairs content that democratic societies presumably need in order to function.[97] The concern is that the new economic environment for media does not adequately support news coverage of such complex issues as public health, poverty, environmental degradation, immigration, capital mobility, international governance – in a word, globalization in all its dimensions. A second concern is the scarcity of public-affairs media choices at the local level. The United States, for example, is a rich country with a vibrant media market, but most Americans have a choice of only one local newspaper – and in many communities, none. Local markets cannot sustain more. In transition countries, community radio stations typically were launched with grants from governmental and non-governmental donors, and many failed when funding stopped. Those that survived did so by becoming private and/or commercial stations. Some – Nepal's Radio Sagarmatha, Serbia's B92 and Croatia's Radio 101 – have managed to maintain their commitment to public-service programming, but others have largely abandoned that mission. While they still provide an alternative to government programming, the focus is entertainment;

public affairs programming may continue, but with much less emphasis. In the worst cases, news is given over to sensationalism or divided along ethnic or religious lines.

The problem with product diversity, then, is its attachment to the logic of markets and its singular emphasis on competition. Over time, increased competition is likely to drive overall quality down rather than up, with the end result being a media system that continues to have product diversity, but that provides little of the news and information that democratization presumably needs (idea diversity) and where consumers may reduce rather than increase their consumption of information (thus diminishing access diversity). Even as Daoud Kuttab lauds the variety of choices now available to Arab viewers, for instance, he bemoans the fact that "the private stations depend on advertising" and "the public stations become government mouthpieces. There is little room between these two choices. Only international funding keeps alive a third way."[98]

It must be emphasized here that if market competition has a leveling effect on content diversity, the usual alternative is worse: a media market (and a news and entertainment culture) dominated by the state. In 2001, for example, the Russian company Media-Most lost control over its television station NTV and its publishing house Sem Dnej (Seven Days, publisher of the daily *Segodnya* and the weekly newsmagazine *Itogi*) to the huge and partly state-owned gas utility Gazprom, which technically controlled only 46 percent of Media-Most but in 2000 called in $300 million worth of loans to the company and staged an armed raid on NTV on April 15, 2001. In the weeks before the raid, American media mogul Ted Turner and financier George Soros reportedly offered to buy approximately 19 percent of NTV's shares from its principal owner, Vladimir Gusinsky, for $225 million. The Duma firmly rejected a resolution to provide government relief to the station, leading between 10,000 and 20,000 Muscovites to rally in Pushkin Square on March 31, holding signs that read, "We want our NTV."[99] After the raid that followed two weeks later, more than 350 NTV employees reportedly quit or were fired, some going over to Gusinsksy's cable channel TNT, which reaches only about half of Russia's 145 million people and was also deeply in debt to Gazprom. At one point several of NTV's journalists tried to negotiate a merger with another independent channel, Boris Berezovsky's TV-6, but no deal ever materialized.[100] Eduard Sagalaev, the respected journalist who had led TV-6, was replaced in March 2001 by Igor Shabdurasulov, a former government official, and Berezovsky himself fled the country to avoid criminal charges.

International observers rightfully condemned the "Kremlin's determination to reassert its dominance over the news media,"[101] and today independent media in Russia exist in a far more precarious political environment than they did a decade ago. In truth, however, neither Gusinsky nor Berezovsky were models of professional independence or editorial integrity. NTV had, during the Yeltsin years, openly allied itself with the president's 1996 re-election campaign while denying his challengers airtime; and *Forbes* magazine, among others, had linked Berezovsky to organized crime.[102] Still, NTV had done some distinguished and critical reporting, making its reputation for editorial independence and courage in its coverage of the 1994 Chechen war, and both it and TV-6 had, at least until their demise, managed to keep their distance of the large banking, mining, oil and electricity conglomerates, many of them state-owned, that at the time controlled most of Russia's other major media outlets.[103]

The issues of government interference at NTV played out in dramatic fashion but have not been unique to Russia. Similar conflicts have occurred in Poland, Hungary, Slovakia, Romania, Bulgaria, and the Czech Republic, in each case with government broadcasting councils dominated by the ruling party making top editorial appointments to national television or radio stations. Unlike their Western European counterparts, public broadcasters in Central and Eastern Europe typically lack the layers of administrative insulation necessary to ensure editorial independence. Nor is it unusual for journalists at public stations to maintain close contact with government officials, particularly those who appointed them, or for politicians to telephone editors in advance of an election to complain that coverage of their parties is unfair or inadequate.

Journalists in the region have responded to these pressures in a variety of ways, and with mixed results. In Slovenia, for example, public broadcasters in 1999 published an extensive code of professional ethics, in the process staking out the boundaries that define editorial independence from state and private sources of influence and interference. As impressive as the code is, it is doubtlessly more effective because Slovenian public broadcasters enjoy a source of revenue (surcharges on viewers' electricity bills) independent of the state budget, and because the country's broadcast council is not appointed by the parliament.

Czech public media also earn revenues from a license fee, but the independence of Czech Television came under international scrutiny in late 2000 and early 2001 when the government council that oversees the station dismissed its director and replaced him with Jiri Hodac, an experienced former BBC editor who purportedly had connections with former Prime Minister Vaclav Klaus and his Civic Democratic Party. The journalists at Czech TV suspected government meddling and had their suspicions confirmed when Hodac named former journalist and Klaus economic advisor Jana Bobosikova as the station's news director. She promptly fired several editors and staffers, at which point the editors barricaded themselves in the newsroom and for a period of weeks and broadcast their own "unofficial" version of the news using satellite and cable links. President Vaclav Havel and other prominent Czech writers and artists gave support to the protestors, and at one point some 75,000 Czechs rallied to their cause in Wenceslaus Square, turning the entire episode into an international embarrassment for the government. Hodac eventually resigned, and his cadre of new managers was fired; all the protesting editors stayed on, including those whom Bobosikova had fired weeks earlier.

Presumably the outcome of the Czech Television seizure was a victory for press independence – that was the common consensus in news accounts in the West. But viewed in another light, the "rebels" (as they called themselves) may have paid a bit too dearly for their cause. "The journalists behind the protests did a great job of manipulating their own media," says Jeremy Drucker of *Transitions Online*, a private, Prague-based news organization, "and were not at all independent or objective in their coverage of their own demonstration."[104] Ironically, Hodac had argued before resigning that one of his goals was to make Czech Television more professional. He had also said he wanted to make the service more efficient in the face of increased competition and a continuously dwindling audience share.

The critical point, then, is that while media may be important contributors to civil society, and thus to democratization, they are embedded in economic society. Editorial mission and "quality" count for nothing if they cannot find sufficient revenue sources to sustain themselves. The choice of revenues, in turn, will affect the core editorial mission of a media organization. The choice for policy makers is whether and how to intervene in the media market, a choice that raises first-order questions about the meaning of media independence. Any choice – including the decision not to intervene – will have profound consequences for character of media goods produced, and thus for the character of "democracy" itself. A 2003 USAID conference on media assistance found that its participants could not agree even on the meaning of press "independence," never mind the importance of press independence to democratization:

> ...[T]he purely commercial independent media may not offer an ideal model because some drop news entirely, as Radio Plus did in Kosovo. Even having a media sector that is politically independent of government and economically self-sustaining may not satisfy media development objectives, which include instilling a sense of mission to serve the public with news and information and presenting diverse opinions and voices. In Mongolia, some independent media undermined democracy, one participant observed. In some cases, quasi-governmental media may be preferable if editorially independent of their governments and if better than purely commercial media in giving space to professional news and a plurality of voices.[105]

The final section of this chapter considers more closely this problem of independence and anti-democratic speech. How are media to be made both free *and* responsible to the public?

Media Freedom and Public Accountability

In a free and open society, free expression is thought to serve several essential functions. It allows people to develop their intellectual and spiritual faculties through their own activities and through engagement with others in art, religion, public affairs, and so on. The importance of free expression in this regard is made obvious by the experience of authoritarian regimes, where even in their private lives people must be wary of what they say and to whom, and even those who wish to conform—to say nothing of those who do not—have no *choice* in the matter. As well, free expression promotes the search for spiritual, intellectual, and civic truths, and truth can best be discerned in an environment that allows all ideas to present themselves for debate. Here again, the theory goes, the experience of repressive societies is instructive. Such societies often suppress not only political and cultural ideas, but scientific ones that conflict with official doctrine or the views of powerful institutions like the army, the religious authorities or a ruling political party. Clearly in a society where some topics are off limits and others hold favored positions, truth must take a tortured path to the light.

Free expression is necessary for democratic self-governance, too. Obviously if the people are to be sovereign and free elections are to mean anything, the people need to be able to assemble, to exchange ideas and to circulate information related to public affairs. The press, in particular, must be free to investigate and criticize the government and to check abuses of state power. And finally, free expression works as a kind of social safety valve, and thus works better than suppression in maintaining social order. This view of free expression values tolerance both for its own sake and for its ability to channel dissent into peaceful social change.

Each of these theoretical points argues for a speech system, and a media system, that are as unregulated as possible. After all, to the extent that ideas are public goods, burdening them with regulations serves only to inhibit their production. And a democracy needs ideas. Still, there are fairly obvious and serious objections to all of these theoretical assumptions. Must a free and open society accept the likelihood that some speech will be avowedly anti-democratic, that some people will find self-realization through expression that is anti-social and even dangerous? Is a view of free expression that focuses narrowly on promoting self-government likely to be less tolerant of dissenting ideas in "non-political" areas like art, music, literature and religion—for many people the very things that make democracy worth supporting in the first place? Does "truth" really prevail when confronted with falsehoods? Even under the best of circumstances it is not clear that truth results from an open and earnest search for the truth, and results matter. Perhaps most important, given the concerns of this book, all of these theoretical arguments assume a level of social stability that rarely exists in developing or transition states. Americans may tolerate hate speech they find repulsive; Rwandans, Bosnians and Kosovars have found it fatal.

Free speech norms are not universal, nor can they be. On December 3, 2003, the International Criminal Tribunal for Rwanda found three Rwandan journalists – two broadcasters and a newspaper editor – guilty of genocide; direct and public incitement to commit genocide; and persecution, a crime against humanity. All three were sentenced to life in prison.[106] In the first major international case on media liability since the Nuremberg trials, the broadcasts and print stories published by these journalists was found to be a critical contributing factor in the genocide of approximately 800,000 Rwandans, most of them Tutsis.

In its review of applicable law in the case, the Tribunal looked at prior UN tribunal cases on genocide charges and the decisions of the European Court for Human Rights (ECHR). It did not look at the U.S. standard applicable to the facts of the case, but did imply that U.S. law in incitement cases was not acceptable to the international community. The Tribunal began its analysis of the Rwandans' case by re-examining the Nuremberg conviction of Julius Streicher for publishing anti-Semitic articles in *Der Sturmer*, a Nazi newspaper.[107] Though Streicher was convicted without a showing of a "direct causal link" between the articles and the murder of Jews, the Tribunal determined that his conviction was based on the Nuremberg court's belief that his articles were "a poison injected into the minds of Germans which caused them to follow the National Socialists' policy of Jewish persecution and extermination."[108] The Tribunal then reviewed several court judgments on cases brought under the International Covenant on Civil and Political Rights, and concluded that speech restrictions are permissible when speech is "intimately linked to...the right to be free from incitement to racism or anti-Semitism"[109] and "it was reasonable to anticipate that there was a causal link between the expressions of the author and the poisoned atmosphere."[110] In its review of ECHR precedents, the Tribunal found cases in which liability was imposed without any evidence of causation.[111] Ultimately, the Tribunal defined incitement as "a crime *regardless* of whether it has the effect it intends to have,"[112] though in the Rwandan case it clearly did. In doing so, the Tribunal effectively rejected the U.S. standard in similar such cases, which requires not only a showing of intent, but that the speech in question is likely to cause "imminent" lawless action.[113]

At one point during the trial, the lawyers for Hassan Ngeze, the owner and editor-in-chief of the newspaper *Kangura*, argued that United States law, "as the most speech-protective, should be used as a standard."[114] In rejecting that argument, the Tribunal wrote:

> The Chamber considers international law, which has been well developed in the areas of freedom from discrimination and freedom of expression, to be the point of reference for its consideration of these issues, noting that domestic law varies widely while international law codifies evolving universal standards. The Chamber notes that the jurisprudence of the United States also accepts the fundamental principles set forth in international law and has recognized in its domestic law that incitement to violence, threats, libel, false advertising, obscenity, and child pornography are among those forms of expression that fall outside the scope of freedom of expression.[115]

The Tribunal's rejection of the U.S. standard in incitement cases is especially remarkable considering that based on the court's factual findings the U.S. standard probably would have sustained a conviction in the Rwandan case. So why did the court reject it in favor of its "poisoning the well" standard? One reason is that the European approach to speech law, like the approach taken by virtually all democracies other than the

United States, is to balance freedoms against one another, including the freedom of speech. In the United States, freedom of speech occupies a "preferred position" in the pantheon of rights and social interests. From this follows the second and more important reason: To accept the U.S. standard with respect to incitement, even if it had sustained a conviction in the Rwandan case, would set a precedent that the international community – or at least the Rwandan tribunal – is not prepared to adopt for similar cases with less compelling facts.

The rights of free expression are now included in articles 18, 19 and 20 of the 1948 Universal Declaration of Human Rights,[116] as well as in a host of subsidiary human rights declarations around the world. Just what these rights imply for press freedom, and for the public's rights with respect to the press, is another matter. For all these reasons, then, "freedom" and "responsibility" are perhaps the two words most frequently coupled in media assistance. The coupling reflects the legitimate concern that press freedoms be exercised so as to enhance the prospects for public participation and democratic sustainability rather than to undermine or even destroy them through hate speech, sensationalism, partisanship, unfounded rumor, privacy invasions, and so on.

American journalists, for reasons of historical experience and constitutional principle, almost reflexively regard "responsibility" as code word for government restrictions on media activity whenever the government deems such activity "irresponsible." Partly as a result of this experience, several American NGOs and press organizations active in Europe's transition states have objected to the provision on free expression in the European Convention on Human Rights (Article 10, Section 2), which begins by saying "Everyone has the right to freedom of expression," and then goes on to say that

> the exercise of these freedoms, since it carries with it duties and responsibilities, may be subject to such formalities, conditions, restrictions or penalties as are prescribed by law and are necessary in a democratic society, in the interests of national security, territorial integrity or public safety, for the prevention of disorder or crime, for the protection of health or morals, for the protection of the reputation of rights of others, for preventing the disclosure of information received in confidence, or for maintaining the authority and impartiality of the judiciary.

Despite the obvious potential for government abuse in such language, some forty member countries of the OSCE subscribe to it. Many of the new democracies in Europe have used the same or similar language in drafting their media laws. As a practical matter, most democratic governments take as their official view that "freedom" is the result of non-restrictive government policies towards the media and that "responsibility" is the product of self-regulation, but in both established and emerging democracies this distinction is constantly under challenge. As a number of commentators have observed, one of the common features of an emerging democracy is a greater number of people than ever before who call themselves journalists, but who are untrained and, by almost any standard, unprofessional. In both established and emerging democracies, the Internet exacerbates this trend. Finally, in many advanced Western media systems the ever-widening acceptance of the marketplace as the best arbiter of the public interest has led to greater reliance on sensational over serious journalism and many well-publicized compromises in journalism ethics. Not surprisingly, it has also led to renewed calls, both within the profession and from outside it, for great press accountability. Some journalists reject these criticisms categorically in favor of a more absolutist approach to free expression. Americans in particular take this view, and indeed raised it in the 1997 negotiations with the Council of Europe that gave rise to the OSCE's creation of an office to promote freedom of the media.

Freimut Duve, a German publisher and the former head of the media office of the OSCE, said in a 2002 interview that American free expression law is an artifact of a people with no memory having been invaded and forcibly subdued.[117] Duve's point can be illustrated by the OSCE's involvement in providing international media assistance to Kosovo after the 1998 cease-fire, and a subsequent dispute over the meaning of press freedom that arose between American and European peacekeepers in the province. When NATO troops arrived in Kosovo, there were no virtually no media operations and no functioning public institutions. The province had been decimated by 8 years of fighting and several months of NATO bombing. Two-thirds of the province was in ruins, and one million Albanians – half the population—had fled or been expelled. Unlike Bosnia, where following the 1995 Dayton Accords there were still intact political regimes to interact with the military peacekeepers and international civilian administrations, there was no such infrastructure remaining in Kosovo. As a result, the UN and NATO became the province's de facto government, and its chief administrator, Bernard Kouchner, became its de facto chief executive.

The problem of media rebuilding fell to the OSCE, which imported its media workers who had been engaged in a similar mission in Bosnia. The

OSCE took temporary responsibility for operating television and radio stations, and it announced that Radio Television Pristina (RTVP) would be reborn as public broadcaster on the Western European model; that it would start its own news service; and that the OSCE would train locals to work in these facilities and provide them with financial assistance. The OSCE also created a Media Regulatory Commission whose job included writing a code of conduct for both broadcast and print media. The Commission assumed for itself the power to censor, penalize, fine or shut down any media outlet that violated international reporting standards related to hate speech. In the absence of a functioning judicial system, the UN created its own tribunal and its own appeals court.

A number of problems plagued the OSCE's efforts to carry out its media programs, but a major one was a controversy that arose when reporter Steven Erlanger of the *New York Times* wrote a story that portrayed the OSCE's activities as offensive to free speech principles. Erlanger's story ran under the headline, "NATO Peacekeepers Plan a System of Controls for the News Media in Kosovo,"[118] and it was followed about two weeks later by a *Times* editorial that criticized "Kosovo's Incipient Media Ministry."[119] Kosovo's Albanians, the editorial said, "do not need another group of outsiders to tell them what they can and cannot say.... The best way to combat hate speech is not to ban it, but to insure that Kosovo's citizens have access to alternate views. There is added danger if the regulations are broad enough to bar other ideas the international community does not like. It is risky to…attempt to regulate ideas and expression in a region where these powers have been so tragically misused."[120]

The immediate effect of the *Times'* coverage was to set off a debate within the UN on the OSCE's media role. It also angered local journalists in Kosovo, many of whom had once welcomed the OSCE mission with the hope that it would put end to the kinds of dangerous allegations that tended to circulate in the region's press. The UN responded by withdrawing the OSCE's power to impose penalties on offending media; at most, it was supposed to encourage voluntary ethics codes. More generally, it was limited to the business of "media development." What followed was predictable. In October 1999, a Kosovo Liberation Army news service (the *Kosova Press*, the official paper of the province's new interim government) published attacks on the journalists Veton Surroi and Baton Haxhiu, both from the newspaper *Koha Ditore*, after their paper condemned the practice of revenge attacks and editorialized about rise of Albanian fascism. Surroi had even gone so far as to compare the excesses of Albanian nationalists with those of Belgrade before the war. The *Kosova Press* called Surroi a "traitor" and referred to Surroi and Haxhiu together as "bastard ragtags," "ordinary mobsters," and "the garbage of history."[121] "Such criminals and enslaved minds should not have a place in the free Kosovo," the paper said, and alleged that the two men had collaborated with Serb paramilitaries during the war and were now spies for the international community. "It would not be surprising," the *Kosova Press* concluded, "if they became victims of possible and understandable revenge acts."[122]

Koha Ditore responded by republishing the *Kosova Press* text in full and accusing the paper of "calling for murder."[123] The OSCE could do nothing but express its "serious concern," and the OSCE media coordinator in Kosovo said of the *Kosova Press* that "Goebbels couldn't have done it better."[124] Other incidents followed. In one case a nationalist newspaper (*World Today*) published an article alleging that an American representative of Human Rights Watch was a homosexual after he condemned revenge attacks; in the homophobic and hyper-masculine world of Kosovo, such a charge not only serves to undermine a person's credibility, but poses a threat to his safety.[125] *World Today* accused another human rights worker of being a Russian spy, also a life-threatening allegation.[126] Finally, in February 2000, the UN itself imposed hate speech regulations that allowed for prison sentences or fines for racial, religious, ethnic hate, but only if the speech in question applied to a group. Nationalist newspapers immediately found ways to violate the spirit of the law while keeping to its letter, for example publishing names of Serbs believed to have committed war crimes, along with their home addresses and places of employment.[127] The OSCE objected that such practices were both dangerous and irresponsible, but could not act.

The *New York Times'* position on Kosovo's media situation was a uniquely American one. But it is not the international view, in which principles of free expression are much more likely to be weighed against countervailing social interests and other civil rights, including the right to "security of person."[128] The logic of restricting hate speech – clearly visible in the Universal Declaration of Human Rights – is that without such restrictions certain groups and individuals will be unable to participate equally in society, maintain their sense of personal security or their self-worth as human beings. In such an environment, democracy of a certain kind is impossible. But that judgment depends on the social values – the public interests – one believes should be at the heart of communications law and policy.

Notes

1. David Held, "Democracy and Globalization," Working Paper 97/5 (Leipzig, Germany: Max Planck Institute for the Study of Societies, May 1997), 1, http://www.mpi-fg-koeln.mpg.de/pu/workpap/wp97-5/wp97-5.html (accessed January 27, 2006).
2. See Takashi Inoguchi, Edward Newman and John Keane, *The Changing Nature of Democracy* (New York: United Nations University Press, 1998), ii.
3. Robert O. Keohane and Joseph S. Nye, "Introduction" in Governance in a Globalizing World, eds. Joseph S. Nye and John D. Donahue (Washington, DC: Brookings Institute Press, 2000), 14.
4. Robert A. Dahl, *Democracy and Its Critics* (New Haven, CT: Yale University Press, 1989), 319.
5. Herbert Gans, "Journalism, Journalism Education and Democracy," *Journalism and Mass Communication Educator* (Spring 2004): 10-16, 14.
6. Ann M. Florini and P.J. Simmons, "What the World Needs Now?" in *The Third Force: The Rise of Transnational Civil Society*, ed. Ann M. Florini (New York: Japan Center for International Exchange and Carnegie Endowment for International Peace, 2000), 3.
7. Fritz Scharpf, *Governing in Europe: Effective and Legitimate?* (Oxford: Oxford University Press, 1999).
8. Klaus Hansch, public lecture, European University Institute, Florence, Italy, June 27, 1996.
9. Ann Hudock, "Democratizing the Media," paper prepared for the Aspen Institute/Ford Foundation International Roundtable on Journalism and Freedom of Expression, November 12-14, 2003, 3.
10. James Curran, "Mass Media and Democracy Revisited," in *Mass Media and Society, 2nd ed.*, eds. Curran and Michael Gurevitch (London: Arnold Publishers, 1996).
11. Beata Rozumilowicz, "Democratic Change: A Theoretical Perspective," in *Media Reform: Democratizing the Media, Democratizing the State*, eds. Monroe Price, Beata Rozumilowicz and Stefan Verhulst (New York: Routledge, 2002), 11.
12. Ross Howard, *International Media Assistance: A Review of Donor Activities and Lessons Learned* (Amsterdam: Netherlands Institute of International Relations: Conflict Research Unit, June 2003), 16-17.
13. Robert W. Hefner, "Civil Society: Cultural Possibility of a Modern Ideal," *Society* (March-April 1998): 18.
14. See, for example, Gordon White, "Civil Society, Democratization and Development: Clearing the Analytical Ground," *Democratization* Vol. 1, No. 3 (Autumn 1994): 375-390.
15. There is a large and recent literature on the subject of civil society. For an overview, see John Keane, *Civil Society: Old Images, New Visions* (Stanford, CA: Stanford University Press, 1998).
16. Lester M. Salamon, Helmut K. Anheier, Regina List, Stefan Toepler, S. Wojciech Sokolowski, *Global Civil Society: Dimensions of the Nonprofit Sector* (Baltimore, MD: The Johns Hopkins Center for Civil Society Studies, 1999), 3-4.
17. Ibid., 8-9.
18. See Michael Walzer, *Toward a Global Civil Society* (Providence, RI: Berghahn Books, 1998), 1-7.

19. In democratic theory, civil society is also the essential element in mobilizing opposition to authoritarian or totalitarian regimes, and so at its most elemental it includes ordinary citizens who are not part of any organization but who turn up in the streets in marches, heckle the police, express their opposition to specific government measures, and challenge the regime in mass protests. Their activity is important because groups by themselves, no matter how many or heroic, are insufficient to overthrow a non-democratic regime. The presence of thousands of protesters in the streets force the regime to decide whether it is willing to use massive force to sustain itself, an action that will almost certainly weaken the whatever remaining claim to legitimacy the government has.

20. For discussion on the changing role of government vis-à-vis NGOs, see Jessica T. Matthews, "Power Shift," *Foreign Affairs* (January/February 1997): 50-66.

21. Don E. Eberly, "The Meaning, Origins and Applications of Civil Society," in *The Essential Civil Society Reader: The Classic Essays*, ed. Don E. Eberly (New York: Rowman & Littlefield Publishers, 2000).

22. See Michael Foley and Bob Edwards, "The Paradox of Civil Society," *Journal of Democracy*, Vol. 7, No. 3 (1996): 38-52; and Marina Ottaway and Thomas Carothers, eds., *Funding Virtue: Civil Society Aid and Democracy Promotion* (Washington, DC: Carnegie Endowment for International Peace, 2000).

23. *Malaysiakini* is a subscription- and advertiser-supported online newspaper, available at www.malaysiakini.com.

24. Juan J. Linz and Alfred Stepan, *Problems of Democratic Transition and Consolidation: Southern Europe, South America and Post-Communist Europe* (Baltimore, MD: Johns Hopkins University Press, 1996), 40-65.

25. *The Hindu*, "The mythologies of civil society" (November 5, 1998).

26. For a case study of civil society development under a weak state, See Michael Foley, "Laying the Groundwork: The struggle for civil society in El Salvador," *Journal of InterAmerican Studies and World Affairs* (Spring 1996): 81-83.

27. Walzer, *Global Civil Society*, 1998, 23.

28. See John S. Dryzek, "Political Inclusion and the Dynamics of Democratization," *American Political Science Review* (September 1996): 475-87.

29. For a discussion on the development of civil society associations in authoritarian societies, see Catherine E. Dalpino, *Deferring Democracy: Promoting Openness in Authoritarian Regimes* (Washington, DC: Brookings Institution Press, 2000), 52-72.

30. David Martin Jones, "Democratization, Civil Society, and Illiberal Middle Class Culture in Pacific Asia," *Comparative Politics*, Vol. 30, No. 2 (January 1998): 147-69, 152.

31. Ibid, 159.

32. Basma el Husseiny, Cairo program officer, Ford Foundation, author interview, Santiago, Chile, March 16, 2001.

33. Daniel del Castillo, "A 1,000-Year-Old University Takes on a New and Troubling Role," *Chronicle of Higher Education* (May 11, 2001): A47.

34. John Charles Chasteen, *Born in Blood and Fire: A Concise History of Latin America* (New York: W.W. Norton, 2001), 275-301.

35. Ibid, 287.

36. Ibid, 289.

37. Ibid, 290.

38. Faride Zeran, director, department of journalism, University of Chile, author interview, Santiago, Chile, March 15, 2001.

39. Ibid.

40. Eugenio Tironi and Guillermo Sunkel, "The Modernization of Communications: The Media in the Transition to Democracy in Chile," in *Democracy and the Media: A Comparative Perspective*, eds. Richard Gunther and Anthony Mughan (New York: Cambridge University Press, 2000), 165-94, 177.

41. Ibid, 170-179. Only in the final days of the Pinochet regime, in 1989, did the government authorize the creation of two private VHF television channels, Megavision and La Red.

42. Ibid, 180.

43. Maria Eugenia Hirmas, "The Chilean Case: Television in the 1988 Plebiscite," in *Television, Politics and the Transition to Democracy in Latin America*, ed. Thomas E. Skidmore (Washington, DC: Woodrow Wilson Center Press, 1993), 82-95.

44. See Ken Leon-Dermota, *And Well Tied Down: Chile's Press Under Democracy* (Westport, CT: Praeger Publishers, 2003).

45. Robert T. Buckman and Richard R. Cole, "Birth, Death and Resurrection of Press Freedom in Chile," in *Communication in Latin America: Journalism, Mass Media, and Society*, ed. Richard R. Cole (Wilmington, DE: Scholarly Resources, 1960).

46. *Informe sobre la Tortura y Prision Politica en Chile*, Gobierno de Chile, March 2005. The report is available at www.emol.com/noticias/documentos/informe_tortura/prologo.pdf.

47. Katie Humphrey and Heidi Koester, "The Chilean Press: Diverse Voices and Legal Changes," unpublished research paper, Medill School of Journalism, Northwestern University, May 2005, 13.

48. *The Clinic* (April 28, 2005), 1.

49. *Sistema de Verificacion de Circulacion y Lectoria* (Santiago, Chile: Asociacion Nacional de Avisadores, May 2005).

50. Quoted in Humphrey and Koester, "The Chilean Press," 2005, 19.

51. See Human Rights Watch, *The Limits of Tolerance: Freedom of Expression and Public Debate in Chile*, (New York: Human Rights Watch, 1998), 46-57.

52. See "Chile: Scrap Laws Criminalizing 'Disrespectful' Speech," Human Rights Watch, March 10, 2005, http://hrw.org/english/docs/2005/03/10/chile10287.htm (accessed January 3, 2006); see also Javier Sierra, "Members of Congress Defend Freedom of the Press in Chile," Washington, DC: International Center for Journalists, January 13, 2003, http://www.libertad-prensa.org/congresistas-eng.html (accessed January 4, 2006).

53. Sebastian Brett, Human Rights Watch Chile, author interview, Santiago, Chile, March 14, 2001.

54. Zeran, author interview, 2001.

55. Federico Joannon, managing editor, *El Mostrador*, author interview, Santiago, Chile, March 16, 2001.

56. Tina Rosenberg, "The Monochromatic Media of Latin America," *New York Times* (May 7, 2001): A20.

57. Craig L. LaMay and Burton Weisbrod, "The Funding Perils of the Corporation for Public Broadcasting," in *To Profit or Not to Profit: The Commercialization of the Non Profit Sector*, ed. Burton A. Weisbrod (New York: Cambridge University Press, 1998), 249-267.

58. See Bruce Bimber, "The Internet and political transformation: populism, community, and accelerated pluralism," *Polity* Vol. 31, No. 1 (Fall 1998): 133-160.

59. See William Ratliff, "Development and Civil Society in Latin America and Asia," *Annals of the American Academy of Political and Social Science* (September 1999): 91-113.

60. Brett, author interview, 2001.
61. Dryzek, "Political Inclusion," 1996.
62. See Linz and Stepan, *Problems of Democratic Transition,* 1996, 8-15; see also Michael Bernhard, "Civil Society After the First Transition: Dilemmas of Post-communist Democratization in Poland and Beyond," *Communist and Post-Communist Studies*, Vol. 29, No. 3 (1996): 309-330.
63. Arrow first explained the impossibility theorem in "A Difficulty in the Concept of Social Welfare," *Journal of Political Economy*, Vol. 58, No. 4 (August, 1950): 328-346.
64. Kenneth A. Shepsle and Mark S. Bonchek, *Analyzing Politics: Rationality, Behavior and Institutions* (New York: W.W. Norton, 1997).
65. For a complete discussion of this issue, see Ellen Mickiewicz, and Charles Firestone, *Television and Elections*, 2d Ed. (Durham, NC: DeWitt Wallace Center, Duke University, 1999).
66. *Pell v. Procunier,* 417 U.S. 817 (1974).
67. *Saxbe v. Washington Post*, 417 U.S. 843 (1974).
68. *Miami Herald v. Tornillo*, 418 U.S. 241 (1974).
69. Ibid, at 245.
70. See Rodney A. Smolla, *Free Speech in an Open Society* (New York: Knopf, 1992), 298-302.
71. James Miller, "Democratization and 'Fact-Based' Journalism: Donor Politics in East Central Europe," paper presented at an International Conference of the Association for Education in Journalism and Mass Communication, London, January 5, 2002, 1-23.
72. Ibid., 3.
73. Ibid.
74. Denis McQuail, *Media Performance: Mass Communication and the Public Interest* (Newbury Park, CA: Sage Publications, 1992), 8.
75. J.B. Lemert, *Criticizing the Media* (Newbury Park, CA: Sage Publications, 1989).
76. Anthony Mughan and Richard Gunther, "The Media in Democratic and Non-democratic Regimes: A Multilevel Perspective," in *Democracy and the Media: A Comparative Perspective, eds.* Gunther and Mughan (New York: Cambridge University Press, 2000), 2-4.
77. Ibid.
78. Beata Rozumilowicz, "Democratic Change: A Theoretical Perspective," in *Media Reform: Democratizing the Media, Democratizing the State*, eds. Monroe Price, Beata Rozumilowicz and Stefan Verhulst (New York: Routledge, 2002), 14.
79. That system understood the world's media as consisting of four types: authoritarian, libertarian, social responsibility and Soviet communist. See Frederick Siebert, Theodore Peterson, and Wilbur Schramm, *Four Theories of the Press* (Champagne: University of Illinois Press, 1961).
80. Guy Berger, "Grave New World? Democratic Journalism Enters the Global Twenty-First Century," *Journalism Studies*, Vol. 1, No. 1 (2000): 81-99.
81. Rozumiloweicz, "Democratic Change," 2002, 13.
82. Maciej Wierzynski, Chief of Polish Service, Voice of America, author interview, Santiago, Chile, March 11, 2001.
83. Rosa María Alfaro, president, Calandria, author interview, Santiago, Chile, March 13, 2001.
84. See Lawrence K. Grossman and Newton N. Minow, *A Digital Gift to the Nation: Fulfilling the Promise of the Digital and Internet Age* (New York: Century Foundation Press, 2001).

85. Wierzynski, author interview, 2001.
86. See Berger, "Grave New World?" 2001.
87. See James Curran, "Rethinking Media and Democracy," in *Mass Media and Society,* eds. Curran and Michael Gurevitch (New York: Oxford University Press, 2000).
88. Rozumilowicz, "Democratic Change," 2002, 15.
89. Monroe E. Price, "Sustainability: An Approach Towards a Matrix," discussion paper prepared for the Aspen Institute Roundtable on Journalism and Freedom of Expression, March 13-16, 2001, draft dated February 25, 2001.
90. See Robert M. Entman and Steven S. Wildman, "Reconciling Economic and Non-Economic Perspectives on Media Policy: Transcending the 'Marketplace of Ideas,'" *Journal of Communication* (Winter 1992): 5-19.
91. Daoud Kuttab, director, Institute of Modern Media, Al-Quds University, author interview, March 13, 2001, Santiago, Chile.
92. Ibid.
93. See Benjamin Compaine, "Think Again: Global Media," *Foreign Policy* (November/December 2002): 20; see also Jim Rutenberg, "Fewer Media Owners, More Media Choices," *New York Times* (December 2, 2002): C1.
94. Several commentators have argued that going digital does not mean going democratic. See, for example, Shanthi Kalathil and Taylor C. Boas, *Open Networks, Closed Regimes: The Impact of the Internet on Authoritarian Rule* (Washington, DC: Carnegie Endowment for International Peace, 2003). The Internet has also proved a valuable organizing tool for anti-democratic groups both domestic and international. See James Goodale, "Could the WTC Attack Have Happened Without the Internet?" *New York Law Journal* (October 5, 2001); Todd Lighty and Stephen Franklin, "Activist targets Jihad's Web site," *Chicago Tribune* (January 5, 2003), C1; Sridhar Alathur, "Web of Hate: Religion, caste and nationality are the basis of South Asian hate Web sites," *Indian American* (January 3, 2003): 24. Some literature also argues that the Internet is more likely to promote to political fragmentation than democratic cohesion. See Bimber, "The Internet and political transformation,"1998.
95. See A. Lin Neumann, "The Resistance Network," *Wired* (January 1996) www.wired.com/wired/archive/4.01/countrynet_pr.html. (accessed January 27, 2006).
96. See, for example, Jonathan Zittrain and Benjamin Edelman, "Documentation of Internet Filtering in Saudi Arabia" (Cambridge, MA: Harvard Law School, September 12, 2002), http://cyber.law.harvard.edu/filtering/saudiarabia/., (accessed January 27, 2006); see also Joseph Kahn, "China has World's Tightest Internet Censorship, Study Finds," *New York Times* (December 4, 2002):A1.
97. See, for example, Richard Gunther and Anthony Mughan, eds., *Democracy and the Media: A Comparative Perspective* (New York: Cambridge University Press, 2000), 434-444. See also Alan Albarran and Sylvia Chan-Omsted, *Global Media Economics: Commercialization, Concentration and Integration of World Media* (Ames: Iowa State University Press, 1998).
98. Kuttab, author interview, 2001.
99. See "The News According to Gazprom," *Transitions Online*, (April 9-17, 2001); and "End-TV?" *Transitions Online* (April 2-8 2001), www.tol.cz. See also *Radio Free Europe/Radio Liberty Media Matters*, Vol. 1, No. 9 (April 6, 2001): 4-7.
100. Peter Baker, "Russian Journalists Plan Rival Network: Ex-NTV Staff Facing Many Obstacles," *Washington Post* (April 16, 2001): A12.
101. David Hoffman, "Russian Media Policy Linked to Soviet Era," *Washington Post* (September 14, 2000): A24. See also Susan B. Glasser and Peter Baker, "Russian Network Seized in Raid," *Washington Post* (April 15, 2001): A1.

102. See "Godfather of the Kremlin?" *Forbes* (December 30, 1996), http://www.forbes. com/free_forbes/1996/1230/5815090a.html (accessed November 16, 2005).
103. "Who owns what in Russia's media," Europe.CNN.com, April 18, 2001.
104. Jeremy Drucker, publisher and editor, *Transitions Online*, author interview, Santiago, Chile, March 14, 2001.
105. Ellen Hume, *Media Assistance: Best Practices and Priorities, Report on a USAID Workshop* (Washington, DC: USAID, Bureau for Policy and Program Coordination, November 2003), 13-14.
106. *Prosecutor v. Ferdinand Nahimana, Jean-Bosco Barayagwiza, Hassan Ngeze*, Judgment and Sentence ICTR, Case No. ICTR-99-52-T (2003).
107. Nazi Conspiracy and Aggression, Opinion and Judgment (October 1, 1946), Office of the U.S. Chief of Counsel for Prosecution of Axis Criminality 56 (1947).
108. *Nahimana*, Case No. ICTR-99-52-T, at Sec. 981, citing Nazi Conspiracy and Aggression, 1946; and Office of the U.S. Chief Counsel, 1947.
109. Ibid, at Sec. 989, citing *Robert Faurisson v. France*, UN Doc. CCPR/C/58/ D/550/1993 (1996).
110. Ibid, at Sec. 986, citing *Ross v. Canada*, UN Doc. CCPR/C/70/D/736/1997 (2000).
111. Ibid, at Secs. 993, 994, citing Jersild v. Denmark, 19 Eur.Ct.H.R. 1 (ser. A) (1995); and *Zana v. Turkey*, 69 Eur.Ct.H.R. (ser. A) (1997).
112. Ibid, at Sec. 1029.
113. See *Brandenburg v. Ohio*, 395 U.S. 444 (1969). In *Brandenburg*, the Supreme Court reversed the conviction of a Ku Klux Klan leader convicted for advocating violent action against blacks and Jews. In its opinion the Court said that such speech can only give rise to liability "where such advocacy is directed to inciting imminent lawless action and is likely to incite or produce such action."
114. *Nahimana*, Case No. ICTR-99-52-T, at Sec. 1010.
115. Ibid.
116. See the Universal Declaration of Human Rights at http://www.un.org/Overview/ rights.html.
117. Freimut Duve, OSCE media representative, author interview, Evanston, Ill, April 5, 2001. Duve himself was the son of a Jewish mother, and so as a child was hidden from the Nazis.
118. Steven Erlanger, "NATO Peacekeepers Plan a System of Controls for the News Media in Kosovo," *New York Times* (August 16, 1999): A1.
119. "Kosovo's Incipient Media Ministry," *New York Times* (August 30, 1999): A29.
120. Ibid.
121. Quoted in Stacy Sullivan, "Kosovo," in *Restructuring the Media in Post-Conflict Societies: Four Perspectives*, ed. Monroe E. Price (Geneva: UNESCO, May 2000), 58.
122. Ibid.
123. Ibid.
124. Ibid, 59.
125. Ibid.
126. Ibid.
127. Ibid., 60.
128. Quoting Article 3 of the Universal Declaration of Human Rights. See http://www. un.org/Overview/rights.html.

5

Editorial Mission and the Dilemma
of Revenue Sources

"News is what somebody somewhere wants to sup-
press; all the rest is advertising."—Lord Northcliffe

If media independence depends to a great deal on the availability of
reliable and varied sources of revenue, it is surprising that the literature
on media assistance, and media assistance itself, takes so little cogni-
zance of the economics of news and public affairs information. In many
places, understandably, the immediate challenges to the survival of free
media are still located in rule of law and civil society issues. Where that
is so, independence is not primarily a problem of finance. But even in
those situations, USAID now argues, "technical or financial assistance
should be given only to those media enterprises willing to take concrete
and concerted steps toward economic independence."[1] As already noted,
many non-governmental aid providers have also moved "sustainability"
to the top of their priorities list for assistance. And yet it is difficult to
find in any aid providers' literature much more than brief and vague
exhortations to do better. In a 2004 overview of its media assistance
programs, USAID noted that its own emphasis on economic sustainability had "achieved only limited success"[2]:

> Many media outlets were not interested in economic independence. In former com-
> munist countries, many owners and editors viewed the media as a public good and
> strongly believed that society should subsidize them. Still others found it easier to
> cut deals with special interests rather than take drastic measures to increase sales and
> advertising or reduce expenses. Independent media were also at a disadvantage vis-
> à-vis state-owned media enterprises, which received preferential treatment in many
> former communist countries. As a result, independent media firms had problems
> competing with state-owned media outlets. In countries such as Albania, Bosnia,
> Russia and Serbia, the media market was oversaturated. Too many newspapers,

periodicals, and radio and television stations competed for the same advertising and audience share. Many business training programs designed to improve economic viability were not quite effective: they provided general information, not knowledge that could be put to immediate use. As democracies stagnated in many parts of the world, independent media faced increased political interference and manipulation. Finally, economic viability was hampered by weak country economics.[3]

Numerous media assistance NGOs offer seminars and publications on different aspects of media management (accounting, marketing and research, sales, case studies, and so on), and while some of these products may be excellent, they, too, tend to be general in their approach. The online newspaper in Malaysia may learn something of significant value from studying the radio network in Indonesia or the newspaper in Guatemala, but the particular challenges facing each business are unique. Finally, training programs alone do not address the truly critical economic problem facing independent media organizations in developing societies: access to affordable capital.

This book, again, argues that the relationship between revenue sources and editorial mission (or quality) is a first-order problem deserving more careful attention. Above all, the belief that media rooted in the private, for-profit sector are more likely to be editorially independent may be true, but not necessarily so. Not-for-profit media are not the key to independence and quality either, unless those firms enjoy a monopoly position, with little or no competition from for-profit media. Such a situation is highly unlikely, and the effect of competition, over time, will compel not-for-profits to behave more like their for-profit competitors.

This point should be obvious but apparently it is not. In recent years, journalists and others concerned with what they perceive to be the declining quality of news and public affairs products in the United States have proposed non-profit institutional models as one alternative to for-profit, publicly traded media firms.[4] The idea is at least as old as the 1947 report of the Commission for a Free and Responsible Press[5] (more commonly known as the Hutchins Commission after its president, University of Chicago President Robert Maynard Hutchins), which among its conclusions urged that non-profit institutions invest to "help supply the variety, quantity and quality of press service required by the American people."[6] A current attempt to revive the spirit of the Hutchins Commission – The Commission on the Role of the Press in a Democracy, a program of the Annenberg Foundation Trust, informally dubbed "H2" by many of its participants[7]-- devoted a substantial part of its June 2005 deliberations to the possibility that not-for-profit incorporation might work a remedy for the many perceived ills afflicting journalism today, in particular what one background paper for the conference called "market censorship."[8] "The central idea," as a contemporaneous Carnegie Corporation report on the subject said, is that "a news organization that hopes only to break even can focus less on what will sell and more on the kinds of coverage it believes society needs."[9]

This assertion almost certainly claims too much. It ignores the fact that the amount of revenue needed to "break even" is primarily a function of the larger competitive environment in which an organization works. . In media systems that environment will often have a dominant sector (for example, private for-profit firms or government media) whose operations will affect the costs of labor, equipment, content (for example, newsprint prices or the cost of rights licensing) and just about everything else in the production chain. This has implications not only for media firms who understand their primary role as serving a social mission, but for organizations that seek to assist them. The short of it is that is that the producer of mission goods cannot sustain the business without tax support, substantial donations or, assuming neither of those are available in sufficient amount, something to sell – revenue goods. Revenue goods are those to which one can assign a market value and that can be sold at a profit; mission goods, as economists under them, are those that the market does not value properly and which, as a result, are usually supplied by non-profit firms.

For most public-service media, the financing choice usually comes down to the third option. Tax support and grants are hard to come by, and for reasons already discussed grants are often undesirable as well. But the decision to produce a mix of mission goods and revenue goods has its own problems, chief among them that though they are usually related, they are not the same. To take a non-media example, consider a university performing arts school. Its mission good is the education of students as scholars, actors, singers, dancers, musicians, directors, choreographers, set designers and the rest. The department might, however, use the exact same inputs used to produce the mission good to produce a revenue good – a play, a musical, or a concert – to which the school sells tickets. The revenue from ticket sales covers production costs, and whatever profits are left over, ideally, go to further the mission good – to new lighting, costumes, instruments, books, teachers, and so on.

One sees this in all kinds of performing arts venues, whether university drama departments or world-class orchestras. The mission good for most of these organizations includes finding and developing new artists and performing new works of music and drama, but in order to pay for that good most of the organizations devote most of their public performances to a small and well-worn library of "greatest hits." To take the most obvious example, each December it is all but impossible to find a major American theater or municipal orchestra that does not do a production of Dickens' *A Christmas Carol* or Tchaikovsky's *Nutcracker* Suite. And they do these productions because ticket sales to them will typically generate well more than half the annual revenue for the company. Fine, but what of the orchestra that performs only greatest hits, that all but ignores new artists and new works because audiences are not eager to pay for them? This is a harder problem. For any firm that understands its primary role as producing a mission good, the constant challenge is figuring out what the proper balance of mission goods and revenue goods should be. That challenge will always be easier when viewed merely as a financial matter. Viewed as a qualitative one, it will always be susceptible to differing judgments about the character of the mission good. The small municipal orchestra whose schedule consists exclusively of the best-known works of a half-dozen eighteenth- and nineteenth-century European composers, for example, might argue that it is better to live off that repertoire than to have no orchestra at all.

In the journalism world we see the same problem and the same kinds of conceptual confusion for the same reasons. Most media management training, for example, makes no meaningful or useful distinction between mission goods and revenue goods, but rather assumes that a well-managed and sustainable media firm produces both in some adequate mix. Given the absence of any reliable way to determine the "public interest" the assumption is forgivable, maybe necessary, but at some point it can lead to other assumptions that do not make sense. On its Web pages and in its public presentations, for example, the Northwestern-based Media Management Center employs a slide presentation that explains to news executives how to engage young people newspaper as readers. Among the first few slides is a pair of visual analogies. One is a photograph of an old, grimy street-corner coffee stand juxtaposed with a photograph of the clean, well-appointed interior of a Starbucks store. The second compares an old Ford Pinto with a new Toyota Prius hybrid.[10] The point of the comparisons is to show managers that they must think in entirely new ways about who their customers are, and particularly about the younger generation of consumers whose needs and lifestyles are emphatically not those of their parents. The intent of this photographic analogy is fine, but as an economic proposition it is misleading, if not simply wrong. A cup of coffee, for instance, has none of the characteristics of a public good: You and I cannot both drink the same cup of coffee. An automobile is not an experience good: I do not have to get into a Pinto, never mind drive one, to know it is not a Prius. At every level, the production of coffee and cars is also far more efficient than it was 100 years ago. Reporting, to be sure, has been made more efficient by communications technologies, but reporting (as opposed to mere "communications") is not coffee or cars. To compare these goods is a first-order economic mistake that permits almost any product consisting of ink on paper to pass as journalism. It is only on this basis, frankly, that one can talk about Guatemala's *El Periodico* and *Nuestro Diario* as being in the same business.

The larger point here is that financial independence by itself is not a value worth sustaining. If it were, *Nuestro Diario* would be the shining example of success in a fragile democracy. Of course media that do not enjoy financial independence cannot guarantee their survival, never mind their editorial mission, and will be tempted to compromise or abandon that mission to go in search of more reliable sources of revenue. This is the dilemma of *El Periodico*, discussed in chapter 1, but it is the dilemma faced by *any* high-quality news or public affairs medium, anywhere. Indeed, to examine the dilemma more closely, this chapter takes as a case study a public affairs medium with which most readers will be familiar – U.S. public broadcasting – and the effect of uncertain revenues on an editorial mission that, if vague, is nonetheless emphatically (and statutorily) more concerned with "quality" than the profit-generating goals of its competitors. Before turning to that case study, let us first review the economic factors that constrain news production and consumption.

News and the Problems of Supply and Demand

News is shaped by the economics of information goods, and information goods have many of the characteristics of public goods. That is to say, information is not like cars or Peach Bowl tickets or plumbing fixtures, but rather more like street lights, parks or police protection: one person's use (or consumption) of them does not preclude use by another. Public goods typically also have high fixed costs—for example, the cost of raising, training, equipping and maintaining an army is enormous – and those costs are typically borne by the public in the form of taxes. Without such provision, many among us would happily let others pay for benefits we enjoy. Why should I contribute to the cost of a streetlight, for example, if my neighbors will pay instead? The light will be no less bright because I choose to ride on the investment of others. If too many of my neighbors reach the same conclusion, however, our economic problem becomes a social problem: The street goes dark. Thus the notion of public goods.

News in its various forms can be described as such a public good. The news business has high fixed costs (printing presses and paper, transmitters and cameras, reporters and editors and designers, and so on); the benefits of news cannot be easily limited to a single consumer; and it would be inefficient to try to so limit them. In practical terms, for example, by far the majority of costs associated with printing a newspaper are the human costs involved in producing the first copy, and once that first copy is sent to press the marginal costs of printing several thousand more copies is very small. The marginal costs in broadcast news are even smaller; the production and distribution costs of the program remain virtually the same whether the program is viewed by one person or by one million.

Wherever these characteristics are found in a product, there arises a simple economic problem. If, one the one hand, the producer charges the average cost of the product (the cost of that first copy), many potential consumers will not buy it, either because they are unwilling or unable to do so. Charging the average cost is therefore inefficient (and dumb), because it excludes potential buyers who would happily pay more for the product than it would cost the producer to include them as customers. And from a social point of view, there is another inefficiency, since selling the product at its average cost will result in the product being under-produced. If, however, the producer charges the marginal cost of the product – the relatively small cost of printing all those extra newspapers or serving all those extra viewers – he will not make enough to cover the cost of producing that first "copy" of the product. Our newspaper publisher or broadcaster will go broke.

Because news and other kinds of public affairs information have these public good characteristics, there are few market incentives to produce them. In First Amendment theory and law, this economic reality is captured by the "marketplace of ideas" metaphor, where the assumption is that if as a society we want the benefit of ideas (or as economists would say, the positive externalities of ideas) we should not burden them with regulatory or other kinds of impediments. This is one answer, if an incomplete one, to those who would choose to restrain hate speech or other arguably "false" ideas.

In the realm of democratic theory, information about public affairs – news – is even more problematic because its consumption is an inefficient activity. That is to say, there is not much demand for the stuff, at least not the stuff journalists tend to think we need to know and care about as citizens. Indeed, when journalists anywhere complain about the lack of serious, "quality" journalism available to the public, they state the problem exactly backwards. The problem is not the lack of supply, but the lack of demand: rational people do not follow the news so they can be better citizens, and certainly not so they can be well-informed voters. As economist Anthony Downs demonstrated in 1957, the chances that any single vote will actually make a difference to an electoral outcome is infinitesimally small, and thus the time any of us spends gathering and digesting political information for the purpose of voting can be more productively spent doing other things. [11]Downs called this disinclination to consume news of public affairs "rational ignorance."[12] More recently, economist James Hamilton has called the response of most media organizations – to provide less than optimal amounts and types of public affairs news – an act of "rational omission."[13]

Whether such ignorance is efficient is another thing. One might quarrel with Downs' view of the value of voting, since of course all votes *do* count (or in a democracy are supposed to count) in the aggregate, but as a matter of mathematical probability, Downs is right; the likelihood that any *single* vote will matter to the outcome of an election is infinitesimally small. It is smaller still if one assumes that democratic governance is about more than elections. Beginning with Theodore Lowi, any number of political theorists have argued that meaningful political power in the United States requires the time, expertise and financial resources to access and work the bureaucratic apparatus of government, an apparatus that changes little (except to grow ever larger and more Byzantine) irrespective of who is in charge. This assumption applies to all advanced democracies (Dahl's polyarchies), and I have heard journalists in developing democracies from Malaysia to Guatemala say the same thing – that elections by themselves change little about the character or priorities of government. Without reading so much as a word of political science or economics, most people understand these things intuitively, and so are disinclined to consume public affairs journalism.

If so, our economic problem again becomes a social problem. The journalists in developing countries whom I interviewed for this book consistently told me that the first task for democracy is ending historic divisions of race, ethnicity or class so that people can identify their common interests. (By their words and by their deeds, these journalists, like good journalists everywhere, reject Downs' rational ignorance theory.) To the extent they see themselves as a principal agent of that change, these journalists are right to think that the consumption of public affairs media can have positive externalities for democracy that have little to do with voting, such as the formation and support of civil society organizations. They are also right to think that the disinclination to consume political information can have negative externalities, in the form of misguided policies, demagogic leaders, civic decay and poisonous foreign relations. As discussed earlier, these various externalities are among the explicit reasons given for the provision of media assistance. But as discussed in chapter 4, the relationship between political society and civil society is a complex one, and it is not always clear how or even whether the two are connected. Moreover to the extent there is such a connection, in the form of work done by NGOs, the largest of these organizations often succeed precisely because of their ability to engage political society on its own terms – with lawyers, lobbyists, public relations campaigns, survey research, and the rest.

For all these reasons, most people remain ignorant about public affairs. Like their audiences, journalists and news organizations everywhere know this, if only intuitively, and so they invest relatively little in learning about or covering public affairs with any depth. It is cheaper and more profitable to feature coverage that focuses overwhelmingly on style and presentation rather than substance; the latter requires more resources to produce and is less likely to appeal to broad audiences. When news organizations do treat the news seriously, writes Herbert Gans, "lack of time and space still forces journalist to focus on what I call the Knowns, especially in government, and among Unknowns to limit themselves to those who engage in conflict, break the law, or carry out unusual activities."[14] One indication of news organizations' interest in public affairs is the relatively low pay that journalists in general earn compared to other, similarly educated people in the labor market. In the United States it is not uncommon for the highest-paid editorial staffer in a local newspaper to be a sports or gossip columnist whose province is, essentially, entertainment, but whose value to the paper is his or her appeal to the largest number of potential readers. Celebrity journalists – news anchors, talk show hosts and others—are valuable in the same way. The result of all this is a perverse kind of economic logic: It makes sense to spend lavishly for things that have perceived market value rather than to plow money into things like newsgathering, which may or may not make a discernable difference to a news operation's economic performance.

Other economic characteristics of newsgathering and production also militate against public affairs reporting. One is that news and public affairs information, in addition to being public goods, are also experience goods. That is to say, unlike a motorcycle, a chainsaw or a football helmet, I cannot make a reliable determination about the quality of a media product without first consuming it. As a result, if I purchase and read Newspaper A I cannot know for certain whether I would have been better off if I had instead purchased and read Newspaper B – unless, of course, I do just that.[15] Faced with several media choices, the best I can do as a consumer is to look for signals about content – for example, the length or style of stories, the design or presentation of the product – that conform to my preferences. As a result, producers of media products are compelled to make editorial decisions in an environment in which consumers themselves may have limited knowledge about how different media products serve different preferences. The problem, again, is how to stimulate demand. The editorial responses to this economic problem are familiar to anyone who has ever browsed a newsstand or watched cable television news. Many magazines, including news magazines like *Time* or *Newsweek*, will often spend more to produce a cover than they will to produce the rest of the issue. Cable news programs will repeatedly, sometimes for weeks on end, air the same story about a celebrity trial, a sex scandal or a natural disaster. By the third or fourth airing, these stories offer little or no new information and even re-cycle the same video, but as products they succeed at a large scale and so enjoy network effects: They gain a hugely disproportionate market share even as the incremental costs of producing the story decline.

A third economic factor affecting public affairs and news reporting is that there is in most cases more than one kind of consumer for the product, and each has very different preferences. A newspaper publisher, for example, typically sells his product twice, once to the reader who subscribes to the paper, a second time to advertisers who are in effect buying access to the paper's readers. Terrestrial broadcasters, again, represent a different case, one in which the advertiser is in fact the only customer; the ordinary assumptions about rational consumer choice apply in broadcasting *only* with respect to advertisers. By itself, this kind of externality – when more than one party is affected by an economic transaction – is not unusual. However, as discussed below, this externality can have a profound effect on the content choices made by news organizations – in short, on editorial mission.

The Economic Effects of Competition

Consider the economic choices faced by the organization whose mission it is to publish high-quality, independent journalism (and leaving aside for the moment what that may be). To begin with, the high fixed costs of producing news limits the incentive to invest in a product that only a small market of consumers is willing to buy, and about which consumers have a range of unarticulated, opposing and irreconcilable preferences. From there things get trickier still. As information markets become increasingly competitive and fragmented – that is to say there are more television channels, more newspapers, more magazine and more Internet sites competing for consumers' attention – the incentive to produce high-quality information decreases even further. Put in economic terms, as competition increases in the market for any good, the overall quality of that good is, at some point, more likely to get worse rather than better. The *Economist* once offered this economic explanation for the poor quality of the British press: "American papers enjoy local quasi-monopolies and can therefore afford to be high-minded. In Britain, ten national papers slug it out daily, competing for readers who seem more interested in exciting stories than accurate ones, and in sensationalism than in sensitivity."[16] In such a competitive atmosphere, the magazine concluded, high editorial standards and a "finely developed ethical sense" may be business handicaps.

The same economic logic applies in developing countries. In Indonesia, for example, *Jurnal Perempuan* (*Women's Journal*) and its companion "Radio Jurnal Perempuan" are relatively new, NGO-based public affairs media created specifically for women in a country where, during the tumultuous transition period that followed the fall of Suharto in 1998, the number of Indonesians living in poverty increased from 20 million to 80 million. According to Gadis Arivia, chief editor of *Jurnal Perempuan*, the impact of the change has been felt most acutely by women and children. Unemployment among women is high; contraception, once affordable, has jumped substantially in price even as incomes have fallen; anemia among pregnant women as well as maternal and infant mortality have all significantly increased. So, too, have domestic violence, rape and sexual harassment. On the belief that "democracy without women is not a democracy,"[17] Arivia organized *Jurnal Perempuan* as an NGO engaged in non-partisan "committed journalism" that seeks to demand access for women to decision-making in the public and private sectors, and to encourage "positive representation" of women in the mainstream media.[18]

Jurnal Perempuan, which has received grants from USAID and the Royal Dutch Embassy, is a 5,000-circulation journal read mostly by academics and professionals. The magazine also trains academics and journalists to be more aware of gender issues in their teaching and reporting. That effort includes advocating for women journalists, who make up 30 to 40 percent of the reporting corps in Indonesia but rarely get the best assignments and almost never break into management. A second activity is "Radio Jurnal Perempuan" (RJP), a twenty-minute weekly radio program that airs on more than 100 stations across the country's thousands of islands. The program is distributed on audiotape and now on CD-ROM and, according to Arivia, is heard by 5 million to 6 million women every week. Actually getting the program on the air, however, was not easy. The men who make the programming decisions at radio stations did not care much for *RJP*'s content or its audience demographic, and so "we paid for the first three months to get radio stations to put Indonesian women on the air,"[19] Arivia said. Even now, some stations cut out stories from the program that they don't like. As the program found its audience, "we bargained again and got the price down, and now we don't pay at all. Now we ask our station partners to contribute, and about 60 percent do. We try to attract sponsors and many are interested, but they are not always the sponsors we like. We have The Body Shop, which is excellent. Philip Morris is very keen to advertise and the money is tempting, but it's Philip Morris. Nestle wants more passive and domesticated women than what we cover."[20]

Jurnal Perempuan's mission and its success raises at least two interesting sets of questions, one about its editorial mission and the second about its long-term viability. The editorial questions concern journalism's relationship to civil society and what kinds of journalism best suits the needs of post-transition democratizing societies. The organization's strategy of building a coalition of other NGOs, government funders and private advertisers around the women's movement, for example, would lead many Western journalists to ask whether such activity is an appropriate journalistic exercise or one that compromises (or at least risks) "objectivity" and editorial independence. The issue is important only because it once again exposes the widely differing expectations that funders and recipients have for media assistance, and more fundamentally how they understand "journalism" and what it does.

The economic questions concern whether *Jurnal Perempuan* might one day find itself shut out of the women's programming market as for-profit, commercial stations realize its value and began to offer duplica-tive, if less sensitive or valuable, programming. The implication of this problem is critical: Even if *Jurnal Perempuan* and its radio service remain a not-for-profit, high-quality service with no direct competition, other entrants in the women's programming market will increase the competi-tion for audiences and revenues and thus deprive the organization of the flexibility it now enjoys in soliciting private and public support, a loss that will inevitably have consequences for its mission and its program-ming. In economic terms, the assumption among many aid providers that more news outlets results in a better informed public (and better quality news) is wrong, at least after a point. A town with one newspa-per, for example, is not as likely to have a good a paper as a town with two newspapers, or even three. But in a town (or a small country) with six newspapers, all of them competing for the same market of readers, none are likely to be very good. With a product like news, whose public good characteristics and high fixed costs limit a media company's abil-ity to compete on price, the consequences of competitive pressure will fall on the quality of the product itself. And as news begins to take on the characteristics of a commodity – that is to say, the product available from one vendor is essentially the equivalent to that offered by other vendors – the pressure to cut production costs grows even greater. And again, because of its public good character, news will see that pressure most heavily on the quality of the news – on the resources devoted to reporting and editing the news. The news hole may be cut, and reporters and editors fired.

Of course, news media in highly competitive markets do compete in all kinds of ways, some of them having nothing to do with news qual-ity, but rather with the experience value of the product. The economic value of celebrity journalists, for example, will often have little to do with their ability as reporters or even whether they have any reporting experience at all. Rather they are brands, an instantly recognizable signal to consumers about a particular medium's style, content or point-of-view. In the same way, reality TV shows, round-the-clock coverage of sensational or lurid crimes, exorbitant retainers paid to well known columnists, pundits or even photographers, all make sense in strictly economic terms: they serve to quickly establish brand identity. As this strategy succeeds, competitors are likely to copy it, particularly – if they are publicly traded companies – if they are under pressure to maintain or increase profits. As they do so, however, the news market becomes less idea diverse, and the size of the audience for each individual newspaper or television station will decrease.

One might also choose to build one's brand identity on a reputation for in-depth and sophisticated reporting, but that takes a long time, re-quires significantly greater investment of resources, and carries greater financial risk. A media firm that is privately owned may be willing and able to take such a risk, though its access to affordable capital may be limited. Much will depend on the value of what is likely to be a small market to the investor. If that market is well educated and relatively affluent, as is *El Periodico's*, for example, it may be easier to find capital. Alternatively, a publicly traded firm focused on profits al-most certainly will not take such a risk, or if it does it will provide a distinctly different product. Viewed in this way, for example, the decision by the Fox News cable channel in the United States to feature a stable of politically conservative and always indignant "journalists" is not primarily a news decision, but an economic one. For the same economic reasons that nineteenth-century U.S. newspapers aban-doned political advocacy for "objectivity," Fox News now embraces advocacy: It makes sense to do so in an environment characterized by intense channel competition. Advocacy is not all Fox does, of course, since it, too, needs to pull in the largest audience it possibly can. To do that, Fox News uses bright graphics and employs a rapid-fire style of reporting that has the effect of converting the news, such as it is, into an action movie.

A similar branding process goes on at National Public Radio, whose news programming likewise features a staff of reporters and program hosts whose voices and reputation for intelligence and integrity give NPR a voice instantly recognizable to its listeners and to its advertisers (or as they are euphemistically known, "financial underwriters"). NPR's brand identity, however, is built on more than twenty years of quality reporting, and it is known for a kind of long-form, reflective journalism now practically unknown in U.S. broadcast journalism. NPR's brand is thus of a completely different kind than Fox News', but as a purely economic matter there is no difference: Both Fox and NPR are distinctive products in a media market where distinctions are increasingly few. In almost any city in the United States, for example, one can flip up and down the radio dial and recognize an NPR station almost instantly upon landing on it. Fox News does not occupy quite such a distinctive look and feel in seventy-plus-channel cable systems, but it comes very close. As discussed below, the same cannot usually be said of public television, a fact that has significant consequences for the sources of revenue available to that service.

Doubtless some readers (and particularly the Fox viewers) will object to comparing Fox News and National Public Radio. But the juxtaposition is useful because it illustrates that what journalists (and the public and policy makers) frequently criticize or lament as irresponsible editorial decisions – or, conversely, that which they praise and reward as editorial courage—are at least partly the result of economic choices in a competitive market. Ultimately, what Fox News and NPR have in common is that each has found a profitable niche in the news marketplace. NPR is located in the market for serious journalism, a small market with relatively few competitors – the major national newspapers like the *New York Times*, the *Wall Street Journal* and the *Washington Post*; the *Economist*, the *New Yorker* and *Atlantic Monthly*; Bloomberg; the "Lehrer News Hour" and "Frontline" on public television; BBC news or radio, television and the Internet; ABC News' "Nightline" and doubtless several others – all of which serve the same small strata of elites who want a general news product but also have specialized interests in or knowledge about subjects like foreign policy, health care, finance, law and so on. Fox News occupies the other very successful stratum of news production, at the bottom, along with supermarket tabloids, syndicated talk radio and entertainment-feature television programs.

None of this is to say that editorial mission is a fiction – both Fox News and NPR have clear editorial missions. Neither is it to say, given the concerns of this book, that editorial courage is an act of convenience; to the contrary, it is to emphasize just how critical these things are to journalism in a democracy. Journalists and news organizations that confuse news choices and economic choices, for whatever reason, are far more likely to indulge and defend editorial short-cuts and pandering than are those who understand and can clearly state their editorial mission while *also* understanding the extent to which that mission is linked to revenue sources.

It is in part because of the success of NPR's news and culture programs, but also because of the example of the Center for Public Integrity, a not-for-profit investigative news organization, a number of thoughtful academic and professional critics of the U.S. media system have urged the creation of additional not-for-profit news sources. In June 2005, for example, this proposal was one of many discussed by the Commission on the Role of the Press in a Democracy.[21] Among its working recommendations, the Commission urged the development of additional not-for-profit media with financial assistance from foundations and other philanthropies. A year earlier, a symposium at Louisiana State University brought together several journalists, communications scholars and tax specialists to discuss several similar proposals, among them that "more media outlets should be operated by nonprofits, and public policies should encourage and support this type of media ownership."[22] In the preface to the 25th anniversary edition of his class work *Deciding What's News*, Herbert Gans offered a more cautious recommendation, urging journalism schools to "take a new approach to the economics of journalism" and to "figure out how to set up news firms' content with a lower profit, or more realistically, borrowing the utility model, combining limited profit margins with other incentives."[23]

Without discussing these proposals at length, two things can safely be said of them. The first is that they are not new. In the United States of the late 19th and early 20th centuries, critics of the brassy, populist brand of journalism first pioneered by Joseph Pulitzer also urged the creation of non-profit media as ameliorating force in the media market. Then as now, however, the economics of news production was inseparable from definitions of editorial independence. Pulitzer had bought the *New York World* in 1883 and quickly made it into a paper for the city's working class and immigrant readers. Pulitzer's style of journalism favored spot news, exclusive interviews and human-interest stories – in fairness, much as *Nuestro Diario* does today. In its news columns the *World* campaigned on matters of importance to working people, but it also gave them cartoons, puzzles, short stories and illustrations. The *World*'s critics, many of them writing from the repose of opinion and cultural journals, complained that the *World* trivialized important social issues and that many of its entertainment features were vulgar. At 2 cents and

8 pages, the paper flourished anyway. By 1887 it had a daily circulation of 250,000.[24]

There was another way in which Pulitzer's brand of journalism was distinctive, and that was its independence from political patronage at a time when most of the major urban daily newspaper in the country were openly partisan, allied both editorially and financially with either the Republican Party (54 percent of all U.S. metropolitan dailies in 1870) or the Democratic Party (33 percent of metropolitan dailies in 1870). Newspapers that identified themselves as independent of the two major parties comprised only 13 percent of urban dailies in 1870, a figure that by 1880 had jumped to 34 percent. More significantly, by 1880 the independents commanded 55 percent of daily newspaper circulation; they were clearly a good business.[25] Partisan papers faced natural limits on their potential for growth, and in addition posed problems for advertisers whose need was to appeal to all consumers regardless of their politics. Independent or "objective" newspapers were able to serve the market for advertising much more effectively, and the revenues they earned from advertising made it possible for them to exploit improved printing technology and lower paper costs to further increase their circulation (through lower subscription prices) and their advertising revenues. This cycle of investment and growth allowed independent papers to lower their average and marginal costs, and to become highly profitable businesses.

At the same time, the costs of entering the market – and in particular the costs of new printing technology – had effectively ended the days when newspapers had existed as the personal projects of individuals. In this new market, writes economist James Hamilton, independence meant exploiting economies of scale, and "as circulation became paramount, papers chose independence as the easiest way to attain large-scale circulation."[26] From the start, then, "independence" or reportorial objectivity was primarily a commercial strategy designed to boost circulation and revenues, and secondarily an editorial notion. Independent papers covered politics, sometimes vigorously, but were not beholden to any one party or candidate. In the 1890s, and with increasing frequency after 1900, the excesses of Pulitzer's brand of journalism became the subject of commentary in literary magazines and in the *Journalist*, a trade magazine founded in 1883 (and later to change its name to *Editor and Publisher*).[27] William Randolph Hearst had entered the New York newspaper market in 1895 with his purchase of the *New York Journal*, and in head-to-head competition both the *Journal* and *World* rose to new levels of sensationalism, offensiveness and gimmickry, even falsehood.

In response to these developments, there were two general lines of criticism. One focused on the corrosive social effects of such journalism, faulting it not only for bad taste and poor morals, but blaming it for increases in crime and class conflict.[28] Another line of attack, exemplified by E.L. Godkin, editor of the *Nation*, then a conservative weekly publication of the *New York Post*, asked whether such large and unaccountable concentrations of capital and private power were detrimental to democracy.[29] There were several proposals for reform. One was for an "endowed newspaper" that, freed from the demands of the market and the whims of ownership, would also be free to report the news accurately and disinterestedly. The foremost advocate of the idea, sociologist Edward Ross at the University of Wisconsin, argued that the endowed newspaper would also be a "corrective newspaper" that would serve to correct the errors and outright falsehoods in the yellow press.[30] In 1912 Hamilton Holt, the respected editor of a religious journal, put the idea before a national audience of scholars and journalists and asked for a $5 million endowment to launch such a paper.[31] Andrew Carnegie offered his financial support if others would follow suit, but no one did.[32] The proposal died, though the endowment concept would be proposed again (and fail again) with the emergence of broadcasting and the first drafts of national broadcast policy in the 1920s and 30s.[33]

The second thing that can be said of the current enthusiasm for not-for-profit media is that, if Downs is correct, creating them would have little effect on news consumption. (There is also the separate, practical question of who would be willing to provide the enormous subsidies necessary to support such media. Foundations, for example, rarely provide endowments and typically change their funding priorities every few years.) Programming subsidies, whatever their source, may have little or no practical effect because increasing the variety and quality of information does not change the fact that the fundamental market failure is at the point of consumption, not supply. From a democracy-promoting point of view, perhaps, government policy should nonetheless strive to increase both the supply and the consumption of high-quality news and public affairs information, in the same way official policy supports provision of other public goods. But doing so may not work (and realists will also argue that it is not in the government's interest to encourage an informed electorate.) Existing media industry subsidies – the best examples of which are the second-class postage privileges available to newspapers and magazines, and the free and exclusive access to publicly owned electromagnetic spectrum provided to terrestrial broadcasters – have not resulted in greater idea diversity in any of those markets, even if they have resulted in large number of product choices. Other official policies – for example, laws on copyrights and patents – also act as subsidies, since they have the practical effect of raising the cost to use or distribute certain kinds of protected information. Indeed, to the extent that subsidies can be characterized as cost reductions, it is important to remember that a cost "reduction" in any economic system is almost always offset by a cost "increase" somewhere else. U.S. broadcasters, for example, once argued to the Federal Communications Commission (successfully) that the "cost" of the now-defunct Fairness Doctrine, which required them to give equal time to critics who objected to their coverage of a public issue, was their avoiding many public issues entirely.

Finally, and as discussed in detail below with respect to public broadcasting, not-for-profits that compete in mixed for-profit/not-for-profit industries – whether media, higher education, health care, or anything else – cannot avoid the temptation, even the necessity, of mimicking the revenue-producing activities of their for-profit competitors. Such behavior, again, has implications for whatever mission justifies a not-for-profit organization's tax-exempt status.

So to restate the problem: In both developed and developing media systems, the challenge for high-quality, independent news media is to make themselves sustainable in the unique economic environment that characterizes information goods. Political decisions, of course, can either directly or indirectly make that environment more or less hospitable. To consider the effects of those decisions, at least some of them easily predictable by economic analysis, the next section of this chapter takes as a case study the American system of public broadcasting. That system was born in its current form on November 5, 1967, when President Lyndon Johnson signed into law the Public Broadcasting Act, creating the Corporation for Public Broadcasting (CPB). The purpose of the Act, Johnson said, was to "renew the promise of the vision in the word 'television.'"[34]

As Johnson described the new CPB, he called it "the people's Corporation. Fully independent. Broadly representative. Supported by public and private money. Free from interference by private interests, government agency, or political party."[35] Public broadcasting was thus the result of a formal U.S. government policy to promote high-quality, "free and independent" media, the only such time the government has so directly attempted such a policy. In some important respects the experiment has not worked. The reasons for public broadcasting's problems are many, and for readers interested in a more thorough account of them a number of excellent sources are available.[36] But a central problem, if not *the* central problem, has always been a grand confusion about editorial mission and how to finance it. The problem is more acute, and thus easier to grasp, because of the unique economics of terrestrial broadcast television. As a case study, then, public television – in the United States but also in Europe – is a particularly useful medium for examining the relationship between editorial mission and sources of revenue – in short, the dilemmas of sustainability.

A Case Study in Editorial Mission and Financing: U.S. Public Broadcasting

The history of public radio and television in the United States makes clear that their goals were of a particular sort. First, they were to provide programs that were different from what for-profit stations were providing; and second, they were to broadcast them differently – without commercial interruptions. That is, the concept of public broadcasting rested on the belief that the private, for-profit market, while extensive, had failed to provide certain kinds of outputs for which at least some people were willing to pay. How to actually generate the financial support, however, has been the key problem from the start.

When President Johnson signed the Public Broadcasting Act, he set forth an objective for the new Corporation for Public Broadcasting (CPB): "It will have a single purpose: to demand the best in broadcasting and to deliver it for the betterment of our people."[37] Such an ill-defined mission provides little guidance to decision makers. It is difficult for any public broadcasting station, or for the service nationally, to judge whether pursuing or forgoing any revenue-generating opportunity is or is not consistent with the social mission Johnson identified, even though that mission recognizes that the availability of support from any particular source is tightly entwined with decisions on how the funds will be used.

Public broadcasting, like any not-for-profit organization, can generate revenue from either of two basic sources, donations and sales. The collective-type character of radio and television broadcasting essentially precludes selling services to listeners and viewers or charging user fees. There is an indirect way around this problem: A license fee – a tax on television and radio receivers – has traditionally been the finance mechanism for most public broadcast systems in Europe. Such a fee accounts for approximately 80 percent of the revenues of the world's most well-known and well-regarded public broadcaster, the British Broadcasting Corporation (BBC), and those revenues are substantial, approximately $2.5 billion of the BBC's $3.2 billion annual budget in 1996.[38] But the fee is on receivers, not programs, and thus while fees are technically possible they are inherently inefficient. No matter where the fee is set, it will be too high for some people, thus excluding many viewers from watching programs when the cost of serving additional viewers is zero. The annual household license fee in Great Britain, for example, is currently 121, and the cost of collecting the fee and enforcing payment is itself high, approximately 300.[39] The fee currently delivers annual revenues of about 2.8, and during the BBC's 2004-2005 charter renewal, but possibly for the last time. At the next charter renewal, in 2015, the BBC must be able to explain why it should not be supported entirely by advertising or subscription, perhaps with some direct government subsidy.[40]

In the United States, the dominant system of broadcasting has always been private and for-profit, and so license fees do not exist. In that system, advertising is the sole source of revenue, a revenue source which has a profound effect on editorial content. So far as the financial transaction is concerned, the customer in commercial broadcasting is not the viewer, but the advertiser who pays to support the programs. Because advertisers want to reach as many viewers as possible, their measure of a quality program is entirely quantitative – how many people watch it, and is there *any* other program that may attract more viewers? News and public affairs programming, for the economic reasons already discussed, is almost impossible to sustain in this competitive environment. So, too, are fine arts and cultural programs. It was for this reason that public broadcasting was to be non-commercial. For public broadcasters, then, the only remaining revenue options have traditionally been donations from government and private sources, both of which have proved problematic.

Since the 1980s, the fiscal pressure on public broadcasting systems in the United States, Canada and Western Europe resulting from government cutbacks has been significant. In Canada, for example, nearly 80 percent of the Canadian Broadcasting System (CBC) budget came from the federal government in 1994, and the rest came largely from the sale of commercial advertising time. In 1996 a cut of some 12 percent – $127 million – occurred, and by 1998 grants had dropped by about 25 percent even as production and distribution costs had increased. In the United States, federal grants historically have been less central to public broadcast funding.[41] In fiscal 1995, for example, federal appropriations of $285.6 million constituted about 14 percent of CPB's $1.8 billion revenue from all sources.[42] A review of public broadcasting's income over three decades, from 1972 to 2001, shows that tax-based income from all government sources (federal, state and local) declined from 71 percent in 1972 to 46.8 percent in 1989 to 42.9 percent in 2001. The federal contribution to public broadcasting reached a maximum of 27.3 percent of revenues in 1980; since then, federal revenues have steadily declined.[43] That decline has forced public broadcasters to adjust, which they have done by combining decreases in broadcast outputs with intensified efforts to increase revenues from other sources.[44]

Another potential revenue source, private donations, has limited promise. The well-known difficulty of relying on private giving applies to all collective goods; since public radio and television broadcasts are available without a user fee, obtaining private donations involves an act of altruism that runs headlong into free-rider behavior. It is no wonder that public television and radio stations estimate that only some 10 percent of viewers and listeners contribute.[45] Revenue from the sale of broadcast time to private firms for commercial announcements constitutes the financial lifeblood of private, for-profit radio and television, but, historically, it has been anathema to public stations whose goals seemingly precluded the kinds, frequency, and timing of commercials that are most attractive to business advertisers.

There has always been a limited but important market for public stations' sale of broadcast time insofar as stations developed both a reputation for trustworthiness and an audience of affluent listeners and viewers. Some private firms – Mobil Oil, Texaco, AT&T and others – funded programs and in effect "purchased" an identification with these nonprofit broadcasting organizations. This last form of commercial revenue surely holds the greatest financial potential for public broadcasters, even if, under Federal Communications Commission rules, such sponsorship must be constrained in its form, content, and time-positioning (e.g., only before or after a program). With respect to editorial mission (and U.S. tax policy) it is also the most problematic: The more public broadcasters' finances come to mimic those of their for-profit counterparts, the weaker their ability to carve out a unique social role and, hence, to justify any special treatment through government grants, private donations, or tax exemptions and subsidies as nonprofit organizations.

Taken together, private donations and the sale of broadcast time (in the form of program underwriting and corporate sponsorship) now comprise more than half of all income for public broadcasting. Between 1972 and 2001, private donations rose from 28.5 percent of CPB's annual income to 57.1 percent.[46] The meaning of this change is not certain, but two interpretations stand out. One is the argument made by former PBS President Lawrence Grossman, who has said that private donations, whether from individual subscribers or large corporations, help to make public television truly "public" – not dependent on government. In this view, declining tax-based support and rising public support may pose operational difficulties, but nonetheless serve to confirm and enhance public broadcasting's mission. A second, contrary argument is that private support by definition comes with strings attached, and that those strings affect public broadcasting's mission, perhaps adversely. Public broadcasters who seek program support from businesses and foundations do in fact make compromises in program content, and anecdotal evidence says that many worthwhile projects are scuttled, others never proposed. In practice, broadcasters make a determination that a program is worthwhile, then identify sympathetic funders.

Again, however, whether and how that process affects a public broadcaster's editorial mission is difficult to measure given the historic vagueness of that mission. It is very difficult to know whether public television's mission would change, or whether any change would affect programming decisions, if public television's revenues remained the same but simply came from a different mix of sources, or even from sources that were entirely tax-based. Even public broadcasting's most ardent defenders admit that the mission of the institution lacks clear and operational articulation.[47] Further complicating this problem of mission and its implications for programming is that several cable channels now offer similar types of programs, and indeed compete with PBS to purchase them.

The Dilemma of Commercial Activity

Four decades after public broadcasting's creation, an unresolved debate over whether commercial advertising should be permitted, and if so in what forms, illustrates the economic problem that faces any mission-based media organization. For more than a decade now, according to *Current*, the trade newspaper of public broadcasting:

> Managers of some of the biggest PBS-member stations [have wanted] the right to carry ads on-air. Corporate underwriting already provides about 16 percent of public broadcasting's overall revenues, and those managers believe that they could replace much of the lost federal aid if the corporate donors got real commercials instead of restricted underwriter credits.... Most managers appear to oppose commercials, however...more than 80 public TV station leaders officially opposed advertising in September 1995; noticeably absent were executives from 20 of the 30 largest cities.[48]

Revenue opportunities are certainly more limited in smaller cities, and small-market public television and radio stations, many of them licensed to universities or communities, are much more dependent on tax-based sources for revenue that are large-market stations. But it is unlikely that there would be opposition to commercial advertising anywhere were it not that the social/editorial mission for public broadcasting has been so ambiguous operationally.

The remarks with which President Johnson announced CPB's creation in 1967 echoed those made only a few years earlier by President Kennedy's young chairman of the Federal Communications Commission, Newton N. Minow. Speaking before the annual meeting of the National Association of Broadcasters in 1961, Minow had chastened broadcasters for their seemingly single-minded devotion to the needs of advertisers and called television "a vast wasteland."[49] The speech energized the non-profit broadcasting community, then supported primarily by the Ford Foundation, and led the Carnegie Corporation of New York to launch an investigation into the prospects for a new kind of national television service. As the Carnegie Commission foresaw it, the service would be commercial-free and thus offer distinctly different programming than the three existing commercial broadcast networks.

To describe this new service, the Commission chose the term "public television." The choice was intended to imply something broader than "educational television," a service that already existed and which, in Carnegie's view, conjured up images of classroom instruction. As the Commission defined it, public television would include "all that is of human interest and importance which is not at the moment appropriate or available for support by advertising, and which is not arranged for formal instruction."[50] By rejecting advertising, Carnegie reasoned, public broadcasting would be free to do the kinds of programs that commercial television would not. At the same time, however, it recognized that some funding mechanism was necessary, and while it was not averse to government funding, "we all agreed that the federal government was a last resort," Commission member Lee DuBridge said later. "If we could see any other way to get adequate financing, we would be glad to take it."[51] The funding source the Commission recommended was an excise tax on television sets, similar to the license fee commonly used in Europe. The initial tax would be set at 2 percent of purchase price, to rise to 5 percent over time.[52] To augment funds from this new tax, the Commission further suggested that public television seek an endowment of $25 million from "industry and private foundations" with which to insulate itself from political pressure.[53] But when President Johnson signed the Public Broadcasting Act into law, the excise tax was not in it. It had been removed from the bill at the insistence of the Electronic Industries Association, a trade group whose membership included manufacturers of television sets and radios.

Public broadcasting in the United States was thus launched without a secure financial base, and with a relatively small commitment of public funding. The largest single source of CPB revenues has been the public itself, whose contributions ("memberships," or "subscriptions") now account for about 25 percent of CPB's annual revenues.[54] Membership drives are a regular part of the programming, occurring several times a year. No other major public broadcasting service in the world uses such a revenue-raising device, and many people within CPB and outside it think the effort undignified. To a profit-maximizing firm, of course, the issue of whether such fundraising is appropriate or dignified is irrelevant; for a public television broadcaster with vague social objectives, however, such criteria can cause intense debate. This is particularly so when the broadcaster's collective-good nature (which precludes charging viewers) combines with the policy of sharply restricting commercial advertising (which limits revenue from selling broadcast time to private firms) to virtually eliminate conventional user fees as a revenue source. With little access to revenues from direct beneficiaries – viewers or advertisers – finance options are very restricted. The other potential forms, though – private donations, government grants, and sales of ancillary goods, which will be discussed later – have the apparent attraction of insulating revenue-raising from decisions on program quality and content. Or so goes the economic assumption.

The linkage between revenue source and broadcast content in public broadcasting has, over the years, been a volatile political subject. Its volatility has been fueled in part by the original Carnegie Commission's belief that, somehow, non-commercial programming would be better programming. Better than what the Commission did not say. Nor did it provide any clear test of social mission that would focus today's debate over what market niche remains for public television in the new technological world of cable and satellite TV, VCRs, digital video recorders, video CDs, and the Internet. The public policy question is whether that niche justifies public subsidy of a service that is watched by only a small minority of viewers. On average, public broadcasting's nationally broadcast programs earn Nielsen ratings of about a 2 (or about 2 million homes) during the weekday prime-time viewing hours between 7 P.M. and 9 P.M., a figure that would drive private commercial broadcasters to ruin but which is almost identical to the ratings earned by public broadcasting's cable competitors, such as the Discovery, History Channel or Arts & Entertainment networks.[55] The only specific programming recommendations in the 1967 Carnegie Commission report that come close to defining the source of private market failure that might justify public television, publicly financed, were for children's programming and public affairs programming that would go beyond the "bare reporting of incidents."[56] Beyond that, there was little attempt to operationalize important questions about public broadcasting's mission: Who is the public? What are its "needs"? Complicating matters further, the communications core of public broadcasting's enterprise raises, in the United States, legitimate questions about the constitutionality of its receiving any government support at all.

Another common and fair criticism of public broadcasting is that it is "inefficient" and "unorganized." In fact it was designed to be. This is another aspect of the vagueness of its social goal. Efficiency is a matter of achieving goals, and whether public broadcasting is or is not well-organized hinges on how closely those goals are being realized. CPB is a private, nonprofit corporation authorized by Congress to develop non-commercial radio and television services. Public broadcasting, however, is an enormously decentralized and fractious enterprise. PBS itself is a station-owned cooperative organization established in 1969 to acquire and distribute, but not produce, programming. The nation's 356 public television stations are independently owned and operated by 177 different licensees, with each making its own decisions about programming and scheduling; PBS is not a network in the operational sense. By law, federal funding goes directly to CPB, which then allocates it either to individual radio and television stations or to fund programming. Almost half of CPB's 2003 expenditures—$175 million—went to individual public television stations in the form of "community service grants." Another $51 million in community service grants went to the nation's 699 public radio stations. A relatively small sum—$92.7 million—actually went to fund radio and television programming.[57] That funding may go to stations, to PBS or to a related organization, the Independent Television Service (ITVS), or directly to producers.

Over the last two decades, reform of public broadcasting's financing has become unavoidable as a result of the diminished federal government grants and, in many cases, weakened state and local support, too.[58] In 1990, PBS enlisted the Boston Consulting Group (BCG) to appraise its future. The resulting report, "Strategies for Public Television in a Multi-Channel Environment," recommended that to secure donations, especially corporate donations, stations should move away from local programming and toward the "safely splendid."[59] In BCG's view, local programming was not cost-effective because it did not encourage individual memberships or attract corporate underwriters. Local stations, on the other hand, were good at raising money. In the end, BCG recommended against a centralized national television service, but urged that production resources be shifted toward national programming.[60]

Three years later, a report of the Twentieth Century Fund Task Force on Public Television urged that federal funding of stations' operations be eliminated entirely and the resources earmarked for national programs. Once this was done, the task force said, federal funding should be increased. Specifically, "national funding of public television should come from new nontaxpayer sources of funding such as possible spectrum auctions or spectrum usage fees"[61] imposed on commercial broadcasters. "Commercialism," the report said, should be resisted, particularly that which targeted preschool children, one of public broadcasting's core audiences.[62]

Still another oft-proposed response to diminished federal funding, popular with political if not always with fiscal conservatives, has been to privatize CPB.[63] This would convert these nonprofit broadcasters into for-profit firms that might or might not survive in competition with private broadcasters. The public policy issues go beyond the matter of whether public subsidies are efficient; whatever the motivation may be for converting, and whether public policy considers public broadcasting, hospitals, schools, jails or any other segment of the nonprofit sector, conversions have many effects. They alter not merely the finance mechanism for an organization, but also its goals, the constraints on it, and hence the character of its outputs. Conversions also redistribute wealth, shifting assets that were financed in large measure through government and private donations into private ownership, raising questions of equity. Additionally, public broadcast channels are licensed as such and can make no such conversion independently, but must have the approval of the Federal Communications Commission. Finally, many public broadcast licensees – about one third of the total of 177 – are colleges and universities, state or local educational authorities.[64] Many of these entities, some of them predating the creation of CPB, see educational service as their mission – up to and including classroom instruction – and believe that privatization is neither desirable nor likely.[65]

Alternative Methods of Finance for Public Broadcasting

One of the curious features of U.S. public broadcasting, and of U.S. broadcasting policy in general, is its almost willful confusion of terms. It is common, for example, to hear people in the industry, as well as academics and policy makers, contrast "public" broadcasters with "private" ones, a distinction that makes little sense. Few public broadcasters can properly be described as publicly owned. The great majority of licensees, and certainly the principal program producers in the system, are incorporated as *private*, not-for-profit firms, either as public charities or as foundations. The law itself distinguishes between "non-commercial" and "commercial" broadcasters, a distinction that begs the question of why, irrespective of ownership form, a commercial broadcaster could not also be a not-for-profit broadcaster with an editorial mission clearly different from that of commercial, for-profit firms.

In many ways these distinctions are the political legacy of public broadcasting's founding, though as discussed throughout this section there is a good economic case to make, as the original Carnegie Commission did, that reliance on advertising will have (adverse) consequences for programming. All the same, at least one PBS station manager has argued in recent years that Congress should get its terms straight and create, in addition to the non-commercial license category, a new category of not-for-profit licenses that could sell broadcast time to advertisers.[66]

Former PBS President and NBC News President Lawrence Grossman has proposed a mixed economy in public television, similar to that found in Britain, in which PBS would be allowed to operate a parallel, commercial network that would both produce programs and generate revenues for the non-commercial service.[67]

Neither of these ideas has found traction among public broadcasters themselves, and both have been sharply criticized by those who believe that commercial accommodation in public television is suicidal for both the service and its mission.[68] Despite these discussions, public policy has not changed. And so with diminishing federal, state and local funds, and further cuts almost a certainty, public broadcasters have turned their attention to finding new sources of revenue, a practice that is further blurring the distinction between the editorial missions of public and commercial broadcasting.

It is not the first time that alternatives to government funding have received major attention. Over the years a variety of funding mechanisms have been proposed, beginning with the second Carnegie Commission on the Future of Public Broadcasting in 1979.[69] That report urged a spectrum fee on commercial broadcasters as a supplement to general tax revenues, but the recommendation was ignored. A few years later, in 1982, President Ronald Reagan's FCC Chairman, Mark Fowler, called U.S. commercial (for-profit) broadcasters' claims that they serve the public interest (as the statutory terms of their licenses require) a "fiction," and urged that instead of receiving free and exclusive of their channels they pay a spectrum fee and be freed from government content regulation. The resulting revenues, Fowler said, could be used to support public broadcasting.[70] The decision to levy such fees, of course, lay with Congress, which did nothing.

In 1996 this debate arose again, led by Senate Majority Leader Bob Dole, who held up passage of the Telecommunications Act when he realized that it gave to broadcasters additional spectrum, for advanced digital broadcasting, without charge. Dole estimated the value of that spectrum at $70 billion, and suggested that for both economic and First Amendment reasons broadcasters pay for it, though he said nothing about where the resulting revenues might go.[71] Several public broadcasters urged that a portion of them, along with revenues from the sale of several public broadcast television stations in small markets around the country, be used to create a $4 billion trust fund for public broadcasting.[72] Dole's proposal died when commercial broadcasters, led by the National Association of

Broadcasters, threatened to destroy his presidential campaign through negative news coverage and public opposition.[73]

The spectrum and trust fund proposals are but the latest in a long line of other alternative financing proposals advanced over the years. None of the earlier proposals—surtaxes on residential electricity and telephone bills; government matching of private contributions; taxes on license transfers when commercial stations are sold; and taxes on the advertising revenues of commercial broadcasters and cable operators—have come to fruition.[74] Because they have not, public broadcasters have sought to generate their own sources of revenue.

This process began in earnest in 1981, when the Reagan administration ___ened to end federal funding entirely, and, in response, Congress ___d the Communications Act such that "Each public broadcasting ___hall be authorized to engage in the offering of services, facilities ___ts in exchange for remuneration."[75] The same year, Congress ___eral Communications Commission authorized a Temporary ___ on Additional Financing (TCAF) in the Public Broadcast-___nts Act. The TCAF project was an 18-month experiment ___blic television stations around the country were allowed ___rtisements under restricted conditions: advertisements ___y between programs, never during (and then only for ___o advertising at all was to appear in company with

___CC report issued after the experiment, the results ___r contributions during the experiment either stayed ___ Interviews done with 10,000 public television ___ ended found that few discerned any harmful ___ertising; and so long as advertisements did not ___ers did not object to them. Viewers also said ___ents to on-air fund drives.[76]

___ the Commission expressed concern that the ___ from advertising would be outweighed by its ___ on the mission of public broadcasting. The ___pting commercials would be a net money ___ire added production costs, renegotiated ___nues not deemed "charitable support," and ___s a compromise, the Commission urged ___derwriting," a carefully regulated form ___ibly successful one.[77] Advertisers often conclude that underwriting spots are ineffective, and withdraw support. In 1991, for example, corporations provided a total of $17 million to be exclusive underwriters of 20 PBS programs; by 1993, there were only 14 programs exclusively underwritten, with total support of $6.3 million.[78] In 1994, PBS announced publicly that it would reconsider its underwriting guidelines with the intent of liberalizing them. Jonathan Abbott, a PBS senior vice president, told the *Wall Street Journal*, "We want to make sure we're a destination more companies are comfortable considering."[79]

Despite the narrowing difference between commercial television advertising and the forms adopted by public television, and howeve public broadcasting's underwriting guidelines are drawn and redrawn its use of advertising will remain controversial. One of the most heate debates in public broadcasting today is the uncertain conflict betwee the revenue that advertising, in any form, can generate and the publi serving mission that requires financial independence. This debate well underway in Europe, where advertising has increasingly found way into public broadcasting finance. Noting this, some of the la program-producing public broadcasting stations in the United St have urged Congress and the FCC to experiment further with liberali commercial advertising as a revenue source.[80] Enthusiasm for adverti is not universal, however. Opposition can be summarized by the v of Sharon Percy Rockefeller, president of WETA in Washington, I "Commercials would be the death knell of public television. We alr have a vast commercial broadcasting system in this country; we the alternative. And it's the alternative because it's noncommercia so obvious. We put programs on the air for the purpose of the co not for the purpose of making money from commercials."[81]

If on-air advertising is unacceptable, however, less controversi enue streams have proliferated. Stations can now rent out their space; they can accept advertising in their program guides, sell music tapes, transcripts, and classroom materials based on PBS pr They do all of these, and more. PBS itself leases time on its satell sponders through PBS Enterprises, a wholly owned, for-profit su that develops services for use with new communications techn PBS Video sells videocassettes of public broadcasting progra has further created its own home video label—PBS Home Vid allows all public stations to buy its tapes at a deep discount, t them at considerable profit. To boost support for national progr together with four of the service's major producing stations consolidated the sales of underwriting credits in 1997 under the auspices of the PBS Sponsorship group.[82]

With the expanded opportunities, public broadcasters are expanding into an ever-widening array of commercial ventures to raise revenue, presumably for their preferred, mission-related, outputs. In 1998, for example, CPB gave four "strategic business development consultation" grants to public radio and television stations, essentially to develop new commercial ventures. Station WHYY-FM in Philadelphia launched a book club service linked to the highly popular National Public Radio (NPR) program "Fresh Air with Terry Gross"; WHRO-TV in Norfolk, Virginia, developed a World Wide Web consulting service for businesses; several small Illinois public television stations established a teleconferencing business for citizens, businesses and government agencies in rural west-central Illinois; and television station KCET in Los Angeles created a Center for Professional Development to offer multimedia and Internet training to teachers and private industry.[83]

The grants, first awarded in November 1995, were the second round of the CPB Business Development Initiative; the first round gave grants to WPSX-TV at Pennsylvania State University to develop CD-ROM and other electronic publishing; to KTCA/KTCI-TV in Minneapolis/St. Paul to develop online, CDROM and teleconferencing services; to KQED-TV in San Francisco to develop adult-learning services; and to KNPB-TV in Reno to create a retail operation. PBS now operates its own on-line retail operation,[84] and NPR has on-line retail sales of music and books heard or discussed on NPR programs. During the 1990s, major PBS stations located in Boston, Los Angeles and Chicago operated retail shops in partnership with the now-defunct LearningSmith Company and the Store of Knowledge.[85]

Some individual public broadcasting television stations have been especially innovate and aggressive in finding new commercial revenue sources. WTTW-Chicago, perhaps the most notable in this regard, has partnered in the production of programs with MTV Networks, Lifetime cable, and Walt Disney's Buena Vista television unit. In 1993, WTTW briefly experimented with an upscale home-shopping service after the FCC ruled the same year in a different context that home-shopping programming was legitimate public service.[86] Over a period of a week preceding the Christmas holidays, WTTW aired about 40 hours of programming in which it sold items from the gift shops of two

Chicago museums, the Lincoln Park Zoo and the Chicago Symphony Orchestra. Proceeds of the sales were to benefit WTTW and each of the other not-for-profit entities involved. In response to protests from self-proclaimed public interest groups, the FCC eventually found that the station had violated an FCC rule with respect to its programming, though it did not find that the fundraising technique was "too commercial" because its sales did not benefit any for-profit firms.[87]

In another highly publicized case, the thirty-five-station Minnesota Public Radio Network raised about $4 million a year from its for-profit mail-order catalog business during the 1990s.[88] In 1998, with that business causing MPR significant public relations problems, the network sold the catalog business to the Dayton Hudson Corporation for $120 million, giving MPR by far the largest endowment in public radio.[89] Today, MPR operates less conspicuous for-profit businesses, among them the lease of studio space.[90]

With the obvious exception of MPR, the profitability of these many and varied activities is not clear. In the mid-1990s, for example, WGBH reported that net income from its for-profit ventures amounted to no more than about 5 percent of its annual operating budget.[91] At the same time, many people in public broadcasting doubt that these enterprises can be greatly expanded without risking congressional wrath and the hastened end of all federal monies. Several well-known executives in public broadcasting, including former PBS President Ervin Duggan, have vigorously opposed increased commercial activities within the system, but against what has been a strongly contrary trend. PBS's own rules about national underwriting credits, for example, limits such announcements to fifteen seconds, but many stations routinely sell thirty-second spots anyway.[92] They do so because underwriting credits, which are subject to a host of vaguely worded and occasionally bizarre FCC regulations (a credit may include a corporate mascot, for example, but only if the mascot stands still), are, from the point of view of advertisers, worth far less than a "full strength" commercial on a for-profit channel.[93] This is especially so because credits that run during program breaks are far less likely to reach the advertisers' intended audiences.

One practical result of these restrictions is that stations must raise funds separately for each program they produce, a process that has the unintended effect of giving corporate donors' a veto over programs. Presumably the programs most at risk are those that are most controversial politically and culturally – presumably also the very kinds of programming public broadcasting was created to support. In other cases, the too-close identification of sponsors with programs can damage the credibility of the programs that are produced. In one well-known case, for example, television station KQED in San Francisco was embarrassed when it turned out that the Mondavi winery had provided the funding to produce a documentary about the family patriarch.[94] Even more serious have been charges that some public television stations have received money in return for airing privately produced programs that feature flattering profiles of for-profit firms – the same companies that paid to produce the program.[95]

Finally, many for-profit businesses in other mixed industries have attacked nonprofits' increasing engagement in commercial business activities as constituting unfair competition. Public broadcasters have not been singled out for criticism, but their commercial expansion is particularly rapid, and so they are likely to be under growing challenge as political forces bring pressure to define "unrelated business" activities more broadly and then to restrict them.

Despite concerns, public broadcasters have pushed on, more worried about congressional threats to eliminate funding. Not only is public broadcasting entering a vast uncharted sea of commercial activity, but it is increasingly doing so in partnerships with private firms. The barriers between nonprofit and for-profit organizations are falling. It must be noted that this is true not only in the United States, but also in Europe, Canada, and Japan. Because of the increasing number of channels available everywhere, the competition for talent, film and major events, such as sports, has driven their price well above the inflation rate. This is a particular problem for public broadcast systems dependent on the license fee, because the fee is typically pegged to inflation or lags behind it. Public broadcasters have thus had to turn to new sources of revenue, including advertising, to make up the shortfall. In 1994, for example, the BBC created BBC Worldwide, a division dedicated to developing commercial revenues; and in 1995 launched two new commercial ser- vices outside Britain, BBC World, a news channel, and BBC Prime, an advertiser-supported entertainment channel. Both services are undertaken in partnership with private firms.[96]

Revenue Sources and Public Broadcaster Independence

In the end, none of these many experiments can resolve the debate over the social efficiency of allowing public broadcasters to emulate the financial approaches used by for-profit firms. One half of the experiment is easy: to determine whether, and to what extent, commercial advertising or some other measure can actually increase the flow of revenue. The other half is hard: How will the organizations' social mission be affected? That requires understanding what the editorial mission is in ways far more operational than by reference to "the public interest." And here we encounter again legal questions about the appropriate place for the government in the speech market. In the United States, of course, the First Amendment prohibits a more precise statutory or regulatory statement of editorial mission, not only in the context of public broadcasting, but elsewhere. In the absence of such direction, experiments of any kind will do little if anything to resolve disagreements over the appropriate role for advertising or, for that matter, other financing techniques. Until then, it is hard to disagree with former FCC Chairman Mark Fowler's famous proclamation that "the public's interest…defines the public interest."[97] Of course, from the point of view of democracy (and certainly for the democracy promoter), this is an unsatisfactory outcome. Surely democracy requires something more than "Baywatch" reruns on TV and pin-ups in the newspaper.

But this only brings us back to our original dilemma. "Public" radio and television are industries that illustrate well the interplay of outputs and the mechanisms needed to finance them. From an economic perspective, every potential revenue source – government grants, private donations, private sales, or anything else – represents a willingness to pay for some particular output and the ability of its provider to tap into that willingness. Thus the decision by a provider of public radio or television programming (or any other media content for that matter) to reach out to a particular source of funds implies that programming will be of the type that appeals to that source. Decisions about the nature of programming a media organization will provide cannot be made independently of the availability of funding for that package of service. The character of the services being produced and the success of a media organization in generating funding for those services are inextricably entwined; depending on the nature of the "outputs," it can be easy, difficult, or even impossible to finance them through sales to "consumers," whomever they might be.

So public, not-for-profit broadcasters are faced with a dilemma. They can retain the focus on the twin-mission goals of "quality" (as they define it) and avoidance of the commercial funding techniques used by private, commercial broadcasters – they can, that is, restrict their activities to what can be financed through donated, presumably unrestricted, revenue – or they can compromise one or both goals in some measure by increasing their reliance on commercial revenues.

It is tempting for public broadcasters to believe there is no dilemma – that resort to new revenue-generating sources will not necessitate a compromise in quality. Achieving their goal of quality programming is an admittedly ambiguous concept, as both critics and supporters of public broadcasting emphasize; thus any attempt to assess the impact on mission of emulating private stations' commercials is likely to yield – as it has – an argument without end. One intermediate position has been widely adopted by public radio stations—"selling" what amount to personal, rather than business, "commercials" by mentioning donors' names and a brief message concerning their birthdays, anniversaries, etc. But a far greater compromise with the non-advertising goal has been evolving at a rapid rate; some public broadcasters, as already discussed, have dropped completely the goal of avoiding commercials, although at this point still restricting their timing so as not to interrupt programs.

The question is whether the growing commercialism of public broadcasters is making them indistinguishable from for-profit stations, and thus whether they are abandoning their distinct historic position and editorial mission. Will the process of competition for revenues continue to blur the distinction, or will public broadcasting contract or even wither away? What is not clear is whether nonprofit broadcasters have sufficient advantages in the market for private donations—whether because of tax deductibility or altruistic support—to sustain their current level and form of activity, or whether they can be sufficiently innovative in overcoming free-rider problems in ways that will sustain their social role. A critical and enduring question is whether an exogenous drop in government grants can be offset by a partial, never mind a full, increase in private donations. Economic theory suggests there will be only a partial offset because "crowding out" of private donations by public funding is a general phenomenon in markets for collective goods.

To summarize the economic problem, then, any mission-based organization can be expected to pursue a strategy that will optimize the balance of revenue from varied sources, taking into account the effect of each source on the organization's achievement of its goals. This process involves balancing an organization's multiple goals with one another and with the availability of revenues from each source. It also involves recognizing that the pursuit of revenue is a process that not only raises funds but that also can affect achievement of the organization's goals. Revenue, in short, brings both a direct effect on organization behavior, through its impact on the revenue available to pursue the organization's mission, and an indirect effect through the compromises in organization outputs that may be required to obtain the funds. In the case of broadcasting, the unique mission of public, nonprofit, stations – never entirely clear – is becoming even less so. This is particularly true in television, as the technologies of cable and direct satellite have greatly expanded the variety of programming appealing to smaller, specialized audiences. Still, survival is a powerful motivator, and so public broadcast stations are, at an increasingly urgent pace, trying to find funding to offset the loss of government grants. In the process, the fear is that they are becoming more like the for-profit broadcasters whose behavior they were established explicitly to avoid.

As government grants continue to decline, and as competition for private donations becomes more intense between all participants in the nonprofit sector, public broadcasting's mission will come under further scrutiny. This is true not only in the United States, but in public broadcast systems throughout the world. Typically, however, other public broadcast systems have detailed public-service charters specifying programming and service requirements, and an organizational structure designed to meet them. U.S. public broadcasting has neither of these things, in part because it was created as a nonprofit alternative to a dominantly for-profit, commercial broadcast system. Particularly with public television, it is no longer clear what "alternative" the service provides.

As the United States moves toward digital broadcast television delivery, the question of public television's mission is likely to become even more confused. Digital transmission permits a broadcaster to operate multiple channels in the spectrum space currently used to operate one, and the explosion of new profit-seeking channels will further segment the television audience while also increasing the competition among all programmers for the limited supply of existing video content. Further, the transformation to digital broadcasting has required all broadcasters to make huge capital investments in equipment and facilities. Many broadcasters, public broadcasters included, are expected to recoup some of that cost by using their extra channels for non-broadcast operations such as Internet service or telephone paging. The manner in which public broadcasters respond to these new competitive and structural challenges will have a great deal to say about their social and editorial missions in the multi-channel marketplace.

Some readers may object that public broadcasting is an extreme example for anyone interested in promoting free media overseas, and thus not a very useful one, precisely because of the financing limitations public broadcasting faces in its desire to secure editorial integrity and independence. But the history of private, for-profit media in the United States is in many respects more confused; its editorial outcomes are little better, and if any number of communications scholars are to be believed, they are often dangerously worse. Moreover, any short list of the world's "best" news and public affairs media is likely to include at least one public broadcaster, the British Broadcasting Corporation, and very possibly more. It is precisely because of public broadcasting's primary emphasis on editorial quality that its financial difficulties are so instructive. The dilemma of revenue sources that trouble public broadcasters will confront *any* media organization that desires to compete in that market. The regulatory restraints may differ from place to place, but the economics of public affairs journalism – and human nature – do not. Finally, while it is certainly possible that high-quality news and public affairs media would be better able to service their editorial missions in the not-for-profit sector of the economy, as some scholars and practitioners have suggested,[98] such a shift would do nothing to alleviate the financial challenges in sustaining those media. If U.S. public broadcasting is any example, such a shift may even make matters worse. Globally, too, the U.S. concept of a not-for-profit sector, with its tax exemptions and other benefits, is not universal, and certainly not in the developing world.

Finally, an observation: With the singular exception of public broadcasting, the world's elite public affairs media – broadcast, newspaper, magazine – earn most of their revenues from advertising, not subscription or other sales. By contrast, it is the *National Enquirer, Nuestro Diario* and other popular "commercial" media that earn the greatest share of revenues from direct public support, that is, street and kiosk sales. If revenue sources and editorial mission are inextricably bound up, that does not mean that sophisticated, professional and aggressive reporting will not have a market that advertisers want to reach. They will. But the theory of rational ignorance tells us it will always be a relatively small market. In the United States, for example, one can (arguably) count one's fingers the nation's elite newspapers and broadcast news programs (almost all of which are, again, advertiser supported). There are perhaps more elite public affairs magazines and journals, but many of those are subsidized in some way – whether by a single wealthy individual or by a not-for-profit owner such as a university or a professional association – and of course many such magazines do not survive, or do so by publishing irregularly. Many of these publications also serve specialized audiences, too, and not the general public.

Absent a major political, social or economic crisis, there is no economic reason for the market for high-quality journalism to be large. In democratizing societies, of course, there often is such a crisis, at least in the period immediately before and after transition. But as the process of democratic consolidation goes forward, the market for aggressive journalism will decline. For those in the media assistance business then, there arises the likelihood that at least some of the media they seek to develop will either not survive in the long term or, if they do, will do so by dramatically changing the character of their products. Time will tell. In any case, those public affairs media that keep to their original editorial mission and that do survive are unlikely to appeal to a broad public, and thus will always struggle with the dilemma of revenue sources. Some can and do find inventive ways to enhance revenues in a manner consistent with their larger editorial mission. As important, so do the assistance organizations that support them, a subject for the next chapter.

Notes

1.   Krishna Kumar, *USAID's Media Assistance: Policy and Programmatic Lessons,* (Washington, DC: USAID Office of Development Evaluation and Information, Bureau for Policy and Program Coordination, January 2004), 12.
2.   Ibid., xi.
3.   Ibid.
4.   The most sophisticated and useful of these discussions is *News In the Public Interest: A Free and Subsidized Press* (Baton Rouge, LA: Manship School of Mass Communication, 2005). The report is a summary of a March 2004 symposium organized in part by Manship School Dean John Maxwell Hamilton, a board member of the International Center for Journalists and a journalist with extensive international experience.
5.   Robert D. Leigh, ed., *A Free and Responsible Press: A General Report on Mass Communication: Newspapers, Radio, Motion Pictures, Magazines and Books* (Chicago: University of Chicago Press, 1947).
6.   *A Free and Responsible Press* has endured as a source of press criticism, but in every other respect it was a failure. The press itself rejected both the report's recommendations and the qualifications of its authors, whom trade magazine *Editor and Publisher* described none-too-kindly as "11 professors, a banker-merchant and a poet-librarian." A.J. Liebling wrote in the *Nation* that he was "inclined to

wonder uncharitably as I read the book what they had spent the $200,000 on: it contains some sound, unoriginal reflections, but nothing worth over one grand even at *Ladies Home Journal* rates."

7.   Commission on the Role of the Press in a Democracy, Annenberg School for Communications, University of Pennsylvania, Philadelphia. In June 2005, the author was one of about forty participants at "H2" discussions at the University of Pennsylvania.

8.   James Curran, "Comment on Hutchins Chapters 1 and 2," in "Unedited Drafts of Papers Revisiting the Report from the Commission on Freedom of the Press," unpublished discussion paper, Annenberg Trust at Sunnylands Press Commission, June 2005, 28.

9.   See Daniel Ankst, "Nonprofit Journalism: Removing the Pressure of the Bottom Line," *Carnegie Reporter* (Fall 2005): 20.

10.   See "Something to Talk About: Engaging Young Adults in the Core Newspaper," a PowerPoint presentation available as part of the Readership Institute studies of the Media Management Center: http://www.readership.org/experience/default. htm.

11.   Anthony Downs, *An Economic Theory of Democracy* (New York: Harper Books, 1957).

12.   Ibid.

13.   James Hamilton, *All the News That's Fit to Sell* (Princeton, NJ: Princeton University Press, 2004), 8-35.

14.   Herbert Gans, *Deciding What's News: A Study of CBS Evening News, NBC Nightly News, Newsweek and Time, 25th Anniversary edition* (Evanston, IL: Northwestern University Press, 2004), xvii.

15.   One might argue that in the current media environment of bloggers, advocacy groups, and self-appointed media critics, that such evaluations of media are now possible. Certainly many people in these communities seem to believe that media products can be judged without actually reading or viewing them, and that their evaluation of those products are of greater value than the products themselves.

16.   *Economist*, "Stop Press," (March 26, 2005): 58.

17.   Gadis Arivia, editor and publisher, *Jurnal Perempuan*, author interview, Santiago, Chile, March 14, 2001.

18.   Ibid.

19.   Ibid.

20.   Ibid.

21.   Commission on the Role of the Press in a Democracy, Annenberg School for Communications, University of Pennsylvania, Philadelphia., June 12-14, 2005.

22.   *News in the Public Interest: A Free and Subsidized Press* (Baton Rouge, LA: Breaux Symposium, Manship School of Mass Communication, Louisiana State University, March 20, 2004): 14.

23.   Gans, *Deciding What's News*, 2004, 16.

24.   Michael Emery and Edwin Emery, *The Press and America: An Interpretive History of the Mass Media* (Englewood Cliffs, NJ: Prentice Hall, 1992), 174.

25.   See Hamilton, *All the News That's Fit to Sell*, 2004, 52-70.

26.   Ibid., 38

27.   "Editor and Publisher Marks its Sixtieth Anniversary," *Editor and Publisher* (March 25, 1944): 11.

28.   Marion Tuttle Marzolf, *Civilizing Voices: American Press Criticism, 1880-1950* (New York: Longman Publishing Group, 1991), 24.

29.   E.L. Godkin, editorial, *Nation* (May 5, 1898): 336.

30. Edward Alsworth Ross, "The Suppression of Important News," *Atlantic Monthly* (March 1919): 311.
31. Hamilton Holt, "A Plan for an Endowed Journal," *Independent* 73 (1919): 301.
32. Marzolf, *Civilizing Voices*, 1991, 63.
33. Robert W. McChesney, "Conflict, Not Consensus: The Debate Over Broadcast Communication Policy, 1930-1935," in *Ruthless Criticism*, eds. William Solomon and Robert McChesney (Minneapolis: University of Minnesota Press, 1993), 224.
34. Lyndon Johnson, "Remarks on Signing the Public Broadcasting Act," November 5, 1967.
35. Ibid.
36. The best short account of U.S. public broadcasting's editorial and financial dilemmas is Twentieth Century Fund, *Quality Time? The Report of the Twentieth Century Fund Task Force on Public Television* (New York: Twentieth Century Fund Press, 1993). Most useful is Richard Somerset Ward's brief but comprehensive analysis of these problems, contained as the report's appendix.
37. Johnson, "Remarks," 1967.
38. *Economist*, "Time to Adjust Your Set," (December 23, 1995): 69.
39. *Review of the BBC's Royal Charter: A Strong BBC, Independent of Government* (London: British Broadcasting Corp., March 2, 2005), 59.
40. Ibid., 58-63.
41. For comparison purposes, government spending in the United States is $1.06 per head for public television. Japan spends $17.71 per head for NHK, Canada spends $32.15 per head for the CBC, and the United Kingdom spends $38.56 per head for the BBC.
42. *Current*, "The Struggle Over Federal Aid, 1995-1996," (July 24, 1996): 1.
43. See *Public Broadcasting System Revenues 1982-2001*. Available at Current, www.current.org.
44. Federal funding of public television has always commanded bipartisan support, and normally funding has come in the form of three-year authorizations and two-year appropriations. Appropriations do not always match authorizations; the actual appropriation for 1993, for example, was $253 million, well short of the $285 million Congress authorized. In 1993, Congress authorized substantial increases in federal funding for the years 1994-96: $310 million for '94 (appropriation was $255 million); $375 million for '95 (appropriation was $285 million); and $425 million for '96 (appropriation was $275 million). In fiscal 1997, authorized funding dropped to $260 million; in 1998 it dropped to $250 million, and in 1999 and 2000 it held at $250 million. More recently appropriations have been higher, for example $365 million in 2003, though a significant part of those appropriations have been for costs associated with digital conversion.
45. Willard D. Rowland, "Public Service Broadcasting in the United States: Its Mandate, Institutions and Conflicts," in *Public Service Broadcasting in a Multichannel Environment*, ed. Robert K. Avery (New York: Longman, 1993), 182.
46. *Public Broadcasting System Revenues 1982-2001*.
47. Rowland, "Public Service Broadcasting," 1993, 166-167.
48. "Should Public Broadcasting Go More Commercial?" *Current* (May 12, 1996): 12.
49. Newton Minow, "The Vast Wasteland," address to the National Association of Broadcasters, Washington, DC, May 9, 1961.
50. Carnegie Corporation of New York, *Public Television: A Program for Action* (New York: Bantam Books, 1967), 11.

51. *Current*, "The Public Buys In," (November 2, 1992): 2.

52. Carnegie Corporation, *Public Television*, 1967, 68-69.

53. Ibid. The first private contribution to CPB was a $1 million gift from CBS.

54. Memberships comprise a larger portion of revenues for public radio (33.9%) than for public television (22.7%). See Corporation for Public Broadcasting, *Public Broadcasting Revenue Fiscal Year 2002* (Washington, DC: CPB, February 2004).

55. Public television's Nielsen rating varies with its national program schedule, and some programs, such as the 1991 documentary "The Civil War," received Nielsen ratings of 20 and higher—on par with major network sports and entertainment events. For an average rating, see A.C. Nielsen's monthly reports, *PTV Cumulative Audience Ranking by Station Market*. Weekly Nielsen figures are also reported in the industry trade magazine, *Broadcast & Cable*.

56. Carnegie Corporation, *Public Television*, 1967, 96.

57. Corporation for Public Broadcasting, *Annual Report* (Washington, D.C: CPB, 2003), 42.

58. In 2002, the last fiscal year for which full data are available, U.S public television's total income was reported at $1.62 billion, of which the total federal appropriation was $262 million; most of the rest came from membership subscriptions ($370 million), state and local governments ($341 million), businesses ($254 million), foundations ($104 million), and colleges and universities ($141 million). Additional revenue sources included federal contracts, auctions and miscellaneous sources. See CPB, *Revenue Fiscal Year 2002*, 2004.

59. Boston Consulting Group, *Strategies for Public Television in a Multi-Channel Environment* (Washington, DC: CPB, March 1991), 3.

60. Ibid.

61. Twentieth Century Fund, *Quality Time?* 1993, 3.

62. Ibid, 3-6.

63. Bill Carter, "Conservatives Call for PBS to Go Private of Go Dark," *New York Times* (April 20, 1992): A1; See also Laurence Jarvik, *After Privatization: Public Television in the Cultural Marketplace.* (Washington, DC: Heritage Foundation, 1992).

64. Richard Somerset Ward, "Public Television : The Ballpark's Changing," in Twentieth Century Fund, *Quality Time*?, 1993, 143-60.

65. Bill Davis, "Congressional Funding for Public Broadcasting: Will There Be a Public Broadcasting Trust Fund?" *Current* (July 24, 1996): 1-3.

66. Hal Bouton, "Commercials: Divided Views on Fundamental Question," *Current* (May 1, 1995): 1.

67. Lawrence Grossman, "Introducing PTV Weekend," *Current Online*, June 20, 1997, http://www.current.org/weekend/wklg597.html (accessed January 2, 2006).

68. Wick Rowland, "We Take Another Step in a Seductive Dance with Commerce" *Current* (February 10, 2003): 3.

69. Carnegie Corporation of New York, *A Public Trust: The Report of the Carnegie Commission on the Future of Public Broadcasting* (New York: Bantam Books, 1979).

70. Mark S. Fowler and Daniel L. Brenner, "A Marketplace Approach to Broadcast Regulation," *Texas Law Review* 60 (1982): 207-257.

71. Newton N. Minow and Craig L. LaMay, "The Land Grant of the Airwaves," *Wall Street Journal* (January 24, 1996): A26.

72. Max Boot, "Competing with Big Bird," *Wall Street Journal* (October 23, 1996): A27.

73. See James H. Snider and Benjamin I. Page, "Does Media Ownership Affect Media Stands? The Case of the Telecommunications Act of 1996," unpublished research paper delivered at the 1997 Annual Meeting of the Midwest Political Science Association, Chicago, Illinois, April 10, 1997.

74. Richard Somerset Ward, "Public Television," 1993, 150.

75. U.S. Code, Title 47, Ch. 5, Subchapter 3, Part IV, Subpart e, § 399b.

76. Federal Communications Commission, *Report of the Temporary Commission on Alternative Financing* (Washington, DC: Federal Communications Commission, 1984).

77. Ibid.

78. William McCarter, president and CEO, Windows to the World Communications Inc., author interview, Chicago, Illinois, May 10, 1993.

79. "PBS May Ease Rules as Way to Increase Corporate Support," *Wall Street Journal* (June 1, 1994): A3.

80. Craig LaMay, "Thinking the Unthinkable: Is Advertising in Public TV's Future," *Chicago Tribune* (June 8, 1994): A25.

81. *New York Times*, "Reprieve for PBS, but Hunt for Funds Continues," (January 2, 1996): B1.

82. Steve Behrens, "Tour Aims to Correct Ad World's Notions About Underwriting, Introduces PBS Sponsorship Group," *Current* (May 12, 1997): 2. The partner producing stations are WNET in New York, WGBH in Boston, KCET in Los Angeles, and WETA in Washington, DC

83. Corporation for Public Broadcasting, "CPB Leads Public Radio and Television to New Ventures," November 30, 1995.

84. See "Shop PBS" at http://www.shoppbs.org/home/index.jsp?clickid=mainnav_home_img.

85. See "Cut Loose by LearningSmith, WETA Hooks Up With KCET Chain," *Current* (June 23, 1997) http://www.current.org/mo/mo711s.html (accessed January 27, 2006).

86. As part of regulations implementing the 1992 Cable Act, the FCC in July 1993 ruled that more than 100 home-shopping programs were serving the public interest and thus that they were legally entitled, along with local broadcast TV stations, to be carried on cable networks.

87. See Steve Behrens, "FCC Petitioned to Ban Shopping Shows on PTV," *Current* (August 1, 1994): 1; and *Current*, "Chicago Station's Experiment with Home Shopping Violated FCC Rule" (November 8, 1995): 1.

88. *New York Times*, "Public Radio Being Pressed to Turn its Success into More Independence" (March 3, 1996): C1.

89. Jacqueline Conciatore, "Minnesota net endows itself with sale of mail-order firm," *Current* (April 6, 1998) http://current.org/mo/mo806k.html (accessed October 12, 2005).

90. See Minnesota Public Radio's Web page at www.minnesota.publicradio.org.

91. Ward, *Public Television*, 1993, 158. The true reason for the lack of clarity is that existing tax law encourages the confusion. Nonprofits, including public broadcasters, have the incentive to select ancillary business activities that use inputs jointly with their tax-exempt mission-related activities, and then to allocate as much of the joint costs as possible to the taxed sector, thereby showing little or no profit in that sector.

92. Karen Everhard Bedford, "'The Question of Length is Really Settled': It's True that 30-Second Spots Abound on Some Stations, But They Divide the Public TV System," *Current* (February 17, 1997): 2.

93. See Karen Everhart, "Corporate Mascots (Still as Rocks) and Celebs to Appear in Sponsor Credits" *Current* (July 8, 2002): 2.

94. See Steve Behrens, "KQED Drops Mondavi Project in Underwriting Controversy," *Current* (November 25, 1996): 8.

95. One such program is "World Business Review," hosted by former Secretary of State General Alexander Haig, which collected payments from the companies profiled on the program. The financial arrangement was exposed by a National Public Radio program, "On the Media," on February 23, 2002. See Steve Behrens, "Haig's Chats with Executives Seen as '30-Minute Commercial'" *Current* (February 25, 2002): 2.

96. *The Economist,* "Time to Adjust Your Set," 1995: 69.

97. Fowler and Brenner, "A Marketplace Approach," 1982: 210.

98. See *News in the Public Interest: A Free and Subsidized Press*, 2004.

6

Sustaining Independent Media:
Case Studies in Media Firms and
Assistance Providers

"You are going to let the fear of poverty govern
your life and your reward will be that you will eat,
but you will not live." – George Bernard Shaw

So far this book has examined the difficulty of sustaining free and independent journalism in transition societies, particularly those where civil society is weak or impaired. That examination has centered on an economic dilemma: *How are professional and independent news media supposed to sustain themselves financially without giving up their editorial independence?*

This chapter looks more closely at the financial accounting side of civil society and free press promotion. It takes as its primary focus an NGO, the New York-based Media Development Loan Fund (MDLF), and a handful of its many media clients around the world. MDLF is a creation of journalists – most of them from Southeast Europe – whose personal experiences with Western aid programs led them to believe that there must be a better way to use scarce resources to promote independent media. As its name suggests, MDLF uses loans, rather than grants, as the centerpiece of its assistance programs, with the result that the character of MDLF's assistance, and the performance of its clients, is distinctly different from anything in the field. Another NGO, the Gaborone-based Southern Africa Media Development Fund (SAMDEF), is also discussed in this chapter because its does much the same thing as MDLF, and the two organizations are partners in financing projects in the SAMDEF region.

MDLF is by far the larger of these two organizations, both in its geographical reach and its loan portfolio. It is a U.S.-registered, tax-exempt venture capital firm that supports high-quality news organizations in transition countries throughout the world; its goal is to teach those firms financial and managerial discipline, to make them profitable if at all possible, and thus to secure the future for free and responsible journalism in the countries where it operates. Repaid principal goes back into the loan pool, where the money is used again to help new clients, exponentially extending the impact of MDLF's assistance dollars; dividends and capital gains go to support MDLF's operating expenses. Some MDLF clients get grants or other kinds of assistance, but the idea is to wean clients as much as possible from donations and make them full and competitive participants in the market. In time, the goal is for MDLF clients to be able to attract investment capital from more traditional sources. For some of MDLF's early clients in Central Europe this has happened, a successful outcome that raises new problems of how to preserve editorial independence and quality against the expectations of new business partners and shareholders.

The contention of this chapter is that the aid model developed by MDLF and SAMDEF is the most cost-effective at joining civil society and free press goals with a workable financial strategy. The "third way" they have pioneered is not the only funding model worthy of consideration. Grants are obviously another, and in many situations where loans are impractical or impossible, grants will be the only realistic model. Grants can also be used, as MDLF uses them, to supplement the loan program – for example to support journalism training programs at a newspaper that has taken out a loan for a printing press. Still, the loan approach to media assistance is unique in that it takes sustainability as a central objective of that assistance. It also, by design, a form of aid that requires the long-term commitment and attention of the provider, something rare in the assistance world. For aid providers, of course, the usefulness of the model will depend on providers' programmatic goals in the places where they operate; MDLF and SAMDEF are simply very good operational benchmarks for linking editorial mission to financial performance.

Social Entrepreneurship

Though I have never heard anyone in either MDLF or SAMDEF describe their organizations this way, both are examples of what leading business schools now call "social entrepreneurship" or "social enterprise management." So, too, are many of their clients. At its simplest, social entrepreneurship is about managing businesses that have an explicit social mission, usually but not always one that is difficult to sustain in the for-profit economy. As a management idea, social entrepreneurship springs from the policy confusion and the operational realities that characterize what economists call "mixed industries," those in which both for-profit and not-for-profit firms compete. As a practical matter, conflict between non-profit and for-profit firms working in the same industries has increased dramatically in the past two decades.[1] In developed countries, one result of that conflict is that there has everywhere been a transformation in citizens' expectations about the provision of "public" goods and services. For-profit firms increasingly provide goods that were once provided almost exclusively by governments – parks and recreation centers, hospitals and health care, education, prisons and rehabilitative services, sanitation and sewer maintenance, police and even military services. Many of these same services have traditionally been the domain of private, not-for-profit firms, which in addition to facing new competition have been asked to meet the new demand created by diminished state spending on these and other social goods and services.[2] Social entrepreneurship has developed as a practical response to these changes.

In the developing world, the growth of the non-profit sector has been boosted by the emphasis on civil-society promotion, but there, too, there is an increasing emphasis on what might be called social entrepreneurship – to the need to build a sustainable business environment and centers of private enterprise. In perhaps the most well known example of this, the United Nations in July 2003 announced a new commission, led by former Mexican President Ernesto Zedillo and former Canadian Finance Minister Paul Martin, to promote entrepreneurship in poor nations through the introduction of more rigorous financial and managerial discipline in development projects.[3] The sum of these changes in the global economy, writes Lester Salamon and his colleagues, is that the global non-profit sector has outgrown its traditional sources of revenue (government grants and private philanthropy) forcing it to find or create new ones.[4] Social entrepreneurship, unlike traditional not-for-profit management, emphasizes revenue creation, but at its best it does more than that. It is non-profit management that is financially disciplined, customer-focused, and organizationally strategic. It is management that has a long-term plan for fulfilling an organization's mission (a plan, *not* a document), and is willing to take calculated risks to do it. Organizationally, successful social entrepreneurs are characterized by a businesslike board of directors; tight operational controls; a strong, well-educated staff that understands and buys into the goals of the organization; technological sophistication; a strong bias for marketing; and, if at all possible, diverse sources of revenue.[5] In short, social entrepreneurs are not-for-profit firms that behave very much like for-profit firms, but with social mission as their bottom line.

For purposes of this book, the important point about social entrepreneurship is that it is emphatically not what media assistance usually looks like. Neither is it easy to do. Critics of social enterprise management make two important arguments. The first is that mixing mission with entrepreneurship is an invitation to abuse as firms of all kinds (but particularly non-profits) attempt to use social mission as a shield for profit-making activities (and in the United States to avoid paying taxes on any unrelated business income). Second and related is the risk that what were once valuable social missions can be diluted or lost through profit-seeking. In the economics and business literature there is evidence to support both of these criticisms, but both miss a larger point: *Any* revenue good, including grants and donations, can obliterate a firm's mission if it becomes an end in itself, and without a sustainable revenue good the mission is doomed anyway. This is exactly MDLF's premise: Grants and donations are unsustainable over the long term, and only by building the business can clients stay focused on and enhance their editorial mission. In the case of MDLF, its program related investments (PRIs, discussed below) are clearly mission goods: commercial lenders would not make the same investments on the same terms, if at all. PRIs are *also* MDLF's principal revenue good, key to the organization's own sustainability.

More significantly, through its activities MDLF poses a philosophical challenge to the usual strategies for addressing media and civil society sustainability – whether the medium is a newspaper, a Web site, or works of performance art. MDLF is deeply concerned with the editorial integrity of its clients, but as a practical matter its assistance dollars will sometimes support that mission good only indirectly, by helping its clients develop revenue goods. B92 provides a good example: its mission goods include arts and cultural programming that are not yet profitable (and may never be), and which are supported through the production of revenue goods that include B92TV, whose top-rated programs include "Sex and the City" and NBA basketball games. Many if not most MDLF PRIs are focused much more directly on the production of mission goods – for example, sustaining independent journalistic voices in places where there are otherwise none – but the point is MDLF thinks creatively about the mix of mission goods and revenue goods. That is what social entrepreneurs do.

Finally, the discipline that characterizes good management in any firm, for-profit or non-profit, is especially important where markets are unstable, the law in flux, and a media company is still struggling to make its core product sustainable. For many MDLF clients, and for media companies in many transition countries, the daily struggle is still to cover the news, serve customers, find and retain good employees, and keep the lights on – basic things. Beta News Agency in Belgrade, for example, hopes to one day develop financial partnerships with some of the western news agencies that now subscribe to its daily print and audio services, but for now the goal is still to make a profit on those services. Founded by eight journalists in the early 1990s, Beta survived harassment from the Milosovic regime and now competes with, among others, the state-subsidized news agency Tanjug. Average salaries at Beta are 300 euros per month, making it difficult to keep qualified people.

According to Zlata Kures, Beta's business manger, and Dragan Janjic, its editor-in-chief, about 10 percent of Beta's annual revenues still come from donations, but the goal from the beginning, Janjic said, has been for the company "to be in the market." With an MDLF loan, Beta renovated and moved into new offices in February 2003, greatly increasing capacity for its daily service, which includes reports from correspondents in all the countries of the former Yugoslavia, as well as 12 reporting from other parts of Europe. MDLF assistance is also helping BETA redesign its central news desk operations to mirror the kind of "superdesk" set-up used at news organizations like Bloomberg. Beta is an excellent example of the long-term commitment MDLF makes to its clients. Its first loan to the agency, also for office space, was in 1997, at the height of the Milosovic era, when Beta's reporters were working out of a cramped Belgrade apartment and reporters had to take turns working at the desks. With its new offices and equipment, Janjic told me, BETA sees business and financial reporting as its best opportunity for growth, especially as Serbia and Montenegro begins to recover economically from its years of isolation. Janjic and Kures also see revenue possibility in a mobile Internet subscription service. BETA is thus entrepreneurial in vision, but requires the kind of assistance that it can only get from MDLF to convert that vision into a profitable business.

Before examining MDLF and SAMDEF in more detail, let us first briefly examine several other examples of media firms that behave as social entrepreneurs.

Social Entrepreneurship and Media Firms

A media company's social mission is not necessarily dependent on the legal status of the firm, which can be either for-profit or not-for-profit. In the developing world the distinction between for-profits and not-for-profits, at least in the way developed countries understand it, often does not exist anyway. In any case, many media firms and all journalism companies, for-profit or not-for-profit, profess to have a social mission of a kind not typical of firms in other industries, one usually linked explicitly to the strength and character of democracy, or at least to the quality of public life. But no matter how a firm is organized, and depending on how it understands "mission," it can devote parts of its operations to the production of mission goods and others to the production of revenue goods.

Allowing for different judgments as to the value of any given mission, what does social entrepreneurship look like in the media firm? Before turning to examples in developing countries, let us consider a few well-known examples from the United States.

- Harpo, the media company created by super celebrity Oprah Winfrey, consists of four discrete for-profit divisions – Winfrey's television show, magazine, movie production company, and book club boutique – and a non-profit known as the Angel Network, founded in 1997 to provide college scholarships for financially needy students, financial and in-kind support to Habitat for Humanity, and aid to schools around the world.[6] In both its for-profit and non-profit entities, Harpo is dedicated to an explicit social mission: helping women and children develop through education the ability to live productive lives, and more broadly to "to inspire individuals to create opportunities that help underserved people rise to their own potential."[7]
- Sesame Workshop, formerly known as the Children's Television Workshop, is the creator of the children's educational programs "Sesame Street," "3-2-1 Contact," and others. The Workshop is a not-for profit company that describes its social mission as helping children "to learn and grow; to be prepared for school; to better understand the world and each other; to think, dream and

discover; to reach their highest potential,"[8] and its "Sesame Street" program is popular throughout the world, including democratizing and post-conflict societies like South Africa, Afghanistan and Kosovo. The Workshop sells its programming overseas, earns money on royalties, and licenses its "Sesame Street" logo and characters for use with an enormous variety of products, from vitamins to bedsheets. According to the firm's 2002 report, 72 percent of revenues came from such sales.[9] The report also noted the need for new revenue sources, including the introduction in 2003 of "Sesame Street" products for the teen market – t-shirts and jeans, hats and other headgear, watches and hosiery.[10] Another new product, designed to tap into the "adult nostalgia market," are music CDs featuring "Sesame Street" songs performed by the likes of Billy Joel, Paul Simon and REM.[11]

- National Geographic magazine is the widely recognized public face of the National Geographic Society, the world's largest not-for-profit scientific organization, with assets of more than $1 billion. According to the Society's 2003 tax returns, the magazine alone earned $72 million in advertising revenue that year.[12] The magazine is also just one of several revenue-generating programs that include three other magazines, book publishing, television production, school publishing, photography sales, interactive media, public lecture programs, and a catalog sales division. Revenue from these programs support the Society's mission goods: scientific research grants, exploration, museums, geography education, public service awards and grants to schools and teachers.

- *National Public Radio* is a private non-profit created by the Corporation for Public Broadcasting whose mission is "to work in partnership with member stations to create a more informed public—one challenged and invigorated by a deeper understanding and appreciation of events, ideas and cultures. To accomplish our mission, we produce, acquire and distribute programming that meets the highest standards of public service in journalism and cultural expression; we represent our members in matters of their mutual interest; and we provide satellite interconnection for the entire public radio system."[13] NPR relies on a mix of revenue sources, including private donations, government grants and sales of books, music, consulting services and other goods. NPR also sells advertising in the form of "enhanced underwriting announcements" (a term of art that makes sense only to the Federal Communications Commission). Critics decry such announcements as undermining public broadcasting's public-service mission, but as discussed in the previous chapter there is no necessary reason why that should be so – any more than, say, advertising in the *New York Times* is inimical to its editorial mission. Besides, "non-commercial" is not a mission and should not be confused with one.

Entrepreneurial Media in Democratizing Countries

Easily one of the best examples of social entrepreneurship in a transition state is the multimedia firm B92, in Serbia and Montenegro, which began life in 1989 as a student-run, punk rock radio station in Belgrade. During the Milosovic years, B92 became the globally ubiquitous voice of dissent in the former Yugoslavia, and as such received substantial international assistance, both governmental and non-governmental. Today B92 understands its social mission as helping to heal a democratizing Serbia and Montenegro, a mission that includes not just the production of high-quality news and public affairs programming on radio and television, but also cultural centers, music and book publishing, and the provision of legal assistance to local broadcasters throughout the country. With the help of an equity investment from MDLF, B92 is in the process of becoming a private, for-profit firm, and in early 2004 relocated its many disparate operations (formerly hidden from hostile government officials in homes and offices scattered across Belgrade) under one roof in a renovated building in Novi Belgrade.

Some of those operations, according to Editor-in-Chief Veran Matic, cannot be profitable and still serve their social mission, so B92 has put its book, music publishing and cultural programs in a non-profit foundation. The company's profit centers are its radio and television entertainment programs, which subsidize the news and public affairs programming in those media. The profits B92TV earns from "Sex in the City" and NBA basketball games, for instance, covers the costs of carrying live all of the testimony from the Hague War Crimes Tribunal for the Former Yugoslavia, a decision that is not only expensive (since it means forgone revenue opportunities available from other programming), but editorially controversial. Much of the Hague testimony is laced with the same kinds of hate speech that fueled the country's violent disintegration, and the broadcasts have been criticized by other Serb journalists who believe they tear at old wounds better left alone.

Currently the largest obstacle to B92's growth is the still-unsettled state of law concerning the conversion of formerly "socially owned" assets to private ones and the absence of comprehensive broadcast regulation. Without these things it is very nearly impossible for B92 to properly value its various assets, which of course makes it difficult to attract quality investors. For now, MDLF has taken a large equity stake in the company, allowing it to aggressively pursue new business opportunities. In 2003, B92 emerged as the nation's largest private Internet Service Provider; in 2005, the company announced plans to launch a twenty-four-hour cable television channel.

If B92 is a compelling example of social entrepreneurship, it is also a special case. B92 enjoys a measure of international celebrity owing to its long (and colorful) defiance of the Milosovic government, and the United States and the EU, having engaged in two wars in the region in the last decade, have also made significant post-war investments in democracy promotion there. Other high-quality media organizations in Central Europe have continued to struggle financially, and some have remained non-profits. And outside of Central and Eastern Europe – in Asia, Africa and Latin America, where democratization assistance and media assistance have been much less – one can find some of the best examples of social entrepreneurship in media firms. All operate, of course, in unique political and economic environments, and not all are equally successful in developing revenue goods sufficient to sustain their mission goods. Several examples follow.

Transitions Online, Prague

The excellent, subscription-based *Transitions Online* (TOL) provides in-depth, on-scene coverage and expert analyses of the politics and economics of Central and Eastern Europe and Eurasia. Founded in July 1999 by four staff members from an earlier and now-defunct print magazine, *Transitions*, TOL has correspondents based in each of the 28 countries it covers and a global readership of 80,000. TOL has received financial and professional support from the Open Society Institute and technical help from MDLF, but because of its substantial editorial costs (reporters' salaries) the magazine has had to seek additional sources of revenue beyond individual subscriptions, including institutional subscription and research packages for university libraries and Slavic studies departments, the International Monetary Fund and the World Bank. According to founder and publisher Jeremy Drucker, TOL has also tried to develop an online "store," so far without much success, and in 2005 it launched a two-week summer training program for Western journalism students interested in the region. In its first year the program had 26 students who either paid tuition or received foundation-funded scholarships.[14]

El Periodico, Guatemala City

In 2005, *El Periodico* (discussed at length in chapter 1) began to develop new editorial products designed to attract not just new readers but new kinds of readers. The goal is to become "essential" reading (the specific objective of Readership Institute recommendations) for a much larger and more diverse audience, and to compete more vigorously with *Prense Libre*, Guatemala's long-standing paper of record. In 2005 the paper launched a once-weekly supplement for kids and, to a great extent, *by* kids. The supplement, created by Investigative Editor Sylvia Gereda, has an advisory board comprised entirely of teenagers, who drive the editorial content. A second new offering is *El Periodico in Five Minutes*, a daily news digest distributed as part of the main paper. The four-page digest summarizes the day's major stories and features several of the paper's best photographs. The supplement has proven enormously successful with women and specifically with housewives – a readership *El Periodico* has heretofore been unable to reach – and Managing Editor Juan Luis Font is now making plans to distribute the supplement as a stand-alone publication on college campuses. Finally, led by publisher Jose Ruben Zamora, *El Periodico* has developed a special weekly section on business and economics that focuses on economic policies and trends in the region and the world, and on management issues. The supplement is more esoteric, even scholarly, than the usual newspaper business section or business magazine, at times even academic, and is intended to provide unique, added value to the economic elites that comprise most of *El Periodico's* traditional readership. All of these supplements, in addition to boosting subscription revenue, provide additional opportunities for advertising revenues.

Kantor Barita Radio 68H, Jakarta

Perhaps the most impressive radio project in the developing world is Kantor Berita Radio 68H, an Internet-based network that from a small central studio space in Jakarta serves one of the world's largest and most geographically, economically and culturally diverse audiences. The 68H studios are located within the compound of its parent organization, the Institute for the Study on Free Flow of Information (ISAI), a free expression NGO in Jakarta made famous during Suharto's time as home to a *samizdat* media house. Indeed, the station's call letters are its street address – Jalan Utan Kayu No.68H. Today the ISAI compound includes, in addition to the radio station, a theater, an art gallery and a bookstore. In front of the building stands a 70-meter transmitter, supplemented in February 2005 with a second, 200-meter transmitter in another section of Jakarta. The second antenna increases the network's terrestrial reach across Java, the country's most populous island and home to 250 of 68H's 400 network stations. Some network members – in Wamena (West Papua), Soe (West Timor) and no less than three places in Flores – are actually part of the state-run Radio Republik Indonesia (RRI).

As is the case in many developing countries, Indonesia's print media serve a market that is primarily an educated, urban upper class. The cumulative circulation of all papers published in Indonesia hovers around 5 million – barely 2 percent of the country's 241 million people. After the 1998 revolution, then, one of the challenges of democratization was to provide news to the rest of Indonesia's people, and radio was the obvious answer. There are estimated 40 million FM/AM radio receivers in the Indonesia, many of them serving entire families or villages. For reasons of its own, the Suharto regime had licensed hundreds of local FM and even AM stations across the archipelago, though it had banned independent news broadcasts in favor of official news bulletins distributed by RRI. Still, at the time of the 1998 revolution there were 700 radio stations in the country. Today there are more than 1,200 plus another 400 community stations with broadcast footprints of only a few miles.

68H, launched in 1999 by a former *samizdat* journalist, Santoso, sought to link as many of those stations as possible in an Internet-based news network. Most of these stations were shoestring operations with no business acumen (or cash), whose entire operation consisted of a single technical staff member (usually with rudimentary skills), one or two administrative staff, and an on-air personality whose job it was to play pirated music tapes and CDs. If these stations had budgets, there was no line in them for reporters, and there was no obvious way to deliver news programming to them. At the time, the ordinary delivery method required the use of costly terrestrial or satellite relay stations, an option available only to state radio. MDLF proposed digital audio compression, then a relatively new technology, as an alternative distribution method. The idea was not to stream audio – a pointless exercise in a country with an underdeveloped telecommunications infrastructure – but to distribute news programs as compressed files – as email attachments or as easily downloaded FTP files – that could then be rebroadcast in the old-fashioned way, on terrestrial radio.

In financial terms, 68H presents the kind of mixed history common to news organizations in post-authoritarian states. The company began with a grant (not a loan) from MDLF and the Asia Foundation, and then a second grant from the Dutch Foreign Ministry. The company was registered in January 2000 as a business entity under the name PT Media Lintas Inti Nusantara, with 60 percent of shares going to the management and employees, and 40 percent to ISAI as the parent organization. ISAI's share of the company is now 24 percent, though Santoso says that when 68H makes profits a portion are given to ISAI in order to advance the cause of free expression in Indonesia. MDLF, which continues to provide technical and management assistance to 68H, also made a $400,000 equity investment in the station in 2000.

From the outset the idea was for 68H to become an advertiser-supported medium. On the model of U.S. broadcast networks, 68H gives its programming away, relying on advertising sales for revenues. In each thirty minutes of programming, 68H reserves six minutes for advertising. In 2004, when I visited the station, the country had just concluded national elections, and the sale of advertising time to candidates and parties, to national and international NGOs, had sufficed to earn the network its first, small profit. Ordinarily, however, the station in 2004 was selling only about 30 percent of available time, generating enough revenue to cover about two-thirds of its operational costs. Importantly, almost 80 percent of 68H's ad sales are to other non-profits, including in particular the UN Development Program, the UN High Commissioner for Refugees, and the World Health Organization, all of which use 68H to distribute public service announcements. The UNHCR, for example, runs information campaigns for East Timorese refugees in West Timor. USAID does not contribute directly to 68H, but through the Asia Foundation has sponsored programs on legal reform and has underwritten the cost of training journalists in many of the local stations that comprise the 68H network. The U.S. State Department provides financial support to a new 68H service launched in 2003, "Asia Calling," a weekly, thirty-minute English- and local-language program distributed by satellite to more than forty stations across Southeast and East Asia.

Local, national and international NGOs also pay the production costs of programming. An Islamic NGO located upstairs from 68H, for example, pays for a weekly program on religious tolerance, an issue that virtually everyone at the station believes is essential part of its editorial mission in a country where religious fundamentalism has been a source of violence, and in a city (Jakarta) where the largest party in the ruling coalition is the Islamic Justice and Welfare Party. The Indonesian National Commission for Human Rights ran its non-violence campaign on the network, the only way to reach the many conflict zones like Aceh, the Moluccas, and West Papua (Irian Jaya). In Aceh, the youth wing of the second largest national Muslim organization, Muhammadiyah, ran a radio campaign for religious tolerance on 68H. In the same way, a U.S.-based NGO, Family Health International, pays to support programming on sexual and reproductive health. All of these organizations rely on 68H's reputation for integrity and, of course, its wide geographic reach.

Because of all this activity, 68H's marketing director told me, 68H is known to its listeners and to potential advertisers as "NGO radio."[15] That identification is again historic, a result of 68H's long association with human rights and free expression groups like ISAI, and it is consistent with the station's editorial mission, which Santoso described to me as "providing good information, helping the public participate in important political decisions, promoting debate and increasing information access in remote parts of the country."[16] Nonetheless, the network's identification with NGOs has made it difficult for 68H to broaden its appeal to other advertisers. Some large consumer product firms – Unilever, McDonalds, Coca-Cola – have advertised with 68H, but in 2004 only 20 percent of 68H ad sales were to for-profit firms. Advertisers, of course, must be concerned with the appeal of programming, and several 68H's staff whom I interviewed acknowledged that the station's programming made it a difficult sell. The company's marketing director, Elin, described 68H programming as "boring," without a distinctive style or brand identity.[17] Moreover, she said, the sheer number of 68H programs resulted in a programming schedule that was difficult to sell to advertisers. "We go from music to microeconomics," she said, "and it is hard to follow."[18] All the marketing staff I interviewed at the station expressed similar frustrations.

Part of the problem is competition. On the island of Java and in Jakarta particularly 68H has several competitors, including El Shinta, a private commercial station that emphasizes celebrity interviews and sports programming. A second problem for 68H has been audience data. The A.C. Nielsen Company publishes data on radio audiences in Indonesia, but only measures the top ten stations in the nine largest cities, thus overlooking 68H member stations almost everywhere – including Jakarta, where forty-two FM and five AM stations compete for listeners and advertisers. The other data problem is inherent to the size and reach of the 68H network: Until recently, the company had no credible way of showing advertisers when and where – or even if – their advertisements had actually aired. In late 2004, with MDLF's technical assistance, 68H began to provide advertisers digital proof of broadcast, thus greatly increasing the company's potential for sales revenues. 68H splits advertising income between Jakarta and the member stations according to a number of factors that include the stations' profiles, the volume of 68H programming they air and the volume of programs they produce for the network. On average, however, about 35 percent of advertising revenue goes to member stations. For many of them, especially the smaller and more remote ones, that revenue is the key to their own sustainability.

Malaysiakini, Kuala Lumpur

Across the Strait of Malacca from 68H is another exemplary news organization (and another MDLF client) *Malaysiakini*, a six-day-a-week, online-only newspaper. As developing democracies go, Malaysia is unique in several respects, not least that it is economically well off. In 1957, the year of its independence from Great Britain, Malaysia was a third-world country poorer than Ghana or Rhodesia, with no industry, no foreign investment and no infrastructure. The economic stars of Southeast Asia then were Indonesia and the Philippines, both of which Malaysia has since far outstripped. Malaysia is today a net exporter of oil and gas, both of which are nationalized industries, and the colonial export industries of rubber and tin have been surpassed by automobiles, steel and electronics. Malaysia's communications infrastructure is the most advanced in Southeast Asia, the result of a strategic decision made by the country's former prime minister, Mahathir Mohamed, who, in addition to transforming the nation's economy, ruled Malaysia with an authoritarian hand for twenty-two years, from 1981 to 2003.

Malaysiakini is the only independent news source in Malaysia in the sense that is not financially supported by, nor is it associated with, any of the political parties that comprise Barisan Nasional, the coalition that has ruled the country for more than two decades. Under Malaysian law, newspapers can only publish with a license from the government, and the government issues several different kinds of licenses. Political parties, for example, may distribute their periodicals to party members but not to the general public through kiosk sales. The most sought after license, of course, allows for public sale everywhere, but these licenses are few and belong to publishers with strong party connections. Among the country's major papers, for example, the *New Straits Times* is associated with the United Malays National Organization (UMNO, the largest party in the Barisan Nasional), and the *Star* is published by Persatuan China Malaysia (Malaysian Chinese Association), the second-largest party in the coalition. Occasionally someone will print a publication with an ever-changing masthead or at irregular intervals, thus seeking to avoid the letter of the law as it defines "publication," but the government gets around this problem by placing the burden for enforcement on distributors and retailers, which it threatens with fines and possible imprisonment if they are caught selling "illegal" newspapers.

Malaysiakini comes about as close to this line as possible without breaking it. By publishing online only, the paper falls outside of the legal definition for publication, and the paper's owners are betting that the government, having invested so heavily in communications infrastructure to attract foreign investment, will be unwilling to risk the international embarrassment and censure that would follow on closing the paper down. For the most part that bet has paid off, though in January 2003 police raided *Malaysiakini*'s offices and seized all 19 of its computers, including the four servers used for the paper's distribution. The raid was instigated by the youth wing of UMNO, which had complained to the police about an anonymous letter *Malaysiakini* had published comparing the group to the Ku Klux Klan. The paper's co-founder and editor-in-chief, Steven Gan, refused to reveal the identity of the letter writer to the police, prompting the seizures. With assistance from MDLF *Malaysiakini* was quickly back online, and international publicity from the raid had the undesired effect, from the government's point of view, of greatly increasing *Malaysiakini*'s readership.

In many ways, Malaysia embodies the notion of "Asian values" in the way that former Singapore Prime Minister Lee Kwan Yew once described it[19] – a governing system that values consensus over conflict, order over liberty – and for reasons of history, in Malaysia at least, it is a tradition with firm roots. To the extent the characterization is accurate, it has implications for how people understand and respond to social problems. Malaysia is a center for human trafficking in the region, for example, and yet the government treats the women at the center of that trade as criminals. There is little alternative, since no civil society network exists to treat them as victims and there is no place to send them but to jail. A U.S. State Department officer whom I interviewed in Kuala Lumpur told me he had never seen a country with such weak civil society.[20] The country has virtually no indigenous NGOs, and those few that exist have almost no connections to the extensive network of international human rights NGOs.

One of *Malaysiakini*'s mission objectives is to change this culture, to promote civil society organizations and expand civil liberties, particularly the right of expression. *Malaysiakini* itself is tightly connected to the excellent journalism resources in the region, including the Southeast Asian Press Association (SEAPA) and the distinguished Philippine Center for Investigative Journalism. But in its own country one of *Malaysiakini*'s most difficult business problems is a culture in which, as Gan says, "no one is supposed to rock the boat."[21] Because Gan's goal is to do just that, Malaysiakini has found it difficult to hire good employees, particularly on the business side (marketing and sales), and many advertisers are not eager to be identified with the paper. Even some readers, says Chief Executive Premesh Chandran, do not like to admit to the fact that they are subscribers. *Malaysiakini* has repeatedly tried to sell discounted subscriptions to the libraries of private colleges in the country, for example, none of which is willing to purchase one. *Malaysiakini* knows that it has subscribers in several government ministries, but for privacy reasons does not publicize the fact. "Only if we were really forced to do that would we do so," Chandran says.[22]

Malaysiakini began life in November 1999 as a free service, and by the close of 2000 it was drawing 120,000 readers daily and had expanded its editorial staff from three to fourteen. The publication has from the beginning been a mix of news, letters from readers, features and editorials. Its principal value was that it offered Malaysians, as well as others in the region and Malaysians living abroad, a source of independent and uncensored news. In the beginning the idea was also that *Malaysiakini* would get a government publishing license, if not on its own then through a proxy, and that the print product would supplant the online one as the company's core product and main source of advertising revenues. As late as 2003 the company's internal strategy documents assumed a license was still a possibility, if a remote one, and MDLF had established a $250,000 credit line for the paper product that the company was never able to use. The online paper remains the company's principal product and core mission enterprise, but it struggles for readers and for advertising revenue. Despite Mahathir's Multimedia Supercorridor project, less than 25 percent of Malaysians had Internet access in 1999 and only about 40 percent do today. As a result, the paper has had to find other ways to make itself viable, including loans and grants.

Within eight months of its launch, *Malaysiakini* had about 100,000 daily readers, and until the global collapse in the dotcom business the plan was for the paper to be entirely advertiser supported. That plan has yet to work out, and in 2000 the paper began loan negotiations with MDLF, negotiations that fell apart after a former employee publicly accused the company of having received money from George Soros, at the time possibly the least popular man in Southeast Asia. Because Soros has an important historic connection to MDLF the negotiations were postponed, but as with the 2003 police raid, the publicity from the Soros affair attracted international publicity and some new grants.

Unable to generate sufficient revenues through advertising, *Malaysiakini* in February 2002 began to make its core news services available only to subscribers at a rate of R10 (10 ringits, or approximately $2.50) per month or R100 (about $25) annually. For another R300, subscribers could purchase access to all of *Malaysiakini*'s archives. A small amount of free content remained in order to attract readers, and in the first six months after the transition the paper gained 700 subscribers, and by the end of 2002 it had 1,500 subscribers. But the subscription model experienced and continues to experience several implementation problems: multiple readers using the same password; the difficulty of online credit transactions, owing both to the low penetration of credit cards in Southeast Asia (at between 5 percent and 20 percent of Internet users) and to high levels of credit card fraud; and the fear among readers that online subscriptions would be monitored and possibly penalized by the government.

By October 2003, *Malaysiakini* had only 2,000 subscribers and had been compelled to cut staff from thirty people down to about twenty-four. The 10 percent conversion rate it had hoped for when it moved to subscriptions came in closer to one percent, and one of the paper's problems, as it turned out, was that it simply did not know much about its audience. It had assumed, owing to the medium in which it published, that its readers were mostly under thirty, but when the paper surveyed its subscribers it was stunned to find that it had almost no readers in that demographic. Rather the average *Malaysiakini* reader is considerably older, male, and well educated, and many prefer to read the paper in their native Malay or Chinese rather than English. In response, *Malaysiakini* developed both Malay- and Chinese-language versions of the paper, but the additional production costs were not offset by increased revenues. By the close of 2003 the paper was running monthly deficits of between R50,000 and R60,000 ($13,000 to $15,000); had an annual deficit of approximately R588,000 (approximately $145,000); had subscription growth of only about 3 percent per month; had no advertising growth; and did not have a marketing manager.

At the time Chandran estimated that in order to break even the paper would need 10,000 subscribers or would have to greatly increase its subscription price. Internally, discussion at the paper turned on just what *Malaysiakini*'s core product was and how the company should position itself in the market. The paper considered a range of positions from low price/mass market to high price/niche market and the consequences for those choices on the character of the news product and, of course, the character of Malaysian democracy. Eventually the decision was to maintain *Malaysiakini* as a mid-price/medium market publication, but to increase subscription rates by as much as 50 percent.

In the end, Chandran and Gan have chosen to aggressively pursue a number of projects designed to derive new revenues from the existing business. MDLF has participated in a number of these revenue experiments, variously by supplying lines of credit, loans, technical expertise or management advice. Not all of these projects have panned out, but in the way good firms do *Malaysiakini* has learned from all of them and it has not been reluctant to pull the plug when new ventures have failed to establish themselves. In 2001, for example, *Malaysiakini* launched a weekly intelligence brief, *SAM*, priced at $1,000 annually and targeted at business and political elites. A number of foreign embassies subscribed, but the project struggled to maintain quality and Chandran closed it. The same year, however, *Malaysiakini* developed, with a grant from MDLF, a classified advertising management program, "My1Ads," and more recently MDLF provided substantial seed funding that *Malaysiakini* used to develop the Southeast Asian Centre for e-Media (SEACeM), a technology development venture that "seeks to assist Southeast Asian independent media and civil society organisations to utilise electronic media technologies in their work by providing training, consultation and media solutions, as well as acting as a platform for regional cooperation."[23] SEACeM includes a number of links to non-profit civil society organizations; to *Malaysiakini*'s own online book retailer, Kinibooks; and to the profit-generating core of the business, Manage4Me, a package of proprietary software tools for online publishing, subscription and advertising management, and payment.[24]

In 2006 *Malaysiakini* will launch Asia247.tv, a P2P webcasting system that will allow virtually anyone with a video camera to shoot and broadcast news. This exercise in "citizen journalism," Gan says, is both good for democracy in Malaysia and good for business. Among other things, the expectation is that Asia247.tv will appeal to the younger audiences – as viewers – that the magazine has had such difficulty attracting as readers. *Malaysiakini* now also includes regular reports from a blogger. Editors review his work and check his sources, but the idea is to appeal to a broader readership.

Social Entrepreneurship in Media Assistance:
The Media Development Loan Fund

While the Media Development Loan Fund is a not-for-profit firm, it does not behave as most non-profits do; it is an entrepreneurial organization, just as it expects its clients to be. Formerly registered with the Internal Revenue Service as a private foundation, MDLF changed its legal status to public charity in January 2002.[25] MDLF makes both loans and grants to independent news media in emerging democracies with the goal of helping its clients generate sufficient revenues to sustain and grow their businesses, thereby improving the larger environment for free media and free expression in the countries where it chooses to operate. MDLF's focus in media assistance is exclusively with high-quality journalism, not arts, culture or entertainment, though any of those things may be organic to a loan client's editorial mission and its profitability. MDLF also provides services in support of its investments, chiefly business and financial consulting, technology training and development.

MDLF's largest offices – neither with more than six or seven full-time employees – are in New York City and Prague. New York is home to MDLF's internal administrative functions, including its loan invoicing and collection department. MDLF's deputy managing director its inside counsel are both based there. Prague is the operational center for vetting potential clients and their loan proposals, and is also home to MDLF's technology development and support operations, known as CAMP (discussed below). MDLF's finance director and his staff are based in Warsaw, where they do business plan development and monitor clients' finances; another MDLF financial analyst is based in Moscow. Ordinarily, all of these offices are involved in at least some aspect of preparing loan proposals for review by MDLF's investment committee, a process described in detail below.

MDLF partners with other assistance organizations in its work, but three relationships have been particularly productive. One is with the Open Society Institute, which provided the original funding for MDLF and continues to subsidize a significant portion of its operating costs. A second, in several of the countries of the former Yugoslavia – Bosnia and Herzegovina, Serbia and Montenegro, Croatia and Macedonia – is an MDLF partnership with the Swedish Helsinki Committee for Human Rights, which helps identify candidates for a special MDLF loan pool created for the region by the Swedish International Development Cooperation Agency (SIDA). Until 2003 a third partnership was the Moscow-based Media Viability Fund, a joint program of MDLF and the Eurasia Foundation that identified prospective loan clients in Ukraine and Russia. MDLF now operates under its own banner in those states, and maintains a less formal working relationship with the Eurasia Foundation in the CIS region. In addition, MDLF has worked with the Asia Foundation, UNESCO, Panos South Asia, Press Now, the U.S. State Department, and Internews Russia, among others, providing services that range from administering grants to evaluating other organizations' project proposals. In 2005 MDLF announced an "Independent Newspaper Development Initiative" with the Paris-based World Association of Newspapers. The Initiative relies on WAN to identify sources that can make significant loans to MDLF, at low or no interest, and which MDLF can then loan to clients at below-market rates, thus earning a profit. WAN will also be able to provide additional sources of training and management expertise to MDLF clients.

The most important of MDLF's assistance tools are program related investments (PRIs), instruments that by their nature encourage the kind of long-term and studied engagement that media assistance so conspicuously lacks. Program related investments are a feature of U.S. tax law created in the late 1960s that allow non-profits to make interest-bearing, revenue-generating investments in other firms, both non-profit *and* for-profit, whose work will further the stated social mission of the non-profit investor. PRIs are typically low-interest loans to or equity investments in organizations that have large-scale capital needs and either no access to financing or access only on onerous terms.[26] PRIs help recipients by allowing them to bridge gaps in credit, to accumulate assets, and, eventually, to leverage additional financing from more traditional sources. More significantly, PRIs help recipients build managerial capacity in their businesses and to increase productivity. For providers, PRIs deliver both financial and programmatic returns; they make limited financial resources go further in the service of the provider's non-profit mission, in significant part because the return on investment can be reinvested.[27] In effect, then, the award of a PRI instead of a grant fundamentally changes the relationship between provider and recipient from one of donor/supplicant to a partnership: the funder takes a long-term interest in the financial and programmatic health of the recipient, which to pay back the loan must develop greater financial discipline and more strategic management. Put another way, a well-executed PRI operationalizes the proverb that is it is better to teach a man to fish, and thus feed him for a lifetime, than to give him a fish and feed him for a day.

PRI's are themselves odd fish, however. For public policy reasons, a non-profit generally is barred from making high-risk investments that, if they were to fail, would damage the organization's financial health and thus its ability to serve its mission. PRIs are the exception to that rule, permitting non-profits to make high-risk investments *so long as they are connected to the production and furtherance of their mission good* as opposed to being merely a revenue good (that is, a profit center unrelated to the mission good).[28] Again, these investments can be in for-profit firms and for a variety of reasons frequently are. For-profit firms often have technical expertise or specialized skills that non-profits do not, or (as with MDLF's media assistance goals) the mission good desired by the donor specifically requires changes in the for-profit sector that can only be accomplished through direct involvement in that sector. Sometimes, too, government regulation favors the for-profit firm or sector (as with international development banks, for example), or for policy reasons does not allow a non-profit to accumulate the substantial amounts of capital necessary to produce its mission good. For example, many environmental NGOs are intensely interested in the creation and adoption of environmentally friendly technologies, but simply do not have the financial resources to develop and market them.[29]

The majority of PRIs, approximately 80 percent, nonetheless go to non-profits, and they are sometimes made through intermediary organizations (MDLF, as discussed below, makes PRIs directly from its own loan pool and also as an intermediary for others).[30] In the United States, the creative pioneer in making PRIs has been the Ford Foundation, which has viewed them as a way of stretching its assets to meet its charitable goals in both domestic and international projects.[31] Domestically, Ford along with MacArthur, Rockefeller, Russell Sage and a handful of other foundations have used PRIs to spur community development by providing loans in poor or depressed neighborhoods – capital for low-income housing, small-business and job creation, education, arts and culture, religion, environmental protection and other engines of civil society growth.

A critical and much-commented-on feature of that growth has been the attendant increase in the managerial capacity of the entrepreneurs who get the loans. MDLF's experience with its clients illustrates the point, but given that return it seems noteworthy that so few PRIs have been made in the field of journalism assistance.[32] In the 1998-99 Foundation Center report on PRI trends, for example, the 35 largest providers include only one specifically with a media focus – MDLF.[33] The same report discusses PRI financing by major program areas, and at best the "arts, media and historic preservation" category comprises only about 9 percent of total dollars and total PRIs; it is impossible to tell from the Foundation Center data what part of the category consists of journalism projects, either in the United States or overseas.

MDLF's program-related investments take the form of loans, equity investments, or, where loan collateral is a problem, finance lease programs in which MDLF will purchase equipment and then essentially sell it to a client through the terms of the lease.[34] MDLF also makes technical assistance grants in support of its PRIs, and it makes a few, narrowly focused grants in areas where it has special expertise. Through its New Media Fund, for example, MDLF makes grants to support projects in which the Internet or other digital technologies are critical to a news organization's operations – online news magazines, radio stations and syndication platforms, virtual radio networks, wireless ISPs and web-publishers.[35]

Mission

The Media Development Loan Fund's principal activity is at once easy to understand and counterintuitive: It is a *not-for-profit* firm working to build economically sustainable, mission-driven, *for-profit* media firms in countries transitioning to democracy. As such, some of the more interesting questions about financial sustainability in this report concern

MDLF itself, not its clients. Several of its original clients are already self-sustaining, while others are getting there.

MDLF's literature describes the organization as a venture capital firm like any other, except "where venture capital firms seek profits, MDLF seeks another kind of return: a strong and independent press." For research purposes, the most reliable and least-embellished statement of any non-profit's mission is ordinarily contained in the letter from the Internal Revenue Service establishing its tax-exempt status. MDLF's letter from the agency states that MDLF will

> make a series of low- (or no-) interest loans to organizations in the media field (e.g., newspapers, television stations, radio stations, etc.) in various regions of the world, primarily Central and Eastern Europe and the former Soviet Union, Latin America, Southeast Asia and Africa. (Most, and perhaps all, of these organizations are for-profit businesses.) Your primary purpose is to assist in the development of non-governmental, non-partisan, pluralistic, tolerant and non-extremist printed press, radio and television in societies that have historically been 'closed' (or non-democratic). Through the creation of indigenous independent media in these countries, you hope to speed the institution-building process toward open societies and democratic systems.

The IRS designation letter goes on to say that the terms of MDLF loans

> will be significantly more favorable than would be available (if at all) from commercial lenders. You will select loan recipients based on the following criteria: (i) whether a loan to the proposed recipient will promote independent, fair, honest and responsible journalism in the affected region; and (ii) whether the proposed recipient has sufficient managerial expertise and financial stability so as to make repayment of the loan likely.

Origins

The managing director of MDLF is forty-one-year-old Sasa Vucinic, who began his career as a journalist in Belgrade at the age of sixteen. During the Tito era, Vucinic developed his skills at the weekly newsmagazine *NON*, which lived at the edge of the civic space tolerated by the regime. Vucinic later became a lawyer and the youngest-ever editor-in-chief of *NON*, and he enjoyed the shortest tenure in the job – six months before the government dismissed him. In 1989 he was one of the founders of radio B92, serving as editor-in-chief and general manager until 1993, when he left to join the Open Society Institute as a media consultant working with radio start-ups in the former Soviet Union. In that role Vucinic met former *Washington Post* reporter and editor Stuart Auerbach, who also worked as a consultant for Soros, and together they came up with the idea for what is now MDLF.[36] As Vucinic described it to me, MDLF was created to make the most efficient use of the limited funds available for media development. "Media assistance usually consists of grants and they are usually small, with the result that the problem never gets solved," he said. "It's like treating a toothache with anesthesia. Our goal is to fix the business."[37]

Vucinic approached George Soros with the idea of a loan fund. Soros was skeptical but gave him $10,000 to investigate the idea further. Vucinic then spent three months learning as much as he could about the subject, research that included extended visits to the PRI departments at both the Ford and MacArthur foundations and discussions with OSI lawyers. When it was done, Soros was still unconvinced but nonetheless on May 1, 1995, gave Vucinic control of an existing but dormant OSI program known as the Fund for Independent Media, with $500,000 to its name.[38] Soros described the donation as "a rope you can use to hang yourself."[39] The trustees of the old fund resigned, including Soros himself, new trustees were appointed, and the organization's name was changed to the Media Development Loan Fund. On December 1 of the same year, the renewed organization received IRS approval as a 501(c)(3) not-for-profit, and in 1996 made its first loans to the Slovakian newspaper *SME*.

Today, the most concise summary of MDLF's success are the eighty-three color-coded push-pins stuck into the large map of the world that hangs in the New York office of Harlan Mandel, the organization's deputing managing director. The pins represent MDLF clients who have received PRIs, grants or other kinds of assistance in partnership with other funders and foundations. Some of those clients have received more than one loan, and some have received – and paid off –several. In the ten years since its founding, MDLF has made $55 million worth of investments in forty-seven media companies in seventeen countries. Approximately $47 million of that has been program-related investments in the form of direct loans, finance lease arrangements or equity investments. The balance has been mostly grants: $6 million has gone to training programs, $2 million to software and technology development on behalf of MDLF clients. Over the same period, MDLF has been repaid more than $13.4 million in principal and collected $3.5 million in interest and dividends. The greatest share of MDLF loan dollars – approximately $26 million – have gone to print media, with the balance going to broadcast media (television and radio), news services and on-line media.

The largest number of pins on Mandel's map are blue, twenty of them representing magazines and newspapers with outstanding PRIs. Sixteen white pins represent MDLF's New Media Fund portfolio, which consists primarily but not exclusively of grants. Five green pins indicate television stations with PRIs; four red ones mark radio loan clients; and eighteen yellow pins identify special projects that sometimes involve no funds whatever, but training or advisory partnerships. Most significant, perhaps, are the sixteen orange pins representing clients that have successfully paid off one or more loans; many of those also represent media organizations that are now profitable. Four black pins denote defaults, and in every case but one MDLF has recovered most of its assets. The one sour case, a 1997 loan to a Skopje, Macedonia, broadcaster for transmitters, was a case of fraud, and MDLF is working to get Macedonian courts to enforce a New York court judgment against the owner (who diverted the entire loan to a meat-importing business).[40]

Given MDLF's origins and staff expertise (and the interests of its donors), the greatest concentration of its loan projects and dollars is not surprisingly in the countries of the former Yugoslavia (approximately $17 million) and the former Soviet Union (approximately $14.1 million). In recent years, MDLF has expanded its loan operations to Southeast Asia, South Africa, and Latin America. Asia has received the smallest MDLF investments, just under $1 million between 1996 and mid-2005, though those investments have benefited two of MDLF's most impressive and technologically sophisticated clients, the online newspaper *Malaysiakini* in Kuala Lumpur, and the radio network 68H in Indonesia. Through its New Media Fund, MDLF also makes grants in all these regions, plus the Middle East, the only region in which the organization has made no PRIs (unless one counts Armenia as a Middle Eastern country).[41] MDLF has provided technical assistance to two excellent news organizations in the Middle East: Ammannet, a producer and distributor of Internet and FM radio news programs in Jordan; and the Human Rights Media Network, a Lebanon-based NGO that monitors human rights and publishes on the Internet (www.rightsmedia.org). As of June 2005, MDLF had approximately twenty-eight loan clients around the world that between them had forty-six open loan projects.

MDLF loans cover a range of needs, from working capital – funding to pay for salaries, paper, marketing and so on – to equipment. Interest rates are typically low, between 2 percent and 10 percent, with most now at 5 percent or above. The smallest loan to date was $5,000 to a Russian newspaper (*MIG*) in Astrakhan that needed to pay for newsprint and related expenses. MDLF's largest PRI, an equity investment estimated at more than $6 million, went to B92 in Belgrade between 2003 and 2005. The average range for MDLF program-related investments is $150,000 to $800,000, and a typical loan goes to purchase a printing press.[42]

MDLF equity investments have typically been part of a long-term plan to help developing businesses streamline ownership structures and secure control as they transition from multiple owners to a few, or from "socially owned" firms to privately owned ones. The notion of social ownership was an artifice of control under the old communist regimes that allowed the government to shut down an operation by arbitrarily seizing space and equipment in the name of the public. In the transition period, as companies have tried to convert these ill-defined assets to private control, privatization laws have had the sometimes perverse effect of subjecting these fledgling news organizations to power grabs by interests in and out of government who wish to use them for their own ends – or to kill the company entirely. MDLF's objective has been to help these firms – for example, the magazine *Novi list* in Croatia and B92 in Serbia – to gain control of their own stock by blocking hostile takeovers or at least placing controlling shares in friendly hands until the companies have the resources to buy them back. Equity investments are, of course, more complex than straight loans, and thus more costly to structure and administer.

Governance

MDLF is governed by a six-member board of directors, the chairman of which is American University Law Professor Kenneth Anderson, an expert in micro-finance and human rights law. Vucinic participates on the board in an ex-officio capacity. With respect to loan operations, the board approves prospective applicants, determines whether or not to accept contributions from other organizations, determines MDLF's interest rate policy, and regularly evaluates MDLF's loan portfolio. Anderson and two other members serve together as an executive committee of the board, a group empowered to act on any matter requiring an immediate response. Finally, the board has the discretion to appoint an ad hoc credit advisory committee comprised of outside financial experts to evaluate MDLF's lending strategies and interest rate policies.

The board members themselves are mostly journalists or civil society activists, not management specialists, so while they identify both the countries in which MDLF will operate and the editorial worthiness of prospective clients, decisions about business plans and other financial matters are delegated to a separate investment committee, or loan panel. Ordinarily, MDLF staff comprise the investment committee, with assistance from MDLF's finance director. The balance of the committee is a mix of those who have worked on an application and others who are either fresh to the project or bring special expertise to the discussion. Except for a few permanent members, then, the composition of the committee will vary from meeting to meeting, but the idea is to have adequate financial, legal, managerial and regional expertise to evaluate an application properly. If a project involves a new country, a new medium (no longer likely) or a kind of financing MDLF has not done before (for example, convertible bonds), the managing director has the discretion to include additional participants as he sees fit.

To ensure the integrity of MDLF's mission, all board members, employees and consultants are required to disclose any personal or financial interests in a project, and to recuse themselves from participation in the loan process if the board believes there is a conflict of interest or the perception of one. Vucinic, for example, does not participate in discussions of projects and clients in any part of the former Yugoslavia, where he has extensive personal and professional ties. MDLF staff are also required to keep in strict confidence all financial data supplied by potential clients, to protect them from competitors and from hostile governments.

Loan Clients

To qualify for a loan, a potential MDLF client first has to be located in a country transitioning to democracy that has been cleared by the MDLF board; and for the board the first threshold requirement is that a country's commercial law environment be sufficiently open and functional that MDLF can gets its money back in the event of non-payment or default. In some cases the board will investigate a country as a potential loan site without having first identified an applicant there because, as MDLF counsel Elena Popovic told me, "It's just important to be there." Nicaragua and El Salvador, for instance, have been approved by the board, but as yet MDLF has no loan clients in either place. More often a country receives board approval because a prospective client is located there.

Some transition countries do not qualify for loan projects (in which case potential clients are still eligible for grants if grants are appropriate).

MDLF has reviewed Albania four times for four different projects, for example, without reaching a favorable decision. Despite having bilateral investment treaties with the United States and others, Albania's judicial system is too corrupt to satisfy MDLF's board that it could enforce a contract there. Still other countries do not qualify because loan applicants there can find affordable capital – for example, the Czech Republic, Hungary, and Slovenia.

Once a country has been approved, a potential client must meet three MDLF "mission" requirements:

- *Editorial quality.* A client must be a professional and responsible news and public affairs medium that serves a local or national audience and that meets all applicable laws concerning registration or licenses in the place where it does business. A client need not be exclusively a news organization, but a "significant part" of its regular fare – which can range from news summaries to documentaries to photojournalism – must demonstrate "fact-based, honest, unbiased, fair, non-partisan, investigative and responsible journalism."[43] Additionally, an applicant must have "a proven record of offering coverage of different political opinions, promoting human rights and the rights of ethnic minorities, and promoting inter-ethnic coexistence."[44] Among other things, this normative language helps to sort out media that cannot qualify for MDLF assistance. NGO media in developing countries, for example, often produce content whose primary audience is not local or even regional, but international.[45] That said, MDLF tries to apply these standards in a realistic way. So while most MDLF clients are, in Mandel's words, "stellar, combining quality and courage,"[46] the standards for what constitutes a professional news medium are somewhat less in Ukraine and Russia, where, because of the difficult political and economic environment for journalism, the goal for a local publisher is to provide "a decent local newspaper."[47]
- *Editorial independence.* By this MDLF means no government ownership, no political party ownership or affiliation, no oligarchic ownership (of the kind commonly found in Ukraine and Russia), and no foreign ownership. The foreign ownership restriction clearly means no multinational media conglomerates, but beyond that is the least rigid of MDLF's requirements. Sometimes issues of ownership are complicated precisely because of the kinds of restructuring discussed above. In other cases, "foreign" ownership may be the guarantee of a news organization's independence. The *Phnom Penh Post*, for example, is owned by expatriates. The *Post* is the only self-sustaining paper of record in Cambodia (the other, *The Cambodian Daily*, is NGO-supported) and though it is

not an MDLF loan or grant client, it does use MDLF's "Digital Kiosk" to sell subscriptions. (Digital Kiosk is an e-commerce site where MDLF clients can make secure online transactions with subscribers, and where MDLF itself sells a handful of case studies on management, some written by clients.) In any case, the critical test of ownership is that it must allow a media organization to preserve editorial independence while helping it to create capital investment.

- *A business track record.* A news medium ordinarily must have been in operation at least one year and have a record of "promoting democratic institutions and practices" and "exercising principles of free, independent and responsible press."[48] Except in one unusual case involving a newspaper in Montenegro (*Vijesti*), MDLF does not fund start-ups. *Vijesti* was launched at a crucial time when the province was testing its independence from Milosovic. The public there needed an independent voice to explain events, MDLF Senior Counsel Elena Popovic told me, "so we jumped."[49] *Vijesti* also grew out of the remnants of *Monitor*, a reputable monthly newsmagazine, and so its staff had strong record. But the one-year requirement is intended to ensure financial and editorial commitment by the client and thus as well as to protect MDLF's own not-for-profit status under U.S. law.

Beyond these editorial prerequisites are several financial ones. Potential applicants have to be able to show themselves a plausible loan risk – which in MDLF's case means they must have a transparent management structure led by capable people who can be trusted to use a loan for its stated purpose, and to repay it. More pointedly, transparency means a firm must make available to MDLF unrestricted access to all of its accounting records. MDLF's mission requires it to balance editorial goals with higher-than-usual financial risk, but it is not casual about the risk it assumes. It monitors its loan portfolio using a standard risk rating scale and maintains a loss reserve fund to ensure protection of its funds and the uninterrupted maintenance of its loans. The loss reserve fund is not an actual pot of cash, but an accounting device whereby the value of PRIs on MDLF's books is adjusted to account for risk of loss. The adjustment varies, but in 2002 was approximately $3.5 million; the figure is adjusted at least three times a year based on recommendations from the finance director to the executive committee, and is reviewed by MDLF's auditors.[50]

Very often, MDLF has already visited prospective clients before there are any discussions about financial assistance. MDLF sometimes identifies potential clients through its own fact-finding efforts, but it also relies on its principal programmatic partners – the Swedish Helsinki Committee (an NGO), OSI's Network Media Program, the World Association of Newspapers, the Eurasia Foundation, Internews Russia – to serve as additional eyes and ears in the places where it operates, particularly in Europe and Russia, helping not only to identify prospective clients but to vet them – finding out about their editorial product, their owners, and so on. Prospective clients can also identify themselves through a preliminary application form available on MDLF's web site – a very short form that asks for contact information about the news organization and a brief description of its operations. In any case, once a prospect is identified the staff will prepare for the board a profile of the client, if necessary sending someone to visit the organization. The staff recommendation to the board includes:

- a description of the organization and the quality of its news and public affairs programs, with special emphasis on investigative reporting;
- a discussion of the political role of the firm, including some assessment of its place in its home country's social and political milieu; MDLF's partners often play a vital role here, as can local NGOs;
- an assessment of the firm's business performance and the likelihood of its long-term market viability;
- a discussion of the firm's operational and editorial strengths and weaknesses;
- and a description of what the loan would be for, how much is needed, why it is needed, and how it will contribute to the firm's sustainability.

The Business Plan

If the board approves a media organization for further consideration, the next step is to prepare the loan proposal for review by the investment committee. The central feature of the loan proposal is the business plan, which consists of a description of the investment and a detailed financial analysis of the company's current condition and future prospects. Reportedly, the process of drafting the business plan – which typically requires the assistance of MDLF staff and several drafts – is the longest part of the entire loan process, but for the clients also the most revealing and beneficial. "At first clients think the business plan is a ritual," Vucinic told me, "then they understand to their horror what they need to do. Most do work through it, and the research tells them a lot about their business."[51] Though MDLF staff will assist with the business plan, clients themselves must prepare it and then defend it before the investment committee without the benefit of outside consultants. "For all first-time loan clients," Mandel says, "we require the company's senior management to attend the investment committee meeting in person," and the bulk of the meeting "consists of the committee members grilling the management on the plan and the assumptions behind it, both to test the plan's merits and to ensure that the management really knows and understands what's in the plan."[52] Konstanty Gebert, a columnist for Gazeta Wyborcza in Poland and a consultant to MDLF, says that applicants who do not get their loans, or who for whatever reason choose to forgo them, nonetheless report that the preparation of a business plan was singularly useful.[53] One MDLF client, the iconoclastic Feral Tribune in Split, Croatia, discovered to its complete surprise in the process of doing market research that its primary audience was not the young and the hip, but significantly older readers.

To begin the business plan drafting, MDLF sends clients a template. The responses it receives vary in sophistication – the first draft from the Montenegro newspaper *Vijesti*, for instance, consisted of two hand-written pages – but eventually develop into something much more substantive and compelling. *Vijesti* took its first loan from MDLF in 1997 and would not have survived without it. Recently the firm sold 50 percent of its equity to WAZ (Westdeutsche Allgemeine Zeitung), a German media group, and paid off its last loan four years early. MDLF, in turn, reviewed the terms of *Vijesti*'s sale to WAZ to ensure that its former client was being treated fairly.

MDLF allowed me to review on a confidential basis portions of two loan proposals, from each of two different clients in two different regions of the world. What each proposal lacked substantively the other contained, and between the two of them it was possible to understand what a complete proposal would look like, the unique nature of MDLF clients, the enormous efforts MDLF staff invest in teaching its clients "how to fish," and some of the risks inherent to MDLF's not-for-profit mission.

One proposal was not really a proposal at all, but a collection of summaries prepared for the investment committee and excerpted from a much larger document. As such it did not include the full-dress business plan with all of its components.[54] The client in this case was seeking financing to purchase a piece of equipment that would allow it to vertically integrate its operations, increase its independence from other vendors (including state-owned ones), improve the quality of its output, and diversify its revenue streams. The company's summary financial statement showed it had increased annual revenues by 10 percent in 2003 and projected that revenues would increase by a staggering *90 percent* in the first two years of the loan, with a significant part of that increase (roughly a third) attributable to new business made possible by the new equipment. A year after the proposed investment, the gross margin was projected to be about 70 percent of sales. This projected growth was reflected in the summary balance sheet, which showed the new revenues producing – apparently for the first time – positive cash flow in year two of the loan. From these data, it would be possible for someone evaluating the company's business plan to calculate a break-even sales point for the enlarged business.

There were a few red flags in the summaries, all of them presumably addressed in the larger body of work from which the summaries were excerpted. Some language in the narrative, for example, *seemed* to suggest that the figures in the financial statement were not in constant dollars but adjusted for inflation. If so, the magnitude of the firm's growth, if any, might be considerably smaller than indicated in the business plan. Another cautionary note concerned the capability of existing management and the availability of qualified new employees. Finally, nowhere in the summary was there a *quantitative* statement about the client's market. From this I assumed that extensive market data for this client and location were either not available or, more likely, that available data were incomplete and probably unreliable[55]; in any case, the subject of market threats and opportunity was not addressed through a traditional SWOT analysis, but by a narrative that described the competition and made it clear that there really was none that would be able to do what this client proposed to do with the acquisition of new equipment. At one point, for example, the summary asserted that the equipment would enable the client to increase prices without losing any sales volume, a claim that in a competitive market would be very unlikely even with a small price increase.

The second proposal MDLF provided me did not include narrative but did include the full-dress business plan – the 100-plus pages of detailed financial reports arrayed on spreadsheets that are doubtlessly the source of client "horror" Vucinic spoke of in our interview. The business plan included a financial statement, balance sheet and cash-flow forecast, each laid out on a *monthly* rather than an annual or even quarterly basis, and shown over a three-year period from January 2000 to December 2003.

Cash-flow analysis is one of the first concerns of a commercial lender, which cares about securing the loan but makes its money on the monthly interest payments; for MDLF, cash flow is key both to its mission good (its clients' sustainability) and to its revenue good (its own sustainability), and so, Mandel told me, "We're intensely concerned with it, and probably force our applicants to analyze it in much more depth than a bank would. We won't approve a loan if we're not convinced the project can generate sufficient cash flow to [repay it]. And the investment committee will run various performance scenarios through the business plan to see how they will impact cash flow."[56]

The second proposal also included detailed analyses of the firm's capital expenditures and working capital, as well as a summary statement of its assets and liabilities. The working capital spreadsheet (also showing data on a monthly basis over a three-year period) included costs for everything from ink to marketing costs, insurance to salaries. While I did not see them, my understanding is that a similar series of reports were prepared for the other client whose summaries I reviewed, in the same exacting detail, with discrete analyses of each of the firm's existing products and services, as well as the new ones made possible by the new equipment.

In sum, then, the documents I reviewed represented conscientious and thorough efforts to explain how the proposed MDLF investments would improve a client's business performance *and* make the business more financially stable. The full-dress proposal provided a level of financial detail in excess of what many commercial lenders would require. And both sets of documents provided data with which anyone could calculate ratios and percentages over time and figure out which direction these companies were moving and the magnitude of that movement – the essential purpose of a business plan.

Loan Review

Once a loan proposal goes to the investment committee, the committee's job is limited to approving or rejecting the proposal on its financial merits (including an assessment of a client's trustworthiness and managerial ability). The committee may table the proposal if it thinks it lacking in some essential detail, but the editorial worth of the organization and its project is presumed (from prior board approval). Whatever decision the committee makes, the record of its deliberations must specify the amount of the loan under discussion; a tentative repayment schedule; the interest rate; the type, form and size of any collateral; and any guarantee or conditions attached to the loan (discussed below). Every member of the committee must sign that record.

If a loan is approved, MDLF's director of operations in Prague will send a letter of commitment to the client in which she will outline the terms and conditions stipulated by the investment committee. The applicant must then respond with within 90 days or the investment committee must review the project again; if during that time new information becomes available that might have affected the committee's decision, the managing director has the right to cancel the loan or ask the investment committee to reevaluate the proposal. Final agreements between MDLF and the client get worked out between MDLF's lawyers and local counsel in the country where the client is located. If within a year it becomes clear that the financial needs of the client are greater than contemplated by the original proposal, the managing director and financial director, acting together, have the discretion to increase the loan amount by 10 percent. (Acting together these two officers may also approve small loans, in amounts approved by the board, without a meeting of the investment committee.) MDLF's executive committee can authorize an increase of 25 percent of the original loan amount, but any greater increase requires a new meeting of the investment committee.

Loan Conditions and Monitoring

Typically the conditions MDLF will attach to a PRI are for mandatory technical assistance or managerial consulting. If a loan is for equipment worth more than $50,000, for example, MDLF may require training and employee certification as a condition for releasing any funds for the equipment's purchase or lease. MDLF also provides for consultants in management areas like finance or marketing, usually with the result that the loan client realizes the long-term need for such expertise. MDLF may at times also offer editorial consulting services to clients, though clients are free to reject them. MDLF's board will make small grants to cover these kinds of loan requirements, though it prefers clients get money for that purpose from other assistance organizations or from MDLF partners.

MDLF prefers to disburse its PRIs in portions (or tranches), ideally in such a way that proper use of and reporting on one portion becomes the condition for disbursement of the next. Like any lender, MDLF assigns an account manager to monitor each loan and imposes penalties on late principal and interest payments – fees, higher interest rates, and so on. In addition to making their regular payments, clients are required to submit monthly financial reports to their account manager. The format of the report will vary with the media organization – primarily because reports track the key performance measures outlined in clients' business plans, which will vary with the client and the purpose of the loan – but must include information about any major managerial or financial changes. Internal MDLF auditors monitor some borrowers, and all borrowers have to make available to the auditor their accounting records, tax and legal documents, and anything else MDLF thinks important. On an annual basis, clients must provide MDLF's counsel proof that they are in compliance with local and national laws. Finally, MDLF staff visit each client at least one a year, and in some cases much more frequently. Those visits allow MDLF not only to observe business operations, but to ensure that its clients are maintaining, if not improving, their core editorial mission.

If a loan client stumbles financially because of economic or other difficulties outside its control, MDLF believes that *its* core mission requires it to sustain the organization (and the loan) using whatever reasonable means it can. It may provide additional managerial or technical assistance, including providing on-site, long-term consulting help, or it may restructure the loan. After the Russian ruble crashed in 1998, for example, MDLF's Russian clients had no way to meet their monthly payments – which must be made in U.S. dollars – so MDLF restructured their loans and extended their payments. If, however, a client is no longer bona fide, is grossly negligent, or has in some way misused the loan funds, MDLF will begin legal proceedings to recover its funds or its capital. In one such case, for example, MDLF recovered equipment it had leased for a Russian television station after a dispute between shareholders caused the station to default on its payments. MDLF can write off a loan if at some point it appears that there is no hope of recovering the loan; to date its write-offs total about $350,000.

Loan and Grant Support

Related to its monitoring process and central to its core mission, MDLF provides it clients with a variety of tools to help them build their businesses. The most significant of these is the Center for Advanced Media (CAMP), which operates out of the Prague office. CAMP is a technology-development and training service that works with MDLF clients to identify and adapt cost-effective technological solutions to the various problems – from poor infrastructure to regulatory and economic barriers – experienced by media organizations in developing countries. CAMP has, for example, has been central to the development and operations of, among others, Radio 68H in Indonesia; Ammannet in Jordan; the Human Rights Media Network in Lebanon; Radio Ecclesia in Angola; the Radio Hai Network in Armenia; the Virtual Radio Network in Nepal; and Drik, a photojournalism service and the main Internet service provider for the NGO community in Bangladesh. Importantly, most of these clients are recipients of MDLF grants, not loans, and several of those grants in some way involve partnerships with local or regional NGOs, or with government aid organizations. The Radio 68H project, for example, involved grant funding from both the Asia Foundation and the Dutch foreign ministry; Radio 68H is also an MDLF PRI recipient. All of these projects, however, depend for their success on software and hardware solutions developed at CAMP.

The basis of CAMP is open-source software development – the creation of technologies that any media organization can freely use and adapt to its particular needs. This cornerstone of this software production effort launched in 2001 and known as "Campware" (see www.campware.org). The driver for Campware was the recognition that most off-the-shelf software for print and broadcast media is beyond the financial reach of independent media in transition states. It is also proprietary, requiring constant updates and refinements that only add to the cost of its implementation. Most available open-source software, on the other hand, has been written by technological sophisticates with little or no concern for the needs of end users. Both products are written overwhelmingly by and for Western users, and so neither are particularly well suited to the editorial and budgetary requirements of news organizations in transition states; for the same reason, neither commercial software nor open-source software tends to feature multilinguality or Unicode support, an essential thing for users in the developing world. As a practical matter, then, media in developing countries have long resorted to software piracy, an act that is both anathema to MDLF's mission and that provides a ready pretext for hostile governments to shut down newsrooms and seize their computers.

CAMP's first software release, in March 2001, was "Campsite," an automated web publishing platform that can be used with any language and that includes both subscription and indexing features.

Several MDLF clients operate Internet sites using campware products, including *TOL*, which publishes only online. In 2003 CAMP created an open-source customer management software called "CReaM," which MDLF clients *Feral Tribune* (Croatia), *Noseweek* (South Africa), *El Periodico* (Gutatemala), Ammannet (Jordan), Makfax News Agency (Macedonia), and Beta News Agency (Serbia) all use to develop sales databases and marketing strategies. CReaM allows users to track sales orders, payments, shipments, services, online and print subscriptions, and the effectiveness of promotional campaigns. The software also has a customer service function, with a full-fledged email program built in and templates that anyone can use to create HTML newsletters. A more recent CReaM spin-off program designed for print media, "Dream," is an open-source distribution management system that allows publishers to track relationships with distributors and vendors.

Arguably, CAMP's most impressive open-source innovations are those it has developed for its broadcast and Internet media clients. "LiveSupport," for example, is a broadcast management tool that supports open-standard audio formats and multilingual metadata information (smart playlists, XML news feeds, file storage) and allows for remote control of radio stations through the Internet. The software was developed with a particular client in mind – Radio 68H, a radio network based in Jakarta and which provides news programming to more than 400 stations scattered across the Indonesian archipelago, a geographical sweep roughly the same as the distance from London to Tehran. For 68H, both the sheer technological challenge and prohibitively high costs of program distribution required several technical innovations if the enterprise was to work commercially. LiveSupport is one of those innovations, providing electronic proof of broadcast for advertisers, who otherwise have no way of knowing if an ad they paid to air in a remote radio station actually did air – never mind at when and with what programming LiveSupport embeds a distinctive, non-reproduceable digital tone to each advertisement, logs the tones and compiles time (accurate to the second) and programming data from those tones daily. The data are secure and encrypted, so stations cannot defraud the system, and advertisers can monitor directly the play their ads receive. LiveSupport is now also used by Radio B92 and Ideeleradio, a human rights radio service in Lima, Peru, and operated by a Peruvian NGO, the Institute of Legal Defense. LiveSupport, like all CAMP products, is free to anyone who wishes to download and use it, and users are encouraged to make code changes and additions to the program as their operations require. Its distinctive value is both its extraordinary quality, much of it the result of CAMP's developing, for a fee, features that meet specific client requests, and of course its cost. As of this writing, a comparable, commercially available radio automation program made in Greece, Jazler, charges clients a license fee of approximately 780 Euros *per station* to use.[57]

Social Entrepreneurship in Media Assistance:
The Southern African Media Development Fund

The Southern African Media Development Fund (SAMDEF) was founded in 1998 by the Media Institute of Southern Africa Trust Fund Board, along with two other organizations: the Media Institute of Southern Africa (MISA) and the Southern Africa Institute of Media Development (SAIMED). All of these organizations derive from the 1992 Windhoek Declaration, discussed elsewhere in this book, and each has a distinct purpose: MISA is an advocacy and educational organization; SAIMED teaches management skills to journalists; SAMDEF is a financing body, similar in operation though much smaller than MDLF, and with a specific geographic remit – the eleven nations that comprise the South African Development Community (SADC).[58] According to SAMDEF chairman Bojosi Otlhogile, vice chancellor at the University of Botswana, the need for SAMDEF was the same as that for MDLF: media firms in the region typically lack not only support in law, but access to affordable capital and an internal capacity to manage their businesses. MISA created SAMDEF as a loan fund to meet equipment and infrastructure needs, and with the expectation that the organization would also generate the revenues necessary to cover MISA's operating and program expenses.[59]

SAMDEF is like MDLF in that media "sustainability" and democracy promotion are the linked objectives of its business. The organization's published mission is to "achieve the growth of successful, vibrant, dynamic, diversified and sustainable media enterprises which optimise value to shareholders and contribute to strengthening democracy in the region."[60] When the organization was new it offered both loans and grants, but confusion among aid recipients about what kinds of projects qualified for grant assistance quickly put an end to the grant program, and SAMDEF instead focused on loan, equity and debt financing. Unlike MDLF, SAMDEF will invest in start-up media firms with little or no track record. It will also invest in a broader range of media enterprises, not just news organizations (MDLF is presumably limited in this respect by the terms of its IRS non-profit authorization), and so has financed a range of companies that include advertising, public relations and entertainment firms. In 2003-2004, SAMDEF made loans (calculated in Botswanan pula) totaling P15.2 million, with the largest pieces of that portfolio (P13.3 million) invested in just four countries: Botswana, Zambia, Tanzania and Zimbabwe.[61]

The first major donation to SAMDEF's loan fund, and the largest to date, came from the Open Society Institute-Southern Africa. Other original donors to the loan fund were Free Voice, a Dutch government-funded NGO that provides media assistance primarily in the Southern Hemisphere; and the Netherlands Development Finance Company. Despite these grants, SAMDEF President Charles Mundale believes the organization can only be sustainable over the long term, and more importantly serve its clients well, if it moves away from what he calls the "NGO model" toward something more traditionally entrepreneurial. When I met Mundale in 2004 his goal was to diversify the fund's investments into other industries but to retain "media" as the central fund. In SAMDEF's existing media portfolio, Mundale says, "60 to 70 percent of the portfolio is with strong media houses that could probably get loans from commercial banks if they wished."[62] Most of these firms, Mundale says, were built with loans from SAMDEF, and that they have not yet availed themselves of commercial lenders is to SAMDEF's continuing benefit.

It is also the unfortunate consequence of the economic and political environment in which these media operate, which makes them, if not risky investments, not very attractive ones for traditional lenders. In Southern Africa as throughout the continent, the private sector is dwarfed by the public one, and private media firms are everywhere tiny compared to the large, state-owned media monopolies with which they compete. For example, in Botswana – SAMDEF's home and since its independence in 1966 Africa's longest-standing multiparty democracy – more than 60 percent of the population works in the public sector. The nation's mines, the principal source of income for the country, are 51 percent government owned. The government is the dominant television and radio broadcaster; and the government newspaper, the *Daily News*, is given away for free. Indeed, the government prints so many copies of the paper that every day bound and unread piles of them can be found tossed around Gaborone's streets and public buildings. The *Daily News* competes with private publishers for advertising, which it sells at 20 percent below market rates, and in 2003 the government's Science and Technology Ministry began a campaign for "cost recovery" in which it withdrew all government advertising – about 25 percent of the revenue base – from the private press. In December 2004 the ministry announced its intention to purchase its own printing press so that the government could compete with the two privately owned presses in the country.

One of those private presses is owned by *Mmegi* (the *Reporter*), Botswana's best independent daily newspaper, published six days a week. The new competition from the government, said *Mmegi*'s editor, Titus Mbuya, will almost certainly mean the loss of several publishing contracts.[63] Already facing competition from presses in nearby South Africa, *Mmegi*, like most of Botswana's privately owned media, thus face economic pressures that make sustainability very difficult to achieve – in a country whose media Freedom House ranks among the "freest" in the world. Next door, in Zimbabwe, SAMDEF has provided financial assistance to the privately owned *Daily News* even though there is virtually no possibility of financial return. SAMDEF made the loan, according to Bojosi Otlhogile, simply because "it is important to be in Zimbabwe."[64] It is not an exaggeration to say that in Southern Africa the term "independent" means simply that a media firm is not state-owned. Editorial quality is a concern, too, but it is also a luxury many private firms cannot afford.

SAMDEF makes its money in three ways. The first is to act as a guarantor for loans made by commercial lenders to media firms: SAMDEF puts the money for the guarantee into a certificate of deposit and earns interest on it while the client repays the loan. SAMDEF will also attach a surcharge to its guarantee, perhaps 1 to 2 percent of the loan amount, to cover administrative costs and in some cases to make a small profit. Ordinarily borrowers can cover these costs, but where they cannot SAMDEF will structure the payments to include them. The third revenue stream comes from operating as a secondary lender and adding to the interest rate. MDLF, for example, has made back-to-back loans in Southern Africa using SAMDEF as its intermediary. MDLF may loan to SAMDEF at 5 percent, for example, and SAMDEF will re-loan the money at a rate 1 percent to 10 percent higher, depending on the client and the size of the loan. MDLF relies on SAMDEF for the same reason it relies on partners in other regions: SAMDEF has first-hand knowledge of the borrower, the local and regional market, the law, and so on. The price of its involvement, in short, is the cost of securing the loan.

In 2004, SAMDEF's media portfolio consisted of about forty different loans to twenty different clients (some on their second or third loans) at rates of between 5 and 10 percent per annum on the dollar, usually a point to several points lower than loans available from commercial lenders. Most loans are made for a term of three years, though for larger loans the term will run to five years. The interest rate depends on several factors, not least of them the currency in which a loan is made. When SAMDEF began in 1998, its mandate from MISA was to loan in U.S. dollars, Botswanan pula or South African rand wherever possible since most economies in the SADC region had highly volatile local currencies. The idea was to cushion SAMDEF against foreign exchange losses, but the policy only worked when the dollar was appreciating against the Pula, SAMDEF's chosen unit of account. More than 56 percent of SAMDEF loans are in dollars, and between March 2002 and December 2004 the dollar depreciated 5.8 percent against the pula, resulting in substantial losses – a little more than 6 million pula, or nearly $2 million. In 2005 the Botswana government devalued the Pula, and as of this writing SAMDEF enjoys an exchange gain on its dollar denominated loans. The larger point remains that managing exchange rates is a critical activity for SAMDEF (MDLF has no such problem, since it loans in dollars and is repaid in dollars).

Sustaining the Funders

Despite the success that MDLF and SAMDEF have had with their clients, the big question about their future concerns their own long-term sustainability. Their funding model clearly works for their clients, but it is an open question whether either organization can generate enough interest from outside funding sources, for-profit or not-for-profit, to support the costs associated with their work. In 2001, MDLF's Vucinic told me, he had an opportunity to speak to top executives from several multinational media firms at the Davos conference, and to his surprise and dismay, after he finished his presentation not a single person asked a question. In a 2003 interview, Kenneth Anderson, the American University law professor who serves as MDLF's board chairman, described the organization's capitalization challenge as two pronged: "We act like a venture capital firm but get the returns of a bank, that is to say, modest. At the same time, MDLF does not have the typical exit strategy of venture firms. Often there is no one available to buy MDLF's equity."[65] Against those financial realities, both functions of MDLF's journalistic mission, it is extremely difficult for the organization to attract capital.

In 2003, SAMDEF was largely dependent on OSI, which had promised a matching grant of up to $1 million a year for three years. Under the terms of the OSI proposal, qualifying matching funds included investments from commercial lenders, from other donors, and interest paid on existing loans. The unique nature of the matching program was such that Mundale thought SAMDEF would in time have to become a more traditional lender; in other words, he thought it unlikely that some other large donor would come forward, never mind with the kind of generous terms offered by OSI. In 2003, OSI gave SAMDEF a $10,000 grant to pay for a review of its investment strategy. "We must always re-evaluate," Mundale told me, "and it's not just re-evaluating the loans. Of course as financial managers we review all our projects and report to our board quarterly. But reviewing our lending model is another thing. There we review the needs of donors and clients, the impact we make on the media, and our own capitalization."

By the fall of 2005, SAMDEF had yet to see a new donor come forward, so Mundale has pushed forward with a plan to create and manage a pension fund. The fund will pay a fixed rate on investments and loan funds at a rate one to two percentage points higher.

MDLF's financial challenges are larger because it is a much larger firm. Its operating expenses include staff and office in New York, Prague, Warsaw, and Moscow. MDLF raises funds separately to pay for operating costs, with an understanding that OSI will cover operating costs it cannot meet through interest payments. In 2002, OSI paid for 65 percent of those expenses, or $1.5 million out of $2.6 million. As one might suspect, MDLF's operating expenses are unusually high because of the nature of the work it does and the extraordinary due diligence required to make PRIs in the countries where it has clients. The personnel and processing costs for making PRIs are much higher than those required for making grants: PRIs require expertise in finance; legal counsel at both the point of origin and the place where the loan will be made (MDLF engages local legal counsel in every country where it makes PRIs); and significant time and money in investigating prospective clients, verifying their ownership, and documenting the social value of their operations. Perhaps the most significant cost of all is the monthly monitoring of each client's business performance over the life of a PRI, a task that often includes MDLF assistance. For most grant-making organizations, monitoring is a much less costly activity because it is usually a passive one, digesting grantee reports once or twice a year.

Additionally, MDLF's mission activities can entail costs that a commercial lender would avoid. Lease arrangements for a printing press, for example, are sometimes necessary because local law requires loans to go through a national bank, a requirement that raises the interest rate and the cost to the borrower. MDLF will thus purchase the equipment itself and lease it back to the news organization, but that process increases MDLF's own costs. Honoring the letter of local and national laws, a strict MDLF requirement, can also be also costly. In one Southeast Asian country where MDLF does business, for example, foreign ownership is limited to 20 percent of a company and must be divided between two investors.[66] When MDLF needed to take a 39 percent equity stake in a client there, local lawyers advised a nominee arrangement whereby a local person would hold company shares on MDLF's behalf. The practice is common but illegal under regulations that have not been changed since the country was a European colony, so MDLF acquired convertible bonds that can be made liquid or, when the law changes, converted to equity. These kinds of arrangements are expensive to execute, but for reasons both principled and practical MDLF cannot subvert the rule of law it is trying to support. If it did, it could not in good faith expect the countries where it does business to enforce a contract with a wayward client.

MDLF has three principal sources of revenue – grants to and program-related investments in MDLF, and PRI revenue.[67] Several different organizations contribute to MDLF's PRI pool, either through donations or through program-related investments of their own. In the latter case, MDLF is an intermediary, having itself received PRIs from the MacArthur Foundation, SIDA and OSI. Of these lenders, only MacArthur has charged interest (2 percent per annum); the other loans were interest-free. With its own PRIs, MDLF sends repayment on principal back into the loan pool, while other revenues – interest on loans and leases, dividends and capital gains from equity investments – go to operating costs.

As with most non-profits, an endowment would be the best way to ensure the MDLF's long-term viability, but no one I spoke with at the organization thought that likely. Among other things, MDLF would have to convince potential donors that a PRI is the most efficient way to employ limited resources. Put another way, MDLF must convince a donor that it cannot receive a higher return (and thus have more funds available for its program or mission goals) by investing its money elsewhere. The donor has to consider whether a PRI will tie up money that could be used for projects that better serve its mission, and it has to decide what loss of principal and interest, if any, it would be willing to accept as part of a PRI program (its own or MDLF's). A host of other questions attend that analysis: [68]

- *What is the volume, character and return from loans?* In the case of MDLF, for example, the great majority of its loans appear to succeed (i.e., generate a return) such that the Fund can make money by servicing demand. But how much additional loan volume is necessary to cover operating costs? At what volume is the break-even point, and if MDLF cannot break even, where will the necessary subsidy come from to sustain the organization?
- *What are the organization's assets and liabilities?* What is an organization's net worth, and are its assets valued appropriately? How much of its net worth is liquid, and is net worth growing or shrinking? What are the organization's liabilities, and when does its own debt mature? Are the maturities of the organization's loans and debts coordinated? Does the organization have many sources of capital or just a few? If a government agency or large donor is contemplating an investment, what percentage of the recipient fund's total capital will that investment represent?
- *How good is management, both the board and day-to-day? What are the investment risks?* Do the funding organization's managers actively pursue capital, and does the organization make loans carefully? How efficiently does the fund service its debt, i.e., bill clients and collect payments? Can the fund collect bad debts and how aggressively does it do so?
- *What kind of losses are possible or even likely?* What reserves are available to cover losses, and how is the reserve calculated? Does the fund get collateral for its loans? How are risks allocated among the fund's creditors?
- *What is the mix of a funding organization's permanent and PRI capital?* Permanent capital is that which a firm can use at its own discretion to cover operating costs and losses, and it can make that money on its loans, through grants, or some combination of the two. Permanent capital provides institutional resilience that PRI capital does not, allowing a firm not only to cover operating expenses but to provide a cushion against loan loses, poor cash flow, or (unlikely in MDLF's case) a downturn in lending activity; that, in turn, allows the firm to take the risks required to meet its non-profit mission. Second, a firm can actually have *too much*

permanent capital – the whole point of equity, after all, is to use
it productively.

In MDLF's case, the answers to some of these questions are contained,
in small part, in the discussion of MDLF's mission and operations above.
Ironically, MDLF's fund-raising challenges had until recently been made
difficult by the fact that it has purposely maintained a very low profile.
Like any financial institution, it does not reveal information about its clients without authorization, and for many of its clients public knowledge
of their relationship with MDLF could subject them to hostile actions
from their home governments or from competitors. MDLF thus is often
a hidden partner to its clients, which while understandable and perhaps
necessary, is emphatically *not* the normal choice of external relations
strategies for a non-profit firm that is itself dependent on donations from
outside funders.

In 2005, MDLF hired its first communications director to help remedy
this problem, and it also took its appeal for funds directly to the general
public. When I met Vucinic in Prague in 2003, he discussed the possibility that MDLF might issue what he called "social responsibility" bonds,
and in early 2006 MDLF began offering "Free Press Investment Notes."
The idea is that these bonds will raise funds for MDLF's PRI pool and
be both affordable and attractive to socially conscientious investors
in the United States and Europe. The minimum investment is $1,000,
and purchasers can choose an interest rate from zero to three percent,
and terms from one to ten years. Longer terms (five to ten years) are
eligible for the higher rates. The idea replicates a number of existing
social investment programs, such as the Community Investment Notes
offered by the Calvert Foundation in the United States.[69] Calvert, in fact,
manages the Free Press Investment Notes program for MDLF through
its Community Investment Service Center in Maryland.

Whatever else can be said of the assistance models represented by
MDLF and SAMDEF, both organizations provide a disciplined way of
understanding and solving the problem of media sustainability in transition societies. Both take a long-term view of political transition. Their
concern is *market sustainability*, and they are one of the very few media
assistance organizations – if not the only ones – that have offered more
than vague prescriptions on the subject. Inherent in their activities is an
understanding that the "third wave" of democratization has passed into
some new phase, the outcome of which will take years to unfold. Some

of the countries in which MDLF works, for example, are down the road
– usually not very far – toward democratic consolidation, while others
are stuck in a political gray zone. Others – Guatemala, for example – may
yet lapse into authoritarianism. Recognizing this, Harlan Mandel told me
in early 2006, the term "transition state" has now passed from MDLF's
lexicon in favor of "developing state," which is broad enough to capture
the wide variety of circumstances in which MDLF works. Whatever the
case, through its PRIs and other activities MDLF has made a long-term
commitment to the notion that wherever democracy has a chance, the
odds for success are better if indigenous, professional and financially
independent news organizations are there to tell the story. And all the
stories that follow.

Notes

1.   See Burton A. Weisbrod, "The Future of the Nonprofit Sector: Its Entwining with
      Private Enterprise and Government," *Journal of Policy Analysis and Management*,
      Vol. 16, No. 4 (1977): 541-555; see also Henry Hansmann, "The Role of Nonprofit
      Enterprise," *Yale Law Review* 89 (April 1980): 835-899; and John R. Emshwiller,
      "More Small Firms Complain About Tax-Exempt Rivals," *Wall Street Journal*
      (August 8, 1995): B1.
2.   Lester Salamon and his colleagues write that the global not-for-profit sector of
      the economy has grown dramatically over the same period, such that if it were a
      national economy it would rank as the world's eighth largest. See Lester L. Sal-
      amon, Helmut K. Anheier, Regina List, Stefan Toepler, S. Wojciech Sokolowski,
      et al., *Global Civil Society: Dimensions of the Nonprofit Sector* (Baltimore, MD:
      The Johns Hopkins Comparative Nonprofit Sector Project, 1999), 9.
3.   See Felicity Barringer, "UN Will Back Entrepreneurs in Bid to Lift Poor Nations,"
      New York Times (July 27, 2003): A5.
4.   See Salamon, et al., *Global Civil Society*, 1999, 1-41.
5.   For case studies and analysis of social entrepreneurship, see Peter C. Brinkerhoff,
      Mission-Based Management, 2ⁿᵈ edition (New York: John Wiley & Sons, 2000);
      Peter C. Brinkerhoff, *Social Entrepreneurship: The Art of Mission-Based Venture
      Development* (New York: John Wiley & Sons, 2000); J. Gregory Dees, *Strategic
      Tools for Social Entrepreneurs* (New York: John Wiley & Sons, 2002); J. Gregory
      Dees, *Enterprising NonProfits: A Toolkit for Social Entrepreneurs* (New York:
      John Wiley & Sons, 2001).
          Some of the most well known examples of social entrepreneurship are in micro-
      finance. One of the more famous case studies is Chicago's ShoreBank, a for-profit
      firm (with a non-profit subsidiary) dedicated to revitalizing the residential and busi-
      ness districts in the city's poor and racially segregated neighborhoods. ShoreBank
      was created in 1973 with the mission of connecting the "unbanked" – generally
      low-income people without credit or banking accounts – to mainstream financial
      services and facilitating saving and income accumulation in low-income house-
      holds and neighborhoods. Since its inception, ShoreBank has lent approximately
      $1.5 billion to 13,000 families, for-profit and non-profit companies in the South,
      Near-South and West side neighborhoods of Chicago, and reports a repayment
      rate of 98.5 percent. Like MDLF, ShoreBank provides it clients with advice and

support along with its loans. Its "socially responsible investments" now include sustainable development projects in Cleveland, Detroit, Michigan's Upper Peninsula, the Pacific Northwest, and also overseas, in Romania, Northern Ireland and Bangladesh.

6. See Oprah's Angel Network at http://www2.oprah.com/uyl/angel/uyl_angel_about.jhtml.

7. Ibid.

8. See Sesame Workshop statement of mission at http://www.sesameworkshop.org/aboutus/intro.php. (accessed Feb. 3, 2006).

9. *Sesame Workshop Annual Report 2002*, 6. Available at http://www.sesameworkshop.org/aboutus/pdf/SesameWorkshiop2002.pdf (accessed January 11, 2006).

10. Ibid., 8.

11. "Hot Topic Success Sparks Expansion of Sesame Street Teen Program," Sesame Workshop Press Release, June 4, 2003, http://www.sesameworkshop.org/aboutus/inside_press.php?contentId=9345821 (accessed February 5, 2006).

12. The National Geographic Society's most recently published 990 form is from 2003 and is available through www.guidestar.org.

13. NPR's mission statement is available at http://www.npr.org/about/nprworks.html. (accessed February 5, 2006).

14. Jeremy Drucker, editor and publisher, *Transitions Online*, author interview, Prague, November 5, 2005.

15. Sri W. Roshalin, marketing director, 68H, author interview, Jakarta, Indonesia, November 14, 2004.

16. Santoso, director, 68H, author interview, Jakarta, Indonesia, November 13, 2004.

17. Sri W. Roshalin, author interview, 2004.

18. Ibid.

19. See Fareed Zakaria, "Culture is Destiny: A Conversation with Lee Kuan Yew," *Foreign Affairs* (November/December 1994): 189-194.

20. Frank J. Whitaker, press officer, U.S. Embassy, Kuala Lumpur, interview with author, September 13, 2004.

21. Steven Gan, editor-in-chief, *Malaysiakini*, author interview, Kuala Lumpur, Malaysia, September 3, 2004.

22. Premesh Chandran, chief executive, *Malaysiakini*, Kuala Lumpur, Malaysia, September 2, 2004.

23. See http://www.seacem.com/

24. See http://www.manage4me.com/

25. The change of non-profit status makes it easier for private foundations in the United States to support MDLF because they are not required to carry out expenditure responsibility for grants to public charities.

26. PRIs employ a range of instruments in addition to loans and equity investments, including loan guarantees, linked deposits, and real estate mortgages. According to the Foundation Center, the value of PRIs made by the top 135 providers in 2000-2001 was more than $421 million in 667 different PRIs, up from $148 million in 1998 and $279 million in 1999. The majority (90 percent) of PRIs are made by private foundations, roughly 20 percent of them to intermediary organizations. PRIs vary in size, but of those from major providers, the majority (62 percent) are for $100,000 or more. In 2000-2001, only $28 million in forty-five PRIs went to overseas recipients. See *The PRI Directory, 2003 Edition* (New York: The Foundation Center, 2003); see also "PRI Financing: 1998-1999 Trends and Statistics," available at the Center's web site, www.fdcenter.org; and C. Mandler,

The PRI Index: 500 Recent Foundation Charitable Loans and Investments (New York: Foundation Center, 1997).

27.   For tax purposes, income from a PRI is treated just like any other investment income, but when the principal is repaid it counts as a negative distribution. In effect, then, a provider must recycle PRI funds to another charitable purpose – loan or grant – in the year the principal is paid.

28.   See Internal Revenue Code 4944 (c): "No significant purpose [of a PRI]... is the production of income or the appreciation of property." In determining whether a PRI meets a non-profit's charitable purpose, the relevant questions are whether the interest rate is at or substantially below market, and if at market whether the risk is higher or lower than a commercial lender would tolerate; whether the market and the client are new; and whether the client has a lower than ordinary level of capitalization and/or lower than ordinary collateral or prepayment requirements. For an excellent, short discussion of PRI requirements and uses, see Milton Cerny, "Creative Uses of Program-related Investments," *Journal of the International Center for Not-for-Profit Law*, Vol. 1, Issue 3 (1999): 7-12, http://www.icnl.org/journal/vol1iss3/PRI.html (accessed February 7, 2006). For a comprehensive treatment of the subject, see Christie I. Baxter, *Program-Related Investments: A Technical Manual for Foundations* (New York: John Wiley & Sons, 1997).

29.   See Frances Brody, S. Miller, C. Morduch and J. Weiser, "Foundation Investments in For-Profit Enterprise," in Baxter, *Program-Related Investments*, 1997, 331.

30.   The term intermediary does ***not*** mean subsidiary. Irrespective of the source of funds, MDLF makes the decision about whether to approve a PRI. MDLF borrows some of its funds and takes grants for others; some donors do set priorities for the funds they provide (for example, by region or media type), but otherwise donors are not involved in evaluating loan projects.

31.   Scholarly sources on the subject identify the Ford Foundation as the most authoritative source of knowledge and experience on PRIs. Ford's PRI program began in 1968 and by 1992 had a loan portfolio of $92.7 million. The Ford Foundation funded both the Project on Social Investing at the Massachusetts Institute of Technology and research by the Foundation Center on trends in PRI funding. Ford remains one of the leading PRI providers, and one of a very few – along with MDLF – that makes overseas PRIs.

32.   One authoritative source on PRIs describes them as "powerful" but "underutilized"; see Paul E. Lingenfelter, "Program-Related Investments: Do they Cost, or Do They Pay?" in Baxter, *Program Related Investments*, 1997, 441. In an Aspen Institute monograph, Titus Levi writes that during a conference discussion about PRIs "few participants" knew about them and that PRIs "remain small and underpromoted"; See Levi, *Mission-Driven Media* (Washington, DC: Aspen Institute, 2002), 10.

33.   MDLF is not alone in making media-related PRIs. The U.S. Corporation for Public Broadcasting, for example, has received PRI assistance from the Ford Foundation "to enable it to compete more effectively with larger, national media outlets." See "Asset Building and Community Development: Program-related Investments" on the Ford Foundation's web site, at www.fordfound.org/program/economic_pri.cfm.

34.   Finance leasing is a standard method of financing large equipment purchases, and is advantageous to the lender because it holds title to the equipment and thus has great security in the investment. When the client "buys back" the equipment, it pays cost plus interest.

35.   MDLF also has a grant program specifically for Indonesia.

36.   Auerbach died unexpectedly in December 2004.

37. Sasa Vucinic, managing director, Media Development Loan Fund, author interview, Prague, September 16, 2003.

38. The Fund for Independent Media was a 501(c)3 trust that George Soros had established in 1993, one of many trusts the philanthropist established at the time. The activities proposed for these trusts were later consolidated as programs within OSI, leaving a number of unused trusts – and funds – on the shelf.

39. Sasa Vucinic, author interview, 2003.

40. See Kenneth Anderson, "Not So Friendly to Investors," *Washington Times* (November 2, 2005): A23.

41. Reportedly, MDLF's board at one time discussed the need for investment projects in the United States, but rejected the idea as inconsistent with its core mission.

42. As is often the case in transition countries, printing presses are owned by governments or others closely aligned with them, thus giving them life-and-death control over media in need of their services; the purchase or lease of a press is thus the first practical step toward long-term financial and editorial independence. Owning a press also allows a firm to earn additional revenues by printing for third parties.

43. Media Development Loan Fund 2004 brochure, 4. The printable brochure is available at http://www.npr.org/about/nprworks.html. (accessed February 5, 2006).

44. Ibid.

45. NGOs can, however, qualify as MDLF clients. The Instituto de Defensa Legal (IDL) in Lima, Peru, is an NGO with a human rights and media component, with a monthly magazine, a radio network and an on-line presence. In Lebanon, the Human Rights Media Network (HMRN) is a project of local NGO, the Multi Initiative on Rights: Search Assist and Defend (MIRSAD). MDLF provides New Media Grant Fund support to both IDL and the HMRN.

46. Harlan Mandel, deputy managing director, Media Development Loan Fund, author interview, New York, NY, September 4, 2003.

47. Ibid.

48. MDLF 2004 brochure, 4.

49. Elena Popovic, general counsel, Media Development Loan Fund, author interview, New York, NY, September 4, 2003.

50. MDLF's risk rating evaluates each potential borrower by financial performance (earnings, cash flow, assets and liabilities, debt capacity), industry position, management and reporting, collateral (value and liquidity), and guarantees.

51. Sasa Vucinic, author interview, 2003.

52. Harlan Mandel, author interview, 2003.

53. Konstanty Gebert, columnist, *Gazeta Wyborcza* , author interview, Santiago, Chile, March 11, 2002.

54. The essential items in a loan application to a commercial lender are the profit-and-loss statement (sometimes called the financial statement, or statement of operations); balance sheet; cash-flow statement; break-even analysis; and management plan.

55. In the United States, for example, loan proposals will usually rely on industry data available from both the Department of Commerce and the Department of Labor.

56. Harlan Mandel, author interview, 2003.

57. See http://www.jazler.com/.

58. To qualify for SAMDEF assistance, media firms must be located in Angola, Botswana, Lesotho, Malawi, Mozambique, Namibia, Swaziland, South Africa, Tanzania, Zambia, or Zimbabwe.

59. SAMDEF's mission statement says the organization "seeks to strengthen, through financial, technical and training support, the capacity of the region's independent

media to become self-sustaining enterprises. This includes the capacity of the region's independent media to effectively produce, manage, market and distribute their products – be they newspapers, books, broadcast programmes, films, intellectual property or hard or software – in conformity with the goals of the 1991 Windhoek Declaration on Promoting an Independent and Pluralistic African Press." See www.misanet.org/samdef.html (accessed December 11, 2005).

60.   SAMDEF's mission statement, as well as a detailed explanation of its services, is available at the firm's web site: http://www.samdef.com/vision.htm (accessed February 7, 2006).

61.   "A Review of SAMDEF's Unit of Account and Lending Currency," AssetMan Consulting, Gaborone, Botswana, May 2005.

62.   Charles Mundale, chief executive officer, Southern Africa Media Development Loan Fund, author interview, Gaborone, Botswana, December 3, 2004.

63.   Titus Mbuya, managing editor, *Mmegi*, author interview, Gaborone, Botswana, December 4, 2004.

64.   Bojosi Otlhogile, vice chancellor, University of Botswana, author interview, December 3, 2004.

65.   Kenneth Anderson, chairman, Media Development Loan Fund Board of Directors, author interview, Belgrade, Serbia, November 6, 2003.

66.   MDLF requested that I not identify the country so as to protect the identity of the client.

67.   Typically, non-profit firms also have significant non-cash donations – for example, volunteer labor, free or discounted equipment or services – that for-profit firms do not have. Donations of this kind are not counted as income but in fact are.

68.   This list of review questions is compiled from Baxter, *Program-Related Investments*, 1997: 265-325, 329-330; see also Lingenfelter, "Program-Related Investments," 1997, 441-449.

69.   See the Calvert Foundation's website at www.calvertfoundation.org/individual/investment/investmentnotes-index.html (accessed January 25, 2005).

Conclusion

For journalists in both developing and developed countries, the stark reality is that economic demand and public policy are rarely supportive of good journalism. The irony of this, as both development theory and free expression theory recognize, is that neither markets nor governments work very well in the absence of reasonably complete, accurate and timely information. So though the "public interest" may not be susceptible to definition in economic terms, for journalists the thrust of the thing is straightforward: It is about serving the information needs of listeners and viewers so that the actions they take as citizens have real meaning. How to sustain this mission is the problem.

As noted throughout this book, many assistance providers have in recent years cast a critical eye on their own work, and they have given special emphasis to the problem of long-term benefits in media projects. In February 2002, for instance, members of the IGO and NGO media assistance and development communities met at Oxford University to discuss several aid issues, among them "business management development."[1] The program was conceived partly as a response to a World Bank conference of the same year, "Building Institutions for Markets," one part of which focused specifically on the poor record of long-term success in media projects.[2] Third-party assessments have been less charitable.

Making matters more difficult, democratization aid's traditionally heavy emphasis on free markets and economic development arguably has left journalists in many countries in situations where their media markets have been commercialized but they have won little if any autonomy from government. Especially for journalists in Thomas Carothers' gray-area states, the few inches of breathing space that have come with political liberalization have been offset by having to negotiate competitive pressures in markets where the rules still heavily favor state media and entrenched elite interests. According to a 2001 World Bank report, for example, the largest media firms in ninety-seven mostly developing countries are owned either by the government or a family.[3] Television remains the least democratic of all media in this regard. These difficulties are compounded in countries like Indonesia or Russia, where governments have sought to re-regulate the media and rein in what they view as media excess. In others, political liberalization has simply meant the exchange of one source of repression (the state) for another (local government officials, gangs, religious authorities or civil society actors). In several regions of the world – Southeastern and Eastern Europe, Latin America, parts of Asia – the official censorship of a previous age has been replaced with organized violence – including murder – as a form of media "regulation."

In many developing countries, then, it makes little sense to talk about financial sustainability as an assistance goal. Obviously it is important for a media organization to be managed well, and management training – already a staple of media development efforts – needs to be continued and enlarged. Journalists themselves need to become much more engaged in that enterprise. But in many places management training will not be enough. At its worst, the current emphasis in the aid community on economic sustainability risks being counterproductive, a mirror of the same one-size-fits-all paradigm that has too frequently shaped democratization programs generally. As a practical matter, it may also be an indication that traditional sources of media assistance are shifting their priorities, redirecting aid, and in some cases reducing what they give. In the aftermath of the 2001 attacks on the United States, and the wars in Afghanistan and Iraq that followed, U.S. democratization spending has necessarily reflected new foreign policy objectives, with the administration of George W. Bush redirecting funding to Muslim countries. USAID spending on democracy programs went from $671 million in 2002 to $1.2 billion in 2004, with almost all of the new spending in Afghanistan and Iraq.[4] The National Endowment for Democracy received $80 million in 2005, twice its 2002 budget, but the entire increase went to President Bush's Middle East democracy initiative, leaving democracy spending elsewhere in the world either flat or reduced; in 2004, for instance, the administration cut democracy program spending in Eastern Europe and the NIS states by 38 percent and 48 percent, respectively.[5] The largest part of that spending had gone to Serbia and Montenegro under the Support for East European Democracy Act and to Russia and the NIS states under the Freedom Support Act. The president's 2006 budget also proposed cutting the budget of the Asia Foundation by 23 percent, from $13 million to $10 million.[6] Over this same period, many private donors have re-trenched as the result either of financial setbacks or new priorities, sometimes both. The Freedom Forum, for example, abruptly ended its international programs in 2001, and other foundations have seen their grant-making ability sharply reduced by losses in the market. Against these developments, it is hard to quarrel with the emphasis on market viability.

Still, however, too great an emphasis on financial sustainability ignores the fact that many countries are not transitioning to anything that might be called a democracy. Their civil society organizations are often hostile to democracy, their governments and economies are weak, and many have no significant past experience with democratic institutions or process, or even a functioning bureaucracy. As Carothers writes, the "precarious middle ground between full-fledged democracy and outright dictatorship is actually the most common political condition today of countries in the developing world and the post-communist world."[7] If this is to be the norm, at the very least it means that financial sustainability for any media organization – for-profit or not-for-profit, commercial or non-commercial – requires a multi-faceted development strategy that will allow the company to diversify its revenue sources. Partnerships, joint ventures, learning projects and other innovations, where they work, have to be a part of that strategy. So, too, do more traditional tools – training and exchange programs, fellowships, grants and loans.

Finally, the crisis of editorial integrity that faces journalists in many developing states is not unique to them. Journalists in developed countries find themselves in economic and political environments that do not encourage the production of high-quality news and public affairs content either. Ironically, they do so at a time when the future of democracy in the world has become less certain.

The Global Crisis of Journalism

News media in developed democracies are faced with the same economic and editorial challenges as their colleagues in developing countries, if not always the same political ones. In the United States, for example, the current interest in non-profit organizational structure for media companies arises from structural changes in the news industries in the West, encouraged by public policy, that have had the effect of undoing traditional editorial mission.

Consider just one example: In the United States there has been a dramatic transfer of newspaper ownership from family-owned, privately-held firms to publicly traded companies over approximately three decades, between about 1970 and the late 1990s. Some of these companies were sold by families faced with the prospect of paying inheritance taxes; others went public to generate capital for acquisitions, to reduce debt or to avoid hostile takeovers. The newspapers of some of these publicly traded companies – particularly McClatchy, the Washington Post Company, and the flagship newspapers of the New York Times Company and Dow Jones – are among the most distinguished in the country. Others – Gannett, Knight Ridder, E.W. Scripps, the Tribune Company, A.H. Belo – will also produce exemplary journalism.

But doing good work has not been not good enough. Knight Ridder reporters, for example, were widely credited in 2004 with having alone debunked the George W. Bush administration's evidentiary case for its 2003 war against Iraq in the months before the war began, even as senior editors at the *New York Times* allowed a credulous reporter to use anonymous administration sources to trumpet the government's case in the paper's news columns.[8] Knight Ridder won several awards and professional accolades for its reporting, but less than a year later the largest shareholder in the company, Private Capital Management (PCM), demanded that the company either seek a single buyer for all of the company's 32 newspapers or sell the company off piecemeal, paper by paper.[9] Citing "unacceptable operating margins," PCM urged Knight Ridder to immediately sell the *Philadelphia Inquirer*, the Miami Herald and the San Jose Mercury News, the company's most respected newspapers.[10] At the time PCM urged the sell-off, Knight Ridder had just posted a dividend on a 2004 profit margin of 19 percent.[11] PCM's demands were widely noted within the industry: The company also holds a 35 percent share of McClatchy and 13 percent of the New York Times Company, second only as a shareholder to the controlling Sulzberger family.[12] In December 2005, the union that represents workers in the newspaper industry, the Newspaper Guild-Communications Workers of America, announced that it would try to find an equity partner to help it buy eight of the Knight Ridder papers so as to avoid "serious social and economic harm" to the regions served by those papers.[13]

The move to public ownership, while by no means the only factor influencing change in the U.S. newspaper industry, has had a singularly transforming effect on the economics of editorial judgment and thus on public-service mission. Above all, write Gilbert Cranberg, Randal Bezanson and John Soloski,

Ownership of the companies by thousands of passive investors interested in financial return, not news quality, has distorted the direction of change caused by economic and technological forces, and thus the capacity of newspapers to continue to perform their historic and constitutionally protected role as the foundation of a free press.... For the public companies, with but few exceptions, the business of news is business, not news. Their papers are managed and controlled for financial performance, not news quality. Central corporate control over operating newspapers is rarely focused on news content; it is instead strictly financial, measured by such neutral criteria as revenue growth, operating margins, advertising rates, and the like. But it is understood by all that financial controls enforced by the parent company compel known changes in size and quality of editorial staff, content, newshole, priorities for coverage, market segmentation, etc.... The most important short-term strategy for increasing margins is cutting costs, and this consists principally of cutting personnel. News personnel are often seen not as contributing to revenues or margins, and are therefore cut heavily.[14]

The other strategy for revenue growth and increased margins has been the same used by the first independent papers of the nineteenth century: market segmentation, a process by which newspapers seek to deliver to advertisers the most affluent audiences possible. Today, however, general circulation increases no longer translate into higher advertising rates unless newspapers can show that the increased circulation is among an advertiser-desired demographic. Similarly, circulation among low-income readers or other, undesirable demographics can actually drive advertising rates down. According to former *Chicago Tribune* editor James Squires, former Gannett CEO Allen Neuharth once proposed raising the per-copy price of newspapers to one dollar, not only to increase revenue but to eliminate from the circulation base "the unwanted low-income reader."[15] Advertising revenue for the publicly traded newspapers has steadily climbed over the past four decades even as the newspapers' share of the total advertising market has declined. Zoned editions of newspapers distributed to wealthy urban suburbs have been a major factor in that growth.[16]

Consolidation in the newspaper and other media industries has resulted in new forms of both horizontal and vertical integration, and extraordinarily powerful media firms. The Tribune Company, for example, went public in 1983. At the time it acquired the Times Mirror Company for $8 billion in March 2001, Tribune owned three other newspapers in addition to its flagship paper, the *Chicago Tribune*, and twenty-two television and four radio stations around the country. The Tribune also owns the Chicago Cubs baseball team, is a leading academic textbook publisher, a television program producer and syndicator, a cable television programmer, and owner of a variety of on-line businesses from classified advertising to grocery delivery. With its purchase of Times Mirror, the Tribune Company acquired the *Los Angeles Times*, *Baltimore Sun* and *Newsday* in New York along with four other daily newspapers, twenty-four shopper newspapers in southern California, and several consumer magazines. More significantly, the Tribune Company's combined media properties make it the single largest media provider, in terms of audience reach, in four of the United States' five most populous states: Illinois, New York, Florida and California.

From a macroeconomic perspective, consolidation of this type raises difficult policy questions for a democracy. The first is how to reconcile the conflicting objectives of a regulatory system. If, for example, the regulatory goal is to ensure the sustainability of good quality local media, consolidation may be a poor policy choice; if, on the other hand, the policy objective is to ensure the competitiveness of national media companies in a global marketplace increasingly dominated by multinational firms, consolidation is unavoidable. From the broad point of view of policy makers, the critical question is what the relevant competitive marketplace is and what constitutes "too big" in that market. In every communications sector companies have gotten bigger over the past two decades, but often their share of their traditional markets has declined over the same period. Worldwide there are more than 100 media companies with more than $1 billion in revenues; by that measure media as an industry are still fragmented compared with other industries such as pharmaceuticals, banking or aerospace.

It matters as well what the outputs of competition actually are. As discussed in chapter 4, increased competition in the news industry, much of it made possible by advances in technology, have also created a huge array of new content choices. Much of that content, even perhaps most of it, is nothing that a democratic society needs to function and may even get in the way of public understanding of important issues. But there is also much *more* content – more print publications and television programs created specifically for racial and ethnic minorities, more news and public affairs, more children's fare, more documentaries, and infinitely more digital information sources – than were available twenty years ago. Indeed, it was only a little more than two decades ago – in 1984, a year ordinarily associated with totalitarian thought control – that there were in the United States one telephone company, three broadcast television networks, and one major computer manufacturer (IBM). There were far fewer broadcast radio and television stations on the air, and cable was still under the boot of broadcaster-influenced government regulation. No one thought then that this universe of media companies was particularly public-spirited or idea diverse. They appear that way only in the soft glow of nostalgia.

Finally, despite the growth of these conglomerates, there can still be strong inter-media competition – between competing units of the same conglomerates, or between similar units in different conglomerates – that make for a "healthy" media system. Even as these large firms buy companies they are looking to sell other parts of their business that no longer fit their strategic objectives. In particular, they are interested in creating firms that are both horizontally and vertically integrated, controlling both several production units in the same business and the means of distributing those products. Around the world many of these firms – most famously, for example, General Electric in the United States and Berlusconi in Italy – are multi-sectoral organizations with substantial operations in other industries such as real estate, mining, manufacturing and military defense contracting. From a journalist's point of view, this is just the problem: In the West, the media mogul archetype is no longer Joseph Pulitzer or Robert McCormick (and forget Lord John Reith), but Jack Welch and Silvio Berlusconi in pursuit of strategic fit and maximum return. All these companies will manage to stay in business, and many will do very well. The question is whether they will manage to stay in journalism.

A second question, given these trends in the developed world, is what developing media systems might learn from them. For news organizations in developing societies, financial sustainability – establishing themselves as viable participants in competitive markets – is just the first step. Eventually they, too, will find that growth in larger and even more competitive markets may require editorial compromises once thought unthinkable. Social entrepreneurship, discussed in chapter 6, can help to reconcile these conflicting pressures, and to the extent such a thing is possible the best of international media assistance programs have much to teach journalists and policymakers in the United States about the business of journalism – and perhaps about journalism itself.

But social entrepreneurship can only do so much, and it cannot make up for policy choices that make serious commitment to editorial quality economically a business liability. In the United States, for example, the business of journalism would be transformed overnight if public policy created economic incentives to think long term, and the best way to do that would be to change the way news organizations think about costs and expenses. Any business that has to think in terms of quarterly profit reports will naturally see things like employee training, research, product development – and even adequate numbers of experienced reports and editors – as hits to the bottom line. Viewed over a longer reporting period, these same things can improve a company's performance, its product and its profits, and some can be capitalized as expenses rather than as costs that reduce profits. Another policy choice that affects editorial performance is that which allows media firms to be bought and sold speculatively. Speculation can make markets work more efficiently, but it can also create distortions that make them less efficient and which produce negative externalities. Where that occurs the usual policy remedy is taxation – financial penalties. In the name of the "public interest," for example, broadcast companies in the United States were once subject to requirements that they be held for a fixed period before they could be sold, but those requirements disappeared in the deregulatory 1980s. Obviously it is difficult to determine what a proper holding period should be, and it is also possible that the levy of penalties for irrational or damaging speculation could have undesired chilling effects on trade and make it difficult for firms to raise capital. But a country that chooses as a policy choice to impose no constraints on the transfer of media companies, and which subjects them to constant demands for profits, will get the media system it deserves.

In the absence of wise policy, mission-based media companies in the developed West may do well to learn from their colleagues in developing countries around the world. There are already some notable instances of this. The San Francisco-based Independent Press Association (IPA), for example, makes relatively small loans (no more than $50,000) to its members – "alternative" newspapers and magazines in the United States – to help them "rise to the next level" by expanding or diversifying their revenue sources through direct-mail and marketing campaigns, or by making small capital investments in things like fulfillment software or computers. The IPA was created in 1996 and counts in its membership well-known publications like *The Nation* and *Mother Jones*, and about 400 others that include quarterly and online titles, many of them regional or urban-based publications for ethnic- and racial-minority audiences. Applicants to IPA's Independent Press Development Fund, like MDLF clients, must present a business plan and show themselves capable of repaying the loan, though they usually do not need collateral. Loans are short-term, no longer than eighteen months, and made at a fixed rate of between 8 and 8.5 percent per annum, or slightly below commercial lending rates.[17]

Another non-profit organization, Public Radio Capital (PRC), was created in 2002 to help U.S. public radio broadcasters acquire additional stations through the use of tax-exempt bond financing. According to its Web site, PRC's mission is "to help strengthen our country's democratic traditions by protecting and expanding public radio's critical role as a trusted source of news analysis, and to increase the availability of a wide variety of public radio music formats. This is at a time when public radio audiences continue to grow, and there is a demand for more locally-owned and operated media to deliver quality services."[18] PRC helps these broadcasters prepare and plan their acquisition strategies, evaluate acquisition opportunities, ascertain market values, align their organizational mission with their acquisition goals, develop a business plan, and resolve the legal and regulatory issues that come with adding new channels.

The Global Crisis of Democracy

The research and reporting for this book began in the mid-1990s, when democratization was a less controversial topic and a more celebrated one. Third wave enthusiasm and the euphoria that began in 1989 became more subdued with the U.S. invasion of Iraq in 2003 and the insurgency that has followed. Though President George Bush talked about the need to bring democracy to Iraq, critics of the war claimed that democratization in the region was, at best, an after-the-fact justification for an invasion that failed to find weapons of mass destruction, and, at worst, a rhetorical cover for a cynical mix of oil politics, an almost theological belief in American exceptionalism, and imperial American ambition. Whatever one's view of the war, afterward the United States *had* to install some sort of successor government (as it had also had to do in Afghanistan in 2002), and while some failures in both places are now widely attributed to policy incompetence and political opportunism, not all can be blamed on the administration.

Democracy in the Middle East is, as it is everywhere, the least bad system. And it may be a very bad system if one assumes, as Mr. Bush and journalists continually do, that democracy can be reduced to voting – "the freedom to hire and fire your government," as the *Economist* put it in its defense of the war.[19] Of course, democracy depends on much more than political institutions and political society. What there is of civil society in the Middle East, for example, is rooted in mosques and in militant organizations like Hezbollah or Hamas, and so it should not be surprising that democratic choices in Iraq, Egypt, and Palestine thus far have produced leaders who are hostile not only to the West, but to the values of democracy itself. But what is the alternative? Excepting foreign policy "realists," few would argue that it would be better to maintain indefinitely the Middle East's authoritarian regimes, assuming such a thing were possible. If Mr. Bush has proven anything through his prodding, it is that democratic choices are not always wise ones.

Moreover if Mr. Bush's adventures in Iraq have created a security crisis, the crisis of democracy is larger and more complex, and it predates him. Consider, for instance, the developing world's largest experiment in democratic transformation, the European Union. The EU parliamentary elections in June 2004, in addition to sending large numbers of vehemently anti-EU delegates to Brussels, constituted the world's biggest-ever multinational democratic vote and the world's second-biggest democratic vote (after India's).

The enlargement of the EU from nine countries in 1973 (when it was known as the European Economic Community) to ten, twelve, fifteen, and currently twenty-five countries, represents in some obvious respects a triumph. Whether it represents a triumph of *democracy* is harder to say. The 1991 Maastricht Treaty was not an overwhelming success when it was put to voters, and the recent enlargement was possible only because the Irish, who had rejected the Nice Treaty when they were first asked to vote on it in 2001, were compelled to vote a second time so as to come up with a more acceptable answer. In the European Parliament elections in June 2004, voter turnout was abysmal—an overall average of 45 percent—with the weakest turnout in several of the new member states. In Poland, for example, only about 20 percent of eligible voters cast ballots. Meanwhile, in old and new member states alike, voters showed their unhappiness with the EU by supporting nationalist, populist, and anti-EU parties. Of the new members elected to the 732-member Parliament, more than a quarter (as many as 200) came from parties opposed to union. And in twenty-three of the EU countries, the largest party in the national government saw its share of the vote fall.[20]

The good news, perhaps, is that a voter turnout of 45 percent, even when adjusted for states like Belgium and Luxembourg where voting is compulsory, is still better than Americans can muster for their legislative vote: Only 39 percent of eligible U.S. voters turned out for the 2002 congressional elections. Moreover, the European Parliament's many new members, even if they make decision-making more difficult, will fairly represent the disorganized range of European public opinion on matters related to European unity. The bad news is that their representation grows increasingly weak. The low-turnout in 2004 marked the sixth-consecutive drop in parliamentary elections since they began in 1979; moreover European-wide elections draw far fewer voters than national elections on the continent do. The "Euro gap," as it is called, averages 21.9 percentage points in the 15 states that were members prior to May 2004, 29.1 percent in the ten new member states.[21]

Central and Eastern Europe is a particular challenge for the EU. Without question, many of the new member states in the region have made remarkable economic and political progress in a stunningly short period of time, but the costs have been high. Some of the "reforms" that were endorsed in principle by expert advisors from the West have done a lot to undermine public confidence both in the market and in democracy. Most notoriously, the process of privatization in some countries was really just a looting of state assets, with the result that the economic and political power once concentrated in state hands is now inequitably concentrated in a few private ones. Crony capitalism is combined with political systems in which many former communist officials remain in power, now as "democrats." Some of the EU's newest members (some of which are also now NATO members) have doubtful democratic credentials and none-too-stable politics. Latvia, for example, has had twelve governments since 1993, the most recent installed in March 2004. Over the same period, Poland has had eight governments; the Czech Republic and Hungary each has had five.

But the core of the "democratic-deficit" charge against the EU is that it is remote from citizens not just physically, but psychologically. Anthony Smith has questioned why a citizen of Germany, France, Spain, or Poland would choose to identify with Europe over his own culture and history: "Without shared memories and meanings, without common symbols and myths, without shrines and ceremonies and monuments, except the bitter reminders of recent holocausts and wars, who will feel European in the depth of their being, and who will willingly sacrifice themselves for so abstract an idea? In short, who will die for Europe?"[22] Timothy Garton Ash has written that "there is no European *demos*, only a European *telos*."[23]

Other writers have disputed Smith's emphasis on the "natural links" of culture and history, or have argued that such links are no less artificial, no less imaginary, than the kind of civic nationalism on which European union is based, in which allegiance is not to national identity or kinship but to a set of civic values and norms and the institutions that embody them. Civic union, indeed, is a central purpose of the European project, an effort to avoid the destructive intolerance of societies divided by ancestry, blood ties, and skin color. As former British European Commissioner Lord Cockfield once said, "The gradual limitation of national sovereignty is part of a slow and painful forward march of humanity."[24] Is it part of the march of democracy, too?

Finally, of course, the work of European union is not done. One of the biggest remaining challenges is Turkey, which was granted accession status in 1999. The historic gateway between Europe and Asia, Turkey is part of both lands and at home in neither. Since World War II, Turkey's foreign policy has sought to link the country organically to Europe, but it is a Muslim country outside of Europe's traditional borders, and many Europeans strongly oppose its EU candidacy. That opposition has intensified as Europeans perceive themselves threatened by militant Muslims already living in the West.[30] Others point with concern to Turkey's weak human rights record, particularly with respect to its Kurdish minority; its poor record on matters of free expression; its history of military interventions in domestic politics; and the influence of anti-democratic, Islamic fundamentalist groups in the country.

Arguably, Turkey's democratic credentials are no worse than, for example, Croatia's, another accession country. But even those who support Turkey's EU candidacy will acknowledge that admitting it to the Union will provoke a strong negative reaction from, and new support for, nationalist and anti-immigration movements already doing quite well in Western Europe. As an EU member, Turkey would within a generation surpass Germany as most populous country in the EU, and as such it would also have the largest number of votes in the EU's legislative bodies, the Council of Ministers and the European Parliament, in a Union that already accounts for as much as 50 percent of new domestic law in its member countries. As one politician told the *Economist*, "Letting Turkey into the EU would mean more Le Pens and Haiders."[26]

As a study in democratization, the EU is particularly compelling because it is a smaller version of the evolving, non-hierarchical network of institutions – nation states, international governmental organizations, non-governmental organizations, transnational corporations – that together form a largely un-elected and unaccountable system of global governance.

At the core of this system are nation states, which act as they always have, both unilaterally and in cooperation with one another as they choose or must, but any number of commentators have offered up the theory that the era of Westphalian states that defined the world in terms of "national interests" and "national sovereignty" is fading or dead. As one commentator notes, nation-states have succumbed to "the postmodern cosmopolitan culture that some think the pinnacle, others the nadir, of human progress. It is a pastiche of cultures, rather than based on one, specific culture. It is eclectic in nature, disinterested in place and time, has no concern for ethnic or national origins and is blissfully ignorant of history."[27]

Anthony Smith has argued that this is a nonsensical "dream confined to some intellectuals.... We can discern no global identity-in-the-making, nor aspirations for one, nor any collective amnesia to replace existing 'deep' cultures with a cosmopolitan 'flat' culture."[28] As far as anyone can see, Smith says, the nation-state will remain the foundation of the world order. Certainly quite a few people are banking on it. It is a common observation that the process of globalization has created a simultaneous and contradictory one of localization, as people began to search for or renew cultural identities. Quebec in Canada and Chiapas in Mexico, for example, lobby vigorously for international support and recognition of their independence movements. Quebec has put the matter to referendum twice, with independence losing by only a narrow margin the second time; a third vote could easily succeed. Other national groups—the Kurds, Palestinians, Chechens, Albanians, and Tibetans, to name a few – want an autonomous territory with defined boundaries and the usual instruments of governance and sovereignty, for instance a currency and an army. Some of these national groups are scattered across multiple states, as the Arabs, the Albanians and the Kurds are, or they exist, sometimes with their own laws, territory and culture, within larger states, as, say, the Scots and American Indians do.

What, then, lies ahead? Some commentators, Robert Keohane and Joseph Nye among them, are cautiously optimistic about the future of global democracy,[29] while others are deeply pessimistic. Some – Samuel Huntington and Robert Kaplan – have described a future characterized by war and general lawlessness.[30] Others believe as Cicero did that the world will insist on being governed, but that it will not insist on democracy. Dahl worries about a third transformation in governance that will result in "de facto guardianship" at the international level, a world run by unaccountable, unwise, and self-interested elites.[31] More darkly, the British writer Hedley Bull argued almost 30 years ago that global governance will be a chaotic mix of competing authorities and conflicting allegiances reminiscent of the Middle Ages.[32] Mary Kaldor, Helmut Anheier, and Marlies Glasius have described what they call a new phase of "regressive globalism," a form of "displaced, latter-day quasi-imperial, nationalist, or fundamentalist thinking in the context of global capitalism."[33]

Even among those who believe that the global democratic impulse cannot be restrained, some see plenty of potential for violence. Huntington, for instance, argues that the so-called "democratic-peace hypothesis"— the idea that democracies do not fight other democracies, and therefore the greater the zone of democracy in the world, the greater the zone of peace – is probably wrong.[34] This is what *New York Times* columnist Thomas Friedman once called, more colloquially, the "Mickey D's theory of world peace," the idea that countries with McDonald's restaurants do not go to war with each other.[35] Friedman later qualified this theory after NATO bombed Belgrade, which has many McDonald's restaurants, including one only blocks from the army, police and state broadcasting buildings NATO destroyed in 1998. But to the extent that democratization is an irreversible global phenomenon, it seems at least possible that the consequences of that process may not be what democratic theorists would expect. On what basis, for example, would a democratic China, or a democratizing Middle East, be friendly and unaggressive toward the United States?

The democratic-peace hypothesis is limited above all by a lack of evidence to support it. Until the middle twentieth century, there were so few democracies in the world that they did not have much opportunity to fight one another; during the second half of the century, almost all of the world's democracies were part of a United States-dominated alliance against the Soviet Union. Moreover, as Edward Mansfield and Jack Snyder have argued, what evidence does exist suggests that democratizing countries, because they are unstable, are more likely to engage in wars and other violent conflict than either stable democracies or stable autocracies.[36] Amy Chua, further, has written that within many developing countries, contrary to all conventional wisdom in the foreign aid community, the combined pursuit of democracy and free markets "may catalyze ethnic tensions in highly determinate and predictable ways, with potentially very serious consequences, including the subversion of markets and democracy themselves."[37]

Against all this, the need for rigorous and serious journalism is greater than ever. But what are journalists realistically supposed to do? One thing they *cannot* do is continue to make arguments for editorial virtue absent some understanding of the economics of their industry and the policy choices that shape media decision making about the products they provide for their audiences. Editorial virtue of one kind or another has been and in many instances remains the single rallying point in media assistance. When, for example, the Knight Foundation reviewed the journalism assistance field in 2002, its summary report was tellingly titled "The Media Missionaries."[38] It has to be emphasized that the report's leading recommendation was that long-term economic sustainability be moved to the top of the priority list in program design, implementation and evaluation, but the report said almost nothing on the "how" of that subject. Internationally, this silence struck some aid recipients as emblematic of the larger problem that has bedeviled media assistance. As Chinese journalist Yuen-Ying Chan told me in late 2005, "We don't need more 'missionaries' from the West. We need long-term investments, we need commitment that goes beyond making the donors feel good about themselves, and we need to grow our businesses."[39] This means more than training programs, however superb the training. It means much more than grants. It means that both assistance providers and recipients must think in new and inventive ways about how to finance a public-service editorial mission. The era of assumed virtue is over.

Notes

1. "Global Media Assistance Strategies: The role of media in economic and democratic development" unpublished research paper (London: Programme in Comparative Media Law and Policy, 2002). The paper was presented at a conference sponsored by the World Bank and USAID at the World Bank Conference Center in Paris, Feb. 4 and 5, 2002.
2. See "Anarchy is not a Business Plan: Practical Pointers on the Business of Media," *Global Issues* (February 2003). Available at http://usinfo.state.gov/journals/itgic/0203/ijge/gj05.htm (accessed February 12, 2006).
3. Simeon Djankov, Caralee McLeish, Tatiana Nenova, and Andrei Schleifer, *Who Owns the Media?* (Washington, DC: World Bank, 2001). Available at www.economics.harvard.edu/faculty/shleifer/papers/media_september_2002_JLE.pdf. (accessed February 12, 2006).
4. Peter Baker, "Funding Scarce for Export of Democracy," *Washington Post* (March 18, 2005): A1.
5. Ibid.
6. Ibid.
7. Thomas Carothers, "The End of the Transition Paradigm," *Journal of Democracy* (January 2002): 5-21, 18.

8. See Michael Massing, "Now They Tell Us," *New York Review of Books*, Vol. 51, No. 3 (February 26, 2004): 3.
9. Frank Ahrens, "The News Hounds: Investors and Falling Stock Prices are Dogging the Industry," *Washington Post* (November 3, 2005): D1.
10. Ibid.
11. Ibid.
12. Ibid.
13. Joe Strupp, "New Twist: Guild Leads Effort to Buy 8 Knight Ridder Papers," *Editor & Publisher* (December 22, 2005). The Guild proposed to buy the *San Jose Mercury News, Philadelphia Inquirer, St. Paul Pioneer Press, Akron Beacon Journal, Duluth News Tribune, Lexington Herald-Leader, Monterey Herald, and Grand Forks Herald;* see also Strupp, "Guild Still Seeking Investors for Knight Ridder Purchase," *Editor & Publisher* (December 29, 2005).
14. Gilbert Cranberg, Randall Bezanson and John Soloski, *Taking Stock: Journalism and the Publicly Traded Newspaper Company* (Ames: Iowa State University Press, 2001), 7-12.
15. James D. Squires, *Read All About It! The Corporate Takeover of America's Newspapers* (New York: Times Books, 1993), 92.
16. Cranberg, et al., *Taking Stock*, 2001, 24-25.
17. See the IPA's Independent Press Development Fund web page at http://www.indypress.org/site/programs/loanfund.html (accessed February 11, 2006).
18. See Public Radio Capital at http://www.pubcap.org/index.html (accessed February 11, 2006).
19. *Economist*, "The One Thing Bush Got Right" (February 4, 2006): 9.
20. *Economist*, "The voters take their revenge" (June 19, 2004): 49.
21. Ibid., 50.
22. Anthony Smith, *Nations and Nationalism in a Global Era* (Cambridge: Polity Press, 1995), 139.
23. Timothy Garton Ash, "Europe's Endangered Liberal Order," *Foreign Affairs*, Vol. 77, No. 2 (March/April 1998): 59.
24. Quoted in Alan S. Milward, *The European Rescue of the Nation-State* (Berkeley: University of California Press, 1992), 2.
25. See Patrick Tyler and Don Van Natta, Jr., "Militants in Europe Openly Call for Jihad and Rule of Islam," *New York Times* (April 26, 2004): A1.
26. *Economist*, "Too Big for Europe?" (November 14, 2002): 43.
27. Peter van Ham, "Identity Beyond the State: The Case of the European Union" (Copenhagen: Copenhagen Peace Research Institute, June 2000): 8-9. Available at http://www.ciaonet.org/wps/vap01/. (accessed February 2, 2006).
28. Smith, *Nations and Nationalism*, 1995, 24.
29. See Robert Keohane and Joseph Nye, *Power and Independence,* 3rd edition (New York: Addison-Wesley, 2000); see also Keohane and Nye, "Introduction," in *Governance in a Globalizing World*, eds. Nye and John Donahue, eds., (Washington, DC: Brookings Institution Press, 2000), 7-12.
30. See Robert Kagan, *The Coming Anarchy: Shattering the Dreams of the Post Cold War* (New York: Vintage, 2001); and *Samuel Huntington, The Clash of Civilizations and the Remaking of World Order* (New York: Simon & Schuster, 1998).
31. Robert A. Dahl, *Democracy and Its Critics* (New Haven, CT: Yale University Press, 1989).
32. See Hedley Bull, *The Anarchical Society: A Study of Order in World Politics* (New York: Columbia University Press, 1977).

33. Mary Kaldor, Helmut Anheier, and Marlies Glasius, "Global Civil Society in an Era of Regressive Globalization," in *Global Civil Society Yearbook 2003* (Oxford: Oxford University Press, 2003), 3.

34. Samuel Huntington, "Culture, Power, and Democracy," in *Globalization, Power, and Democracy*, eds. Marc F. Plattner and Aleksander Smolar (Baltimore, MD: Johns Hopkins University Press, 2000).

35. Thomas Friedman, *The Lexus and the Olive Tree: Understanding Globalization* (New York: Doubleday, 2000).

36. See Edward D. Mansfield and Jack Snyder, "Democratization and War," *Foreign Affairs*, Vol. 74 (May/June 1995): 79-97.

37. Amy L. Chua, The Paradox of Free-Market Democracy: Indonesia and the Problems Facing Neoliberal Reform (New York: Council on Foreign Relations, 2000), available at http://www.cfr.org/publication/8695/paradox_of_free_market_democracy.html (accessed February 12, 2006).

38. See Ellen Hume, *The Media Missionaries: American Support for International Journalism* (Miami, FL: John S. and James L. Knight Foundation, May 2002). Available at http://www.ellenhume.com/articles/missionaries1_contents.html (accessed February 12, 2006).

39. Yuen-Ying Chan, director, Journalism and Media Studies Center, University of Hong Kong, author interview, Prague, November 3, 2005.

Index